ROME OF THE RENAISSANCE

Paolo Portoghesi

ROME OF THE RENAISSANCE

Translated by Pearl Sanders

Phaidon

The drawings in this volume were executed
by the studio of Enzo Di Grazia with the assistance
of the Consiglio Nazionale delle Ricerche, through
the Institute of Humanities of the Faculty
of Architecture, Milan Polytechnic. The perspective
reconstructions and diagrams are the work
of Germano Foglia.

The photographs were made especially for this
volume by Eugenio Monti, Paolo Portoghesi, Oscar Savio,
and Giorgio Stockel.

Design by Diego Birelli
Art director: Electa Editrice

Phaidon Press Limited, 5 Cromwell Place, London SW7

Published in the United States of America by Phaidon Publishers, Inc.
and distributed by Praeger Publishers, Inc.
111 Fourth Avenue, New York, N.Y. 10003

First published 1972
Originally published as *Roma del Rinascimento*

© 1970 by Electa Editrice. Industrie Grafiche Editoriali S.p.A. - Venezia
Translation © 1972 by Phaidon Press Limited

ISBN 0 7148 1419 9
Library of Congress Catalog Card Number: 73-138246
All rights reserved

Printed in Italy by Fantonigrafica®, Venezia

CONTENTS

PREFACE

Two images, both by Michelangelo, the *Pietà* in St. Peter's, made in the closing years of the fifteenth century, and the *Rondanini Pietà* on which the sculptor was working in the year of his death, indicate the distance covered between 1503 and 1564, the two dates which define the chronological limits of this book. The same activity, sculpture, seems to have changed fundamentally in its motivation, its style, and its objectives. In Michelangelo's early work, 'sculpture' and 'form' were synonymous; he used 'form' to dominate the material and make it coincide with an image that was communicable because it was absolutely clear and well defined. But by the time he came to the *Rondanini Pietà*, sculpture signified a process of thought, a dialogue between the artist and the stone, and free from the presence of witnesses or patrons; here the stone was scrutinized and made to yield all its latent possibilities in order to express the conception of the artist rather than the world of actual experience. In both cases the validity of the equation: to make = to know, which was the starting point of humanist culture, remained unchanged; but by the latter date it was no longer possible to speak of 'knowing with certainty' since the norm had now become to 'know in doubt', and this led to a search which admitted of no conclusion.

It is true that the case of Michelangelo is so exceptional that it cannot be taken as a yardstick for sixteenth-century culture as a whole, and moreover in architecture, which by its nature is an art of permanence, it is extremely rash to seek any such direct terms of comparison in order to explain historical changes. The two *Pietàs* must therefore be viewed not as examples of two different artistic cultures, but as testimony to the profound change which had taken place in the human condition. This change could not, of course, be ignored by architects, although their work did not reflect it to such a high degree of intensity.

The close connection that existed between political and artistic events becomes apparent to us as soon as we try to divide the chosen chronological span into clear-cut periods. Not only the subjects for buildings suggested by patrons but also the direction taken by formal research changed radically at least four times during the sixty-two years with which we are concerned. Each of these changes coincided with crucial events taking place more or less simultaneously in the political and religious spheres.

The first easily defined period coincides with the papacy of Julius II and the years of Bramante's activity in Rome.

The Pope's plan to create a *renovatio urbis*, able to express in symbolic form the restoration of the political prestige and territorial integrity of the State of the Church, found in Bramante a sympathetic interpreter. Each of the Italian cultural centres had developed its own individual interpretation of humanist classicism, which was based on a compromise between the ideas emanating from Florence and local tradition. In opposition to this pluralism

Bramante pursued the aim of 'restoring the central authority' by making a new and more thorough examination of classical sources and using the knowledge gained in this way to effect a return to the kind of structures and spatial effects found in the architecture of ancient Rome.

The dream of a state which could acquire sufficient authority to enable it to take a decisive place in the balance of political power was matched by an aspiration to a new objectivity, based on a unification of style and renunciation of the terminological and decorative variants in which so much of the architectural activity of the late fifteenth century had been dissipated. One can even see a similarity between the mass of unresolved contradictions with which the political career of Julius II came to a close, and the uneasy legacy left by Bramante to his pupils: an optimistic pragmatism, refusing to be put to the test of theoretical proof, had condemned the activity of both men to fragmentation and incoherence.

The papacy of Leo X and the first years of that of Clement VII—separated by the short but significant interlude of Hadrian VI—are conventionally believed to represent a *plenitudo temporum*, the summit of the period of Roman classicism. But in reality this plenitude rested on a frightening political void. The optimism which led Julius II to work towards his aim of 'transforming reality' was succeeded first by the astute passivity of Leo X—who treated Luther's revolt as a drunken brawl among monks—and then by the impotent ineptitude of Clement VII and the horror of the Sack of Rome. After the short illusory respite of *pax gallica* proclaimed by Francis I after the Battle of Marignano (1515), there began as early as 1521 and even before the death of Leo X, the struggle between France and the Empire which lasted almost forty years and saw the power of Charles V grow to such an extent that the position of the Holy See was reduced to that of a vassal state of the Emperor. For the majority of Italians, therefore, the so-called plenitude was illusory and erroneous, existing as it did within a precarious and equivocal situation.

During these years the city was replanned and enlarged beyond the curve of the Tiber. At the same time the authority of the papacy was consolidated by the presence of an exceptional concentration of intellectuals and artists. Leo X had brought about the political union of Rome and Florence, and this resulted in such a large influx of Tuscan citizens that a city within a city was created and Rome acquired a durable position of cultural supremacy. Whereas Bramante strove to create a synthesis in which the Florentine tradition acted as a starting point for his own fundamentally opposed methods, his pupils, Antonio da Sangallo, Raphael, and Peruzzi, saw this Florentine tradition return to impose itself with the full weight of its authority. Florence came to resemble a colony which outgrows its mother country, and compared with her achievements Rome seemed merely a centre for the absorption and consumption of Florentine culture. On the other hand, just because Rome, unlike Florence, was not subject to the narrow limits of a city-state, she could offer Tuscan artists something new and extremely significant—a larger scale, the urban dimension of a capital city.

The papacy of Leo X is generally considered to mark the climax of sixteenth-century classical culture. In fact, the classicism of Bramante was based on contradictions and contained within itself the seeds of unrest which had manifested themselves even before 1520; it was therefore a programmatic rather than a real classicism, continuously challenged by practical activity and so insecurely founded that just when it seemed on the point of being transmuted into certainty, it began to inwardly disintegrate.

Castiglione's letter to the Pope sets out a programme of classical renewal, but postulates the application of a scientific method of analysis to the heritage of Rome which should be promoted by the State as a definite political act. This idea was typical of the Utopian outlook prevailing at the time, but was contradicted by the facts of history. Just as the Italian Renaissance as a whole became aware of its historical distance from Ancient Rome at the very moment of its declaration of belief in the myth of renewal, so too the period of Roman classicism signified both the ephemeral affirmation and the impracticability of a classicism

Perspective reconstruction of Bramante's first design for St. Peter's.

Perspective reconstruction of Bramante's final design for St. Peter's.

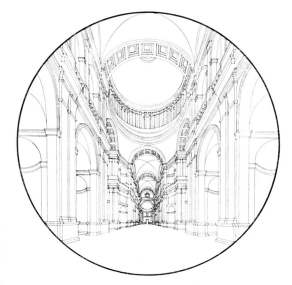

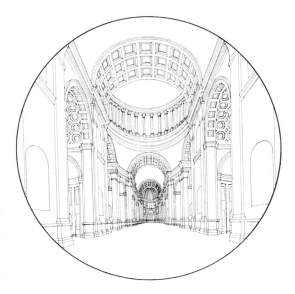

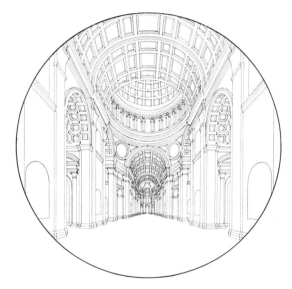

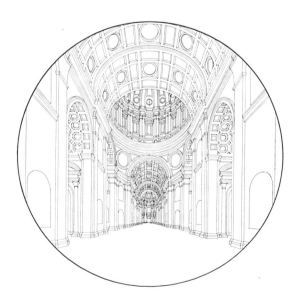

symbolizing a return to the serene 'infancy of the world' and of an intellectual experience extending above and beyond the present crisis.

To find a historical motivation to account for the exceptionally high level of cultural activity in the first twenty years of the sixteenth century is far from easy, either from the standpoint of the autonomy of the arts or by seeking a facile sociological explanation. However, the complex cultural developments which took place in the period under review can be better understood if they are analysed against the background of historical events and the interplay of forces which determined their pattern. Such an analysis points to the conclusion that the hopes, the myths, and the illusions which were pursued in artistic circles in reality concealed other hopes, other myths, other illusions nurtured by men of power in their vain hopes of future dominance. What did Rome, the State of the Church, the home of religious institutions, really mean to the great aristocratic families and financiers of the central regions of northern Italy? To them Rome was first and foremost an instrument of international power which, if wielded successfully, could be used to extend their own sphere of influence. Through their members who entered the College of Cardinals, the great families were able to increase their power, and by supporting one or other of the important factions which held control of the political balance of Europe, could participate actively in the game of official diplomacy. The great bankers were both the indispensable administrators and the beneficiaries of that formidable draining of capital which the church exercised over the whole Christian world. Without their assistance it would have been an arduous task to collect the enormous dues that were absorbed by the church—tithes payable on the possessions of the clergy, annates due to the Holy See by men newly elected to high office in the church, and the infamous sale of indulgences. It was this last abuse which attracted the greatest attention at the time of the rebuilding of St. Peter's and was one of the prime causes of Luther's revolt.

At the beginning of the sixteenth century, after the activity of Duke Valentino and the successful policy of Julius II had restored the church to a position of prestige and strength, this new security lulled people into the belief that Italy could continue to flourish economically and enjoy cultural supremacy by maintaining anachronistic political structures and standing by passively as the great national centres of Europe consolidated their power. Italy's claim to an aesthetic civilization was used to provide her with an alibi for her political incapacity, while the Albertian myth of an all-powerful Beauty which could defend itself against every attack had nurtured Italy's mistaken belief in her own stability. This belief was to be tragically shattered by the horrors of the Sack of Rome. Italy's greatest period of cultural achievement thus coincided with the awakening of an exceptional interest in Rome among the powerful Italian families, to whom the city represented the object of their plans for dominance (the inconsistency and fallaciousness of these plans had already been openly denounced by Machiavelli).

The third identifiable period began in 1527 with the Sack of Rome and ended in the 1540s, during the papacy of Paul III Farnese (1534-49). The dominant political figure was now Charles V. After the church had been split apart by the Schism, he tried to restore the religious unity of Europe by instituting a Council at which a dialogue could be maintained between Catholics and Protestants. At first Paul III encouraged the Erasmian school of orthodox reformers and brought to the fore men such as Contarini, Sadoleto, and Pole, who seemed equipped to face the crisis with courage. It was at this time, after the long silence following the Sack of Rome and the consequent exodus of artists, that architecture enjoyed a period of renewed fertility and expansion, when the stresses of the past years became transmuted into new forms, apparent especially in the work of Peruzzi.

Around the year 1540, three factors—the confirmation of the Jesuit Order, Charles V's failure to achieve the religious agreement he had sought at the Diet of Regensburg, and the establishment of the Inquisition (1542)—marked the beginning of a defensive and authoritarian policy which was later to determine the whole course of the Council of Trent.

When, weary of the long struggle, Charles V accepted the Peace of Augsburg, thus acknow-ledging the perpetuation of religious division and abdicating the unity of his empire, he was merely ratifying the progressive erosion of that dynamic element which had made the first fifty years of the century a period still great with possibilities for the future of Europe.

The gradual introduction of repressive policies in the field of religion corresponded in architecture to a flourishing crop of academies and the formulation of rigid rules of style. Two complementary directions were followed by architects: the obedience to strict rules leading to a rigid functionalism, and Manneristic licence leading to a decorative style of literary derivation. Until 1546 Antonio da Sangallo reigned supreme as the most important architect in Rome. On his death Michelangelo was summoned to complete the buildings he had left unfinished, and this position now devolved to him. The rebellious radicalism which had led him to participate in the Erasmian circle of Vittoria Colonna was now put to the service of architectural research.

The papacy of Julius III (1550–5), which coincided with the abdication of Charles V and the Peace of Augsburg, marked a pause in the defensive policy of the church. Artists began to question the church's autonomy and attempted to reinstate the values of human-ism. The Villa Giulia is the outstanding example of this trend, but in the architecture of the interior the disparity of aims between Ammannati and Vignola indicates what was to become the prevailing trend within the next decades: to deny and suppress the unrest and doubt revealed in Mannerism and to continue, in a deceptive and milder version, the tra-dition of sixteenth-century classicism. The last ten years of the chronological span covered by this book mark the triumph of conservatism and the final end of any attempt at mediation between Catholics and Protestants. While the Peace of Câteau-Cambrésis confirmed the power of Spanish influence in Italy, Paul IV Carafa, who had encouraged Paul III to establish the Court of the Holy Inquisition, imprisoned in Castel S. Angelo Cardinals Moroni and Pole as exponents of the Erasmian school of orthodox reform. With the conclusion of the Council of Trent (1563) and the political influence of the Jesuits and of Carlo Borromeo, there came into being the repressive climate of the Counter-Reformation, when any rebel-lion against the dogmatic centralism of Rome was bloodily suppressed.

In a letter dated 1 May 1564 Annibal Caro wrote: 'I do not know what news to give you of Rome except that the decorator of fountains and candlesticks (Cardinal Borromeo) has begun to refashion it completely; and Rome does not suffice for his zeal; he wants to do as much for the whole world.' This is the letter of a disorientated survivor from a period which saw a complete reversal of values, a man disillusioned by the advent of a 'new bar-barism' and by the final disappearance of that 'sweet liberty' which had been enjoyed by intellectuals at a time when the Church had deceived herself into believing that the revol-ution of humanism could be compatible with her own temporal interests.

THE LEGACY OF THE FIFTEENTH CENTURY

When, after one of the shortest conclaves in the history of the Church, Cardinal Giuliano della Rovere became Pope Julius II on 1 November 1503, the city and state of Rome were undergoing a period of stress and uncertainty. A number of political and economic developments were in progress, but their effect on the urban scene could not be considered even provisionally satisfactory. A programme aimed at restoring the universal authority of the Church by consolidating a state structure able to compete with the European powers had begun to emerge in the middle years of the fifteenth century; later, through the political activity of the Borgias, this programme, though variously interpreted, had always been pursued with vigour and determination. It was this uneasy legacy which awaited the new Pope.

In the cultural and social activity of the city, the *renovatio Romae*, initiated at the time of Pope Martin V, was also awaiting a decisive impetus. In fifty years a little of the dust and mud of Rome had been shaken off, but her prestige was still far below that of the great centres of Italy. And although so many classical models were close at hand, the architectural growth of the city had been along more or less provincial lines; there had, it is true, been some quite important research and experimentation, but this was insufficient to enable Rome to play a decisive part in the rich Italian panorama.

For Julius II, the structure of the city represented a symbolic expression of the universality of the Church and authority of the Papal State. In this view he was following the path indicated by Popes Sixtus IV and Nicholas V, as is shown in his papal bull of 19 February 1513 with its explicit reference to 'predecessors' and to the memory of 'Wise Solomon' who, 'although not illuminated by the light of Christianity', had spared no sacrifice in order to 'build unto the Lord a house worthy of His name'. Julius II's awareness of the political significance of architecture and the process of urban reorganization may be viewed as a further stage in the programme which was solemnly established by Pope Nicholas V on his deathbed, as we read in Manetti's biography. This document may be considered the first organic expression of the plan to make of Rome the political symbol of a religious capital, and it was this plan which inspired her popes with a coherent vision for three hundred years of architectural activity.

Nicholas V considered the value of restoring the city to her monumental splendour to be primarily one of reinforcing the faith of the multitude. 'The immense, supreme authority of the Church of Rome', he declared, 'can in the first place be understood only by those who have studied its origins and developments through the medium of the written word. But the masses of the population have no knowledge of literary matters and are without any kind of culture; and although they often hear men of learning and erudition state that the authority of the Church is supreme, and lend their faith to this assertion, reputing it to be true and indisputable, yet there is need for them to be awestruck by grandiose spectacles, lest their faith, resting as it does on a weak and unstable foundation, might with the passage of time be finally reduced to naught. However, the grandeur of buildings, of monuments which are in a sense enduring and appear to testify to the handiwork of our Lord, serves to reinforce and confirm that faith of the common people which is based on the assertions of the learned, so that it is then propagated among the living and in course of time passed on to all those who will be enabled to admire these wonderful constructions. This is the only way to uphold and extend the faith so that, preserved and increased in this way, it may be perpetuated with admirable devotion.' In other words, a city which would be a *Biblia pauperum*, its architecture a language understood by all, as described four hundred years later by Victor Hugo in *Notre Dame de Paris*.

However, the architecture produced in the fifteenth century, which by its nature was an abstract representation of space, was not yet at a stage where it could completely fulfil and become identified with this purpose; this stage was not reached until the Baroque period, when art accepted the devices of rhetoric and became an instrument of popular persuasion and propaganda. From around 1450, when the influence of Florence first made its mark on Roman architecture, until the period of Baroque classicism, after 1750, a path can be traced which follows the course of a culture able to lay claim to an autonomous development and continually evolving techniques within the ambit of the demands made upon it by the papacy.

In this course of events, the short period of Julius II's pontificate marks a significant climax, when for a brief and unrepeatable instant the interests of learning and the arts seemed to coincide with those of religious power. For the political purpose of restoring the State of the Church to a central function in the balance of European power, it no longer sufficed for Rome to be just one of the cultural centres of Italy, with the special role of being the most important consumer of ideas originating in Florence and mediator among the ambitions of rival courts. It was essential for Rome to become the focal point of European culture, so that the prestige of her image should be so great that it would symbolize the political prestige of Catholicism.

As the custodian of the classical heritage, Rome had a claim to a universality of culture; this same universality now became the ideal which inspired every architectural project, and the unifying factor in all artistic controversy.

Rome in the Early Sixteenth Century

'The city which he found plebeian, bare and dirty,' said Tommaso Inghirani, speaking to the College of Cardinals in commemoration of Julius II's papacy, 'he made clean, dignified and worthy of the name Roman. If all the buildings which arose through the work of the Savonese over a period of forty years were put together, they would form the real Rome. The rest, if you will excuse the expression, were nothing but shacks.' By referring to Sixtus IV della Rovere and his nephew Julius II as 'Savonese' (Tr. note: Savona was the birthplace of the Della Rovere family), Inghirani was drawing attention to the continuity in the urban development policies pursued by these popes. The direction and limits of this continuity may be correctly assessed only by making an analytical reconstruction of the appearance and architectural features of Rome in the first years of the sixteenth century.

The Rome of Nicholas V was a small town of 17–20,000 inhabitants, but in only seventy-five years its population, as revealed by the census of 1526–7, had grown to 55,000. This more than doubling of the size of the population did not correspond to a proportionate increase in the occupied area of land, but to a process of reorganization and modest expansion.

Rome, from a late fifteenth-century engraving.

Principal urban structures in the Rome of Julius II.

The information provided by this census makes it possible to discover the population density for each of the districts of sixteenth-century Rome, which with some differences correspond to the present-day districts. The density varies from a maximum of 33,000 to a minimum of 549 persons per sq. km. in the Ripa district. A significant figure, 682, relates to the Monti district, which comprised the whole of the vast area enclosed by the Aurelian walls, the zone now bounded by Via XX Settembre, S. Stefano Rotondo and the Capitol. After the process of expansion in an easterly direction had already begun, an area equal to about a fifth of the whole territory enclosed by the walls housed a paltry number of 'hearths', 476 (less than 3,000 inhabitants), only a third of the number found in the Ponte district (1445, corresponding to 7,626 inhabitants), which occupied an area fifteen times smaller (4.32 as against 0.28 hectares).

In 1527, besides the left-bank districts (Borgo, Trastevere and Ripa), five others still had a population smaller than 10,000, although they occupied territories much larger than those of the central districts: Monti, Trevi, Colonna, Campo Marzio, and Campitelli.

Together these peripheral neighbourhoods had a population of under 5,000. A study of views of Rome covering the late fifteenth and early sixteenth centuries indicates that at least until 1550 no vast territorial expansion took place, but that growth was essentially qualitative and increasingly polarized by the important monuments of the old city.

To those who know the present firmly integrated structure of the city it is difficult to imagine how Rome must have appeared in the early years of the sixteenth century. If we wish to discover its essential features then, bearing in mind the winding ribbon of the Tiber, we must refer first to the Vatican complex. This formed a magnetic pole which, through a series of convergent channels, seemed to draw into itself a dense, homogeneous mass of buildings enclosed by the bend of the Tiber. This mass grew thinner towards the east, remaining within the line of the Via Lata (the present Via del Corso), while to the south it was bounded by the Capitol, another ideal pole of the urban system, although endowed with a much smaller power of attraction, as can be seen by the paucity of the population before 1527 in the Campitelli district at the foot of the hill.

Trastevere, lying on the opposite bank towards the lower bend of the Tiber, still maintained a separate identity even as an administrative unit and was joined to Rome by the bridges of the Isola Tiberina (Island of the Tiber) but had no links with the Vatican. Other thinly populated districts arose here and there around ancient monuments, especially near the Quirinale and the Colosseum.

In the larger nucleus comprised within the bend of the Tiber, structures were heterogeneous and confused; the only noticeable pattern was the series of irregular streets leading out from the Vatican, on one side towards the Campo Marzio, and on the other towards the Capitol and Isola Tiberina, linked by a small number of intersecting roads, the most important of which was the Via dei Pettinari, opened by Sixtus IV.

The characteristic element of the urban scene, even in the most densely populated districts, still remained the medieval private dwelling consisting of single-family houses which backed on to each other and which were often separated by narrow gaps. This was still the general pattern in the time of Pius V. It was punctuated by an incredible number of towers, bearing witness to the warlike customs of the medieval barons. Towards the end of the fifteenth century, the tower no longer served any strategic military purpose and came to represent an emblem of nobility and social distinction. Of the vast number of these edifices which were built, the Millini tower, still standing on the corner of Via dell'Anima and Via della Pace, seems to express with its ornamentation of sgraffito plasterwork the new symbolic significance this architectural feature had acquired.

If one can easily reconstruct the appearance of the fifteenth-century city by piecing together fragments which have survived, or borrowing elements from the neighbouring villages of Latium which have retained their original medieval structure, it is far more difficult to reconstruct the role played in this context by the remains of the old city, at the time when they had not yet been reabsorbed into the urban scenography in which we are now accustomed to see them. Some parts of Via del Pellegrino, or Via dei Cappellari, or the remaining side of Piazza Giudea, can give us some idea of the atmosphere and modest, not to say homely, scale of the city of Sixtus IV, while a visit to the Corte degli Acetari, with its obtrusive and all-enveloping character, could still provide a meaningful picture of the characteristic process of integration of the urban structure. In its arbitrariness and spontaneity, it was able to portray a way of life which took its cohesiveness from the neighbourhood framework. This way of life came to an end in the fifteenth century, when the popes sought to achieve a unified reorganization of the town and saw that this could be obtained by stressing the continuity of the line of the street and making it serve as a co-ordinating factor in the urban perspective.

The Function of Ruins

When we compare the role played by ruins in the fifteenth century with their present-day function, we observe that there has been a profound change in the situation. Apart from the question of the difference in context, this change lies less in the number of ruins laid bare, than in their structural relationship to the landscape, to other buildings, and to natural scenery considered as a background to the extraordinary images designed by time. In the present city, the network of streets provides a continuous point of reference which is the conditioning factor of every architectural anomaly and places each of the disparate monuments in an ordered visual setting. To us, therefore, the ruins serve as documents of the past, taking their place in the interstices of a homogeneous pattern. Through the systems constructed by archaeologists, order has been brought into the diversity of the superimposed strata which correspond to the various epochs of history. Certain paradoxical juxtapositions, certain sharp contrasts of scale, can still produce a dramatic effect, or else reduce the ruin to the role of an unrelated object which may, however, still serve to form a number of new and unforeseeable relationships. But, in general, the remnants of the imperial city as we see them today are like historical documents which have already been classified in the archaeologist's laboratory.

In Rome of the Renaissance, however, the ruins were in essence features of the landscape. They mingled with the natural scenery and in a sense were themselves elements forming that scenery, since the uneven terrain, the chasms and hillocks which abounded, were often indications of the site of buried monuments or unexplored subterranean caverns. The case of Testaccio offers the most irrefutable proof that the work of man, when transformed by time, can come to be identified with nature and itself form a natural landscape. As an agent of the transformation of the earth's surface, man was seen engaged in a heroic struggle with the destructive forces of time and decay. This dramatic image showed man in all his grandeur and frailty, suggesting at one and the same time the heroic ideal of the classical tradition and the Christian message of the vanity of all mortal striving.

Although he did not reach Rome until 1580, Montaigne has left us a precious testimony of the role of ruins in the urban setting of the time. His secretary has given us the following account of Montaigne's first impressions of Rome: 'Of Rome he said that nothing could be seen but the sky beneath which she had once stood, and the place on which she arose; that the science relating thereto was abstract and theoretical, offering nothing to the senses; that those who declared that one could at least discern there what had been left of ancient Rome were exaggerating: the ruins of so tremendous an organism would have shown far greater honour and respect for her memory; whereas what remained was only her grave. In hatred of her long dominion, the world had first smashed and broken in pieces all the members of that admirable body; and since, dead as it was, cast down and disfigured, it could still inspire fear, had then buried even the fragments that remained. As for the small signs of her decay which still appear upon her coffin, they were preserved by fate in order to testify to the infinite grandeur which so many centuries, so many conflagrations,

the conspiracy of the whole world, had so many times joined to cast down, but had failed to destroy in all its parts. But it was probable that the disfigured members which still remained were those least worthy, and that the fury of the enemies of her immortal glory had first reduced to ruin that which was most beautiful and most noble. And as for the buildings of this bastard Rome which were now being built on top of the old ruins, although they did contain some qualities which could enrapture our present times, they were more likely to remind us of the nests which sparrows and rooks were building in France on the walls of churches demolished by the Huguenots.' Although Montaigne had seen the new St. Peter's and the Renaissance buildings, his Rome was still dominated by the absurd disproportion that existed between a city no longer visible, which had once been the capital of the world, and a small town perched like a parasite on top of the old buried structure. The old was like a shadow cast over the new, a shadow which the writer saw projected against the sky. The sky too, seen through the tall gaps between chains of broken arches, acquired a heroic quality and set a dimension that the new architecture was inadequate to attain.

The *Journal* imparts very vividly Montaigne's sensation of stepping onto a soil which was not formed by nature, of passing through valleys and hills created by ruins: 'It often happened that, having dug to a great depth, one at last uncovered the capital of a tall column which still stood upright at a lower level. No other foundations are needed for the houses than some ancient ruin or arch such as are seen in every cellar, otherwise they stand them on top of the old foundations or on some wall which is still standing. But on the actual ruins of the old buildings—in the haphazard pattern in which they arranged themselves when they collapsed—they have placed the foundations of their new palazzos as on solid and secure boulders. It can easily be seen that several streets lie thirty feet below the level of the present ones.'

In this account it is interesting to observe how the writer not only marvelled at the buried city but also seized upon the manifest relationship which bound the new city to the old. The utilization of ruins to serve as foundations for new buildings was in fact a law of architecture which had governed the development of the city since medieval times. To this phenomenon was due the presence in the new town structure of certain grandiose vistas and epic dimensions which would otherwise have been inexplicable, such as the vast scale of Piazza Navona, Castel S. Angelo, and the long rectilinear line of the Corso.

The Architectural Culture of the Fifteenth Century

In the late fifteenth and early sixteenth centuries, at the time of the papacy of Alexander VI Borgia, Rome was just one of several Italian cultural centres which were trying to work out their own interpretation of the new humanist ideology of a return to classical sources. Although Rome possessed an undoubted advantage in that her architects could continually refer to original buildings, she did not achieve a position of supremacy from the point of view of either quality or quantity, while in the search for an original alternative to Florentine ideas, Urbino, Venice, Milan, and Mantua could all lay claim to greater importance at the start of the new century.

Elevation, Palazzo Sora (1 cm = 3.5 m).

Rome, however, possessed what could be termed an 'architectural culture', that is, a coherent body of local tradition in technique and style. This culture was conditioned by the familiar presence of classical monuments, but the use of certain materials (brick and Travertine) and the fashion for late-Gothic elements (the polistyle pilaster and mullioned window, for example) provide a clear indication of the distinctly cosmopolitan nature of the local culture. The best proof of the firmly grounded autonomy of the local tradition is to be seen in Rome's resistance to the direct penetration of Florentine models, which were elsewhere accepted unreservedly. Although there was no lack of Tuscan architects in fifteenth-century Rome, they always had to take the indigenous tradition into account.

One of the reasons for Rome's incapacity to find a clear alternative to the Florentine tradition and her reluctant acceptance of a compromise position is to be sought in the tendency of fifteenth-century popes to see architectural problems as an aspect of town planning and as part of their policy of carrying out a functional reorganization of the city. As we shall see, the great innovation introduced by Julius II corresponded to an explicit change of direction in this policy. For the Brunelleschi school, architectural activity represented the creation of built forms possessing a significance which transcended the immediate problem of fulfilling the requirements of a particular theme and style. Such an attitude had no place in Rome, whether in the Vatican buildings, the Palazzo Venezia, or the churches built by Sixtus IV. The case of Leon Battista Alberti, too, is indicative of the changing pattern. He was a guest of Rome for many years, wrote his *De Re Aedificatoria* and probably also planned many of his greatest works during his stay, but did not succeed in producing any buildings of his own there. It may be believed that he provided inspiration for other architects concerned with projects such as the Palazzo Venezia, the basilica of San Marco, or the restoration of S. Stefano Rotondo, but it must be acknowledged that there is no trace in any of these buildings of the highly personal imprint of Alberti. This seems to indicate that although Alberti was appreciated by the court in Rome for his unsurpassed knowledge of classical sources and for his inspired works of archaeological restoration (for example, the enclosed garden of Palazzo Venezia), the court did not consider this humanist-architect to be the man who was best fitted to give architectural expression to the ideals of the time.

Without the presence of outstanding personalities, Roman fifteenth-century architecture consists for the most part of a series of experiments which could not be organically integrated, although they did possess considerable individual value and contained the seeds of future development. These experiments can be summarized under the following headings: *Value of the Material.* The architectural tradition of Florence, as seen in the works of Brunelleschi, is linked to the preference that was systematically given to the juxtaposition of pale plaster and sandstone, with the wide use of a special hard, weatherproof, sandstone on exteriors. The two contrasting tones resulting from this use of materials—a light background forming a contrast between the closely integrated dynamic structure and the framework surrounding it like a diaphanous cloud-filled sky—represented an essential feature of a line of development which led from Brunelleschi to the Michelangelo of the Sagrestia Nuova, and later to Mannerism. In Rome this technique had no adherents, partly owing to the rival attractions of travertine, a rough-textured yellowish stone which offered little in the way of effects of contrast. The juxtaposition of travertine and plaster did not represent a real departure from the juxtaposition of plaster and sandstone. On the contrary, it provided an illusion of continuity, while the choice of materials for exteriors, travertine

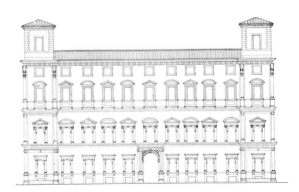

together with brick, which had been used to such effect in classical buildings, made for a contrast of grain and texture rather than colour.

Roman fifteenth-century architects understood the particular qualities of their materials and exploited their possibilities in order to create a unified homogeneous structure, imparting an immediate sense of stability.

In such façades as S. Agostino, S. Maria del Popolo, or S. Pietro in Montorio, the linear design formed by the 'edges of surfaces', to use Alberti's definition, did not gain a position of importance. The texture of cavities, the veins of the travertine, the faint shadows, were all of an importance equal to that of the mechanics of proportion, and already introduced the overall impression of a luminous mass. In the interior of S. Maria del Popolo, the very rough texture of the travertine in the polistyle pilasters accentuates the impression of durability and strength in the structure and, at the same time, introduces a natural element into the geometric design which creates a strong contrast to the plastered ceiling. The same could be said of the barrel-vault of the porch of Palazzo Venezia. Although the design is so hesitant that the possibility of a contribution by Alberti must be excluded, it can be seen that the technique of vaulting over boxed centering which was to be of such great interest to Bramante, had now been completely recovered.

Traces of Late-Gothic Influence. After the rural atmosphere of medieval Rome, the fifteenth century still retained some remnants of a courtly past. These could be seen in the profusion of intricate tracery, brackets, mouldings, sgraffito plasterwork and mullioned windows of undoubted German derivation. Of course, this archaic propensity did not represent the whole heritage of the fifteenth century to be passed on to the sixteenth, but some traces of it certainly remained: for example, the mullioned windows of the Villa Madama (the brackets in Raphael's design published by J. Shearman) and the fashion for painting the exterior of houses in fresco which reached its climax at the beginning of the new century. However, the construction of S. Maria dell'Anima and the restoration of S. Giacomo degli Spagnoli illustrate the enduring success of a model directly connected to the tradition of the Hallen-Kirchen.

It is difficult to say with certainty how the fashion for wall graffiti arose. In 1262, as U. Gnoli relates, the Act dividing up the property of the Orsini family refers to a 'domus scaccata quae erat in Ponte', which was probably decorated with pictures drawn in black and white, as were so many soft fabrics of the period. About the year 1480, in the courtyard of the palazzo of Domenico della Rovere (today Palazzo dei Penitenzieri), Pinturicchio painted a complex design incorporating niches, statues, partitions and friezes, traces of which have been uncovered in a recent work of restoration; it is quite likely that this was the model which inspired the fashion for the painting of exteriors which was to attain its climax in the work of Polidoro and Maturino.

The Direct Consultation of Antique Sources. In spite of the lack of outstanding personalities and a precise line of research in Roman fifteenth-century architecture, certain features found in classical buildings, as well as their proportions, were gradually absorbed into contemporary buildings, usually as a result of direct contact with the original sources and without the intervention of theoretical concepts.

In Florence, the imitation of the fixed rules governing classical models had been the objective of architects such as Brunelleschi and Alberti; to this was added in Rome an imitation of the effect. The adaptation was thus made directly, without the compulsion exercised by rules of style, but with a certainty which came to architects through their daily contact with the original sources.

A typical example of these direct influences is the composition consisting of an order projected onto and interpenetrated with the arch, in the manner of the Tabularium, the Colosseum, or the Theatre of Marcellus. This type of structure was typical of Rome and in fact represented one of the specific contributions made by Roman civilization to the classical system of architecture, but had been rejected in Florence, at least in its serial application. The fresco of the *Trinity* in S. Maria Novella, for example, already included an arch supported by columns within a framework of wall pilasters, but this was a case of an inversion of the composition of the Tabularium which provides a contrary plastic effect.

Leon Battista Alberti in the Tempio Malatestiano (where he examined theoretically the relationship existing between column and walls) selected for the sides of the building an unbroken rhythm of massive arcades, without dividing them into separate orders, while for the façades he freely superimposed the two systems (arcades and orders) without the use of a linking intersection. Later in Mantua, where this type of linking section was adopted and systematized, the use of columns was abandoned and the consequent plastic effect was created by the standardization of the system of superimposed structures, thus producing a revolutionary change of style. In Rome, however, the system as applied in its original form can be examined in three works produced in the last years of the fifteenth century which may be considered forerunners of sixteenth-century fashion: the courtyard of Palazzo Venezia (1457–61), the façade with open gallery of S. Marco, and the benediction gallery added to the Vatican by Pius II. In the two first examples there are many obvious ingenuities, indicating that the buildings were derived directly from classical models without the intermediary of theoretical concepts. Particularly noticeable examples include the protrusion of the columns to about half their diameter (whereas in Roman models it was always greater), the presence at the bottom order of the courtyard of Palazzo Venezia of tall column bases independent of the pillar behind them, and the absence of tapering in the columns of the Loggia of S. Marco.

Another feature derived directly from classical sources is the repetition in the Palazzetto Venezia of the architrave of simplified corbels found in the Colosseum which, with the variant of the double *fascia*, was to become typical of the style of Bramante. In the interplay of superimposed orders, the grandiose scale of the design was well adapted to providing this type of cornice with the value of a more sharply-defined terminal, thus indicating the conclusion not only of one order but of a series of superimposed orders. One can also observe here a direct link with the roof of the nave of S. Maria del Popolo, where four connected cross-ribs rest their weight on pedestals above the half-columns, which serve the double function of supporting their weight and lending thrust towards the polistyle pilasters. Only in the Urbino church of S. Bernardino do we find again in the fifteenth century a technique which leaned so heavily on Roman classical models. In spite of the episodic treatment of form, S. Maria del Popolo could represent for sixteenth-century architects the example of a new and unpreconceived relationship with the technical problems of vaulted systems.

PLENITUDO TEMPORUM

From the 'Great Hope' to the 'Great Fear'
The climate of *renovatio* which imbued Rome in the ten years of Julius II's pontificate cannot be entirely understood without reference to the messianic expectation with which the new century was awaited and the widespread anxiety to know what was in store. Everyone was anxious to discover whether, as certain prophets had declared, they were at the start of a new golden age or a period of catastrophes, as suggested by those who were worried by myths of the millennium.

In fact the period of anxious waiting and questioning had been initiated more than twenty years earlier by astrologers, prophets and philosophers. The conjunction of Saturn and Jove in Scorpio under the ascendant of the fifth degree of Libra which occurred in

1484 had alarmed the astrologers, who interpreted it as a sign that a far-reaching religious change was due to take place within the next twenty years.

In his *Oraculum de novo Saeculo*, written in 1496, Giovanni Nesi foresaw the start of a happy era, with the rebirth of the political power of Florence, the conversion of Moslems, and the salvation of the Church. At the beginning of the sixteenth century, Florence would already have rejected such an optimistic vision as an anachronism, but it still seemed a possibility in Rome. The myth of *renovatio Romae* was in fact partly encouraged by the realization that Florence was not likely to retain her position at the axis of the Italian political balance of power; it became the last of the optimistic myths current when the Renaissance was at its height.

The plan to establish a solid political structure on the foundation of the new humanist culture and so to guarantee world peace had failed in Florence but could still be realized in Rome under the leadership of a resolute and aggressive pope. This seemed to be the great certainty—or at least the great hope—which dominated public opinion in Rome at the time of Julius II. Egidio da Viterbo, the General of the Austin Friars and an influential adviser to the Pope, became the mouthpiece of this attitude. In his *Schechina*, a work of cabalistic inspiration, he stated that ten Sephirot governed the ten epochs of the world, and that the last of these was about to commence. In this new era the propagation of the Holy Scriptures would put an end to religious strife. The discovery of the New World would coincide with the early defeat of the Ottomans, and in this way the final reunification of the human family would be brought about.

Julius II's interest in *renovatio Romae* was inextricably linked to his programme of *renovatio imperii*, that is to say, the transformation of the State of the Church into a strong and unified monarchic state. In its general tactics, the policy of Julius II was to counter the violent course of events which were then altering the balance of European power. This policy was continuously being modified and revealed an obvious contradiction between a constant strategic policy and a tortuous line of tactics. It is apparent from this contradiction that the Pope had to endure a dramatic inner conflict caused by his realization that in order to carry through his political programme he would need an entire lifetime, not just the few years of life which remained to him.

Julius was elected in November 1503 at the age of sixty, and even before he could give thought to forming a policy, he found himself faced with the problems connected with a basic reorganization of public offices. In the same month as his election, an epidemic of plague broke out which forced him to take refuge in Castel S. Angelo.

In the spring of 1504 an event occurred—an attack on the papal cortège by a group of starving citizens—which illustrates how seriously the economic situation had deteriorated. The internal problems of the city did not, however, cause the Pope to neglect those of the state. From the first, his major concern was to curb the expansionist policy of Venice; but since he was unable to deal with this problem until he had consolidated his own power, he began to concern himself with other contributory factors to the disintegration of the state authority. He first eliminated the danger of a counter-attack by Cesare Borgia, who was captured by the Spaniards in the spring of 1504, and by a series of marriages formed alliances between his family and the Orsini and Colonna families.

After the first phase of the consolidation of his power and political reorganization had been achieved, the Pope, in line with the tradition of his uncle Sixtus IV, instigated an urban policy and set the stage for a flourishing period of cultural expansion which was to result in the removal of the seat of the papacy from Florence to Rome. From as early as 1503, Bramante and Giuliano da Sangallo were at his side. It was probably in 1504 that the Belvedere was adapted to house a large open-air museum for the display of his admirable collection of antiques.

In April 1505, plans were made to complete the construction of Via Alessandrina in Borgo. In the same year Julius summoned to Rome two sculptors who were his friends

Andrea Sansovino and Michelangelo Buonarroti. Both were asked to make a commemorative monument, Sansovino the funerary monuments for Cardinals Ascanio Sforza and Girolamo Basso della Rovere, and Michelangelo the future tomb of the Pope himself. The plans for his burial then developed to include the restoration of the basilica of St. Peter's. With extraordinary courage, the Pope began to have the old edifice demolished and with the help of his advisers started to plan afresh the construction of the most important church in Christendom.

Meanwhile in 1506, after the epidemic of plague had passed, Julius II carried out a rapid and highly successful excursion against the Baglioni and Bentivoglio families and conquered Perugia and Bologna. The triumphal procession of the victorious Pope passed before the Vatican beneath a reproduction of the arch of Constantine, and other temporary arches were put up along the route which led from S. Maria del Popolo to St. Peter's. Even Pasquino forgot his irony and celebrated the victory with enthusiasm. After 1507, the Pope's building policy became part of a wider concept of town planning. A project for a citadel, to be erected near St. Peter's in order to house the Curia, was considered and later abandoned. Plans which were carried to completion, however, included the construction of the Via Giulia, the replanning of the Lungara and improvements to Via dei Banchi and Via alle Botteghe Oscure.

The work on Via Giulia and the Lungara represents a definite intention to restructure the urban scene, and reveals the existence of an organic plan for the replanning of the city. The two almost parallel streets run along either side of the Tiber and are conceived in a close relationship to the river; together with Via dei Pettinari which joined the Ponte Sisto at Trastevere to the Capitol–Vatican axis and Via Alessandrina, the two streets formed a kind of rectangular through-way traversed by the Tiber. Since it was the Pope's intention that the Lungara was to continue as far as S. Maria in Trastevere and reach the still uninhabited part of the district and the harbour of Ripa Grande after first touching the Aurelian and Portuense, it becomes apparent that the purpose of the new road system was to create a new structure within the disordered conglomeration of populated nuclei which Rome still represented, so as to support and allow room for expansion in the largest of the districts formed by the uneven pattern of the medieval road system. This result was to be obtained by only tangentially touching this nucleus. Julius was anxious to construct a link between Borgo and Trastevere and seemed to wish to endow the Tiber with a central function in order to reduce the isolation of the Vatican and of the populous Trastevere district, which even in medieval times had been a city within a city. Efforts to make the river navigable, as well as the projected construction of a bridge at the intersection of Via Giulia, belong to the same urban and economic plan.

A boldly conceived design has been discovered by L. Frömmel in the Uffizi. It was proposed to insert a large piazza half-way along the straight line formed by Via Giulia, to face the Palazzo dei Tribunali as far as the Palazzo della Vecchia Cancelleria (today Palazzo Sforza Cesarini), to be connected with the 'canale dei Banchi'. This plan to provide the city with a secular centre corresponded to a programme for developing the city as a mercantile and banking centre. The desire for a unified city was the main driving force of those other urban projects of Julius' which were not restricted by the system of roads radiating from the river course, but were concerned with restoration and improvements to the interior of the urban road network. Of particular significance is that of Via dei Banchi, with its implicit recognition of the importance being assumed at that time by the Roman offices of the great bankers of Europe, including Fugger, Chigi, Spannocchi, Calvi, and Spinelli.

A stone affixed to a house in the present Via dei Banchi Nuovi by the builders Domenico Massimo and Girolamo Pico recalls in elegant Roman letters how the Pope, 'having established the dominion of the Holy Roman Church and liberated Italy, beautified this city of Rome which seemed rather a city of conquest which he divided, broadening and tracing roads, as befitted the majesty of his reign.' It is significant that the phrase *occupate similiorem quam divise* was taken from the Fifth book of Livy which relates how, after the destruction of Rome by the army of the Veientes, the city was rebuilt in a most disorderly way as the result of haste and the lack of firm control, and no attention was paid to the alignment of streets and private property. Referring to this historic tradition, the inscription thus implies praise of Julius not only in his care for the city, but also for his inflexible authority, since in order to attain his ends he had not hesitated to destroy the homes of nobles and cardinals.

Meanwhile in 1508, while work was in progress on the construction of the law courts which were to give Via Giulia a centre and almost a reason for existence, the Pope profited from the collapse of the power of Duke Valentino, and with utmost urgency set about reconquering the cities of Cervia and Faenza which had fallen into the hands of the Venetian Republic. Barely a year after he joined the League of Cambrai with Louis XII, Ferdinand, and the Emperor Maximilian, the expansionist aims of Venice were finally crushed at the Battle of Agnadello (14 May 1509) and the Pope could turn his attention to more ambitious schemes. Now that his state was consolidated, it was necessary to save Italy's position in the balance of power by reducing the power of France. For this purpose he broke away from the League of Cambrai and turned to Ferrara, an ally of Louis XII, and personally led the siege of Mirandola; he evinced such daring that he forgot his age and pastoral dignity and scaled the walls himself. This was in the year 1511. France reacted strongly and made an attack on the papal policy—from the religious as well as strategic point of view—at a Council which she convoked at Pisa. Julius was thus forced to come to terms with Spain, Venice, and the Swiss cantons, under the so-called 'Holy League'. So, with the well-worn slogan of 'out with the barbarians', the seeds of future Spanish rule were sown in order to avoid French domination. In April 1512 the French defeated the army of the League at Ravenna; but this was a Pyrrhic victory and Louis XII chose to avoid risks by leaving Italy and his Duchy of Milan.

Close to death, Julius could still hope in spite of his defeat. He was dissatisfied with what had been achieved and perturbed by the growing strength of Spain, so made another of his 'leaps of scale'. Abandoning the narrow Italian viewpoint for a broader European one, he tried to put into operation a long-cherished plan—to lead a new crusade against the Ottomans. Egidio da Viterbo did his utmost to ensure that this projected crusade would dominate the deliberations of the Lateran Council, which was convoked in the spring of 1512. From the very first session, held soon after the defeat of Ravenna, he declared that this defeat was a divine sign pointing to the fact that the best way to achieve the reunification of Europe was by an alliance between Church and Empire, each with clearly defined separate roles. In the years 1508–13, the most intense and dramatic period of the papacy of Julius, Rome became the centre of Italian culture. Raphael came to Rome at the end of 1508 and by the beginning of the following year was already working on the Sala della Segnatura.

It was probably also in 1508 that Bramante began work on the construction of S. Pietro in Montorio. The rebuilding of St. Peter's continued at the same time. In 1512 a heavy programme of building work was initiated in the palace of the Vatican, and the spiral staircase of the Belvedere and the S. Damaso loggias were added. When Julius II died in February 1513, Rome was another city compared with its appearance ten years previously. Another great enemy of the Pope, Machiavelli, acknowledged that whereas at one time 'even the smallest baron thought he had the right to disparage the papal power, now it can incur the respect of a king of France'.

There has been much diversity of opinion over the policy pursued by Julius II. From the time of Erasmus to Guicciardini, Machiavelli, and historians of modern times, opinion has been divided as to whether his strategy was that of a genius or of an infantile and impulsive man. But whatever the effect of his activity in the political sphere, there can be no doubt that he earned himself a decisive place in the role of mediator between the factions of culture and of power—one of the most important functions performed by the Roman Church in the fifteenth and sixteenth centuries.

The papacy of Leo X signalled a pause in both political and urban initiatives. The bold, impulsive activity of Julius II was followed by a policy of astute passivity. Whereas Julius always looked impatiently to the future, his successor remained completely immersed in the present and concentrated all his ambitions in forging a dynastic link between Rome and Florence, a link which proved successful from both the economic and artistic points of view.

The first important project initiated by Leo X was begun soon after his election. It was the construction of new buildings for the University of Rome, facing the old church of S. Eustachio. In this gesture of sympathy and encouragement for learning, the Pope showed an awareness of the mood of the time.

Meanwhile, in the political sphere Leo made an agreement in 1514 with Francis I, the new French king, lending his support to the king's reconquest of the Duchy of Milan. The Swiss force which tried to oppose this move was defeated at the battle of Marignano. Under the peace of Bologna (1515), the Pope yielded Parma and Piacenza to France in exchange for French recognition of the Medici regime in Florence and the granting of the Duchy of Urbino to his nephew Lorenzo. At the same time, Charles V of Hapsburg, who became ruler of the Netherlands in 1515, inherited the kingdom of Spain from Ferdinand in the following year, and in 1519, after the death of Maximilian, obtained the imperial crown with the support of German financiers and Flemish bankers.

The years of the papacy of Leo correspond almost exactly to the *pax gallica* which followed the battle of Marignano, but during these peaceful years a tragedy occurred, the full gravity of which was not immediately apparent in Rome—the revolt of Luther and the beginning of the Reformation.

The Lateran Council set up by Julius II in 1512 was reopened by Leo and continued its activities until 1516. Some desire for reform was expressed, though cautiously, by its members and in 1517 there was established in Rome on the initiative of Carafa, who was destined to become the champion of the repression of heretics, a congregation of priests and laymen called 'the Oratory of Divine Love', for the purpose of fighting religious decadence. This was in the very year when Luther affixed his ninety-five arguments against the sale of indulgences to the door of Wittemberg Cathedral. At first the Pope's attitude towards Luther had been one of indifference; but in 1520, after the rebel monk had issued his third pamphlet casting doubt on the orthodoxy of the church, he had been compelled to intervene and in his bull *Exurge Domine*, threatened Luther with excommunication. Leo X died in December 1521 before the schism had become irreparable. The last duel at which he was present, the Diet of Worms, could still give him an illusion of victory. Luther was banished, but returned to Wittemberg and remained safe in the castle of Wartburg. There he spent his time in solitary meditation, translating the Bible, giving a unified form to the German language, and making the Reformation the catalyst of the national German conscience.

The dramatic events taking place in the church thus remained in the eyes of the Medici Pope a remote background which he still mistakenly believed he could exorcize. Only the most sensitive minds were fully awake to the situation, while the Roman court was absorbed in cultural matters and tended to shut its eyes to reality. 'The Pope', wrote the Venetian ambassador Marino Giorgio in 1517, 'is a kind and very liberal man, who holds every serious effort in horror and loves peace ... he loves the sciences, possesses a good knowledge of literature ... and above all is a fine musician.' In the same account we read that immediately after his election Leo X had said to his brother Giuliano: 'Let us enjoy the papacy since God has given it to us'. Whether it be true or false, this anecdote expresses the view of the papacy which was held by many learned ecclesiastics of the time. It represented to them the acquisition of an exceptional degree of personal power which could be used in order to carry out dynamic projects, to promote culture and the arts, and to establish in the small community of the court a style of life based on an aesthetic ideal of learning and courtesy.

During the papacy of Leo X, scholars continued to come to Rome from all parts of Italy and any traces of provincialism remaining—including literary provincialism—quickly disappeared. Intellectuals were attracted by the air of liberty which had been observed by Erasmus in 1509, when he wrote to his host Cardinal Guibé after his departure from Rome: 'If I had not suddenly torn myself away from Rome, I could never have brought myself to leave. There one can enjoy sweet liberty, rich libraries, pleasant interchange of conversation with men of culture, the company of many scholars, and the spectacle of ancient monuments.'

In architecture, one of the first ideas to interest Leo X was the extension of the Medici palace, and the designs made by Giuliano and Antonio da Sangallo have come down to us. Of particular interest is Giuliano's plan to connect the building to Piazza Navona by a large space enclosed by an arcade: this was the first attempt to restore the open space of the Roman circus to an organic part of the city, when it was still so clearly beyond the scale of the medieval structure and even of the Renaissance buildings.

In 1518, under the direction of the *magistri viarum*, Bartolomeo della Valle and Raimondo Capodiferro, work was begun on Via di Ripetta. In order to solve the technical and aesthetic problems connected with the standardization of the corresponding network of old streets, the Pope called in Raphael and Antonio da Sangallo the Younger. The funds to pay for this work were raised by an extraordinary tax called 'prostitute tax' because it hit the inhabitants of the district which was much frequented by prostitutes. Much of the land situated near the street was let on long lease by the hospital of S. Giacomo and by Agostino Chigi. To acquire plots and build on them, co-operatives of master builders and architects were established; many of their members lived in the vicinity and the church of the guild of masons (S. Gregorio) was also nearby. Baldassarre Peruzzi and many members of the Sangallo family owned houses in the street. Around 1517 it was also decided to rebuild the hospital of S. Giacomo as a centre for the treatment of venereal diseases.

The new Via Ripetta represented a continuation of the urban policy of Julius II and at the same time an alternative. This road corresponded to the Via Giulia, as an artery following the course of the river; but it also served a contrary function in that it directed urban development northwards, away from the most densely populated area at the bend of the Tiber.

The large works of construction begun by Julius were abandoned and fell into neglect, including work on St. Peter's. Leo X concentrated on beautifying the Vatican, and instituted a competition for the national church of Florence, which brought Jacopo Tatti unexpectedly to the fore.

The pontificate of Hadrian VI marked a break in the development of papal policy. Elected almost by chance in the hope that he could heal the rift between the two sides dominating the conclave, the Cardinal of Toulouse was known especially for his incorruptible character and for having been preceptor to Charles V. His election caused dismay among the colony of intellectuals and artists, for whom it presaged the end of their 'sweet liberty'.

Since the new Pope had not taken part in the conclave and was still in Spain, the most absurd rumours were current in Rome regarding his supposed intention of transferring the apostolic seat. Sanudo recalls that a large poster was affixed to the Vatican with the words: 'This building to let'.

It was difficult to understand how, in a conclave composed almost exclusively of Italians, the man chosen to be Pope was a cardinal born in Utrecht. This choice ran counter to a tradition which had lasted without a break for 461 years, whereby non-Italians were always excluded from the supreme ecclesiastical authority. Although the initiative behind the election came from Cardinal Medici in the hope that it would result in peace between the two sides, it may be said that this unexpected decision revealed a sense of uncertainty and disquiet concerning the possibility of continuing to interpret ecclesiastical power as being equivalent to monarchic power, as had been the policy of the last few popes who were all members of the great Italian aristocratic families.

Hadrian VI was elected in 1522 and had barely one year and eight months in which to tackle the serious problems which afflicted the church. In so short a time he could only become more and more tragically aware of his own powerlessness, and the words he wished to have engraved on his tombstone: *Proh dolor, quantum refert in quae tempora vel optimi cuiusque virtus incidat* (cf. Forcella III, 447) convey the sense of the contradictions in which he felt himself imprisoned. The start of his pontificate was darkened by a terrible epidemic which forced him to take refuge in the Belvedere and caused the majority of his cardinals to leave the city. In a letter to Luigi Gonzaga dated 12 August 1522, Castiglione gives a vivid description of the anxiety which lay over the city: 'I am extremely healthy (thank God) and so are all ours. The plague does enormous harm, but has not yet affected persons of the nobility. It is a very cruel fact that nearly all those who fall ill, even of some other disease, are allowed to die of cold and lack of other necessities, since everyone refuses them aid, while those affected by the plague are too afraid to say anything, so that it is an evil thing: this quite apart from the lack of great provisions. I think forty thousand people have left Rome. Each day certain Companies walk in procession to the principal churches, some carrying a head of St. Sebastian, others a figure of St. Roch, and stop outside the infected houses, and say certain prayers, and call on the mercy of God. But those who made Anna weep greatly (Maria Polissena, Castiglione's sister) were a great number of little children all naked from the waist upwards, who walk in procession beating themselves and calling on the mercy of God, saying: Spare, O Lord, thy people; and with them there are some who make them go in order, and walk with them and feed them ... There are stories of many miracles here in Rome; among others, a woman who was walking in procession carrying a child who had the plague, and the other women knew it, and this woman went in great faith and having arrived at S. Agostino, placed this child, who had the inflammation (the sign of the plague), on the altar of Our Lady, and he was immediately cured. Many other tales are told. I am staying here in Belvedere, a very remote and safe place, and meet very few people, so that your mind may be at rest ...'

Hadrian was eager to reform the organization of the church, but found countless obstacles in his path. At the same time, he was unable to do anything to prevent the schism becoming aggravated, while the struggle between France and the Empire continued to be waged on the soil of Italy. In addition, the problem of the Ottoman threat, to which he was particularly sensitive, was worsened by the conquest of Rhodes in 1522.

Although the austerity and gloom which marked the time of Hadrian's papacy were prophetic—destined to be fulfilled, barely five years later, in the dreadful events of the Sack of Rome—the policy of the Pope aroused only annoyance and derision. People declared, 'Rome is no longer Rome', and looked on with amazement as the Vatican, which had always been thronged with prelates, scholars, and artists, became a cultural desert. It was considered absurd that the Pope should have once thought of going to live in a little house with a garden, far from the ceremonial of the palace which was held to be the finest in Europe. Hadrian undoubtedly saw culture and art as mere instruments of his power. As soon as he was elected, he barred the doors of the Belvedere where the Laocoon was kept, saying that such figures were after all merely pagan idols. Raphael's pupils who were engaged on the Room of Constantine were dismissed, and even the learned Sadoleto left Rome. Referring to his letters, the Pope remarked with great reservation that they were the 'letters of a poet'.

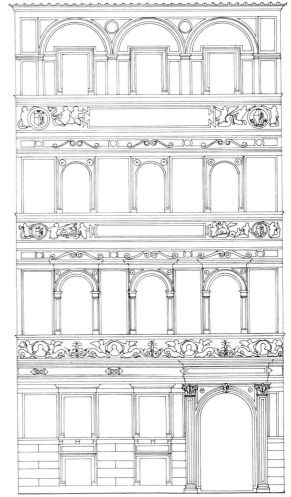

Exterior of the Casa Sander in Via dell'Anima. Typical example of a bourgeois residence decorated with frescoes erected in the early years of the sixteenth century.

It is therefore not at all surprising that Hadrian did not concern himself with urban problems. Even the good intention he did express—to continue work on St. Peter's—could not be put into effect owing to general political difficulties. However, architectural activity did not entirely cease during those years; among other projects, mention should be made of the Palazzetto Leroy and the Villa Lante on the Janiculum.

The election of Clement VII was welcomed enthusiastically by the courtiers of Leo X, most of whom had left the city; however, it was not, and could not be, a return to *plenitudo temporum*. In a few years the situation deteriorated rapidly and it became increasingly obvious that the process which had threatened the 'sweet liberty' of the intellectuals was an irreversible one. Clement, more suited to submit to history than to dominate it, was a Pope whose reign, as described by Berni, was 'composed of respects / Of considerations and discourses / Of yets, of thens, of buts, of ifs, of perhapses / Of countless other ineffectual words ...'

The first political problem Clement had to face was the decision of Francis I to move into Italy in order to recover the land which had been lost to France by the conquest of the Duchy of Milan and the betrayal of Duke Charles Bourbon, who entered the service of the Emperor in 1523. The Pope was intimidated and, acting shortsightedly, broke his links with Spain, while on 24 February 1525 the French army was defeated at Pavia and Francis I taken prisoner. After a short period of imprisonment, the King returned to France, dissolved the agreement at the price of which he had obtained his freedom, and formed the 'League of Cognac' with the King of England, the Venetian Republic, the Duchy of Milan, and Clement VII.

Although a serious Ottoman offensive was taking place in Hungary which brought Turkish troops to the gates of Vienna, Charles V easily succeeded in routing the Italian princes and humiliating the Pope.

An army of fourteen thousand pikemen, drawn from the regions of Germany which had been converted to Protestantism, descended on Italy, broke through the resistance of the troops led by Giovanni delle Bande Nere at Borgoforte, and in the spring of 1527 came within sight of Rome.

The principal cause of the catastrophe was the death of the Connétable of Bourbon. Leaderless, the pikemen and Spaniards put Rome to siege and made a bivouac of the basilica of St. Peter's. 'Everywhere are shouts, the clash of arms,' wrote the Frenchman Grolier (cf. Gregorovius IV, No. 734), 'the wailing of women and children, the glare of flames, the crash of falling roofs; out of fear we resist and look on, as if we alone have been spared by fate so as to witness the ruin of our country.' In his autobiography, Sebastiano Schertlin of Burtenbach described the most brutal week of the siege in these words: 'In 1527, on 6 May, we took Rome by assault, mortally wounding more than six thousand men. We sacked the whole city, taking in all the churches and on the land whatever we could find, burning much of the city. We behaved strangely, and broke up and tore to shreds everything relating to accounting, records, and affairs of the court' (cf. L. v. Pastor, IV, 2, p. 270).

The Pope and his cardinals remained in Rome, barricading themselves in Castel S. Angelo where they endured the siege. They put all their trust in the army of the League, but when at last this army arrived in the vicinity of Rome, it came to the conclusion, after long deliberation, that it was not able to intervene. In *Orlando Furioso*, Ariosto describes the situation in these lines: 'See the murders and robberies / Everywhere mark Rome sorrowful; / And by burning and rape divine / And profane things are destroyed equally. / In the camp of the league he sees the ruins close by / And hears the weeping and crying / And where he should go forward, turns back, / And lets the successor of Peter be taken.' On 5 June 1527 the Pope surrendered and two days later left for Naples with his cardinals. 'Among them', commented Schertlin of Burtenbach, 'there was great sorrow and they wept bitterly; we all became rich' (L. v. Pastor, IV, 2, p. 275).

Between 1522 and 1572, Clement VII had followed the urban policy of Leo X, building the third road of the 'trident' of the Campo Marzio, Via del Babuino, which follows the Pincio and connects the Porta del Popolo with the Trevi district. He also replanned and paved the Piazza del Popolo and the last section of Via Ripetta. In the years immediately preceding the Sack, the Papal Mint was constructed in the banking district, and the Palazzo Niccolini was built nearby, perhaps by Jacopo Sansovino. Meanwhile, above the Theatre of Marcellus, Peruzzi built the Palazzo Orsini, and in the studio of Antonio da Sangallo designs were made for the Pozzo house and the Palazzo Ossoli near the Campo di Fiori.

Thus there irrevocably came to an end a type of relationship between culture and power which had characterized an epoch and was based on the autonomy of culture and on its specific cognitive value. In the future, the Church came to realize more and more clearly that the mediatory role she had adopted between culture and power politics was turning against her own interests, and threatened to lead her into a revolutionary situation which she would be unable to control.

THE UNIVERSAL LANGUAGE

Culture and Architecture between 1503 and 1527

When in 1508 Julius II decided to entrust the decoration of his Vatican apartments to Raphael, then newly arrived in Rome, and ordered work to stop on the paintings begun by Perugino, Sodoma, and Lotto, he was guided by the certainty that he was witnessing the birth of a new culture which would leave behind as an anachronistic survival the pluralistic dispersive trends which had marked the end of the fifteenth century. The enormous political contradictions which had overshadowed the early years of his papacy seemed about to be resolved, so that Julius II, and Bramante who inspired his cultural policy, were encouraged to believe that the contradictions which had weakened late-humanist culture were about to be resolved also. The fact, however, that both the Pope and the circle of intellectuals close to him were under the same illusion meant that the development of the arts came to symbolize an ambitious political programme, prefiguring the reforming and restoring zeal of the state authority which was to pave the way to the 'fullness of time'.

In this ideological context, architecture was called upon to fulfil a distinctly political role, though not yet in a rhetorical or propagandist sense. The universal problems of dignity and order which architects were called upon to solve were of the same nature as those posed in all other disciplinary fields, while architecture's specific qualities of concreteness and social adaptation ensured that this art should enjoy a kind of supremacy as a creator and experimenter in new forms.

Roman classicism thus came into existence not, in the manner of other schools, as the result of a slow maturation of contributory factors, but by the presence at a particular moment in time of definitive political purpose, together with exceptionally gifted men of culture drawn from the most diverse origins. The movement grew especially out of the alliance of two generations: the generation of Bramante and Giuliano da Sangallo, both born in 1444, to which Julius II also belonged, and that of Michelangelo, Raphael, Antonio da Sangallo the Younger, Baldassarre Peruzzi, and Sansovino, all born between 1475 and 1483.

In the first decades of the sixteenth century, the figurative arts and architecture in Rome enjoyed great independence, but at the same time were confronted with problems which transcended the individual disciplines. They were independent because of the great respect accorded to intellectual research, but they were also interdependent since society saw them as an indispensable means to self-realization.

Owing to this special status of intellectual activity and the nature of architectural research as a reflection of society, there arises the need to draw conclusions from the analyses aimed at identifying the autonomous values of architecture in a comparative synthesis which would recompose that unity of culture attested countless times in the course of the analysis.

For all the leading figures in classical architecture, the most urgent decisions to be made with regard to style presupposed the clarification of a two-sided relationship: that with the Tuscan humanist tradition, and that with the classical heritage. There are obvious analogies to be drawn here with the literary debate taking place on the subject of the vulgar tongue versus the restoration of Latin. Such analogies can be useful provided they are not automatically applied. It is clear, for example, that to look in sixteenth-century architecture for any differences corresponding to the very precise distinction that existed between the vulgar tongue and Latin would be to force the analogy too far; but it is true that the aspiration towards universality shared by supporters of both languages was also deeply felt by architects when they were faced by problems which were sometimes similar to those faced by the supporters of a learned universal language, and at other times resembled those facing the partisans of a reform of the vulgar tongue.

The linguistic debate, which was the most urgent problem affecting Italian literary culture in the first decades of the sixteenth century, must be viewed in relation to the polarity between cosmopolitanism and nationalism which dramatically expressed the uncertainty felt by the Italian people as they were torn between their aspirations towards a national consciousness and the pull of the many cultural centres of the city states. In both tendencies, national supremacy was sought; on the one hand by emphasizing Italy's direct descent from classical civilization and her specific function of restoring the language of the Golden Age to its original integrity to act as an instrument of universal communication among men of learning, and on the other, by valuing the vulgar tongue as a personal heritage with a classical quality of its own.

In both cases there followed in the sphere of culture an objective which was unattainable politically, and the instruments perfected by humanism were employed in order to codify absolute values through the rules of syntax and grammar. For Latinists, the problem of 'classicism within classicism' was created, as they considered how to restore the language of the Golden Age before Latin had become decadent and corrupted through the process of evolution; for supporters of the vulgar tongue, there was the analogous problem of regional dialects and orthodox Tuscan set against eclectic tendencies. In both cases, the central problem lay in the supposed opposition of the Platonic theory of types—namely, an ideal type of beauty attainable by synthesis and not by reference to any concrete model—and the recognition of stylistic models in the works of the great masters of literature, taken as examples of absolute perfection to be imitated.

The dispute concerning imitation—which was of such importance to the theory of architecture also—had at the end of the fifteenth century caused Poliziano to take up arms against Paolo Cortese. Now, at the beginning of the sixteenth century, Bembo took up the argument with Gian Francesco Pico della Mirandola.

'You told me', Poliziano had written, 'that having studied Cicero, I do not express myself like Cicero. But I am not Cicero, and it is through Cicero that I have learnt how to be myself.' Paolo Cortese replied: 'I want, O my Poliziano, to be not as the monkey in his likeness to man, but as the son in his likeness to his father. The former is a ridiculous imitator who copies only the deformities and defects of the body correctly while the latter portrays the face, the gait, the condition, the motion, the form, the voice, and finally the form of the body, and yet in this resemblance still has something of his own, something natural and individual, so that if placed side by side they would appear very different ... It is of the greatest interest to know whether one wants to imitate someone or no one. I myself declare that not only in oratory, but in the other arts also imitation is a necessity. For all knowledge is acquired with the aid of previous learning and nothing can be in the mind which has not previously been perceived through the senses.'

An unprejudiced humanist attitude enabled Poliziano to appreciate the late Latin authors as well as the classical ones, whereas for the Ciceronians the chronological limits of the Golden Age were as fixed as the columns of Hercules. 'Finally, I would not insist on the fact,' wrote Poliziano in an essay on the writings of Quintilian and Statius, 'that in the century of these authors, oratory had already become corrupted. In fact, if we look closely we will not say that it is corrupt and decadent, but will understand that it was only the type of oratory which had changed. Nor shall we say that what was different was worse: in truth there is greater learning, more frequent delight, many aphorisms, many choice images, in these late authors; no sense is lethargic, no form inert, and in short not only are they healthy, they are also strong, joyful, warm-blooded and colourful.'

The debate between Bembo and Pico followed almost the same lines. At the time of his first stay in Rome, Pietro Bembo expressed enthusiastic admiration for the oratory of Egidio da Viterbo and declared himself a Neoplatonist (with the result that Castiglione portrayed him ironically in *The Courtier*, having him recalled to reality by the Duchess of Urbino who turned to him saying: 'Take care, master Pietro, that with such thoughts your soul does not become separated from your body'). In his quarrel with Gian Francesco Pico, however, as a literary man by profession he supported an anti-idealistic viewpoint—that of the single model: 'But I come back to what I was saying about the imitation of all good writers; and I ask you again if you want us to imitate all good writers so that we copy the complete style of each one of them; or if you consider that one must take from each one only the best part; and in this way form a unique, entire style out of the best features of many different styles? Consider in which of these two ways you would like your dogma to be taken. It is inconceivable that you would wish it to be in the first. And what could be more absurd than to take diverse and multiple forms, diverse even among themselves, which are followed by many, and to try to incorporate them into a single form? *It is as if in building a single church you were to take from everywhere the many examples of different churches made in various styles and methods.* If then you want it to be in the second way, in the first place it is not imitation to take from the many parts which constitute the style of a writer one thing and repeat this thing in other cases until you make of it a style of your own. This would be more like refashioning or, if one may use the expression, taking alms. This is what men did in times of famine, taking what was needed not from one but from many. Imitation embraces the whole form of a work, asks that its individual parts be integrated, is directed to the entire structure ... If you consider well, there is no way of imitating the individual good parts of each one. What is good and excellent in a writer is the result of all the parts; all the qualities and also the defects, if there are any defects, together produce it.'

Pico answered with the same degree of assurance, insisting on the fallacy of imitation based on a single model, which would be an attempt to seize the unattainable, that reflection of the idea which illuminates the works of man and can only become weak and exhausted in the imitated object. 'It is in our minds that the perfection we have to imitate is to be found,' he wrote, 'not in any model ... you cannot find among men a body so beautiful in all its aspects that it should be copied; I marvel then that you have been able to find a beautiful body of oratory to imitate in a single writer when you should have learnt even from your own Cicero that this is impossible. In addition these sublunar things ... cannot be blessed on all sides, since mother nature distributes her gifts not to one only but to all, and to each person lavishes particular virtues. For this reason the beautiful type of oratory which you seek must be looked for in nature herself and especially in the mind where lies its close origin and and from where are derived words and letters.' The dispute between Pico and Bembo was not so much an ideological debate between Platonism and Aristotelianism, as between two opposed points of view: that of the philosopher and that of the rhetorician, the practitioner who has discovered in his own experience processes and norms whose value he would not wish to deny even if they do not fit in with abstract theories. It is interesting that, at least during his Milanese period, Bramante was of the same opinion as Pico, as can be seen from the opinion that he expressed regarding the tiburium for the cathedral, where he proposed to take the best features of several designs entered for the competition. Bembo had previously stayed in Rome at the time of Julius II, but his influence on the cultural scene became more marked after Leo X appointed him, together with Sadoleto, to the post of Secretary of Briefs. This gesture gave official recognition to the political importance of the purist restoration of Latin, and to the strange phenomenon of Ciceronianism. If the political ambitions of Julius II had been to a large extent frustrated, the hope of preserving for the church the role of arbiter in European disputes was still firmly maintained, and Latin acted as a unifying instrument which was invaluable in ensuring that she preserved her right of tutelage.

In order to be acceptable as the universal language of scholars, Latin had to be purged of the corruptions of medieval usage and restored to its time of greatest splendour. A work of scientific restoration was therefore instigated in Rome, where the language was treated in the same way as an architectural monument which had to be restored, and brought back to the form it had developed in the century of Augustus. For the Church to direct this research into 'classicism within classicism' meant to deny the validity of the evolution of Latin as it had come to be used by the Church herself, and to devalue church Latin by acknowledging the independence of its linguistic form from its historic content; but it meant also that the Church was able in this way to reassert her position as an arbiter beyond party disputes.

Like every dogmatic position, Ciceronianism degenerated into a fetishism of rules and intolerance. Erasmus, who during his stay in Rome had enjoyed the 'sweet liberty' accorded to intellectuals, has left us a witty satire of Roman literary society in his *Ciceronianus*, published in 1528. Here he ridiculed the fashion of disguising the objects and ideas which were part of contemporary and Christian life in words of Latin and pagan usage. The aspect of Roman Ciceronianism which was most nationalistic and self-congratulatory, foreshadowing the lamentable use which was to be made of this imperialist doctrine as a justification for fascism, culminated in the ridiculous expulsion of Christophe Longueil. He had come to Rome in 1511 in order to study Cicero and was about to receive Roman citizenship at the Capitol when he became the object of the anger of the 'Romanists' for having in his youth spoken of the superiority of the Franks over the Romans.

The problem of the *conflict between model and ideal type;* that of the *single model* and that of *distinguishing a Golden Age within the classical heritage* and therefore a purified linguistic repertory, with all archaic forms and involved imagery expunged—all these ideas were present in the architectural debate of Roman classicism. But architects found themselves faced with difficulties greater than those confronting men of letters, and they approached them far more pragmatically. The fundamental contradiction which led to the extension to the field of architecture of the principle of the Golden Age lies in the disparity between the evidence of the monuments themselves and Vitruvian theory, and the difficulty of dating the monuments. In architecture, scientific method was far behind literature and in fact it did not possess a method of its own. The task of filling this gap was to be the greatest ambition not only of Bramante, but also of the generation of his pupils, and later developed into the cultural and political programme which was initiated by Raphael with the help of Castiglione.

Within the Vitruvian theory, which was made up of a collage of heterogeneous ideas, contradictions abounded, creating questions of interpretation which were insoluble. In the first place, the exposition of the theory of orders as a résumé of experiments evolving over a period of time did not correspond to the theory of the single model, and set a pluralistic principle at the basis of architectural stylistic conventions. By systematically choosing the Corinthian and Composite, fifteenth-century architects had interpreted the thoughts of

Vitruvius relating to the other orders, and especially the difficult Doric, as a historical digression concerning experiments which had since been improved upon.

By restoring the Doric, with metopes and triglyphs, in the Tempietto of S. Pietro in Montorio, Bramante was declaring his refusal to make a choice among the orders, and recognizing that several correct solutions were possible corresponding to the genres of architectural parlance, which were exactly similar to the literary genres. Once the misconception had been removed that real classicism could be attained by choosing from among the repertory of the orders, sixteenth-century architects tried to define classicism as harmony and purity, as the refusal to permit contamination between the genres. But a comparison between the Roman monuments as they actually appear and the Vitruvian theory of the inner coherence of genres, which prescribed for each order rules governing the inclusion and precise arrangement of accessory architectural features such as doors, windows, pedestals, etc., immediately made clear the impossibility of reducing the classical heritage to a body of unambiguous rules, even after all archaic and decadent works have been expunged from it. The attempt to organize the classical repertory in a systematic fashion was destined to create a number of problems of far greater magnitude than those which had given concern to the grammarians. The nature of the architectural discipline and its social role precluded its limitation to a purely restorative function, as was the case with Latin; apart from the question of what was correct, architects were forced to meet entirely new demands and, in addition, the aesthetic and technical experiments which had now become such a well-established part of the social heritage could not be entirely ignored, nor could they easily be adapted to a system of orthodox classicism. In essence, architects had to make the kind of choices which corresponded to those confronting both the supporters of Latin and the supporters of the vulgar tongue. Renaissance architecture could not fail to take some account of the heritage of the Middle Ages, which continually re-emerged at the level of economic structure and typology, and there was thus a continual attempt to combine the Latin of the classical tradition with the vulgar tongue of the late–classical, Romanesque, and Gothic architectural traditions. At the beginning of the sixteenth century, it did seem that the Utopian ideal of a total restoration of the classical style was about to become a reality; but such a restoration could take place, and then always deceptively, only in restricted and experimental cases, for example in the Tempietto of S. Pietro in Montorio or the theatre of the Capitol. In the large–scale subjects handled by Bramante, architectural and figurative elements far removed from the Golden Age are found together with classical ones. Hence arises the contradiction connected with the difficulty of translating into architectural 'Latin' aesthetic functions and values which derive from entirely different sources. The forced quality of the translations which were attempted reproduced that paradoxical contamination which was the object of Erasmus's derision.

In literature, some of the arguments raised in the debate regarding the vulgar tongue coincided with those of Ciceronianism; they concerned grammatical rules and the single stylistic model. Besides these, however, the debate also centred on the question of the Tuscan origin of the language and the significance of the other Italian regional traditions. There was a close analogy here to what was taking place in architecture in relation to the Tuscan tradition and the problem of linguistic unification. In this literary debate the leading figures, Bembo, Castiglione, and Calmeta, were exponents of Roman culture, bound by links of friendship to artists and architects.

The ideas of Calmeta, the author of a lost work, are propounded by Bembo in *Prose della Volgar Lingua* and concern the creation of a 'courtly language'—a kind of Esperanto to be constructed out of the linguistic usages of the Roman court. 'Our Calmeta calls courtly language', writes Bembo, 'that spoken in the Roman court, and says that since, when one mentions a court, everyone must believe that one is speaking of the court of Rome as it is the most important of all, courtly language means the language that is used in Rome, not, of course, by Roman men, but by men of the court who stay in Rome ... he calls, I say, that language ... which is used at the court in Rome, not Spanish or French or Milanese or Neapolitan by itself, or any other, but one that is born from a mixture of all of these and now is among the people of the court almost equally common to each one of them.' In opposition to the paradoxical notion of a language created by a small minority of dignitaries and courtiers, a class language artificially imposed from above, Bembo upheld the historic vulgar tongue, not so much in its social reality as in its literary essence, as a tradition which had grown and become an institution through the work of writers, and which needed only a precise grammatical codification in order to acquire full dignity. Since the vernacular was a reality which it would be ridiculous to oppose, one must strive to improve it by standardizing it and creating parameters of judgement which would make it possible to distinguish what was correct from what was not. Failing this, scholars who were concerned only with Latin and Greek would be like those who, 'giving great attention and study to other tongues and practising them masterfully, do not care if they cannot reason in their own, and resemble those men who have built for themselves in some remote, isolated district vast and costly palaces worked in marble and resplendent with gold, while in their own city they live in wretched hovels'. For Bembo, to be concerned with the vulgar tongue meant to analyse linguistic structures and establish criteria of judgement, to acknowledge the fundamental role of the Florentine tradition while at the same time accepting contributions from other regions, and to determine models of perfection which would act as standards of comparison. Dante and Petrarch were taken as examples to point the contrast between, on the one hand, emphasis on content and the inventive use of language, and on the other, mastery of form and polished style. These two lines, taken from Canto 29 of the *Inferno*, served to stigmatize the hazard of inelegance: 'and the nails so tore down the scabs, as the knife the scales of the bream'. 'Which poet,' wrote Bembo, 'not only had he kept silent when he could not say what he wished to say gracefully, would have done better both in this and in many other parts of his compositions, but again, had he taken the trouble to say in more elegant and refined words that which anyone would have known how to say if they had taken thought, while he spoke in such coarse and dishonoured words, he would have been of far greater fame and esteem than he is... Not so did Petrarch, who, not speaking of that which could not be expressed in elegant terms, yet if among what was well said there was some minute expression which could be said better, he changed it and rechanged it, until it could not be said better in any way at all.'

Regarding the supremacy of the Florentine tradition, while Bembo did not dispute it, he made a distinction between the language as it was fixed in literary masterpieces and as it was spoken in Tuscany. He considered that because of its popular nature the latter was unacceptable as a model and was a corrupted form of the fourteenth-century language. Therefore contemporary Tuscan writers were more to be pitied than envied, since, possessing from birth such a renowned linguistic regional heritage, they used it instinctively, without comparison to literary models. In the debate on the vernacular there thus entered the concept of a Golden Age and linguistic involution. 'But how many times does it happen that the manner of the language of past seasons is better than that of the present, so that we too should write in the style of past seasons, Giuliano, and not in that of our own time. Just as much better prose and verse would have been written by Seneca and Suetonius and Lucan and Claudian and all those authors writing after the century of Julius Caesar and Augustus, and after that pure and happy age until modern times, if they had written in the manner of their classical writers, Virgil and Cicero, which they did not do, preferring to write in their own; so we too will in the same way do much better if we will write in the style of Boccaccio and Petrarch than if we use our own, since there is no doubt that they expressed their thoughts much better than we do.'

Castiglione showed a more unprejudiced attitude towards the question of the supremacy of Tuscan. In the preface to *The Courtier*, after speaking in favour of locutions directly derived from the Latin, he expressed his impatience with purists in these words: 'I will say no other than this, that to remove all argument, I confess to those who rebuke me that I do not know this, their so difficult and recondite Tuscan tongue; and I say that I have written in mine, and as I speak, and to those who speak as I speak: and in this way I do not think I have harmed anyone.' The biggest difference between architectural and literary culture with respect to the problem of the vernacular lies in the fact that whatever kind of relationship one may wish to establish between the concept of a national language and the studies of Renaissance architects, it is clear that for them the Golden Age was not a past to which they could look, but a present, an experience to be lived. The position of independence from the Tuscan tradition which was sought by Roman architects corresponded not so much to a desire for a vast field of choice, as to the conviction that this tradition could be of value only as a preparatory stage, to be left behind by the advent of a universal language which would combine the qualities of a scholarly and a popular language: something which on the literary plane would represent a concept of language separated from any concrete peculiarities, a synthesis of Greek, Latin, and the vernacular, in which the constituent elements have lost all their autonomy.

Calmeta's idea that the Roman court should fulfil a central function in the reform of the language corresponded to the ambitions of Bramante and his pupils, and in some aspects is to be identified with the programme of Roman classicism. What was not possible on the literary plane was achieved in architecture, not in the way imagined by Calmeta, through a synthesis of the Romance languages and Italian dialects, but by comparing the achievements of humanist society with those of the best period of the classical tradition. The cosmopolitan pluralism which had characterized late fifteenth-century Roman architecture—apparent in the Gothic taste of Pius II, the international style of the churches constructed at the time of Sixtus IV, and the practice of introducing the late-Gothic mullioned window into domestic architecture—represented for architects of the early sixteenth century an error that had to be overcome. A universal language could not be born out of a contamination of languages, but from an intuition of the ideal unity which linked them all in the purest and most absolute of all languages, that of antiquity, from which the others were derived as deviations and corrupted forms.

This close comparison between the problems of literary culture and those of architectural and artistic culture would be meaningless were not the principle of unity the dominant theme of Renaissance culture. The unity of culture through design, through number, through harmony, was only the reflection of a vaster unity of a cosmic nature which cut across the boundaries between religion and philosophy, between art and religion, between past and present. In the same way as Plato and Moses, Hercules and Christ, hermetism and revelation, prophecy and cabbala, end by becoming one with each other, since truth is indivisible and reveals itself in infinite ways, so too literature, art, and architecture are primarily projections of the human spirit which are transformed into aesthetic value by diverse means on the surface, but are fundamentally alike. It suffices to reflect on the frequency with which men of letters adopted architectural metaphors and the tendency of theorists of architecture (this was particularly apparent in Serlio) to compare architecture with the spoken language. It is with these points in mind that this rapid survey of the terms of the literary debate can help us to understand the attitude towards tradition held by the leading figures of the Roman classical school: Giuliano da Sangallo, Bramante, Raphael, Peruzzi and Antonio da Sangallo the Younger.

For Bramante, a direct knowledge of the ancient world was a need which arose in him at the time of his maturity, after a period of activity and experimentation. When, at the age of fifty-six, he finally settled in Rome at the beginning of the new century, his style was already full of contradictions. Although he was not of a philosophical turn of mind, he had formulated a conception of architecture in which light was the prime reality, giving shape to the structure. Such works as S. Satiro, the apse of S. Maria delle Grazie, or the

Prevedari engraving, appear to translate the Neoplatonic and Early-Christian conception of light into architectural terms. 'He who desires to construct a building which is worthy,' wrote St. Ambrose, 'before laying the foundation, thinks where he can give it light' (Heptameron IX, 33). Bramante, 'before laying the foundation', that is, at the moment of conception, visualizes his building as a luminous spectacle, an optical reality which may not even correspond to concrete and tactile reality. The perspective choir of S. Satiro is not only a stratagem, but an indication of a way of thought in which a technical experiment with painting does not weaken and confuse the architectural structure, but enriches it by juxtaposing real spaces and illusory spaces. At the same time, Bramante's line of research was directed towards constructing a pseudo-classical system in many respects resembling Mantegna's, where, as Fiocco has written, 'the conquest of forms conceived in the round and of the surrounding area conceived geometrically is resolved without the aid of scientific theory, by translating and hence superseding the form through the use of colour to suggest construction, and superseding the linear perspective by means of aerial perspective'.

The first years of Bramante's stay in Rome seem to have been spent in meditation, when he was engaged in absorbing the local tradition. In spite of traces of Lombard influence, the Cloister of S. Maria della Pace is built on the simple, rustic lines of many Roman late fifteenth-century buildings.

It was his meeting with Julius II which transformed Bramante's attitude towards history; the slowness and caution which had marked the initial period of self-criticism were replaced by the dynamic energy out of which Roman classicism was born. The significant feature of this new development was the rediscovery of the Doric, as formulated by Vitruvius; this indicated at one and the same time a rejection of Florentine convention relating to the supremacy of the florid orders, and a determination to return to classical sources without passing through any intermediary.

The Doric is the most structural of the orders, the one in which the connection between the parts is the most intricate and involved, but also the most firm and unambiguous, and where Alberti's distinction between *pulchritudo* (*quidem certa cum ratione concinnitas universarum partium in eo, cuius sint, ita ut addi aut diminui aut immutari possit nihil quin improbabilius reddatur*) and *ornamentum* (*ornamentum autem afficti et compacti naturam sapere magis quam innati*) no longer has any meaning, since decoration and structure have become identical. The abandonment of the decorative ornamentation which was typical of the Lombard style meant also a return to the Brunelleschi tradition and to some aspects of the Urbino tradition, but with new instruments of expression derived from Alberti's rediscovery of the spatial and plastic *effect* of the Roman monuments. Compared with Giuliano da Sangallo who represented the direct continuity of the Florentine tradition, which had become weakened by an excess of theorizing, Bramante shared the attitude of Bembo towards the dogmatism of the supporters of the Tuscan tradition: language does not exist in the abstract but in the concrete examples of actual models; Brunelleschi constituted an essential point of reference; but those who continued to work in his manner have weakened the force of his example. For Giuliano, the classical world was a composite of fascinating and mysterious images which could be incorporated into architectural discourse in the same way as quotations are used in literary discourse. His subtle, evocative drawings transport us to a historical perspective, a far-off and heroic setting, such as we find in the paintings of Mantegna. For Bramante as for Brunelleschi, the classical world was there to testify to an absolute truth, which was expressed in historical texts from which a series of universal laws could be derived.

For Giuliano, Brunelleschi was the model of a system. For Bramante he was the model of a method. Bramante's purpose was to continue research into classical architecture in order to complete the still fragmentary picture built up by the humanists. Apart from the geometrical reality and logical coherence of this architecture, it was necessary to study the optical value of form, its control, and the spatial nature of architectonic phenomena. But Bramante's declared intent to reintegrate more fully the classical heritage was contradicted by an alternative requirement—that of taking into account the medieval, and in particular, Gothic, tradition, at least insofar as its great technical achievements were concerned. To continue the literary metaphor, the problem here was no longer that of distinguishing the classical stage of classicism, or—which is the same thing—of leading the vernacular towards a Golden Age of its own by comparing it with the ancient languages. In relation to the Gothic tradition, Bramante raised the problem of contamination, a problem similar to the one posed by Francesco Colonna in *Hypnerotomachia Poliphili*. Arguing empirically, as Castiglione had done before him, Bramante claimed the right to use linguistic survivals. The contradiction, or rather the 'downfall' of Bramante, does not consist in the fact that he sought a synthesis between the classical and the Christian traditions, but that he deluded himself that this could be achieved without radical innovations, by adopting forms which were incongruous when related to the type of the structure. The work of synthesis which was to succeed for Michelangelo in St. Peter's through the stylistic inventions of the serried rhythm of the giant order and neo-Gothic rib-vaulting resolved in the round failed for Bramante in at least two cases: the Palazzo dei Tribunali ('a castle' decorated with orders) and the exterior of St. Peter's. Here, the plan oscillates between bare, Byzantine-type volumes and laborious classical ornamentation, marking the final defeat of his research into the façade in the Menicantonio sketchbook, where the bell-towers resemble stacks of Chinese boxes, simply because the 'structuralism' of the superimposed orders have lost all sense of unity and appear as a mere collection of autonomous units. If in some respects the position of Bramante appears to coincide with that of Bembo, in particular in terms of technical concreteness and reliance on rules, in other respects they are clearly far apart. This is shown by the unprejudiced attitude of Bramante towards stylistic difficulties. The outstanding example is the spiral staircase of the Belvedere, an over-praised work, in which pictorial and architectonic qualities are not successfully combined except through a contradictory 'optical' solution. We have already pointed out that the sense of continuity evoked by the succession of supports for the spiral staircase was imperilled by the change in the capitals of the columns. The sudden bringing together of different types of columns surmounted by an identical architrave presents a perfect parallel to the case of the lines of Dante quoted by Bembo as an example of excess. In this case, too, a purist would have preferred the author to have 'kept silent when he could not say what he wished to say gracefully', or that he had said it 'with more elegant and refined words'. The clashing dissonance results from the need to lead the view of the staircase from inside the well up to the level of the superimposed orders; but by subordinating the fundamental image of the staircase, which is that of movement, to the static and entirely accidental viewpoint of the centre of the well, the result is an amusing experiment rather than an important demonstration of the contradictions implicit in the classical system. In this case, too, the rejection of stylistic invention limits the value of the experiment, as in the case of a chemical reaction which fails to be produced owing to the absence of a catalyst. Here the mixture of genres is certainly without a Shakespearian breadth of vision, and seems more of a self-mocking diversion to which it is unjustifiable to ascribe the value of a precursor of Mannerism. The solution to the problem found by Vignola at Caprarola fifty years later was the answer provided by a great Petrarchist to the Dantean excess of the Belvedere spiral staircase. However, any link between Bramante and Dante is purely superficial, since far from being an example of spontaneity and aggressivity, the Belvedere staircase, as Serlio correctly saw, represents 'the most artificial architecture of Bramante'. When seen against the background of his most fundamental source of inspiration, universal language, the Roman work of Bramante appears extraordinarily incomplete and riddled with contradictions, far removed from the clarity of thought of classical literary men, although it was nourished with far more vigorous qualities. To define his historic role, we can quote Hegel's *Enzyklopädie*: 'Only when the multiple is urged to its highest degree of contradiction does it awaken and become animated and finds there the negativity which is the immanent pulsation of self-propulsion and vitality.' The strength of Bramante lies in the shortness and incompleteness of his activity, as well as in the intensity of certain successful results, which have acted as examples, and the vast scope of the problems he faced. If the work of Bramante had not possessed this character of an open heritage, making use of heterogeneous trends, it could not have nurtured the exceptionally fruitful 'succession' in the work of his pupils who for another thirty years were to carry forward his research.

Raphael was the favourite pupil of Bramante. While striving together with Castiglione to construct the myth of his master as a 'unique model', as the *Petrarch of architecture* he tried to surpass him by finding a clearer answer to the questions concerning the universal language which, as we have seen, lay at the centre of Bramante's self-criticism.

For the purely structural use of orders as objective instruments borrowed direct from ancient sources, Raphael substituted a subtle control of form according to a system of rules which was applied most successfully in the Chigi chapel. Bramante's impartial choice of minor features in the composition, such as portals, windows, etc., gave way to the delicate Petrarchism of the well-turned expression, the carefully chosen and beautifully pronounced phrase. On the other hand, in late works such as the background to the *Expulsion of Heliodorus* and the Villa Madama, he seemed to return critically to the themes treated by Bramante in the Belvedere and St. Peter's, bringing a new complexity to the simplicity of the master.

But the originality of Raphael's contribution to the dispute concerning tradition is to be sought in the realm of theory, in the letter which Castiglione wrote together with him to Leo X, where they suggested to the Pope that the spontaneous efforts of intellectuals should be put to political use and that the restoration and examination of the ancient monuments should be undertaken with the same rigour as is applied to catalogue and protect a valuable heritage, and as befitted the universal political significance of Rome and the Apostolic See. Writing to Castiglione in 1514, after having referred to the 'great weight' of the task of planning St. Peter's, Raphael added: 'But in my thoughts, I fly much higher. I should like to find the beautiful forms of ancient buildings, though I know not if the flight will be like that of Icarus. A great light on them is held out to me by Vitruvius, but I do not know if it will suffice.' During the last years of his life, Raphael was dominated by the desire to study the classical heritage more deeply and far more systematically than his predecessors had done. Winckelmann speaks of an album, still existing in his time, which contained a minute and complete relief of the Temple of Hercules at Cori. Bembo, writing to Cardinal Bibbiena in 1516, speaks of an excursion he made to Tivoli with Raphael in the company of Navagero and Beazzano, for the purpose of studying the classical monuments. Raphael himself, in a letter addressed to his misanthropic friend Fabio Calvo, who was staying as a guest in his house, writes of having been in the company of 'master Fulvio', that is, the antiquarian Andrea Fulvio, 'seeking the beautiful antiquities (which) are in these vineyards', and added that he would go and take them from his hand 'by order of Our Lord'.

The treatise of Vitruvius was not taken by Raphael as a 'unique model'. Because of its theoretical nature, it had to be interpreted and proved by comparison with the actual texts. 'By continually reading good authors and comparing the works with their writings,' we read in the letter to Leo X, 'I think I have gained some knowledge of that ancient architecture.' Raphael devoted himself to this task with enthusiasm, formed a friendship with Fra Giocondo, the author of the first illustrated edition and the first Italian translation (which he himself annotated minutely), with Fabio Calvo, who was also working on another translation of the Roman treatise in 1516, and with Andrea Fulvio who in 1527 had published *Antiquitates Urbis*, where he reconstructed the form of the imperial city in the light of the new sixteenth-century architecture.

The letter to Leo X was certainly the result of the great friendship between Castiglione and Raphael. At the close of a letter written by Castiglione to his mother in 1520, there is further evidence of this friendship, when he briefly announces the death of his friend in movingly sincere terms: 'I am well, but I do not feel as though I am in Rome, now that my poor Raphael is no longer here. May God keep his blessed soul.'

In the letter, the style and concept can be recognized as Castiglione's, but the substance of the argument, intensely technical and without either the rigour or abstraction of a theory, could be only Raphael's. The classical tradition is seen as an enclosed system, perfect and incorruptible. In the chronological course of Latin literature, the Golden Age followed an archaic age and preceded a period of Mannerism. To this was contrasted the absoluteness and incorruptibility of architecture, based on the 'certain reasons' referred to by Alberti. 'And although letters, sculpture, painting, and almost all other arts had long been in decline and deteriorating up to the time of the last emperors, yet architecture was maintained in good reason and building continued in the same manner as before: and this was the last of the arts to be lost, as can be learnt from many things, among others from the Arch of Constantine, which is well composed and constructed in all that pertains to architecture, while the sculptures on the same arch are very inferior, with no good art or design in them.' Only the fall of the Empire and the advent of the Barbarians, by destroying the political balance, had been able to threaten the classical system of architecture viewed as a heritage of objective scientific rules. Like other arts, architecture is a product of concord and peace and the direct result of good government. The great originality of Raphael's letter lies in the clarity with which he stated the problem of classical restoration and placed it alongside that of the civil Renaissance. Rome was the 'ancient mother of glory and the Italian name', and by saving the relics of her grandeur the memory of 'those divine souls' was kept alive so that they could 'excite and arouse to virtue the spirits who are today among us'. The protection of the cultural heritage was more important as a political than a cultural necessity and represented the corollary of a programme consisting of 'scattering the holy seed of peace among the Christian princes'. The ancient monuments, symbols of *pax romana*, were the living proof of how important peace is in the lives of men, 'because just as from the calamity of war is born destruction, the ruin of all the disciplines and arts, so from peace and concord is born the happiness of nations'.

'Keep alive the example of the ancients so as to equal and surpass them': this was the exhortation addressed by Raphael and Castiglione to Leo X, a reflection of the optimistic attitude which was still possible at the time. The wording is interesting because it reveals that the 'surpassing of the ancients' was still not an accomplished reality but only an aspiration, and that in order to be effected it was first necessary to 'equal' them—an implicit criticism of the Florentine humanist tradition. The conviction expressed by Alberti in his dedicatory letter to the *Book of Painting*, that the surpassing had already occurred with the construction of Brunelleschi's dome and the works of Donatello and Masaccio, was remote both in time and in the cultural assumptions on which it rested. The humanist culture had been only the first step in a process still far from complete. 'The modern buildings', we read in the letter to the Pope, 'are well known, both for being new and for not yet having entirely attained either the excellence or that immense expense which one can see and observe in the old. For although in our days architecture is very alive and has come very close to the manner of the ancients, as is seen in many fine works of Bramante, nevertheless the ornamentation is not of such precious materials as in the old, where it seems that with infinite expense they put into effect that which they imagined, and only by desiring it could break through every difficulty.'

The difference between the position of Bramante and that of Raphael in their attitudes to the problem of the classical and the Florentine traditions emerges clearly from these words, which are very close to the spirit of Raphael's own works of architecture. To the pure structuralism of Bramante, Raphael wished to reintroduce the decorative and material values of classical architecture—to add, not substitute, since some of his own works, S. Eligio, for example, were actually a later expression of the same structuralism. His passion for stuccowork and for grotesques, his return to the florid style of the Augustan period, reveal a criticism of a schematic approach and of a theory of design existing independent of the material. The reduction of colour to chiaroscuro and shading, an indifference to decorative detail, had implied the rejection of fullness of expression which for Raphael was the mark of classical maturity. The aim of 'equalling the ancients' comprised in his view the rediscovery of surface and colour values and the harmonious siting of the building in its natural landscape: it was these qualities which were to inspire the designs for the Villa Madama.

An extremely interesting indication of the historical view of Roman classicism can be found in Raphael's description of Gothic architecture, which he carefully distinguished from medieval barbarism. He showed no lack of comprehension for 'the manner of German architecture', but considered it to be inferior to the classical style, where the architects of the ancient world 'as well as the structure of the whole edifice, made very beautiful also the cornices, the friezes, and the architraves, and in short all the ornaments...' Raphael seemed to admit—and here the influence of Bramante was decisive—that in the 'structure of the whole edifice' even the Gothic architects had attained remarkable results, but he could not excuse their lack of grandeur and measure. 'Yet there was some reason behind this architecture since it was created out of trees not yet cut, whose branches they bent and drew together to make their pointed arches. And although this source is not entirely to be despised, yet it is weak, for huts made out of linked beams serving as columns with their tops and coverings, as Vitruvius describes of the origin of Doric work, would stand up better than the pointed arches, which have two centres: and again, according to mathematical logic, much more support would be given by a half-circle, where each of its lines is drawn towards a single centre; and apart from its weakness, the pointed arch does not have such grace in our eyes as we find in the perfection of the circle; and it can be seen that nature seeks almost no other form.' The supremacy of the classical style was thus explained rationally in terms of imitation, to the advantage of the system based on the circle as against the unstable pointed arch, since architectonic value depends on reason and a structural link with nature.

Baldassarre Peruzzi, the most gifted and most unfortunate of Bramante's pupils, was the one who almost certainly exercised the greatest influence on his master, but unfortunately we know less about him than about any other of the architects of the Roman classical school.

His relationship to the classical world can be studied not only in the few works of architecture he left, but also in a rich collection of drawings and sketchbooks; but the fragmentary nature of this body of work, the lack of even the slightest theoretical comment, and the considerable distance in time separating the most important buildings he designed—la Farnesina and Palazzo Massimo—makes it difficult to reconstruct his critical thought. The writings of his pupils, Serlio and Cataneo, do not help much either, although they both devoted themselves to theoretical activity. Both the open-minded experimentalism and the avowed fidelity to Vitruvius evinced by Sebastiano Serlio (who by holding this ambiguous position seemed to wish to defend himself against any accusation of deviationism) seem extraneous to the thought of Peruzzi, and the arid didacticism of Cataneo under the influence of the Counter-Reformation seems even more remote.

It can be seen from his buildings, measured drawings, and plans that Peruzzi, more than any other of his contemporaries, had through a systematic process of exploration slowly acquired a global knowledge of the remnants of Roman architecture, which was not merely schematic. He was interested not only in the most famous of the monuments, but also in those which were least known, and especially those which differed from conventional patterns and thus demonstrated the anti-dogmatic aspect of his research. We do not possess objective evidence as to whether or not Peruzzi shared Raphael's opinion of classical architecture, which he described as an enclosed system with neither dawn nor twilight, but his predilection for 'exceptions' within the classical repertory leads us to believe that he had a clear picture of the profound stylistic differences between the various historical periods and could appreciate them without dogmatism, in the manner of Poliziano. His early contact with Francesco di Giorgio Martini had a marked influence on Peruzzi and isolated him in Roman society during the first years of the century. The Aristotelian foundation for his thought and the generalization of deductive processes, without leading him to the casuistry of Serlio, enabled him to continue his archaeological research side by side with a study of a type of composition to be based on a geometrical system, and in this he came close to Leonardo.

Observe, for example, in the Uffizi drawing No. 529 (drawing XXXVII) how the problem of incorporating polygons into a continuous pattern, first used decoratively as if new applications for the caisson motif were being sought, became suddenly a pretext for research into the placing of three-dimensional units in space, thus leading to a 'spatial narration' obtainable by means of a succession of areas of different geometrical shapes. The plans for a large monastery, published here for the first time, represent one of the rare cases of composition based on the rules of plane geometry and bring an independent approach to some of the ideas of Francesco di Giorgio. The primary element of the composition is the simple structure, of constant thickness, which is then varied to form a network of closed and open spaces surrounded by peristyles and open to the exterior. The circle, the octagon, and the hexagon are combined like the acts of a drama which is rigidly governed by the rules of the unities. The combination of spatial units was elaborated further in the plans for S. Domenico di Siena (Uffizi No. 339 and Oxford, Ashmolean Museum) where circular, oval, and rectangular spaces succeed each other along the central axis, creating a vibrant rhythm and an illusion of depth recalling the expedients of a theatrical setting (drawings XXXI-XXXIII). Psychological attention to the spatial exploitation of proportions attained the maximum degree of refinement in Peruzzi, as is shown by the frequent notes he inserted in his plans regarding the triple relationship of height-width-length of the rectangular areas. These relationships were always chosen with great care and were linked to the theory of music, being varied in their sequences to create an impression of diversity and of unity in multiplicity.

In connection with the debate on language, Peruzzi's research did not lead him in the direction of definitive systems and absolute theories, such as those held by men of letters. Among his contemporaries, Peruzzi was basically the architect most bound to the tradition of critical humanism and the least likely to abandon this tradition for the safe shores of academicism. A Leonardo-like passion for technology, which never became sterile in its application, urged him to abjure easy solutions and to bring equal interest and intellectual effort to bear on the problems of a dam, a lock, a gigantic dome, or an enormous conglomeration of interconnected volumes. Peruzzi's heretical passion for the hexagon, for the oval, even for the triangle (drawing XXVII), his represen tation of space by means of successive graduated roofs (drawings XX, XXI, XXVI) which both hold back and impel a broad-eyed view, constituted at one and the same time an archaic return to the architecture of Urbino and a foretaste of Borromini. However, these factors also symptomized the uncompromising nature of Peruzzi's architectural thought and his taste for a dogmatic and imitative type of classicism.

In his attitude towards the orthodox theories of Vitruvius, Peruzzi adopted an intermediary position. He certainly studied the writings of the Roman theorist in depth and analytically, but even at the time of his maturity when he had absorbed minutely all their teachings, he maintained a position of jealous defence as regards composition. In the Palazzo Massimo, for example, the disparity between the tapered wall pilasters of the porch and the rectangular pilasters of the façade, the placing of the stupendous Ionic portal in a Doric context, the shortening of the Doric cornice of the courtyard, were all deviations from the laws of Vitruvius which obeyed a logic of composition inherent in the individual nature of the task in hand. It was in this fidelity to the occasion, this close adhesion to the theme, that Peruzzi expressed his idea of a universal language as something which became continually transformed and recreated in the linguistic act. Grammar provides the canvas onto which the action is grafted; every rule must be set against the theme and 'chosen' (in its slight curvature, the *ovolo* of the Doric capital is not a model but a type which can be created in countless diverse ways, only one of which, however, can correspond entirely to the demands of the particular context into which it is to be inserted). From the theory of the unique context was born the last great work of Peruzzi, the Palazzo Massimo. It was the most intense and personalized example of Roman classicism, now under threat, expressing an Erasmian faith in critical humanism, which was the enemy of all conformity, all soothing obedience to rules, but was far from any artificial upheaval or irrational apology for unrest.

Antonio da Sangallo's approach to architecture was dictated by a prophetic intuition of the new role which was to be assumed by the figure of the artist-technician in bourgois society after the period of critical humanism had come to an end. He was interested only in the discipline to which he devoted his life, but interpreted this discipline in a pragmatic sense and included all its ramifications: in other words, he saw himself not only as a planner and executive director, but as a practical organizer, a builder, technician and economist. He was thus at the opposite pole to Alberti, who had advised the architect not to 'dirty his hands' with economic matters, so as not to be drawn into inferior activities. Sangallo entered whole-heartedly into this type of compromise. He associated himself with contractors, took on work on his own account, and surrounded himself with a band of craftsmen who between them covered the whole range of building work—the construction of models, which in his view had the value of the didactic moment in the planning method, the cost accounting, surveying, executive planning, and signing of contracts. For Sangallo, architecture was no longer a liberal art but a profession in the modern sense of the term, an economic and cultural activity which needed well-equipped technicians who could fulfil this ambivalent task. Sangallo's harsh criticism of Bramante and Raphael which appears in his works and letters was a criticism of Renaissance encyclopaedism and the theory of design which placed all three figurative arts on an equal plane. For Sangallo, architecture was connected with painting only in the sense that both arts were means of portraying reality, and he believed that architectural drawing should be something quite different from a branch of painting and should serve a precise technical purpose. We need only look at the drawings made from the Antique by Giuliano and Antonio da Sangallo the Younger to become aware of the abyss which separates the intellectual of the time of Lorenzo de' Medici from the man of action whose attitude foreshadows not only Domenico Fontana but also the artefacts of the Industrial Revolution.

In the work of Sangallo there is an open contradiction between quantity and quality. As was the case with the pictorial work of Raphael, a vast quantity of commissions did not permit the architect to execute all the work personally, so that he was forced to assemble a legion of helpers and to work out an easily applied system of paradigms which could be produced in large quantities. The problem of language and its universality was conditioned in Sangallo by a new type of relationship with society. Since, like most enterprising businessmen in bourgeois society, he aspired to a social prestige which would compare with that of the aristocracy, Sangallo took a firm step away from the inter-class limbo of the intellectuals. His simple, dignified building models were successful because they met the minute requirements of the ruling class, without the intermediary of intellectualistic concepts. The concentration of his interests on the types of architecture represented by the town and country palazzo and the urban villa, and his artistic successes in these fields, were related to his own ambition of 'possessing' buildings of this type, an ambition which was partly satisfied in the two edifices (the most ambitious remained unfinished) which he constructed for himself on the Via Giulia, the most eminent and most modern street in Rome.

For Sangallo the universality of the language coincided with his capacity for meeting technical, economic and social demands. Bramante's insistence on pure structuralism became part of this programme, but had to be directed towards purely pragmatic ends. In the very remarkable stylistic invention of the so-called 'Sangallesque' palazzo, there come into play not only problems related to form, but economic problems and those concerned with the rationalization of building processes as well. The abandonment of orders, the linking of windows by simple bands, the lateral closure achieved by the rusticated corner-stones, these were not only stylistic inventions but represented easy means of piecing together simply-made parts without incurring the slightest problem of tolerance or disparity between structure and decoration. Ackermann has effectively described the Sangallesque palazzo, attributing to it unlimited possibilities of extension in the construction of the façade. The present writer does not feel able to accept this hypothesis completely, because the careful choice of proportions which informs the façades of Sangallo reveals his interest in a final and unalterable result, in line with the Albertian theory of *nihil addi*; but a comparison with modern building processes is fully acceptable and is confirmed by the pertinent remarks made by Giovannoni in connection with the use, in the house of Viacampes, of a series of small gates of a type which often recurs in anonymous productions of the period.

For Sangallo universality of style coincided not only with the observance of practicality and dignity but with the objectivity of the planning process also, an objectivity which was explained by a correct choice of syntax and of words in relation to their frequency and ease of use. On countless occasions, including his town-planning projects, Sangallo concentrated his inventive research at this level and adopted structures which had already been tested; one could say that he forced himself to give the viewer the impression of seeing something familiar.

The most intellectual side of Sangallo's activity was to be seen in his passion for Vitruvius. This was attested not only by his enthusiastic preface to an edition of the treatise, but to an even greater extent by the constant process of self-criticism which characterized his career and was particularly evident in the design of the orders and the accessory features of the architectural structure (doors, windows, etc.). Commenting in a written note on one of his youthful designs, he recognized its immaturity and criticized it severely, saying that he had not yet come to a proper understanding of Vitruvius. His research advanced from two bases: that of functionalism, from which arose the interesting inventions of the Palazzo Farnese, the S. Spirito gate, and the Palazzo Baldassini; and that of Vitruvian orthodoxy, which explains the polished and impeccable detail of his most inventive works. The homage he paid to the authority of Vitruvius and his erudite exposition of absolute forms was the antithesis of his professional pragmatism and technical proficiency. In this dichotomy, there is already contained, as we shall see, the premise for the academic involution of classicism; but Sangallo remained at the threshold of this process, from which he was protected by his great vocation of an architect, a creator of the urban form through the invention and slow progressive perfection of its constituent elements. It is certain that when one walks about in the Renaissance district of Rome, one finds oneself in a city whose decisive imprint, so far as quantity is concerned, was received from Sangallo. We need only consider the innumerable rusticated corners echoing each other from one corner to another of the buildings which compose the pattern of the city. This organizing element acts now as foreground, now as perspective reference, now as a distant visual memory. It is the mark of Sangallo, a testimony to his vocation to construct from a practical basis, resisting the temptation of a Utopian vision, and to create a city which remained a concrete reality.

'What I call a century is not the ordinary measure of time, but those great stages in humanity in which new ideas appear and the face of the world is transformed. This comes about through a slow and constant elaboration of all social elements which work in it unconsciously; but before striking the mortal blow at the crumbling edifice, a man is awaited who is destined to personify that whole movement, to which so many elements conspire unknowingly, and who is destined to give it his name.' What De Sanctis has written with reference to Machiavelli could equally be applied to Bramante in his relationship to sixteenth-century architecture, which he inaugurated during his stay in Rome with a group of works destined to have a lasting influence on the future of architecture. It is only in recent times that the dating of the Tempietto di S. Pietro in Montorio, given as 1501, has been questioned; this dating has given credibility to the myth that Bramante experienced a sudden conversion from the pictorialism of his Lombard style to a rigid classicism, which came to him as a consequence of a direct acquaintance with the ancient monuments and his analytical study of them at the dawn of the new century. '... He resolved', writes Vasari in his *Life* of Bramante, 'to give himself up entirely to architecture when he left Milan. He came to Rome before the Holy Year of 1500, where being known by some of his friends both from the district and from Lombardy, he was asked to design at San Giovanni in Laterano, above the Holy Door which is opened for the Jubilee, a coat of arms for Pope Alexander VI, worked in fresco with angels and supporting figures. Bramante had acquired in Lombardy and earned in Rome a certain amount of money, which he spent very carefully, since he wished to live on his income and at the same time refrain from work so that he could be free to examine all the ancient buildings of Rome. And having put his hand to it, he went his way in solitary meditation, and in a short space of time he examined all the edifices that were in that city and outside in the country as far as Naples, and wherever he knew that there were ancient things. He examined what was at Tivoli and at Hadrian's Villa.'

The date of 1500 or 1499 for Bramante's transfer to Rome is confirmed indirectly by the last document which concerns his activity in Milan—a payment for the model of the monastery of S. Ambrogio—dated 20 December 1498, and by the fact that in the year 1499 Ludovico il Moro left Lombardy. But if this date can be accepted for Bramante's final move to Rome, this does not invalidate the possibility that he may have stayed there on a previous occasion. Support for this hypothesis is provided by the fact that in 1493, during one of his prolonged absences, Ludovico instructed his ambassadors to look for him in Florence and Rome, while a sonnet written by the architect in 1497 is marked 'in Terracina', which indicates that it may have been composed at Terracina, the locality south of Rome where he could have gone to see the ruins of the Temple of Jupiter. The suggestion recently put forward by De Angelis d'Ossat that Bramante may have stayed in Rome around the year 1493 would, on the other hand, confirm Vasari's note to the effect that Bramante participated in certain decisions concerning the plan for the Palazzo della Cancelleria.

The traditional attribution of the Tempietto di S. Pietro in Montorio to the years 1500–2 is based partly on the evidence of the inscriptions on two stones which can be seen in the underground chapel of the temple. De Angelis has rightly pointed out the unreliability of this evidence, and suggests that the inscriptions do not relate to the building constructed by Bramante, but to an earlier temporary construction. The present author finds that the evidence of the inscriptions is very fragile, and on the basis of all the contributory factors—the silence of Albertini, Vasari's notes on the building which he places among those produced in the time of Julius II, after the Palazzo dei Tribunali, and a stylistic analysis which reveals its close connection with certain features of St. Peter's—agrees with the hypothesis of De Angelis, which therefore precludes the possibility that Bramante experienced a sudden and complete conversion to classicism. We shall now see that a much more reliable explanation can be reached by studying the course of what may be described as the 'Roman self-criticism' of Bramante.

An interpretation of sources lends credibility to the hypothesis that Bramante's Roman activity began about 1493, as a member of a team responsible for the technical supervision of the building works for the palazzo which Cardinal Raffaele Riario was constructing near the Campo de' Fiori. This bold enterprise was based on a paradoxical architectural programme which reveals the extent of the patron's open-mindedness: the extension of the palazzo attached to the church of S. Lorenzo in Damaso was to end by totally absorbing the religious fabric inside the new building, thus reducing its importance to that of a palatine chapel.

The demolition work to make way for the new buildings began in 1484, and it was in 1489 that there took place the game of dice at which the Cardinal won the fabulous amount of fourteen thousand ducats (from Franceschetto Cybo, nephew of Innocent VIII) which made it possible to pay for this ambitious building programme.

We know from the inscription engraved on the façade that the work of construction was completed in 1495. Since the inscription mentions the church as well, it may be assumed that by this date the whole building was almost completed. However, on the architrave over some of the windows of the façade looking towards Corso Vittorio, there can be read the name of the patron (who is given the title of Bishop of Ostia, which he did not obtain until 1511), thus providing evidence that some of the less important work was still in progress at the time of the papacy of Julius II.

Vasari mentions Bramante's work on this project in the second edition of his *Lives* in these words: 'Having grown in reputation, he found himself engaged with other excellent architects on a large part of the Palazzo di S. Giorgio near the Campo di Fiori, which although it was later done much better, was nonetheless and is still, for its grandeur, considered a comfortable and magnificent dwelling; and this building was executed by a certain Antonio Montecavallo.' The fact also that this note was omitted from the first edition of the *Lives* and did not appear until the second, indicates that its source was well authenticated and that its early omission aroused a reaction among those who were better informed.

On stylistic considerations, we cannot ascribe this work to Bramante himself, and it would seem more likely that he acted only in a consultative capacity. For although the geometrical composition of the façade, especially in the courtyard, bears some resemblance to the Milanese works of Bramante, taken as a whole the palazzo does not fit in with the architect's self-critical approach. The principal façade has no sense of plastic unity and is composed of bands possessing a marked horizontal development. It is not so much in the style of the façade of a palazzo as of a wing adapted to the scale of a town house; the subtly designed plan conceals a complex and heterogeneous organism which is not projected onto the urban area. Compared with the complex harmonies composed by Bramante, the Cancelleria is more like a simple melody, a delicate and insistent repetition of modulated notes.

The harmonic composition of the coupled order was not matched by a primary structure strong enough to gather and conclude a succession; the slight protrusion of the two final projecting sections can be seen as timid and artificial expedients when viewed from above. Bramante's sense of structure, which he considered an inflexible law co-ordinating the individual parts in a controlled design, is totally lacking in this façade composed of three superimposed bands of equal thickness corresponding to the rusticated base and the first and second orders. Inside these, a complex rhythm of partially superimposed and linked squares governs the succession of wall pilasters and the position and dimensions of the windows. The visual impression created by the façade varies considerably according to the condition of the light; when the air is clear and the sunlight falls directly on to it, the rhythmic design becomes emphasized and overcomes the inertia caused by the large blind

Courtyard of the Palazzo della Cancelleria (1 cm = 5.5. m).

Palazzo della Cancelleria, axonometric of the courtyard.

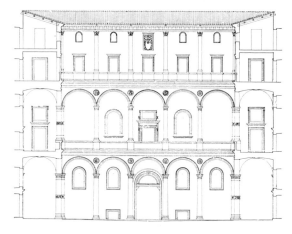

wall; we then become sharply aware of the necessity of the proportions. If, however, the light is only reflected, then the inertia of the mass becomes more powerful than the rhythmic effect of the orders; it is only in the sides of the building, especially in the façade overlooking Via del Pellegrino where an aristocratic restraint comes to terms with the commercial atmosphere of the street, that the rhythm is more strongly marked owing to the contrast between the travertine orders and the brick infill and the complex pattern assumed by the shops.

One may perhaps conclude from a certain ambiguity in the forms of the different façades and contrasting aspects in a single façade that this was a result of teamwork, or at least the pooling of ideas, so that the original conception became superseded.

The most direct influences are those of Urbino, but this fact does not necessarily imply the presence of Bramante, since close links existed at that time between Rome and Urbino and the palazzo built by Laurana and Francesco di Giorgio Martini, which Baldassar Castiglione praised in *The Courtier*, was popular. The contribution of Bramante is to be sought not so much in this influence of Urbino as in certain very characteristic stylistic features.

For example, an important feature of the façade, the terminal cornice, has a close resemblance to that of the cloister of S. Maria della Pace, while the first- and top-floor windows contain more than a hint of the influence of Bramante. The derivation of the former from the Arco de' Borsari in Verona indicates that an architect from the north was responsible for them, while the contrast in scale between the second- and third-floor windows recalls the similar rhythmical contrast in the Doric cloister of S. Ambrogio and the arrangement of the second order of the Belvedere courtyard with little niches placed side by side.

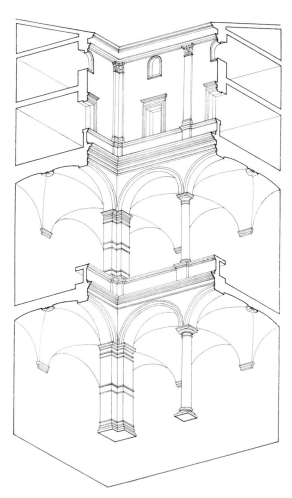

The connection with Bramante becomes clearer in the case of the courtyard, where the syntactic device of an arcade formed by linked archivolts set directly on the capital is handled with extreme proficiency, such as only a lifetime's experience could provide. Bramante had adopted this model for the cloister of S. Maria delle Grazie and in the presbytery of S. Ambrogio, though in the latter case with the addition of Brunelleschi-type dado; if the assumption were made that he contributed towards the collective design this would help to explain the quality and rigour of the result. The proportional arrangement of the orders, moreover, provides a link between the courtyard of the Cancelleria and the cloister of S. Maria della Pace through the chain of squares which cover the interaxial areas of the band corresponding to the shaft of the columns, and through the unusual 3 : 4 relationship which characterizes the rectangles at the base of the archivolts. In its general conception, the courtyard reflects the influence of Urbino in the contrast between the top floor and the empty space beneath it and in the 3 : 5 proportion of the plan which was one of those recommended by Francesco di Giorgio in his treatise.

Viewed as a whole, the Cancelleria, and especially the courtyard, represents a point midway between the architectural culture of Urbino and those elements in it which open the way to the ideas of the sixteenth century. The relationship of the framework to the orders and the wall behind which, from a distance, encloses it was still governed by the crystalline surfaces of the cross vaults and by the discontinuous pattern of the corbels; the columns were thus still cut out of the perforated, lightened wall of which Alberti speaks in his treatise, and mass and surface again became autonomous values which could be counterposed. The solution of the angle problem represents an extreme tendency to charge the colonnaded wall with plastic tension. In the Urbino courtyard, the angle pillars framed each of the four sides of a hollow cube decisively, resolving the dynamic tensions inside an enclosed space; in the Cancelleria, on the other hand, the meeting at right angles between the series was not elided but given plastic expression. The clustered, L-shaped corner pilaster which absorbs the last columns of each two series demonstrates the inadequacy of geometrical proportions as a stimulus to find new solutions to old problems; and to consider the value of the articulated solid, which so greatly interested the first generation of sixteenth-century architects.

43

The Cloister of Santa Maria della Pace

As early as the summer of 1500 Bramante was commissioned by Cardinal Oliviero Carafa to build the cloister of S. Maria della Pace, which is to be considered the first autonomous work of his Roman period. Vasari's lack of enthusiasm was dictated by his evolutionary interpretation of history, and it had a heavy influence on later criticism which always judged this work for its imperfectly-realized classical intentions.

There is no doubt that this cloister marks an important stage in Bramante's self-critical development, but it contains no deviations from the line of research which was later to lead it to assume such an important role in the architecture of the new century. It has been criticized on several counts, namely the anomalous treatment of corners and the placing of the column of the second order above the key of the lower arch, but these features are actually the most significant and revealing choices of the architect. If critical judgement regarding the fundamental stylistic purpose of Bramante is provisionally suspended, and attention is turned to an analytical examination of the handling of the individual problems, then these choices are seen to have a profound logical motivation.

The Typological Problem

In S. Maria della Pace the square courtyard surrounded by simple buildings served the function of a distributive feature out of which virtually the entire area of the living quarters opened out, and it indicated the desire to construct a centralized organism around a hollow space which acted as a source of light and centre of activity. The rooms devoted to collective activity were situated on the ground floor, and the cells on the first floor; in this way a stratification of complementary functions was created.

The contrast and diversity of rhythm in the two orders which make up the cloister can thus be read as the opposition between two spheres which are closely connected but are independent of each other. Moreover, this differentiation is apparent not so much in the reading of the interior of the façades, where the duality is resolved in unity by means of a sound geometrical connecting structure, as in the internal view of the two superimposed loggias. In one, the close connection between the surrounding walls and the external order creates an intricate and rigid pattern which emphasizes the irregularity of the space and its expression in terms of geometrical measurement as a chain of linked units. On the upper floor, on the other hand, where the order is not echoed on the wall, the flat ceiling of wooden beams leaves continuity of development to the enveloping framework and determines the spatial fluidity of the airy annular volume.

A revealing feature of what may be described as the 'intimate' dimension of the second order and of the logic which inspires it is represented by the seats carved out of the thickness of the parapet, which are perfectly adapted to the purpose of reading. They are so well integrated into the architectural composition that they must have been envisaged when the plan was initiated.

The Proportional Problem

To understand the significance of the act of composition for Bramante, one must take into account the precise proportional structure of the image and its variations. On the basis of accurate measured drawings, observation has shown that the latent structure described by the interaxial intervals of the order is based upon the following laws: each of the four sides of the portico is based on a rectangle whose sides are related in the porportion 3 : 4. If the network of twelve squares which result from this relationship are superimposed on the façade, then the surprising fact emerges that the four squares of the base exactly meet the upper level of the impost cornice of the arches. The same 3 : 4 relationship recurs in the impost rectangle of each of the arches, while each of the spans, measured from one column centre to another as far as the upper limit of the cornice, is inscribed in a 4 : 7 rectangle. The span of the upper order measured between the axes and up to the top of

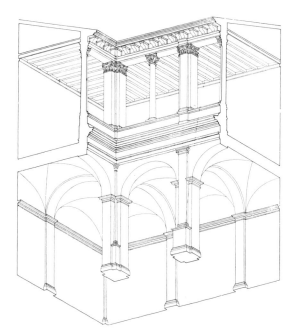

the cornice correspond to rectangles in which the relationship between the sides is 2 : 5. Finally, a 1 : 1 relationship emerges in the square, which could ideally be inscribed between the antae imposed on the pilasters of the second order. These results have been confirmed by the studies of Bruschi made on a different set of measured drawings.

The Optical Problem

The aesthetic value of the image of the cloister, or rather of the complex of images, depends less on the mechanics of proportion than on a very carefully planned optical effect, and it is in this that its fundamental novelty lies. An example of the method employed can be seen in the projecting moulding from which the second order rises, whose height corresponds exactly to that of the incline which joins it to the overhang of the lower cornice as seen by someone standing under the central arcade. Another example is the relation of the wall pilasters of the arcade to the base pedestal of the lower order; these jut out beyond it at the impost, while lower down they are in line with the edges of the pedestal, thus producing an illusory accentuation of the plastic effect.

But the feature which was most clearly conditioned by optical motivations is the much-criticized treatment of angles by means of the projecting corner of the concealed wall pilaster. An alternative to this solution would have been to place two pilasters at right angles to each other or else a single L-shaped pilaster. While the former solution would have heavily overweighed the inner corner, taking light from the loggia, and would have resulted in an anomalous solution to the vaulted roof of the portico (obtained by an arrangement of groined vaults on a square plan), the latter would have implied the same defects, though slightly attenuated, and would also have considerably reduced the sense of continuity in the contiguous façades, as may be seen, for example, in the courtyard of the Palazzo Baldassini by Antonio da Sangallo the Younger. The solution Bramante adopted should therefore be seen not as a stylistic anomaly but as a deliberate choice dictated by the necessity of linking the two perpendicular series of arches and making this aim more important than that of weakening the plastic effect of the corner produced by the disappearance of the wall pilaster, now almost totally immersed inside the two wall areas which meet near the edge. The completely objective solution of this interpenetration must have pleased Bramante because, while it sacrifices the viewer's anticipation of seeing in a corner view the same element of the series, it produces an optical equivalence between the normal pilasters and the corner one, which enhances the diagonal view. This method remained a dominant theme in Bramante's later work. The optical equivalence can readily be observed in the fact that the thickness measured from the centre coincides with that of a normal pilaster. The possibility of a diagonal reading which instead of dramatizing the duality of the perpendicular planes (as is the case in the Urbino courtyard) would reduce this duality until it yields the impression of a continuous structure with a prevailing vertical development, seems to have been Bramante's aim from the very first, and should not be ignored if we wish to judge his work undogmatically.

Relationship with the Classical World

Another supposed defect which, according to those who criticize the cloister from a classical point of view, would seem to limit its aesthetic value, is the anti-classical character of the balusters of the second order which weigh upon the key of the arches beneath them. Now, if by classicism one defines the nineteenth-century interpretation of Greco-Roman architecture, then no exception can be taken to this point of view; but if we wish to see in this choice made by Bramante an attitude of well-considered rejection of a rule which could be derived from the classical heritage, this criticism does not hold, since there are frequent classical examples where the rhythm between superimposed orders is doubled, one at least of which would certainly be known to Bramante because it was still to be seen in his time: the so-called portico of Pompeo or house of Mario, which had been drawn by

Giuliano da Sangallo and reproduced by Serlio in his third book. When we consider the Vitruvian dogmatism of Serlio and the much more open-minded position of Bramante, we reach the conclusion that no deliberate desire to injure classical proprieties was responsible for this choice. In fact, the syntactic choice corresponded to a stage of classicism which preceded the rigid doctrines of the twenties, when architects sought to replace the pluralism of Roman architecture by the enclosed system of the 'Roman school'. The election of Julius II in 1503 brought about a profound change in the life of Bramante: his programme of study and research into the ancient monuments was threatened by the demands made upon him by the new Pope, who wanted his assistance in a number of vast undertakings for which a whole lifetime would not have sufficed. The meeting between the seventy-year-old bellicose Pope and the architect, now aged nearly sixty, developed into a deep friendship based on the complementary qualities in their characters and their shared enthusiasm for a pragmatic and optimistic ideal. As much as Julius's relationship with Michelangelo had been difficult and stormy, so his relationship with Bramante was smooth and undisturbed. The architect became a minister and the Pope's adviser in every great building enterprise. He even supplanted Giuliano da Sangallo in the Pope's favour, in spite of the fact that the latter had been close to the Pope while he was still a cardinal and was so well equipped to play an important part in the *renovatio Romae*.

We have seen Bramante become one of the most influential men in the papal court: the anecdote which relates that he read and commented on Dante at the bedside of the sick Pope provides a revealing insight into their friendship, which went beyond the bounds of specific architectural employment.

But this predilection for Dante acquires a particular significance when one thinks of the imminent fashion for Petrarch which was to mark the second decade of the century under the championship of Bembo, who arrived in Rome in 1512 and was later appointed Secretary of Briefs by Leo X. Some literary historians like to compare the classicism of Bembo with that of Bramante, seeing in both cases the dominant problem to be that of style; but while the author of the *Discourses* favours the 'unique model' which he distinguishes in the work of Petrarch, Bramante was still searching for technical rules and formulae in classicism and considered that a thorough and total interpretation of an individual theme was a more important factor than a personal unity of style, whereby, if necessary, every autobiographical and personal element would be submerged. Bembo blamed Dante for not having remained silent when he could not find a correct and pure form of expression; Bramante would not even have understood the meaning of such a rebuke. In fact he himself, though a great technical innovator, was not a good technician but an impatient experimenter. The ideal of a personal stylistic coherence was, moreover, a problem so far removed from the thoughts of Bramante that it has always aroused considerable perplexity among critics, although this has since been rightly redirected into a revised appraisal of his artistic merits. The truth is that each of Bramante's Roman works represents a discovery of new horizons in research and an extension of the limits of his art; any attempt to separate his personal language from its cultural superstructure must prove even more vain and unproductive than the analogy which has occupied Dantean critics for so many years.

The Belvedere Courtyard
The first result of the collaboration between Julius II and Bramante was the Belvedere courtyard, the monumental link between two separate structures divided by a rural landscape: the Vatican palace, built around the narrow Pappagallo courtyard, and the small Palazzo Belvedere constructed by Innocent on the brow of a hill overlooking the fields of Castello. The two buildings were situated on different levels and were rather irregular in shape, so that the task of linking them appeared difficult and hazardous. The very fact that these separate entities, placed in a natural setting, could be envisaged as forming part of

a single organism indicated a new way of thinking in dimensional terms. It was in the Belvedere, in fact, that the urban dimension of the old city was rediscovered for the first time and as a consequence there began the practice of refashioning the landscape artificially. Just as the construction of Trajan's Forum had entailed the demolition of the Velia, the famous hill separating the Forum region from the Suburra, so, too, the construction of the Belvedere courtyard required a massive replanning of the natural landscape. Just as the Imperial Fora stood out as independent structures in the old city, enclosed within themselves, so this courtyard took the form of an independent enclosed space, arranged to meet a hierarchical viewpoint from one of the windows of the papal apartments. But apart from its conception as an enclosed universe, the Belvedere did have some direct connections with the surrounding landscape, both through the planned openings of the upper galleries on to the exterior and through the state of incompleteness of Bramante's construction, which in its first stage resembled the ruins by which it had been inspired.

The seminal idea from which this magnificent image of the *cortile* was to arise was that of a *passetto*, a 'short walk', a linking passage which was to make it possible to move under cover from the Vatican palace to the Belvedere villa in spite of the difference in the level between the two buildings. The only part which was completed in the Pope's lifetime was the long section facing the fields of Castello, and the three terraces linked by large flights of steps. If the east side of the building had been constructed to match the completed section, an enormous area of about 150 x 300 m. would have been enclosed—that is, an area greater than the present Piazza Navona—and this would have certainly been the largest of the enclosed spaces conceived by western architects after the fall of the Roman Empire. The work remained unfinished for several years, and shortly after it was arbitrarily completed by Pirro Ligorio, as we shall see, its original conception was finally distorted when Domenico Fontana introduced the obstruction of the new library. Even the perspective views of the buildings were irreparably altered by the buttresses in the lower part (the present Belvedere courtyard) and the rustication in the upper part, so that very little has remained in the present construction to recall its original appearance—with the possible exception of the outer wall facing the city with its large rusticated portal: the 'porta Julia', and the famous inscription of Julius II which Bramante seems to have wished to express in some kind of rebus.

Space in Perspective

Many of the old drawings of the Belvedere show an axial view from above, as it would appear to someone looking down from a window of the palace. From this privileged viewpoint the volumetric composition looked clear and harmonious, and could be seen to be based on a double rhythm. The two lateral arcades were interrupted at the level of the first flight of steps by two protruding sections of the building; after this kind of proscenium, a double ramp with a central niche led to a third and deeper platform. At this upper level, the main feature was the concave background, resembling the backcloth of a stage, flanked by open galleries. In the view from above, the various layers of superimposed galleries must have looked like separate horizontal bands sliding one above another to emphasize the effect of depth; a depth increased by the optical illusion produced through the interaction and contrast of light created as a result of placing the longitudinal axis in a north-south direction, and by the light rebounding from the fountain niche and the ramps which are central to the composition.

The Architectural Promenade

The bird's-eye view enjoyed from above satisfied what Serlio described as 'the desire of the sight to extend'. At ground level, a most rich and varied architectural promenade revealed once more Bramante's predilection for the visual multivalence of the structures. The presence of fountains at the centre of the two largest platforms makes clear his inten-

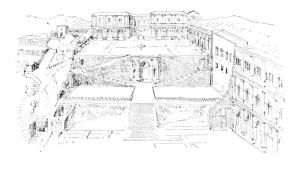

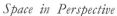
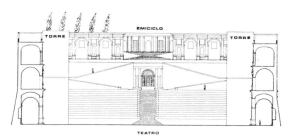

tion to avoid an axial promenade which would repeat with varying conditions of visibility the suggestion of a unitary concept perceived in the view from above. The architect's purpose in this composition seems to have been to counterpose the two piazzas like two opposite poles, leaving to the intermediate platform and to the ramp system (which is closely linked to it) the function of suggesting an axial throughway. This detail, together with the variety of architectural features and the actual dimensions of the area, indicates his intention to distinguish within an overall unity some sub-units endowed with a certain degree of autonomy. So we find again that concern for a psychological characterization of space which was previously observed in the cloister of S. Maria della Pace. Here, however, the sequence is from the monumental appearance of the lower court in the esplanade between the two projecting sections, to the final surprise (note that the single-storey portico was not visible from the bottom of the lower court and came into view only at the top of the staircase leading to the upper level) of the garden enclosed between the open galleries and terminated by the portico. Consider the difference in the relationship between the sky and the architectural image as it appeared from above, where the space was enclosed by buildings on three floors, and as it appeared from ground level where the sky formed the dominant background to a horizontal figure which was animated by the chiaroscuro effects created by the open galleries. These different architectonic rhythms coincide with two distinct models, two forms of reality which come together to form an intricate 'narrative' union.

The Plastic Qualities

The numerous drawings and reliefs relating to the Belvedere and the few fragments which are still standing clearly show that in his choice of architectural devices intended to 'articulate' the very long wings, Bramante set himself the problem of experimenting with new highly organized arrangements of institutional signs of order.

In the grandiose lower area of the courtyard, the arrangement consisted of a continuous section of spans formed by three superimposed orders of wall pilasters.

Whereas for the first two floors we possess exhaustive information from the drawings completed according to Serlio's description, for the third floor there are doubts and contradictions in the iconographic tradition which suggest that Bramante left this part unfinished. The first Doric order contained pedestals and was divided by arches, so repeating the specific composition of Roman architecture in a form which was very much closer to the original classical models than that which was adopted in S. Maria della Pace for the conventional design of the archivolt and the sides of the impost cornice. The anomalous feature of the pedestal allowed Bramante a characteristic proportional composition. Taking as a recurring sub-multiple $1 : 8$ of the width of the arch, all the principal measurements are obtained by whole numbers: the height of the arch is equivalent to sixteen parts, the width of the pillar to which the pilaster is attached equals three parts, the height of the base four parts. The basic relationship can be seen to be that of the octave ($1 : 2$) which is found again between the thickness of the pilaster and that of the pillar behind it.

The link between the superimposed orders was established by Bramante's rigorous application of the principle of 'gradation', which he used inversely to the system found in the Colosseum or Theatre of Marcellus. There is a relationship of one in four between each of the orders and the order superimposed ($3 : 4$) so that each measurement can be deduced comparatively by reducing and increasing by $1 : 4$ the measurement of the corresponding part of the adjoining order.

When we consider the results of the study of classical models undertaken by Bramante during the first years of his final stay in Rome, it seems that the architect had difficulty in grasping completely the logic of the syntactic system, which was not wholly rediscovered until his pupils began to work on it. Faced with the contradictory answers provided by the actual models and the theories of Vitruvius, Bramante chose a system of superimposed

Belvedere cortile, *elevation (after Bruschi)*.

orders which was the inverse of the system employed in the Colosseum, contracting towards the top to emphasize the diminishing perspective instead of acting as a contrast to it. The plastic rendering and visual effect of each of the superimposed intervals was later freely defined on the basis of the diversity of the 'signs' employed: the arcade on the ground-floor level, the wall panel on the upper floor and an open gallery on the top floor. Bramante departed from the most famous classical models by introducing a mixture of orders: above the Ionic he raised a second Ionic order of pilasters in the interior of which the open gallery with the so-called *serliana* motif was divided by Doric balusters. However, it is not impossible that Bramante had envisaged a third Corinthian order, as can be seen in the drawings in the Corner manuscript, and that the present arrangement is to be attributed to Sangallo, who completed the construction.

In the second order an original feature appeared which was destined to enter the official repertory where it continued to play an important part in the three following centuries. The pilasters are outlined by two set back half-pilasters, echoing the central one with a capital but no base. This double figure is accentuated by the projection of the trabeation corresponding to the central wall pilaster, and seems to be the architect's answer to the need to create an intermediary stage between the order and the wall and to strengthen the vertical structure in the background so as to achieve a sense of continuity with the Doric wall pilasters below, which, as we have seen, are one quarter again as large as the Ionic.

With regard to the decoration of the wall panel in the second order, the numerous drawings and the engravings in the third book of Serlio agree in showing a tripartite form consisting of a central window and two small side niches; whereas in the Corner manuscript the windows are classical in design and are each surmounted by a tympanum, alternately triangular and segmented, in the third book of Serlio there appears in place of the windows an empty space with architrave, without cornices and surrounded by rectangular frames which anticipate certain motifs found in Vignola.

Since these panels have been entirely transformed, it is difficult to say which of these two solutions is the more probable.

However, we may be sure that the plan did include narrow, high niches which echoed in a minor key the central empty space, anticipating Raphael's treatment of the Palazzo dell'Aquila. These very delicate niches produced chiaroscuro effects which lightened the weight of the wall and introduced a second (minor) scale into the pattern of the composition, revealing the purposeful intent of Bramante. On the one hand, they conform to the geometrical *certe ragioni* (sure rules), since their top is at half the height of the wall panel (again the relationship of an octave), while on the other they increase the optical illusion of depth in this architectonic expedient which varies according to the choice of one of the possible optical references. In fact the niches are integrated with the central window just as spontaneously as with the intermediary pilaster, and form a point of comparison, now with the pair of lower arches, now with the tripartite arrangement of the upper order conceived by the architect of the serliana.

The ambiguity and contradictory evidence in documents relating to the third order confirm the hypothesis that Bramante left it unfinished.

On the other hand, at least three points of the present Belvedere courtyard preserve the vestiges of the original structure of this part. We see that an Ionic wall pilaster is re-echoed by fillets framing a serliana, while above it a cornice without projecting edges acts as a terminal to the entire system of three superimposed orders. The most striking feature is the contrast of materials between this and the other plane surfaces: whereas the order was constructed in travertine and brick (presumably), the wall backgrounds and all the general framework of the upper story were made out of peperino (a stone composed of lava and tufa) with traces of superimposed plaster which indicate later restorations. In the structure which has been distorted by successive restorations and transformations, there can be distinguished a first stage in which there was built into the peperino framework a serliana with two Doric colonnettes and a central arch; this arch was probably open, but in any case was surmounted by a continuous architrave. Later the side openings were filled in and little arched windows were incorporated; then these windows too were closed in when another superelevation was added.

Even if the third floor was completed after the death of Bramante and the work remained unfinished for some time (this supposition would account for the contradictory evidence and the reticence of Serlio), it is probable that it was completed from the drawings of Bramante by Sangallo and Peruzzi, who strengthened the lower arches when the first signs of instability appeared in the building. If this was the case, then another stylistic innovation may be added to those already noted in this extraordinary conception that was the Belvedere: the repetition of the serliana motif, which was later to arouse so much interest in Serlio and Palladio.

The other basic feature chosen by Bramante for the terminal section of the theatre was the so-called *travata ritmica*, the 'rhythmic frame' previously adopted by Alberti in the church of S. Andrea in Mantua. This may be considered a generalized formula for wall treatment, derived from the tripartite system of Roman triumphal arches. Bramante used it as a system of open arcades on the sides of the upper courtyard, while on the narrow end he filled it in with wall panels, so as to create a sharp distinction between the 'garden theatre' and the enclosed courtyard where the most precious pieces of the Pope's collection of antique sculpture were placed. The terminal exedra was thrust into this rhythmical system, making the panels of the background wall project beyond the meeting point with the large apse which resembled the diorama of a modern stage setting, without any direct connection with the external order. This concealed link made it possible to retain the difference in levels between the buildings, the elimination of which would have presented a considerable syntactic difficulty. In the portico there is an order of coupled pilasters which are much lower in height (about a half) than those forming the 'rhythmic frame'.

The different levels of the portico and the courtyard were joined by a staircase with concentric steps. This consisted of an exceptionally logical sequence composed (according to the reconstruction made by Ackermann which differs very slightly from the drawing reproduced by Serlio) of an upper section of concave steps exactly similar to an amphitheatre, and a lower section of corresponding convex shapes which matched it perfectly; a circular platform provided a linking element and this was probably intended to contain the papal throne when spectacles were held in the courtyard. It is interesting to observe how this ingenious solution enabled Bramante to enhance the intricate and rational interplay of the different levels which is characteristic of the plan of the Belvedere, and also to find subtle relationships between the various devices which connect the platforms and a system of structural analogies: niches, ternary systems (like the group composed of a large niche and two smaller niches) and sloping symmetrical planes such as those produced by the ramps which converge towards their axis.

The sintagma of the rhythmic frame is not treated by Bramante in a synthetic manner as Alberti had done in Mantua, when he made the whole system subservient to a continuous cornice, but analytically, so as to make the observer aware of two aspects of the composition simultaneously: firstly, a continuous wall broken up by large arches and niches and structured horizontally by the impost cornices, and secondly, the pairs of Corinthian pilasters which are made to stand out sharply from the background wall by the projecting bases and by the projecting cornice which has the function of unifying the two contiguous elements while at the same time marking them off from the background, According to the Corner manuscript, the function of unifying and acting as a horizontal link was entrusted to the cornice proper, that is the fillet and the cyma, which did not follow the pattern of the architrave and frieze.

The very clear proportions of the composition underline the impression of two superimposed structures. The measurements of the arches and of the wall intervals coincide,

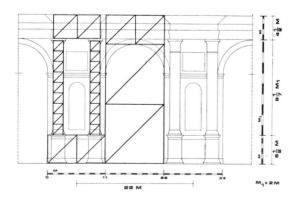

thus creating a very marked rhythm to which Serlio ascribed a symbolic significance as an image of eternity; the pilaster is then subdivided harmonically into vertical fillets of the successive values of 1, 2, 1, 3, 1, 2, 1, so that the proportional relationships are always octaves or thirds. The octave returns in the relationship between the width and height of the arcade which repeats the relationship already met in the lower part of the courtyard, so introducing an element of consonance between these two parts. The different measurements shown in the drawings in the Corner manuscript, which Bruschi has analysed, do not seem to us to invalidate Serlio's analysis, as he must certainly have been well acquainted with the theories of Bramante through Peruzzi.

The Spiral Staircase of the Belvedere

The group of constructions which comprised the 'theatre of Belvedere' have now been irretrievably lost and the few fragments remaining have been taken out of their context and cannot give us an idea of the organic appearance of the whole composition. However, there still exists in the interior of the courtyard a feature which is unchanged and can be appreciated in its original spatial conception, namely the spiral staircase constructed at the point of intersection between the Belvedere villa and the octagonal courtyard, a prototype intended to be reproduced in innumerable replicas and already recognized in the sixteenth century as Bramante's 'most beautiful and ingenious (*artifiziosa*) architecture' (Serlio).

The staircase has a very slight gradient and rises to a height of about twenty metres, with five turns. Bramante was not able to find a similar model in the classical repertory and planned the staircase as a continuous sequence of five superimposed units; in fact, if one looks up from below, the staircase creates an illusion of superimposed cylindrical units, and it is only by concentrating that it becomes clear that this is not a case of superimposed units but of a 'procession' of columns of different types. The architect has divided the forty columns which support the circular vault to the interior of the well into five series of eight units, and has arranged them in a linear order, starting from the sturdiest (a sort of Tuscan Doric) and proceeding towards the most delicate (the Composite order) without varying the height of the column shafts.

The artifice becomes apparent as the viewer walks up and discovers the columns of different diameters and orders which are placed side by side. And it is out of this paradox that the architect's skill as a creator of optical illusions is revealed, as he obeys in turn optical and structural demands and makes them coincide by means of a subtle stratagem.

The aesthetic value of the staircase depends closely on this two-sided image, in which a rigorous synthesis is combined with a flowing narrative movement, touched perhaps with conscious irony. But as already observed, it reveals also the limit at which Bramante's research was arrested, leaving to his pupils a task only just begun.

We should not overlook the possible symbolic significance of the arrangement of the orders, especially if we consider the viewpoint of one of Bramante's contemporaries. We know from Serlio that in the sixteenth century the stratification of the Colosseum was explained as an allusion to the successive historical fortunes of the various nations who followed each other in the dominion of the civilized world. According to this theory, the Romans placed the Composite order, invented by them, at the top in order to express symbolically their position of conquerors. It is not improbable that by arranging the groups of columns of various orders in a number of successive sequences Bramante may have wished to construct a sort of 'historical spiral', illustrating didactically the periods of development of the classical tradition.

The Apse of Santa Maria del Popolo

Between 1505 and 1509 Bramante was engaged on an extension to the church of S. Maria del Popolo, the most important of the Roman churches built in the fifteenth century. He added a large square presbytery with an apse to the original structure which were separated by a barrel-vaulted rectangular area.

The general plan is a repetition of that of the choir of S. Maria delle Grazie in Milan, but the inclusion of the rectangular area radically transforms its spatial effect. The square space here is at the centre of an autonomous organism at the far ends of which are the niche of the apse on one side, and the church on the other.

The organic nature of Bramante's composition is accentuated by the siting of the funeral monuments of Ascanio Sforza and Girolamo Basso, both by Sansovino, which are placed inside shallow niches built into the centre of the inner walls of the domed area, determining a transversal axis which is stressed by the serlian windows above. It is highly probable that Bramante himself worked out this scheme of decoration or at least that he inspired it.

The proliferation of monuments, however, does not submerge the solid structure of the ternary plan according to which they are arranged, and the ceiling frescoed by Pinturicchio follows a rigid geometrical form for which there are no precedents in this artist's rather conventional work in the rooms of the Borgia apartments.

The symbolic schema may have been inspired by Dante but leads us back to Bramante through the clarity with which it is stated and its architectonic quality.

The central domed area is divided by a painted framework in order to accentuate two pairs of symmetrical axes which are defined by dark profiles. The diagonal axes are emphasized by the four tabernacles placed in the corners (which contain the figures of the Church Fathers) and by rotating the large square frame containing the other figurations at forty-five degrees to the walls. At the centre, in an octagonal cornice which reconciles the two different symmetrical systems, there is a *Coronation of the Virgin* against the background of a golden disc.

The hierarchical organization of the whole composition possesses very close structural analogies with Bramante's plan for St. Peter's, and it seems likely that we should look here for a key to the symbolism in the plan for the basilica, where the geometrical figures of the octagon, the square, and the circle were probably chosen to convey certain overtones.

An impression of prolixity of decoration is created by the ceiling and Sansovino's monuments, but this becomes reabsorbed into the grandiose and simplified forms of Bramante's architecture, which attains one of its finest results in this church. The decoration is admitted to the degree in which its role can be exactly circumscribed and defined without intruding upon the calculated hierarchy of the structure. The fact that the architectural form was intended to be the principal element in the aggregate image of the presbytery is demonstrated by the accentuation of light on the niche of the apse, which is illuminated by beams radiating from the two windows built into the right side. These two sources of light act as stage spotlights, creating a remarkable movement over the fluting and cornices of the niche, which reveal the experience Bramante gained as a painter. Only this type of light could create so refined an effect of tonal gradations and inversions as we find here, giving to the apse of S. Maria del Popolo a magical illusion of depth, and then only because the interconnection between the pure forms, the half-cylinders, quarter-spheres, and prisms, was calculated to the ultimate degree of exactitude.

Observe, for example, the relation between the niche and the intervening empty space: this is achieved by means of a continuous modenature, a kind of L-shaped pilaster which articulates the impost cornice it carries; the form of the arch is thus outlined after the initial statement of the projecting edge of the large niche, and is repeated five further times by the concave and convex edges. The five bands of varying width and density form a motif which re-echoes the geometrical plan and this is again partly recalled in a discontinuous manner by the curved lines of the coffers, until it finds a final echo in the large projecting arch, placed at the meeting point with the cross-vaulted nave.

We are reminded of the altarpiece by Piero della Francesca in the Brera, where so many similar features occur: the coffers, the hollow shell, the apse with the barrel-vaulted space

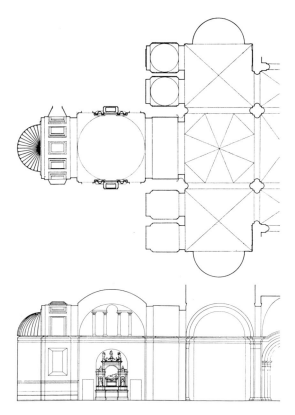

which introduces it; but the architect has added to Piero's prototype not only the power of a three-dimensional structure, but also the value of a light which is intrinsic to the object, no longer a universal light but an adapted light for the purpose of generating an 'effect'.

The Tempietto of San Pietro in Montorio

The possibility that this work was produced at an early date, that is, before the period of Julius II's papacy, must be excluded, and we can date the construction of the chapel of S. Pietro in Montorio either around 1505, if it is thought of as a sort of trial piece for St. Peter's, or else after 1509, the probable date of the *Opusculum de mirabilibus novae et veteris urbis Romae*, if the inexplicable silence of Alberti is taken into account. However, this question is not of great importance in assisting us to reconstruct the course of Bramante's architectural thought, and in the absence of objective proof it seems preferable to set it aside in favour of a consideration of the problems he has raised and solved in this decidedly programmatic work. These are principally: the relationship to the classical tradition; the universality of the new architectural style; the symbolical significance of the model, and its definition in its surroundings.

The Relationship to the Classical Tradition and the Universality of the Architectural Style

The stylistic considerations which influenced Bramante in S. Pietro in Montorio are all of a programmatic nature and, whatever the date of construction, indicate a desire to break away from the traditional norms of the early Renaissance. A fundamental choice, for example, was that of the Doric order, in its conventional form with an architrave and metopes and triglyphs. Vitruvius considered this order to be imperfect owing to the limitations imposed by the rhythm of the triglyphs, and with some few exceptions it was avoided throughout the fifteenth century as it was considered to be ill-adapted to the humanist ideal of refinement and elegance.

A close structural examination of the chapel in all its parts confirms the dual purpose of Bramante, which was to select a platform of absolute objectivity in which each choice could be rigorously demonstrable, and at the same time to escape the dogmatism of the classical school where every new form was condemned. Where it was possible to adopt set patterns, Bramante unhesitatingly relinquished personal invention, as can be seen in the design of the door which was derived from the Temple of Cora, and in some of the details in the interior; but where it was necessary to pursue his research beyond the limits of the traditional repertory, as in the drum and small cupola, new forms emerged spontaneously out of the structural logic of the organism. If a second order had been placed so that it overhung the base of the drum, a paradoxical solution would have been created whereby the limitation of the dimensions would have contradicted the aim of 'thinking on a big scale'; it was necessary to divide the drum less drastically, but in such a way that windows and niches could be inserted into a solid framework. So there came into being the simplified pilasters with moulded niches leading up to a thin projecting ring. These stylistic inventions point to a fruitful area of research directed towards adding to the architectural repertory structures which, though not strictly belonging to the order, were subject to its formal discipline.

The Meaning of a Centralized Structure and the Aesthetic Value of the Chapel

From the time when Brunelleschi had constructed the Angeli rotunda, close to the monastery in which the Platonic Academy was later often to meet, the myth of a centralized organism as a model of absolute organic integration and necessity had gained currency in all the regional cultures and had found its first field of experimentation in the work of painters. Mantegna, Perugino, and the young Raphael had invented models of the greatest theoretical interest; in his treatise, Francesco di Giorgio had declared that the centrally-planned church possessed theoretical superiority and a wealth of symbolic connotations,

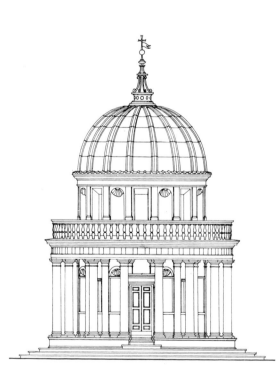

and Leonardo had made abstract studies into the possibilities of ever more complex and articulated centrally-planned symmetries. It is difficult to believe that when Francesco di Giorgio, Leonardo, and Bramante met each other in order to discuss work on Milan cathedral in 1490, this problem did not figure largely in their exchanges of views. Already in his additions to the church of S. Maria delle Grazie, aesthetic and functional considerations had led Bramante to adopt an embryonic central plan for the extension of the medieval church.

In S. Pietro in Montorio, centralization is the dominant theme; it immediately absorbs the viewer and forces him to examine the reasons, the rules, and the properties which govern this structural system. To appreciate Bramante's statement in all its complexity and clarity, it is necessary to envisage how the chapel must have appeared in its original setting. We know from Serlio that this consisted of a concentric circular colonnade incorporated into the interior of the present courtyard. A tentative reconstruction is given on p. 55.

Upon entering the circular courtyard, the viewer would find himself inside a self-contained microcosm which was perfectly defined and enclosed and without any impact from the outside world. It resembled somewhat the present-day Capitol piazza built by Michelangelo, but without the centrifugal allusion of the elements which separate the three buildings of the Capitol and without the dialectical relationship with the movement of the town which is introduced through the opening giving access to the piazza. But the most important difference is that in Bramante's microcosm, the main feature is not a spatial cavity but an object which defines and fills it and becomes the physical embodiment of a form in which the viewer is invited to immerse himself.

As soon as one enters the chapel, an idea of the structure can be gained by considering the series of concentric circles, the discs arranged along a vertical axis which lies along the line of their centre points. If this were in the original colonnade, then we would feel enclosed in a cylindrical form, outside our usual spatial milieu. We would then see fitting like Chinese boxes into each other the circle of the cornice connecting the columns of the colonnade, the decreasing circles of the steps, the circles defining the peribolus of the chapel, those defining the cylinder of the drum, the circles above the drum, and so on up to the sphere which supports the cross.

Marsilio Ficino has written in his commentary to Plato's *Symposium* a page which seems to describe perfectly Bramante's chapel and explain its symbolic significance in areas where proof cannot easily be established. 'And it was not winthout reason', writes Ficino, 'that the ancient theologians placed Goodness at the centre: and in the circle Beauty. I say surely Goodness in a centre: and in four circles Beauty. The only centre of all things is God. The four circles which continually revolve around God are the Mind, the Soul, Nature and Matter. The Angelic Mind is a fixed circle: the Soul, in itself mobile: Nature moves in others, but not through others; Matter not only in others, but also by others is moved. But why do we call God the Centre and those other four circles. Shall we declare? The Centre is a point of the circle which is fixed and indivisible: from where many lines divisible and mobile lead to their similar circumference. This circumference, which is divisible, revolves around the Centre not otherwise than a round body revolves round a pivot. And such is the nature of the centre that, although it is one, indivisible and fixed, nevertheless it is found in each part of many, if not all, of the mobile and divisible lines: since in each part of each line is the point. But the reason why no thing can be unlike its own is as follows. The lines leading from the circumference towards the centre cannot touch this point except by a point of their own which is equally simple, unique and immobile. Who will deny that God is rightly called the centre of all things? Considering that in all things He is unique, simple and immobile: and that all things which are produced by Him are multiple, compound and in a sense mobile: and just as they go away from Him, so too in the way of lines or circumferences they return to Him. In this way the Mind, the Soul, Nature and Matter, which proceed from God strive to return to Him and from alll sides with every diligence they

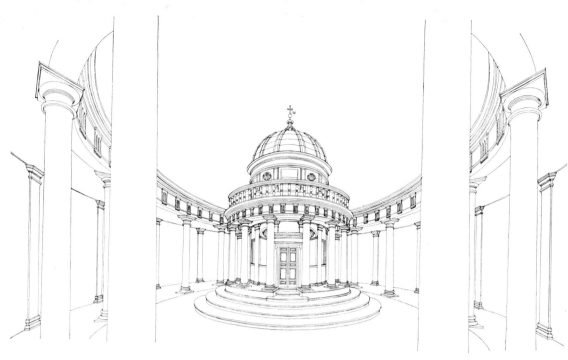

revolve around Him. And just as the centre is found in each part of a line, and in the whole circle: and all lines by their point touch the point which is the centre of the circle, similarly God who is the centre of all things, who is most simple unity and most pure Act, places Himself in all things. Not only for the reason that He is present in all things, but also because He has given to all things created by Him some intrinsic share and very simple and active power which is called the unity of things: from which and to which, as from a centre to a centre of His, all other powers and parts depend on each part. And certainly it is necessary that all created things, rather than gathering round their own centre and their own unity, should come close to their Creator: so that through their own centre, they should come close to the centre of all things.' It would not be difficult to find in Bramante's structure the four circles described by Ficino; but this would be a mechanical and arbitrary operation, while what interests us here is simply to point to possible areas of significance in the ambit of the theories and images which were current in the intellectual circle to which Bramante belonged.

The tendency to relate centrally-planned structures to religious symbolism and to see the dome as an image of the vault of the heavens was present also in the treatise of Francesco di Giorgio, which was probably known to Bramante. The aesthetic objective pursued and attained by the architect was to create an organic and well-balanced structure, the 'concinnitas' of Alberti which was taken to mean harmony between all the parts 'founded upon a precise law, so that nothing can be added or taken away or changed except for the worse' (*ut sit pulchritudo quidem certa cum ratione concinnitas universarum partium in eo cuius sint, ita ut addi aut diminui aut immutari possit nihil quin improbabilius reddatur*). But balance and 'concinnitas' indicate a generic aesthetic ideal, coinciding roughly with an ideal of classicism without historical limitations; Bramante's idea of balance, on the other hand, was that of a 'specific' balance which acquired its historical status in the chapel only to the degree in which it stood apart from acquired tradition and opened up new horizons in research.

The round temples of classical Rome were in the main based on a single volumetric plan. Each part was subordinated to the primary nucleus of the colonnaded drum. The roof consisted of a lid which although supported and not an independent structure, conditioned the equilibrium of the building by leaning its weight on the lower structures and so justifying its design at its inception. To find in the classical repertory an organism based on the interpenetration of volumes one must refer to the mausoleums, although here the relationship between the parts was not based on spatial exigencies of interpenetration but on the superimposing of autonomous blocks; or rotundas, in which the volume of the drum was created by prismatic blocks arranged along lines which were perpendicular to the axis of rotation. Bramante could find examples of this second type in painting, for example, the chapel designed by Perugino for the Sixtine fresco or for the *Marriage of the Virgin* in the Caen museum, or the mausoleums painted by Mantegna, Girolamo da Cremona, and Signorelli. In one case only, Raphael's *Marriage of the Virgin*, the problem was treated in a similar way to Bramante's chapel, and it is not at all unlikely that the admiration felt by the architect for the young painter and the faith he had in him as the successor who would carry on the work he had begun in St. Peter's was born from his realization of Raphael's authentic architectural vocation, as revealed by his altarpeice in Città di Castello. This altarpiece, as can be seen from the inscription, was painted in 1505 and therefore—in this author's opinion—precedes the Tempietto di S. Pietro.

In Raphael's painting, as in Bramante's chapel, the colonnaded peribolus was intended as a transparent screen to encircle the cylindrical nucleus, but whereas in the former case a projected relationship is established between the two parts which is emphasized by the seven beams of the volutes, so that the structure acquires a centrifugal tension, in S. Pietro in Montorio a complete plastic fusion is achieved between the mass of the interior with its niches and wall pilasters and the encircling crown of columns. What interested Raphael was the dialogue between architecture and atmosphere and the connection *a posteriori* between the two prismatic volumes. Bramante, however, was interested in the reciprocal action of these elements, the creation of an effect of concretion between the nucleus and peribolus. If by his invention of the crown of corbels which brought the portico and the drum into a plastic relationship Raphael clearly posed a problem which was to interest architects of the Mannerist and Baroque schools, Bramante rejected this expedient and searched for a deeper and less rhetorical connection, based on the 'clarity' of the law and on a process which might be compared to the simplifications made in the course of algebraic operations. He thus came close to the solution of the problem by eliminating all superfluous considerations and searching for the most elemental forms of expression. The choice of a hemisphere for the extrados of the cupola is a proof of this 'search for clarity' which approaches the elemental forms of geometry as unambiguous statements. It is in this context that an analogy has been made to Leonardo. However, none of Leonardo's many sketches show the theme of centralization developed to the degree of simplicity attained in the tempietto. The extrados of the cupolas seem always to contain a curve which is slightly less than the semicircle. Bramante, however, relies on the absolute value of the hemisphere and enhances it. In fact, in order to produce an optical equivalent to this form, he adds a support a few centimetres large above the cornice to compensate for its submersion by the protruding edge. The upper storey added in the time of Paul V has considerably altered this detail, but we need only examine the numerous sixteenth-century drawings and the engravings of Serlio and Sirigatti in order to reconstruct accurately the original appearance of the structure which was prepared for the attachment of the extrados directly above the cornice.

The Geometric Structure
The accentuated vertical development of the chapel, which may be seen as an innovation with respect to the classical tradition, was the subject of controversy from the time of Serlio onwards. Serlio observed that it was 'of too great a height' and 'exceeded the height of two latitudes', that is to say, its height exceeded twice its width. But his doubts were banished by considerations of the optical value of the form. 'Nonetheless,' writes Serlio, 'in practice, because of the openings of the windows and niches which are there, through which the sight can expand, this height does not offend, and in fact owing to the double cornices which surround

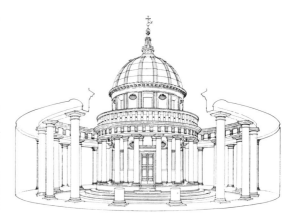

Reconstruction of the peribolus intended by Bramante to encircle the Tempietto of San Pietro in Montorio.

it, which detract greatly from its height, the church appears much lower to observers than it actually is.' In the engraving in the third book of Serlio which shows a sectional view, the proportion between the height and width seems to be one of two squares, but in reality it is 7 : 15 and it seems likely that the additional seventh was an expedient to create the optical equivalent of the desired relationship. The sketch plan of the interior also contains interesting features which, as we shall see, have points in common with the external profile. The height of the internal wall pilasters is the same as that of the columns of the peribolus, but the height of the bases is different, since there are, in the interior, column bases which are equal in height to the whole of the trabeation. From the floor up to the impost of the cornice (the top edge of the wall pilasters), the order fits into a square and, because of the equal height of the base and the trabeation, the same ratio is found again between the width of the cell and the height of the order from the top of the bases up to the finials. If we divide a side of the square into three, we obtain the width of the larger niches, whose height up to the impost of the arch is twice this figure (relationship of eighths). The fascia of the drum shows in section the same 1 : 2 ratio, taking as the upper limit the impost of the second trabeation. The centre of the curve of the cupola is situated on a plane which is tangent to the highest part of the cornice.

In the exterior, taking the space between the columns as a norm, it can be observed that the projection of the portico is contained in a rectangle with a ratio of 5 : 7 between its sides. By subdividing this rectangle into squares, we note that the projection of the portico at each side with respect to the inner nucleus is exactly equivalent to a column of five squares, while the internal nucleus, measured up to the summit of the baluster, is inscribed in a square of five modules per side.

The drum and cupola are then exactly inscribed in another square of five modules, whose base is situated at the point at which the drum emerges from the inclined plane which covers the cornice. Between the diameter and height of the drum measured between the tops of the two cornices there is a ratio of 1 : 2. It is interesting to note that in contrast to the plan of the interior, the width-height ratio of the nucleus is maintained at below an eighth, with a diminution of about 1 : 9, established possibly in order to compensate for the effect of the luminous background which Vitruvius mentioned as a means of softening the outlines.

IVRI REDDO

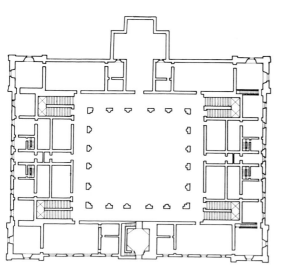

The Law Courts in Via Giulia and the Church of San Biagio

One of the most important projects entrusted to Bramante by Julius II was the construction in Via Giulia of a palazzo intended to house the Law Courts and various administrative offices. Work began on this project before 1509, but it remained unfinished and was later partly demolished. All that is now left to testify to its presence are some fragments of the rusticated wall of the lower part which have often been taken for Roman ruins. To reconstruct the broad lines of Bramante's plan is in the present stage of our knowledge a very difficult task, in spite of the abundance of records relating to it. We have a fairly detailed knowledge of the general plan, but to envisage how it was developed three-dimensionally, we must content ourselves with an engraving on a medal and a few hypothetical notes, since the well-known drawing by Fra Giocondo is entirely extraneous to Bramante's building and refers to a building on Via del Pantheon.

The distribution of the various functions of the building can be clearly deduced from drawing No. 136 in the Uffizi, inscribed 'Palazzo of S. Biagio della Pagnotta (of the loaf of bread) begun by Pope Julius', but the disparity between this drawing and the parts of the building which have survived would seem to indicate that it relates to an early stage of the planning (the drawing is reproduced here).

With regard to the medal, the building illustrated relates to an initial phase of the planning, preceding the stage shown in the drawing.

A distinguishing feature of the building appears to have been the five towers placed at the corners of the large block and at the centre of the façade. At least in the initial stages (the period at which the medal was coined), these towers must have still preserved a medieval character, with battlements and brackets, and for this reason as well as for the greater height of the central tower must have recalled the appearance of the Castello Sforzesco in Milan. The connecting link between the great masses of the walls was to have consisted of three superimposed arches, surmounted by an upper storey of lowered arches which were intended to take up the rhythm of the corbels. In the Uffizi drawing, the towers have lost their validity and seem to be supported by corner pilasters, but very little can be deduced concerning the pattern of the perforations apart from their number (eleven on the principal façade and nine on each side), while the plan for open galleries facing the street seems to have been abandoned in favour of a more solid solution.

This is almost certainly a plan for the mezzanine floor over the shops, and it cannot therefore give us an overall idea of the architect's treatment of volumes.

From the distributive point of view, we are struck by the rigorous symmetry, which would indicate that the building was subdivided according to function into two separate parts. The large number of staircases, four large and four smaller, confirms the hypothesis that this was a structure intended to serve many purposes and that access to each part was self-contained.

A unifying element between the different parts of the building was the large square courtyard with arcades and half-columns. The treatment of the corners with the quarter-columns inserted between two pilasters demonstrates Bramante's fidelity to the system employed in S. Maria della Pace, which guaranteed the continuity of the rhythm between the arches on perpendicular planes.

The fragments of the base which have survived indicate that a radical change occurred in the building programme, as compared with the stage represented on the medal. The corner towers no longer have a smooth battered base, but appear to be defined by vertical edging and marked by monumental rustication of large blocks arranged without regard to dimensions. The effect is comparable to the Palazzo Pitti in Florence, where there is a similar emphasis on the roughness of rustication, achieved by making it project far out of the wall plane; this is corrected by the rounded modelling of the stone and by the corner joint, which consists of a geometrical structure which asserts its power over the brute mass of the stone in a dialectical relationship absent from Brunelleschi's prototype. This carefully worked out solution signifies that Bramante had appropriated both the experience of Claudian architecture and the potentialities inherent in the 'rustic' manner.

Inside the Law Courts complex, Bramante had placed at an angle to the square courtyard a chapel dedicated to S. Biagio, which was later destroyed: that 'unfinished Doric temple' admired by Vasari, which can be reconstructed on the basis of some incomplete measured drawings. Together with the church of S. Celso, the Tempietto di S. Pietro, and the plans for St. Peter's, this chapel was the result of Bramante's experimentation on the theme of the centralized structure. It entailed two major problems: diagonal perspective and the accentuation of the penetrating axis. The central area under the dome has rounded pilasters similar to those in St. Peter's, and is entered by a small nave which breaks the effect of unlimited space and establishes an explicit hierarchy among the three circular apses. The enormous importance of this construction arises not only from its mixture of two systems, the centralized and the longitudinal, which posed a problem that remained in the forefront of architectural thought for the next three centuries, but also from its appearance as an open-planned structure created by the composition of the cupola and supporting pilasters.

The pillars, together with the L-shaped pilasters, define four barrel-vaulted arms, the depth of which can be determined by the intervening wall surfaces in accordance with the specific requirements of the theme. The connection between these sections and the implied aisles is carried out by means of the usual pilaster corner, which here suggests a hypothetical

Axonometric reconstruction of the Church of San Biagio della Pagnotta.

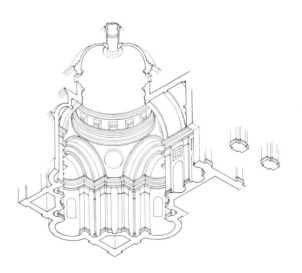

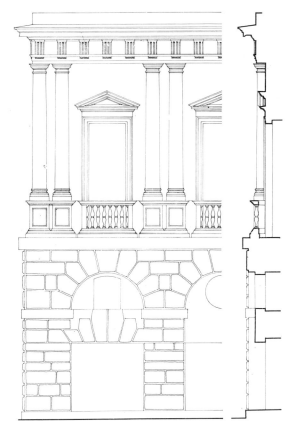

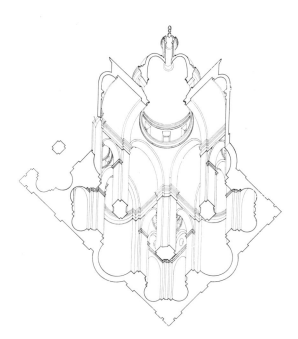

continuation to the primary structure (the baldacchino formed by the dome and the pilasters) further than the pragmatic closure of the secondary structure (the enclosing walls). The reconstruction of the church made by Giovannoni has contributed to propagating an inferior classical version which has been rightly criticized by Förster. The present author believes that the hypothesis put forward here is more faithful to a reading of those measured drawings which have survived in an incomplete state.

A comparison may be made between the volumetric structure of the Law Courts and Bramante's plan for the fortress of Civitavecchia, which can be reconstructed on the basis of a medal coined in 1506. Both the corner towers and the central fortification, without marked variations, were to have a complex pattern of battlements which would have endowed the fortress with a symbolic character recalling the Castello Sforzesco. As far as can be deduced from the medal, it seems that above the turret at the entrance there was to be a gallery covered by a kind of cupola, while superimposed cells on the corner towers bear a resemblance to the bell-towers planned for St. Peter's, although with less vertical development. Since it seems unlikely that the courtyard was constructed during the papacy of Paul III, one must attribute to Bramante also the plan for the internal façades, which in a simplified form foreshadows Michelangelo's system of intersecting orders.

In the palazzo constructed by Bramante on Via Alessandrina in Borgo, acquired by Raphael in 1517, the function and the position of the order have changed radically as compared with previous developments; the problem was no longer to 'measure' the space by means of a frame added to the wall, or to determine the scale of the external area by projecting upper storeys and sub-divisions onto the façade. Here the order is almost completely circular, and by being placed close to the wall, it creates a new spatial dimension. The portico and flat façade are superimposed and fuse into each other to produce a structure which is rich in plastic and illusory possibilities. Compared with fifteenth-century models, we have here a rediscovery of medieval values, such as we find in the rustication of the Palazzo Pitti, or the balance between weight and resistance in certain Romanesque structures. There is no mixture of styles here, and the composition is of the utmost rigour and control, governed by the iron law of the order, although the order has been adapted to create new forms of expression, and by being combined in pairs, maintains on the upper level as well as the lower the strength and the density of chiaroscuro which are necessary in order to bring the two contrasting bands into a unified composition.

A fate very similar to S. Biagio's befell the other small centrally-planned church built by Bramante on the Banchi Canal. We know this church only through incomplete measured drawings, from which we learn that its plan was very similar to that of St. Peter's—a small cross containing four chapels which surround the central dome-covered core. The hand of Bramante can be seen in the elegant arrangement of the niches in relation to the naves and in the cylindrical openings which provided light for the smaller chapels and created a whole network of points of light on the perimeter, thus enhancing the pictorial impression of the space.

The plan for this church may be compared with that of the chapel of the Pietà in the church of S. Satiro, built in the ninth century, where a similar distribution of space is found within a composite exterior.

THE PROBLEM OF ST. PETER'S

The idea of entirely rebuilding the basilica of St. Peter's, by abandoning the 'small improvement' begun by Nicholas V and transposing the early basilica of Constantine onto a heroic plane, came to Julius II as he was undergoing a tragic period of frustration and uncertainty. As he was aware, in the year 1505, not one of the great problems which caused him concern had been solved, while in Rome the plague wrought havoc, and the territorial integrity of the state was threatened from two sides.

The idea seems to have arisen out of the Pope's meditation on death; at first he thought only of his own tomb, which he pictured resembling that of his uncle Sextus IV—isolated like a sarcophagus, but very high in the manner of an ancient mausoleum. Since none of the chapels in the old basilica was big enough to contain such a monument, he had to design a church more grandiose in scale than the present structure. It was probably the vast scope of this new programme of reconstruction which revealed the shortcomings of Rossellino's plan for the restoration of St. Peter's.

Although it seems difficult to accept Vasari's statement that the new church was planned around the focal point of the tomb, it is true that for Julius the mausoleum and the church formed an organic unit. The tomb would probably have occupied one of the smaller chapels; but this chapel had to form a homogeneous part of an entire structure which would be large enough to contain with due proportion the tomb of the apostle Peter at its centre.

The influence which was most apparent during the planning period was that of Neoplatonism, propagated through the medium of Cardinal Egidio da Viterbo, the general of the Augustinian Order and an authoritative exponent of the ideas of Ficino. The choices made in the early stages did not meet the actual needs of restoring the old fabric of the building and of solving the many problems which its renovation implied; no plan was acceptable which was not an expression of the ideal content of the church and the sacred soil on which it stood. The new church had to stand alone, self-contained; at a certain stage it was to become the generating nucleus of a new hypothetical city, since it arose as a pure and ideal statement, a design created with no consideration of material limitations: *omni materia seclusa*, in the words of Alberti. The basilica was to be constructed according to a programme of autonomy, unity, and harmony, which derived from the classical tradition and from the humanist revival of the theories of Plotinus; but to this programme there was added an allegorical current linked to the Medieval Christian tradition indicated in St. Paul's Letter to the Corinthians: *Videmus nunc per speculum in Aenigmate, tunc autem facie ad faciem*. The new church was to represent not only the idea of the Divinity, but also its historical revelation, and the alliance between God and mankind; in this way it would conform to the patterns consecrated by tradition.

The first architect to be employed on the project was Fra Giocondo da Verona, a learned humanist with an expert knowledge of the theories of Vitruvius; but his suggestion that the Basilica of St. Mark's in Venice should be taken as a model and that a replica of its narthex and sequence of cupolas should be made for St. Peter's was immediately seen to be out of touch with the times, and the task of examining the problem passed into the hands of Giuliano da Sangallo and Bramante.

If we accept the hypothesis of Förster regarding the chronology of the plans drawn up by Sangallo and therefore take drawing No. 791 in the Albertina as the first suggestion put forward by the Florentine architect, in competititon with the first plan of Bramante (Uffizi, Nos. 1 and 3), it seems likely that the programme laid down by the Pope presupposed the following basic characteristics:
a) The total isolation of the new structure;
b) The central hemispherical dome;
c) The square plan with inscribed cross;
d) The presence of an indeterminate number of minor chapels.
The iconographical interpretation of this programme presents no difficulty. According to an ancient tradition which was adopted also by the Christian Church, especially in the East, the church is a microcosm reflecting the image of the whole cosmos. According to the Platonic view, the cosmos is represented by the sphere and has completely autonomous

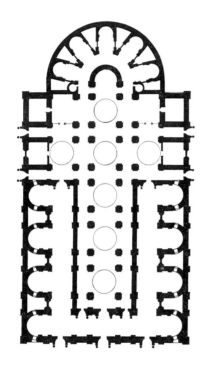

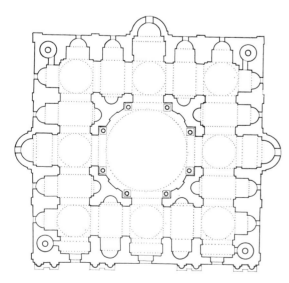

characteristics. 'And so, circle encompassing circle, He made a single, solitary cosmos; a cosmos having the power of being able to remain by itself within itself; a cosmos which knows itself, is in deep harmony with itself' (Timaeus, 34b). 'To the Living One who had to gather in Himself all living things, a suitable symbol will be one which embraces all figures, however many there exist; therefore He chose spherical forms, where the extremes in all directions are equally distant from the centre: a sphere which is as perfect as when it leaves the lathe. God judged this to be the consummate form among all forms, a form which is perfectly homogeneous with itself. And that which is homogeneous with itself is countless times more beautiful than what is uneven' (Timaeus, 33b). Since the dome is also an image of the heavens, and the cube an image of man, the integrated composition of the cube and sphere, the square and circle, represents in abstract form the bond between earth and heaven, made real through the mediation of the cross, which is the symbol of the quaternary structure of the universe as well as of the sacrifice of Christ from which the 'new alliance' takes its origin.

The Neoplatonic theory with which Giuliano seems to have been most in sympathy was that simplicity should be highly valued as a factor in creating a type of beauty which is purer than that resulting from complex relationships of forms, and he envisaged a vast dome-covered area surrounded by an aisle from which opened chapels of alternate dimensions.

From the point of view of *firmitas*, such a structure is impeccable, since the enormous walls separating the chapels create a formidable system of buttressing able to support the thrust of the great seventy-seven-branch dome (about 50 m.); but from the aesthetic viewpoint, the dome and square aisle remain extraneous to each other, while the atrophic arms of the cross are not integrated satisfactorily into the central space.

It was probably in direct competition with this plan that Bramante presented his famous 'plan on parchment', or at least a less detailed first edition of it. The difference in quality between these two plans is immediately apparent. Whereas Giuliano added one structure onto another, relying on the contrasting values to create their effect and seeking mechanically for unity of form through the use of well-defined and simplified structures, Bramante followed Alberti in concentrating on a type of organism built up of linked parts and having a high degree of complexity. His point of departure was the same as Giuliano's— a large dome-covered space; however, the dominating component formed by the dome was not isolated from its context, but instead became the core from which a series of homogeneous spatial developments evolved. The principle of combined development was applied generally. The central area, arrested as it were, in the process of growth, expands in four directions along the arms of the cross. This model was repeated almost identically in the four diagonally arranged dome-covered spaces. The principle of growth along the perpendicular axes was then repeated in a simplified form throughout the whole chain of what could be described as 'mediating spaces', marked by the letter 'c' in the drawing on page 63. Some of these spaces served as passages, others as chapels, and they absorbed the increased thickness of the great spinal walls beside the arms of the cross, which was determined by the 'bevelled' form of the pillars of the cupola. This plan, which introduced the irregular octagon as the basic model for the central space, was a more rigorous version of Giuliano's design in drawing 791 in the Albertina, and remained a fixed point from which the architect did not depart during the whole period of the planning and execution. In this model we can see an intentional reference to the church of S. Lorenzo in Milan and through it a rediscovery of the late-Roman spatial concept which was to become even more noticeable in Bramante's next plan. As far as the structural composition was concerned, the insertion of the octagon led to a binary type of composition, with an alternating pattern of irregular intervals, so projecting into space Alberti's model of the rhythmic frame and at the same time introducing the two diagonals as a determining factor in the spatial perception.

Some critics have seen in the introduction of the octagon an arbitrary subjective choice, but this interpretation does not appear convincing, since the rounding of the angles of the square out of which the octagon is created is the first stage in the process of reducing the square to a circle, the 'squaring the circle' which from the first was the implicit idea behind this type of composition. Moreover the width of the nave and the width of the octagon are related in the well-defined ratio of 1 : 1.5 (diapente).

The most fascinating aspect of Bramante's design on the sheet of parchment is the clarity of the compositional rules and the simplicity of the result. As this author has tried to show in a series of diagrams, the whole structure can be viewed as the product of five spatial cruciform nuclei which are alike in form, or as the aggregate of forty-one sub-units of four types. This means that the model for the spatial arrangements inside the building would result in only four possibilities: the spanning of the cross-vault (b); the octagonal dome-covered areas (a); the niches (d), and the mediating spaces (c). To evaluate the high degree of rationalization involved in such a plan, one need only consider that in Giuliano's drawing in the Albertina, which presents a far more basic and simplified design, an analysis of this type produces the result of six irreducible sub-units.

In fact Bramante succeeded impressively in creating unity within multiplicity by establishing a relationship of homogeneity between the part and the whole which recalls a passage where Plotinus reflects on the relationship between worldly reality and the idea: 'Here below ... each part is always born out of another and every unit is simply a part; there, on the other hand, from the whole the unit is born unceasingly and at the same time it is a unit and a whole; it is true that it looks like a part, but to a discerning eye it is revealed as a whole' (*Enneads* V, IV, 28). We are reminded of another passage in Plotinus by the relationship between voids and solid walls in Bramante's design. It is a complementary relationship depending on dynamic equilibrium and may have been suggested to Bramante by the technique of casting which he had studied in classical monuments. 'But how can that which is corporeal harmonize with what is superior to the body?' Plotinus asks in the first *Ennead*, and taking a comparison from the field of architecture, adds: 'Tell me then how the architect, after measuring the external form of the house against its inner form judges it to be beautiful? The reason lies in the fact that once the stones are removed, what is external is none other than internal form, subdivided, it is true, in the external mass of the material, but existing and indivisible, even if portrayed in multiplicity. Therefore, once the sensitive mind sees in bodies the idea which has bound and dominated unyielding and shapeless nature, and a form which frees itself by being distinguished from all other forms, it then creates a synthesis out of the bodily multiplicity, brings it back and reduces it henceforth to its internal indivisibility; and finally makes it harmonize, become adapted and acceptable to its intimate form.'

Bramante arrived at his desired spatial unity by making use of a number of experiences distant in space and time, while showing an extraordinary ability for synthesis. Roman baths suggested scale and order; but their structure based on a sequence of independent spaces was rejected in favour of the fusion of space discovered by architects of the late-classical period. From the medieval tradition, he absorbed the 'propositional' process for linking the spans of arches, which derived from scholastic logic and the vertical nature of the central spatial area. In the plan on parchment, a symbolic content appeared which was absent from the first plan by Sangallo and might have been included out of an intentional desire to enrich the programme set by his patron. These symbolic features were: the presence of three openings on each of the four façades; the sixteen cells which can be identified around the central spatial area; and the cruciform development of the four satellite areas. In the case of the twelve openings, the reference to the celestial city of Jerusalem is immediately clear and was later confirmed in the urban developments given to the project by Bramante, while the sixteen spatial cells may have been intended to represent the archetypal form of the Temple in Hebrew tradition, which was planned according to the sequence

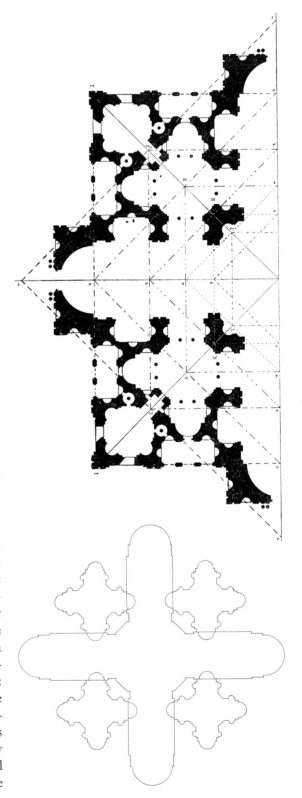

Bramante: Plan for St. Peter's. Diagram taken from the 'plan on parchment', Uffizi 1 A (after Förster).

Geometrical design of the cruciform interwoven structures in the first plan by Bramante.

Design of the spatial units in the first plan by Bramante.

Drawing taken from Caradosso's medal showing Bramante's design for St. Peter's.

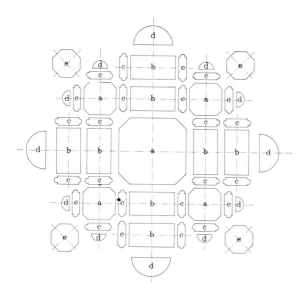

in which the tribes of Israel took their places round the Ark of the Covenant when Moses descended from Sinai. The distribution of the twelve tribes and four groups of Levites is described in detail in the Book of Numbers (1, 2) and at the end of the sixteenth century was the subject of a reconstruction by Villalpando, who used it as the basis for his reconstruction of the Temple of Jerusalem. Bramante's plan was very close to the diagram drawn up by Villalpando (to which reference has recently been made also in order to explain the structure of the Escorial) and corresponded also to the Biblical description. In particular, the four projecting bell-towers appeared to symbolize the tribes of Judah, Ephraim, Daniel and Ruben, who presided at the tabernacle. The fairly convincing attempt made by Wolf-Metternich to develop an elevation from the plan on parchment was based on the supposition that the walls forming the arms of the cross were ornamented by a system of two superimposed orders. Given this type of spatial organization, the treatment of surfaces would have been more representative at this stage than at the final stage of the linear style of Lombard work. What Argan has defined as the 'spectacle of spatialism' certainly expressed the architect's predominant intention and the conditioning factor of every stylistic feature; this can be seen, for example, in the arrangement of the niches and repetition of projecting edges which repeat each other like an echo, as in S. Maria del Popolo. At this stage of his research, Bramante's concept of the exterior seems to have been close to the images of the exterior engraved on medals: bare wall blocks just faintly relieved by cornices—similar, in fact, to the tower enclosing the spiral staircase of the Belvedere, which presented a bare summary of the pattern of interconnected voids planned for the interior. The architectonic orders appear only in the bays of the apses and modify plastically the separate layers as well as the colonnade beneath the dome. This dome became the unrivalled main feature in a composition which was based on large masses, and inspired not from the original appearance of the classical monuments but from their quality as ruins which, having lost all plastic ornamentation, offered a closer image of the spatial quality of the interior, in the sense understood by Plotinus. Bramante's plan on parchment was rejected, but not on artistic grounds. Its acceptance would have entailed a change in the orientation of the church, so that the tomb of the Apostle would no longer have been in the centre. In his *Historia viginti Saeculorum*, Egidio da Viterbo describes the controversy between Pope and architect, from which he himself probably did not remain aloof. Bramante believed that he could not fail if he appealed to the Pope's pride and he explained to Julius II that by following his idea it would be possible to connect the principal entrance to the basilica with the obelisk placed in the circus by Julius Caesar; in this way the Pope's programme of *renovatio imperii* and *renovatio Romae* could be expressed symbolically by establishing a parallel between the achievements of the two Juliuses. But the religious argument prevailed. The tomb of the Apostle had to remain in the centre, the main façade had to continue to face east, and the consecrated area of the old basilica had to remain entirely enclosed within the perimeter of the new edifice.

In order to meet these new demands, Giuliano da Sangallo and Bramante found themselves once again in competition. As seen in drawing No. 8r. in the Uffizi, Sangallo proposed to extend the new church so as to include both the new choir built by Rossellino and the whole area of the original basilica. The large square structure thus attained a size of 700 rods a side (157 metres). In this plan, Sangallo incorporated many of the ideas of Bramante but insisted on emphasizing the separation of the central dome-covered area from the arms of the cross. The major thickness of the wall demonstrates his critical attitude towards the technical aspects of Bramante's plan and his tendency to interpret the internal space as the result of a process of hollowing into the interior of the gigantic cubic mass. The alternative suggested by Bramante formed the basis for the work of reconstruction and sets one of the most difficult problems in sixteenth-century architecture, a problem which will perhaps never be finally solved. Drawings 8v and 20 in the Uffizi show that he favoured a longitudinal plan, viewed as a prolongation of one of the arms of the cruciform structure.

The crossings on the diagonals were no longer octagonal and were ornamented in a way which differed from the treatment of the central space; at the same time the three smaller arms were shorter than in the plan on parchment; they no longer comprised two arch spans but one only. As if to compensate for this decreased size, however, there appeared semi-circular corridors around the apses towards which the space of the aisles flowed: these were the famous ambulatories which—until their final rejection by Michelangelo—continued to be one of the features of the design.

Closely connected to the drawings referred to, but in contradiction to them so far as longitudinal development is concerned, is the plan in the sketchbook of Bramante's collaborator, Menicantonio de' Chiarellis, in which the same features—the ambulatories, the shortened arms, the corner towers—appear in a design which is rigidly centralized, though with an accentuation of the main façade in which the convex apse is enclosed in a protruding cubic volume. It is difficult to discover how these ideas of Bramante developed and changed in order to conform to the requirements of his patron. The work of construction was probably begun with many of the problems which had arisen at the planning stage remaining unsolved, but taking the central nucleus formed by the breadth of Rossellino's choir and the width of the former nave as an essential element from which there could be no going back. This central core, which conditioned the choice of the pattern of the internal order and the form of the pillars supporting the dome, can be studied both in drawing No. 20 and in the drawing by Menicantonio. It differs from Bramante's orginal plan on the sheet of parchment mainly in the change from a system of superimposed orders to a giant order, and in the elimination of the gap between the arms of the cross and the central space which had been created in the original design by the greater projection of the wall pilasters from the central pillars.

Wolf-Metternich has suggested that these variants from the first plan were due to the intervention of Giuliano da Sangallo, to whom the two drawings on sheet No. 8 (r. and v.) in the Uffizi are to be ascribed; this suggestion is very plausible and throws new light on the process of Bramante's thought. To judge from his proposals, Sangallo did not share Bramante's interest in a minute and subtle development of the structure as envisaged in the original plan, and he must have had a decisive influence in the selection of the giant order. At first, Bramante seems to have accepted Sangallo's idea of placing eight large columns at the base of the dome, after the model of the basilica of Maxentius; then he brought his original approach to this new system by treating the order of the aisles after the manner of Alberti: that is, arranging around the central zone eight 'triumphal arches' connected by vast barrel vaulting. A binary system was now envisaged for a single order and adapted to the space of the dome by means of curved wall pilasters, thus transforming the whole cruciform design into a continuous sequence on the single theme a − b − a − b − a − b.

In his designs for the terminal areas of the apses, the function of the ambulatories, and the relationship between the aisles and the smaller polyapsidal spaces, Bramante continued to oscillate between a plan for an uninterrupted sequence of volumes and a plan based on contrasting features. The latter was to be achieved by means of architectonic orders which would act as transparent screens, whose light entablature formed a contrast to the great arched masses of the wall structure. The more radical solution indicated in drawing No. 20 transforms the great arches into triforia by giving linear accentuation to the continuity of the walls of the aisles.

The idea of enhancing the ambulatories with encircling bands of light at the base of the structure in order to lighten both weight and terminal quality represents the final indication of Bramante's clearly formulated stylistic purpose. By adopting the giant order and the feature of the triumphal arch, he continued to rediscover the great organic themes of Roman classical architecture but did not fail to question their validity, applying them through an optical interpretation and a 'modern' sensibility conditioned by the experience he had gained of medieval and humanist culture. Bramante's intervention probably ended in a sus-

Comparison of Bramante's final solutions for St. Peter's (after Förster) (1 cm = 13.5 m).

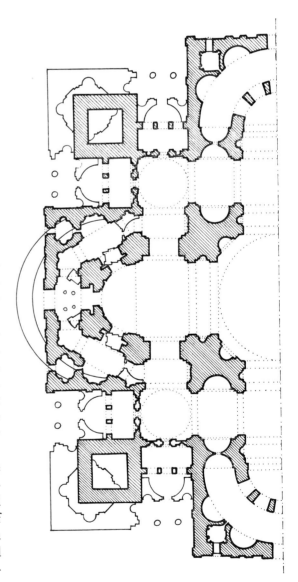

pension of judgement as to the choice between a longitudinal and a centralized solution. Once Sangallo's suggestion that the central organism should be extended to cover the whole area of the old basilica had been rejected, there remained only two possibilities: either to extend the structure lengthwise from the centre (which is presented in such a way that it can be extended in perspective without losing its organic nature), or else to give up the idea of encompassing the whole of the consecrated area. Bramante's preference for the centralized solution seems to be shown in his attempt to find a middle course, as seen in another plan drawn in Menicantonio's sketchbook, where the church appears enclosed within a complex structure on an urban scale. The façade is placed within a grandiose *corte*, a sort of rectangular quadriportico, while all around the body of the church is tightly enclosed in a structure which—like a lingering echo—reproduces the convex forms and diagonal groins of the building. From a dotted outline visible in the drawing there clearly appears the desire to show that in this way the consecrated area of the old basilica, although not entirely contained within the new part, would at least fall within the area of the quadriportico, namely in an area which was still part of the sacred precinct. In an even more organic form, the same idea appears in drawing No. 104 in the Uffizi, where in a version probably preceding the final one, the body of the church is contained by a surrounding square which repeats exactly its cruciform structure and corner towers. This drawing, which may well be the only one where the hand of Bramante can be ascertained, is one of the clearest indications of the whole process involved in the planning of St. Peter's. The church was created in order to solve contingent problems, but had now acquired an autonomous value as a work of architecture and took the Utopian ideas of Julius II to extreme, paradoxical consequences. The abstract idea of central planning gradually led from the aim to improve the basilica itself to an improvement in the whole structure of the Curia, which was placed inside a kind of citadel, similar to the Temple in Jerusalem. The improvement to the Curia led in its turn, as a logical consequence, to an improvement of the city, which appears implicit in the structure where, like a Roman camp, an extension may be made in all directions. The urban Utopia expressed here reveals in its 'impossibility' the extent of the gap between the cultural superstructure and the economic structure.

The hypothesis which governed the plan for the Tempietto of S. Pietro in Montorio, visualized inside a homogeneous enveloping complex which was to re-echo its cylindrical form, was applied again in St. Peter's where the building was not intended as a static (as if seen from a distant viewpoint) but as a dynamic and plastic type of structure. From the interior of the enclosure, the dome would have hardly been visible and even from the exterior the most striking feature would have been the space comprised between the two homologous structures, which would have been represented by this space in the same way as metal repeats the mould into which it is poured.

The critical element of Bramante's legacy is the unsolved problem of the façade. Mention has been made of the indistinct images engraved on dedicatory medals, which are characterized by bare volumes organized around the internal volumes. However, from the very beginning of the building this solution must have appeared unsatisfactory to Bramante, since it subordinated the exterior to the interior too definitely. The most reliable evidence of Bramante's views on this problem can be found in Menicantonio's sketchbook, where a volumetric treatment similar in design to that shown on the medals is relieved by a complex and fragmentary ornamentation. The bay of the façade shows a systematic application of intersecting orders and completely conceals the front apse behind an enormous tympanum supported by a giant order. The very tall bell towers consist of four architectonic orders placed one above the other mechanically and separated by large plinths. Thus a difficult structural problem which defeated even someone as gifted as Antonio the Younger was created there (Parts II and III below).

When Bramante died, Leo X asked Raphael to continue his work, and offered him the assistance of Giuliano da Sangallo and Fra Giocondo. The elderly Florentine architect made

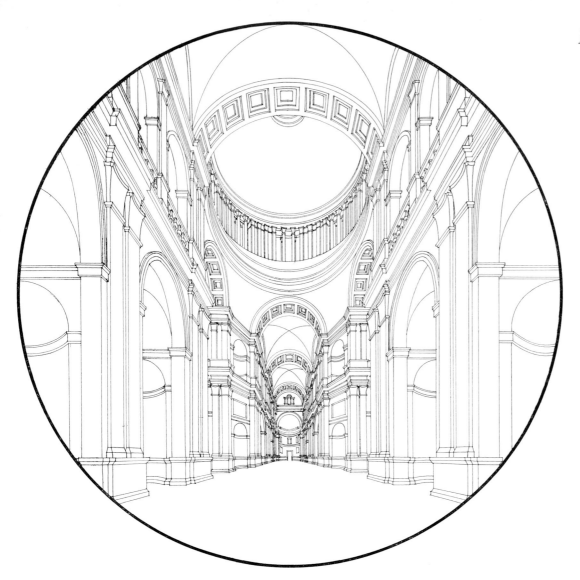

a number of studies in this period related to the longitudinal development of Bramante's plan, with special emphasis on such practical matters as the preservation of Rossellino's apse as it then stood, the restoration of the original basilica of five aisles. Raphael's design is known to us only through the engraving in Serlio's treatise, and in spite of its lack of detail, this engraving shows that the design corresponded in substance to the final longitudinal version of Bramante's plan. The few variants concern the treatment of the external volumes, a more compact and unified result being achieved by the elimination of the open colonnades at the sides of the apses and the introduction into the façade of a row of free-standing columns.

Unfortunately, very little can be deduced regarding the form these external variants took, but they were certainly intended to correct the contradictory elements in the plan produced by Bramante. In the present state of our knowledge and in spite of the unproven assertions of many art historians, it must be admitted that the part played by Raphael in the history of St. Peter's was a very minor one.

We may more easily recognize the considerable contribution made by Baldassare Peruzzi, who worked as assistant to Antonio da Sangallo on the death of Raphael. Pope Paul III confirmed this appointment in 1543 and increased his salary. In the rich collection of draw-

ings by Peruzzi in the Uffizi, a great number refer directly or indirectly to St. Peter's, and in this group of about thirty pages we find what is probably the richest personal testimony to have come down to us concerning the planning of the new church. Unfortunately, we still lack detailed research which could enable the various drawings to be dated and show to what extent the designs were personal to Peruzzi and independent of the ideas suggested by the architects under whose direction he worked.

A series of radical alternatives to the solutions which were adopted might relate to the first period of Peruzzi's activity at the time when he was working in Bramante's studio. In three different designs, he tried to find ways of substituting for the cruciform plan a gigantic rotunda surrounded by smaller spaces. In one of the early drawings, a dome measuring 64 metres in diameter rested on an octagonal drum hollowed out by gigantic niches (about 20 m. in diameter) and communicating with four satellite areas.

An even bolder suggestion occurs in drawing XVIII, in which the dome has taken on colossal dimensions (about 130 metres in diameter) and stands at the centre of an enormous square block measuring 250 metres a side, fifty per cent of which consists of enormous wall masses relieved only by shallow round and oval spaces and narrow passages. In the buildings for which he was responsible, Peruzzi appears mainly as a refined stylist, but in these drawings he evinces a truly amazing resoluteness and ambition. It seems as if he wished to show his disapproval of Bramante for not having taken his programme of 'the restoration of antiquity' to its ultimate consequences and for having sought a compromise solution. For the young architect, the most satisfactory method of treating the construction of the new church was to adopt the compact space of the Pantheon and the Licinian Gardens and extend its height to heroic dimensions. Expressed in these plans was the contrast between the ideal of the sublime and the ideal of proportion, and we see in them an anticipation of 'Piranesian' visions and the indication of the radical attitude Bramante's pupils had already adopted by around 1510. Peruzzi was less interested in the rival merits of the central and longitudinal plans than in the affirmation of his conception of space as an absolutely indivisible unit admitting of no interruption except so far as necessary in order to create a clear hierarchical distinction. In drawing XVIII, he considered the possibility of adapting this spatial conception to a longitudinal design by means of the invention of a façade-porch ornamented by a forest of columns. This porch was conceived like a gigantic funnel which would 'draw in' the viewers towards the narrow central passage leading to the rotunda, a structure comprising decreasing spans similar to Bernini's Palazzo Barberini constructed a hundred years later.

After this critical and Utopian stage, the drawings of Peruzzi document a 'return to the order', an acceptance of the scale and position of the pillars suggested by Bramante. He made many alternative studies for a longitudinal structure with direct communication between the aisles and the satellite spaces on either side of them. The problem of incorporating the columns of the old basilica led to the return of perspective rows which were used as transparent screens separating the aisles. The example to which he constantly referred was the basilica of Maxentius, which was the model for the tripartite division of the nave and the emphasis on the structural elements.

In the perspective of the interior shown in drawing XV (Uffizi No. 25 A), we see that the side chapels are no longer independent units but lateral extensions to the nave, separated by gigantic buttresses. For its highly skilful technique, this drawing recreates the structural quality of the ancient Roman monuments as no other image in this period.

Drawing XVI (Uffizi No. 26 A) showing the external treatment of volumes enables us to appreciate fully Peruzzi's capacity by a process of simplification to master the difficulties created by the vastness and complexity of his subject. For the first time, we are given an indication of the way towards a solution to the hopeless contradictions in Bramante's plan. The abolition of the bell towers and the tripartite division of the colonnade places the three domes which are visible into direct opposition, and by giving each of them a similar base the predominant role of the central block is accentuated by contrast, within an impeccable pyramidal composition of a type dear to Raphael.

It is strange that the only official evidence we have of Peruzzi's plan for St. Peter's—the engraving in the Third Book of Serlio—tends to present a very conventional picture of the architect's work, in contrast to what has been observed in the drawings by his own hand. According to this engraving, Peruzzi—it is not known at what date—designed a central structure closely based on Bramante's last plan, the only variant being the closure of the access at the sides of the apses and the setting of these entries on the principal axes of symmetry. One cannot exclude the possibility that such fidelity to Bramante may indicate that Peruzzi himself made a considerable contribution to his master's final plan. This would support the hypothesis that the famous split perspective shown in the Uffizi drawing was worked out in Bramante's studio.

An interesting footnote to Peruzzi's plans for St. Peter's is provided by drawing XXVIII: this is a very carefully designed plan, perhaps drawn by the Sienese master himself, but signed by Antonio della Valle as his own work. It is one of the most amazing examples of sixteenth-century architecture and is especially interesting because it is the 'opinion' of a dilettante. Della Valle was an accountant at the Vatican and possibly a mathematician; as

Ground plan in Bramante's final design for St. Peter's; from a drawing in the sketchbook of Menicantonio de Chiarellis (1 cm = 45 m).

Project for the construction of a citadel round St. Peter's; from a drawing in the sketchbook of Menicantonio de Chiarellis (1 cm = 28 m).

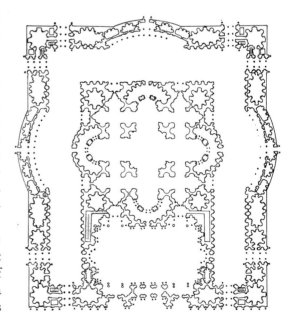

an amateur he took part in the discussions regarding the problems of architectural composition taking place around him in Rome, but was inspired by a geometric 'furore' which was Gothic in origin and entirely free from any classicist inhibitions. The tendency of the Vatican 'accountants' to put aside their professional duties in order to take up architecture was fairly widespread. Another example was the case of Jacopo Melighino, who was assistant to Sangallo at Frascati and the founder of the Congregation of the Virtuous at the Pantheon. Vasari relates that when Pope Paul III was considering designs for the Palazzo Farnese, he looked at the drawings made by Antonio da Sangallo and then said: 'All these are fine, but it will do no harm if we see one other which our Melighino has made. Wherefore Antonio was rather resentful and thought the Pope was making fun of him, and said: Holy Father, Melighino is an architect as a joke. Hearing this, the Pope, who was seated, turned towards Antonio, bending his head almost to the ground: Antonio, we wish Melighino to be an architect by profession, and you see that he gets a salary.' Probably Della Valle did not enjoy such powerful patronage, since it seems that he was never given any professional commissions; however, in his plan he shows a sense of being 'possessed' which is entirely worthy of a Mannerist. The plan was probably designed in the years between 1513-20, because the central part is a faithful reproduction of the structure planned by Raphael and documented by Serlio's engraving. Around this section, however, Della Valle has woven a complex geometrical framework based on a hexagonal plan, on the basis of which a gigantic semicircular area of space is added to this nucleus with a colonnade projecting outwards at the front. Owing to a certain ambiguity in the drawing, it is not clear whether this area of space was to be covered or not, but the consistency of the wall thicknesses and the large circular stairs indicate that he had in mind a half-dome. The most surprising factor—apart from the ambiguity of the drawing—is the ability of its author to carry to their extreme consequences the principle of a geometrical ground plan and his pleasure in the logical sequence which links the parts to the whole. The fact that it was possible in Rome in the years between 1513 and 1520 to think in this way, even from a position of isolation, and to arouse the interest of such an important personality as Peruzzi—who probably amused himself by collaborating with Della Valle—is an interesting reflection of the lively intellectual climate and open-minded approach to problems which were characteristic of the *plenitudo temporum*.

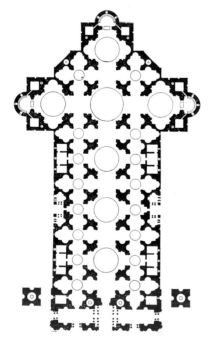

RAPHAEL, OR THE HIGH PERIOD OF CLASSICAL REDISCOVERY

Signs of a marked architectural aptitude can be discerned in the Oddi altarpiece which Raphael painted in 1502 at the early age of nineteen. In the two panels depicting the *Annunciation* and *Presentation at the Temple*, the figures are enveloped in a space which is characterized by columns in perspective which advance from the background. Between the human figures and the columns, a relationship is formed which is based on complementary qualities and proportional affinity. The abstract architectonic element has been charged with a triple function: to clarify the position and intensity of the sources of light (optical model), to make space measurable by the addition of square units (dimensional model), and to collaborate in conjunction with the figures in creating a complex equilibrium (compositional model). In the Annunciation, the asymmetrical arrangement of the figures forms a contrast to the symmetrical framework of the architecture, and serves to emphasize the psychological distance separating the angel who enters and the Virgin, 'static' in her meditation. In the *Presentation at the Temple*, on the other hand, the columns extending into the foreground 'point' the story, creating a tripartite image—hierarchical, narrative, and panoramic—

which guides the viewer's attention in accordance with a precise hierarchy. The assurance with which the painter adopted architectural forms and emphasized their plastic qualities is shown also in his continuation of the architectural structure beyond the area of the internal space: in the *Presentation* especially, where the appearance in the background of the supports for columns beyond two areas enclosed in arches obeys the exigencies of rhythmic design without impairing the rigorous perspective governing the relationship between the row of columns and the head of the priest.

In the *Marriage of the Virgin*, the central building painted in the background gives proof not only of a great skill in using the architectonic image in a pictorial context, but also of an original creative ability in the field of architecture. One of the problems of greatest concern to contemporary architects was faced and solved in an extremely original way, by methods—such as the crown of volutes placed between two faceted volumes—which were destined to have a far-reaching influence. A comparison with the Tempietto of S. Pietro in Montorio, even if we discount the hypothesis upheld by this author that it should be assigned to a later date, does not provide convincing evidence since the same problem has been solved here in a different manner. In place of the circular forms of Bramante which clasp the volume like tight rings, Raphael created two faceted volumes, one compact and crystalline, the other transparent. The common element uniting them is to be found in the value of the temple as a nucleus generating an enveloping centralized space, and in the tendency to view this space as a tree-trunk of infinite dimensions, where the concentric circles, marked by the continuous growth of the structure, are replaced by annular strata of space which impose their own 'visual order'. Just as Bramante wanted to incorporate a second ring of encircling columns around the body of the church, so Raphael arranged the figures in the foreground so as to form one of the concentric layers of his ideal structure. The only building which can properly be compared with the church depicted in the *Marriage of the Virgin* is a church built in a later period, S. Maria della Consolazione, at Todi, which may well have been inspired by this same painting. In this church we find Raphael's faceted treatment of the side apses, his arrangement of the windows, and especially his general volumetric conception which transfigures the landscape by introducing a luminous cell into it.

The geometrical structure of the church provides another proof of the artist's maturity. A sectional view can be obtained by superimposing two rectangles resting on a common base; the vertical rectangle circumscribes the volumetric nucleus terminated by the cell and dome, the horizontal rectangle circumscribes the full length of the circular arcade. At its full height the first rectangle (from the base of the columns to the base of the lantern) attains a ratio between base and height of 1.618 ... equal to the golden section; while if we calculate the height as far as the summit of the top cornice, the ratio becomes 3 : 4 (diatessaron); then by halving this height we obtain the height of the bottom cornice and consequently the line of intersection with the horizontal rectangle which envelops the porch. To obtain the size of the width of the porch (another side of the rectangle), one must add to the two sides two rectangles having a ratio of 1 : (2 + 1 : 8) between the sides. An analysis of the surfaces which close the two drums produces results which are just as interesting: the ratio between the intercolumniation and the height of the shafts is 4 : 5, the ratio between the intercolumniation and the height of the cornice 3 : 5 (almost equivalent to the golden section). In the upper part of the drum the ratio between the intercolumniation and the height of the shafts of the wall pilasters is 2 : 3, and that between the intercolumniation and the total height of the order 1 : 2; the proportion of the space occupied by the window is 7 : 10 (almost equivalent to 1/root of 2). It is possible to make a close examination of the proportions of the building owing to the availability of the original plan, and their complexity shows that the architect's studies had reached a very advanced stage and that he was already well informed as to the Pythagoric laws of Timaeus, which he later transferred to his *School of Athens*.

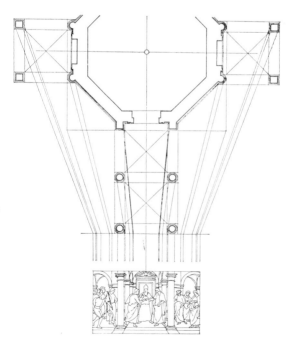

Perspective reconstruction of the architectural background to Raphael's Presentation in the Temple.

In the paintings produced in the years 1504–9, the background of architecture no longer had the determining function it had served in the Brera *Marriage of the Virgin*, yet the painter's experience of composition enriched and secretly nurtured his frustrated architectural vocation. We need refer only to the Borghese *Deposition*, the *Holy Family* in Munich, or *Madonna del Baldacchino* in which a study of dynamic possibilities and the influence of bodies on space acquires a specifically architectonic interest.

Raphael arrived in Rome at the end of 1508 and began to concentrate his activity on monumental painting. It may be presumed that until the death of Bramante he had few opportunities for architectural work on his own account, but his theoretical interst in the subject continued unabated. In the *School of Athens* (1509—10), the *Expulsion of Heliodorus* (1511—12), the *Mass of Bolsena* (1511—12), and the *Fire of Borgo* (1514), architecture plays a fundamental part, even though it is strictly dependent on the pictorial narrative; having abandoned the path of architecture as a volumetric pivot to the composition which had been happily exemplified in the Brera *Marriage of the Virgin*, where the church is an independent organic structure and is defined unambiguously in all its parts, Raphael employs architectonic space to contain the image and serve as an abstract model of the human 'situation' portrayed in the painting.

Much has been written on the subject of the architectural background to the *School of Athens*, especially on the question of whether to accept or reject Vasari's information that it was designed by Bramante and passively adopted by Raphael. There is no actual evidence to support Vasari's statement, while stylistic considerations militate against its veracity. We are a long way from Bramante in this design of the Doric order with anomalous cornice, and the very serrated rhythm of the intercolumniation (the ratio between the intercolumniation and the full height of the order is 1:3) and some incongruities in perspective make it seem unlikely that the architectonic structure was conceived independently of its pictorial context.

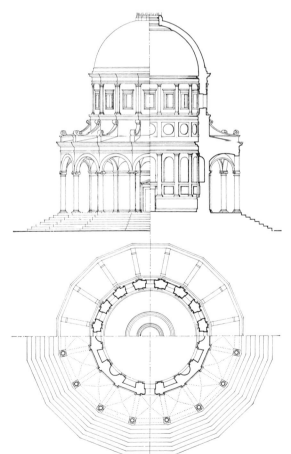

The most striking of these incongruities is the horizontal development of the cornices over the pillars supporting the dome which, in view of the form of the pendentives, should have been inclined. A close reconstruction in perspective of the imaginary building would produce the paradoxical result that the mass of the pendentives would be half deformed or without any support. The attempt made by Theobald Hoffmann to reconstruct a plan of the building without taking account of this incongruity proposed a central dome supported by bevelled piers similar to those in St. Peter's, though without the characteristic L-shaped pilasters to take the archivolts. The incongruity in the perspective indicates that there may have been a modification to the perspective background during the course of the work, and that at an early stage it probably consisted of two free-standing triumphal arches, later joined to each other by the imaginary dome. Raphael therefore did not start with a preconceived idea for architecture, as a kind of container for the ideas of Bramante, but planned the background in conjunction with the figures and modified it freely even during the stage of execution. An intervention by Bramante may certainly be excluded because of the absence of the elaborate ornamentation of the pilasters supporting the cupola. In fact the most noticeable structure visible in the background to the *School of Athens* is that of the three luminous planes which extend in depth to form galleries and triumphal arches. The closer connection between the two first planes through the cupola and the receding of the third into an immeasurable distance fulfil the need to accentuate a movement in depth through a rhythm marked by pauses: a ternary rhythm which becomes the most important element in the picture. However, even if Bramante himself did not intervene in this background, the *School of Athens* expresses Raphael's complete adherence to the ideals of universality taught by his master, and his intentional reference to St. Peter's acknowledged its supremacy as the embodiment of these ideals. However, the vertical composition of the basilica, which was the form chosen in order to worship and symbolize the Deity, was replaced in the painting by a geometrical structure and dimensions which were entirely different. The long narrow aisles (ratio between width and height 2:3 up to the impost of the vaulting and 4:9 as far as the top) gave way to shorter aisles of more massive proportions (ratio between width and height 10:11 up to the impost of the vaulting and about 2:3 up to the top), while the heroic dimensions of St. Peter's (height of nave about 45 m.) have been reduced to the more human scale of the philosophers' gallery (height as far as the top about 7.50 m.)

And it was in this adaptation to a human scale, in this diminishing of heroic tension as compared with Bramante's models of St. Peter's and the portico of the Belvedere (from which there may derive the arrangement of the niches, tightly enclosed by the twin wall pilasters) that Raphael's specifically architectonic intention may be discerned. In other words, he sought for 'grace' through an arrangement of colours which was intended to stabilize an interconnecting relationship with the atmosphere by means of the harmonious dove-tailing of movements.

This same harmonious dovetailing is employed with dramatic intent in the architectural background to the *Expulsion of Heliodorus*, where Raphael's search for 'grace' is expressed in the intense colour harmony between the deep blue, of a type found in Venetian painting, in the last lunette, and the brilliant golds and yellows sparkling with metallic lustre in the double arches at the base of the domes, as well as in the terminal function fulfilled by the lateral arches which have been cut in half so that they almost resemble buttresses. The structural law governing the composition is stated in the foreground by the series of octagons engraved in the floor. With the double symmetry determined by the four intersecting axes, the octagon is the figure which represents both frontality and diagonality— the two principles behind the arrangement of the arches and the angular arrangement of the columns in Raphael's structure.

The passage from the volumetric and extended scene in the background to the *School of Athens* to the intense confusion of architectural elements, without visible wall intervals, was certainly the result of psychological motivation, but also expressed a broadening of the artist's interests to encompass the lesser known aspects of the classical tradition. It is very probable, in fact, that the idea for annular cornices supported by columns was suggested by the ruins of Hadrian's Villa, especially by the recollection of the maritime theatre. If the plastic quality of the structure may be related to the contemporary Palazzo Caprini by Bramante, the complexity of its rhythm and handling of light (with the frontal planes acting as wings which break up the continuity of the horizontal lines) reveal a remarkable originality which belonged to Raphael alone.

Again, the *Fire of Borgo* fresco, in spite of its scenographic composition, has the value of a further experiment into the possibilities of architectonic spatialism.

The architectural structures are interpreted more as surfaces than volumes, and rigidly obey a perpendicular pattern. They create an impression of the wings of a theatre which slide into each other and are moved from the periphery towards the centre and halted in such a way that they create a flowing and dynamic spatialism, comparable to Mies van der Rohe's pavilion in Barcelona which was built in 1929. Even the fragmentary nature of the composition and the marked archaeological flavour did not limit Raphael's awareness of the architectonic possibilities of the theme and led him to undertake his own research into the repertory of Bramante by designing the 'palazzetto of the loggia', where he repeated the binary structure with horizontal superimposed bands found in the Palazzo Caprini. Compared with Bramante's serliana windows in S. Maria del Popolo and the large window of the main room, the window designed by Raphael has more ample and harmonious spatial proportions, anticipating the style of Palladio.

The Church of Sant' Eligio degli Orefici

A famous drawing by Sallustio Peruzzi, now in the Uffizi, provides the only evidence for the attribution to Raphael of this church and enables us to picture the original form of the façade and cupola. We know that the structure remained almost unaltered in the lower part,

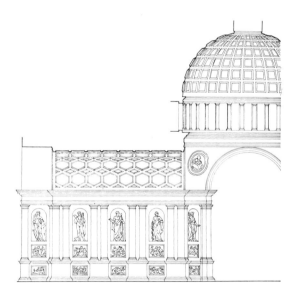

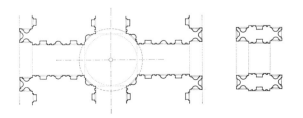

with the exception of the closing of the small niches comprised in the pilasters, which have been identified but not restored in a recent work of reconstruction. The perspective built on two orders of equal breadth (later changed) expressed the architect's tendency to interpret the central structure according to the model of the inscribed cross which Bramante had applied in the church of S. Celso. Although surrounded by other buildings, this little church was made to appear like a cubic block from which only the low cupola protruded. The use of twin Doric wall pilasters, and the upper storey with plain bands were features explicitly derived from the example of Bramante's Tempietto of S. Pietro in Montorio, while the triforium with central arch, which formed a direct connecting link between the interior and the exterior, was related to the windows in the choir of S. Maria del Popolo and the main room of the Vatican. The design of the interior resembled that of the church of S. Maria delle Carceri at Prato, but an even closer resemblance can be seen in Raphael's intentional reference to the simplified composition of the choir of S. Maria del Popolo, designed by Bramante. The wall surfaces in this centrally-planned structure are the only outstanding features, as was the case again in the Villa Madama loggia. The order loses its hierarchical pre-eminence and its function is reduced to that of articulating the inner wall. The projecting bands of the base are thus directly continued in the arches of the short barrel vaulting, with the single interruption of a shortened cornice. The assurance with which Raphael has handled the problem of light, which contributes so greatly to the charm of this building, is demonstrated, even without taking into consideration the possibility of a later covering, by the slightly overhanging cornices, the minute reliefs engraved in the parts which are in shadow, and by the connection between the apsidal niche and the background wall, a connection marked by a subtle pattern of successive narrowing and widening structural elements.

The Chigi Chapel in the Church of Santa Maria del Popolo

If we ignore the unreliable evidence presented by the church of S. Eligio, the Chigi Chapel represents the first concrete opportunity offered to Raphael to translate his architectural theories into three-dimensional form. His choice of model demonstrates his fidelity to the teachings of Bramante, both for its spatial structure, which was integrally derived from the central plan for St. Peter's, and the creation on a small scale of a complex structure. Compared with the slightly later chapel of S. Giacomo degli Spagnoli by Sangallo, the Chigi Chapel reveals a new tendency, a desire to develop the theme in a monumental and celebrative manner, as if the architect wished to affirm the superiority of quality over quantity, or at least the independence of the type from its empirical dimensional reality. The reference to the model of St. Peter's was, in fact, far from implicit initially in Raphael's plan, and this was achieved by an essentially illusionistic method which demonstrated his ability to model space through the chromatic and plastic treatment of surfaces.

The external structure—a cubic block surmounted by a cylinder (from which the hemispherical dome originally protruded)—was adapted to the limits of the space available, which suggested the adoption of a square or octagonal plan. Instead of solving the problem by standing the cupola directly onto an octagonal area, as in S. Maria di Loreto, Raphael chose the cruciform plan and stood the cupola on pendentives above four arches supported by diagonal projecting pillars, exactly as in Bramante's St. Peter's, encased with curved Corinthian wall pilasters at the angles. This choice was not consonant with the shape of the plot, which would have enabled the arms of the cross to be extended in one direction only, but Raphael overcame this difficulty by taking from the background walls in the arches their quality of enclosing space, through the use of colour. Behind the altar the altarpiece by Sebastiano del Piombo, which was certainly painted in accordance with the ideas of the architect, occupies the whole space of the archway and substitutes its illusory space for the actual limits of the architecture, while in the side walls (and barely visible to someone walking through the nave of the church) is a marble polychrome surface, homogeneous

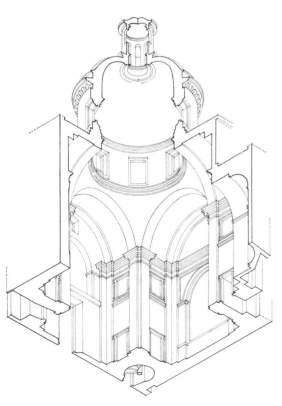

with the blocks of the pyramids, which introduces a neutral note, a kind of provisional limit encouraging the viewer to 'imagine' a possible lateral extension of the space. Compared with the literal and pictorial illusionistic effects of Bramante's choir in the church of S. Satiro, later repeated by Antonio da Sangallo in the porch of the Palazzo Farnese, Raphael has taken a decisive step forward towards a specifically architectonic solution to the problem: a solution developed by Michelangelo in the porch of the Palazzo dei Conservatori, and which later, in the final developments of Central European Baroque, (especially in the work of Kilian Dientzenhofer) inspired the development of the 'miniature church' type in which the principal structure has the form of an endless network, provisionally blocked by wall partitions which are not part of the columnar frame. A sign of the awareness with which Raphael pursued his objective of creating an optical illusion whereby the arches appear to melt into the background can be observed in the contraction of the cornices, which continue in the lateral walls the horizontal pattern of the entablature on the corner pilasters. This detail, which became a valuable stylistic instrument in the hands of Palladio, serves here to make a hierarchical distinction between the walls and the order and to enrich the harmony of the horizontally dovetailing sections, so creating one of the most subtle effects in this chapel.

In order to evaluate fully the novelty and interest to be found in this work, we must be aware of the distance separating it from the examples of Bramante's architecture from which it takes its origin. If we compare it with S. Celso or S. Biagio or the interior of S. Pietro in Montorio, we see Raphael's determination to control the architectonic image down to its most minute expression, and to preserve in his choice of detail the same degree of intellectual tension which he brought to bear in planning the structure as a whole. If Bramante's highest achievements were attained by simplifying or concentrating his interest on one of the aspects of the image, Raphael in contrast excelled in the control of the total organism and attained his desired 'grace' by making the image precise and well-defined. By the use of polychromy, he was able to make distinctions, to comment, to explain the mechanism of the orders, to cause surfaces to surge forward or recede, to clarify the function of the individual parts in the whole organism, and at the same time to soften the cold luminosity of marble by warm tints of brown and red, so as to lessen the contrast between the structural elements and the pictorial images, and finally, to achieve a 'well-composed' totality. In spite of the undoubted classicist origins of the Corinthian order, perhaps the most refined of all the orders employed in Renaissance architecture, the direct quotation from the Pantheon in the linking sections between the pairs of wall pilasters at the entrance arch, and recollections of Egyptian architecture, because of its polychrome surfaces and plastic decoration, the Chigi Chapel still preserves the atmosphere of Urbino, recalling the Perdono Chapel in the Ducal Palace, for example, and revealing Raphael's early architectural vocation and his loyalty to his origins.

Shearman's detailed study of the iconography of the pictorial decoration makes it possible to draw convincing conclusions regarding the symbolic choice of certain architectural features together with the pictorial decoration in order to show the triumph of life over death. The symbolism was drawn freely from both classical and Christian sources. It is in this connection that Raphael incorporated an allusion to the triumphal arch, both in the entrance area and in the short lateral arms containing the pyramids, symbols of existence and ascending development. A less convincing theory has been put forward by Ray, who attributes the anomalous form of the stars in the keystone on the entrance arch to a cryptical allusion to the horoscope of Agostino Chigi (which had inspired the decoration of the Farnesina also), and thus to a pagan identification between the personality and fortune of the great merchant and the attributes of the Divinity in Heaven. But, however we may interpret the symbolic significance of the Chapel, there is no denying the paradoxical results of mixing together pagan and Christian elements. The Christian image of God the Creator, placed at the summit of the dome, is surrounded by images of the Sun

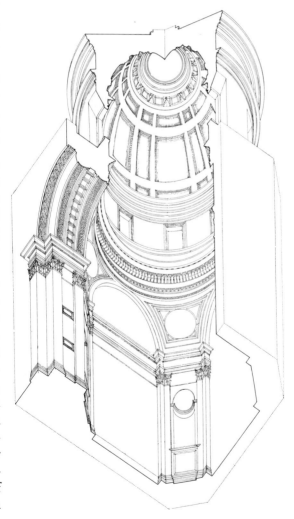

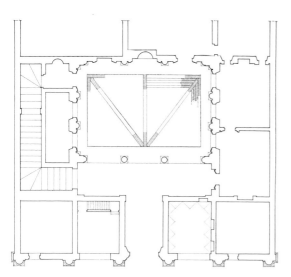

Raphael: exterior and ground plan of Palazzo Branconio (1 cm = 3.5 m).

and planetary divinities, used to signify the divisions of time and exorcized, in the wake of Dantean cosmology, by figures of angels. The reconciliation of the classical world and Christianity, through the medium of Platonic theory, expresses the ideological content of the image; revealed truth is not placed in opposition to the entirely human representations of the religious spirit in the classical world, but is seen as the unveiling of their ideal reality which, before the advent of Christianity, could be only palely evoked by means of allegorical reductions of the divine to human stature. This is the intellectualized and antihistorical interpretation of a culture which, by denying the revolutionary break between the classical world and Christianity, lost the dynamic sense of the latter and saw it as a contemplative and static religion. After listening to a sermon in the Papal Chapel on Good Friday, Erasmus of Rotterdam, who had been in Rome a few years earlier, wrote words which could apply perfectly to this work of Raphael: 'We are Christian only in name, our forehead is marked with the cross, but our mind abhors it; we profess Jesus with our mouths; but we bear in our hearts Jupiter Optimus Maximus and Romulus'.

The Palaces Built by Raphael

Raphael's contribution to urban domestic architecture is represented by three works: the Palazzo Pandolfini in Florence, where numerous features in the style of Sangallo indicate that Raphael may have been freely adapting a plan by this architect, the destroyed Palazzo Branconio, and the Palazzo Caffarelli Vidoni whose attribution to Raphael is uncertain and where, even supposing that the initial conception was his, the influence of his pupils appears paramount. The Palazzo Branconio can be visualized with the aid of many drawings and engravings; it is the most original of the palaces and the one best able to indicate the architectural studies made by Raphael as documented by his paintings and by the few works of certain attribution. The problem before him was to give plastic dimension to the perspective of a street, and the means he chose were of an amazing richness and complexity. For the ground floor, occupied by a succession of shops, he used a Tuscan order combined with a series of arches in the style of a typical classical composition. On the first floor, as in the Palazzo Pandolfini, large windows are enclosed within tabernacles, in a manner directly derived from the Pantheon, and linked by the unbroken line of the entablature. The succession of linked tabernacles is, however, accompanied by a contrasting feature created by the niches, which are lower in height and are placed in the interstices, and by festoons and medallions to fill the spaces between the tympana and the square windows of the mezzanine floor. In the top floor, the openings between the windows and the complex rhythmical succession of rectangles inserted in the band below them (a - b - a - c - a - b - a - c ...) reproduce the intense, vibrant rhythm of the first floor in a more subdued vein.

The view of the Palazzo Branconio as an anticipation of Mannerism can be accepted only if this category is defined in its widest and most generic sense; but it adds very little to our understanding of the reasons which orientated Raphael's research in this particular direction. What interested him was something more than a departure from the norm: it was to bring about a complete return to the architecture of the Age of Augustus and to translate into plastic terms the themes he had already studied in the pictorial decorations of façades. The archaeological reconstructions made by Raphael's friend Fulvio show that even an expert in antiquities could be led to believe that ancient buildings possessed a decorative structure similar to that of the Palazzo Branconio. Even where the canonic order was employed on the ground floor, in a context where the upper storeys have no corresponding vertical ornament, this was not done so as to show disregard of the traditional stylistic structures, but in an unconventional attempt to experiment in interwoven patterns and illusory perspectives similar to those found in decorative Roman painting. Raphael's passionate interest in grotesques, as found in the Vatican loggias, suggested to him that the surfaces should be decorated in such a way that they could multiply to infinity the significant strata of the architectonic structure. The orchestration was based on a multiplication

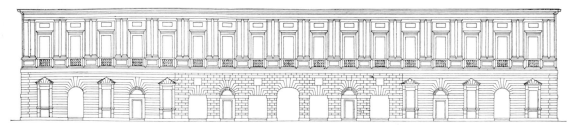

Exterior of Palazzo Caffarelli Vidoni (1 cm = 4.5 m).

Detail of the exterior of Palazzo Caffarelli Vidoni (1 cm = 1.2 m).

Detail of Raphael's Vatican loggias (1 cm = 80 m).

Detail of the exterior of Villa Madama (1 cm = 3.5 m).

of notes and instruments but the clarity of the statement was never lost. One need only examine one by one the superimposed bands which form the façade, the harmonious rhythms, and the superimposed perforations, to become conscious of the coherence of this composition and its roots firmly grounded in the Roman tradition.

Tha Palazzo Caffarelli Vidoni, which may have been planned by Raphael, returns to the theme of Bramante's Palazzo Caprini, but the construction of the order and design of the windows have been simplified. The part of the building most imbued with a personal quality is the ground floor, and this is the part which is least close to the manner of Raphael and seems rather to have been designed by Giulio Romano. The style of Romano is reflected in the design of the large ground floor windows, with rustication enclosed in the tympanum, and the square corbels which anticipate Michelangelo's design for the Porta Pia.

Villa Madama

The most important work of architecture undertaken by Raphael was the villa built for Cardinal Giuliano de' Medici, who later became Pope Clement VII. The villa was left unfinished and was badly damaged during the Sack of Rome. A recently published letter by Raphael contains a minute description of the plan for this villa, and confirms that the drawings by Sangallo in the Uffizi provide an accurate picture of Raphael's general conception. Seen in relation to the tradition of Roman villas of the early years of the century, Raphael's grandiose plan marks a radical leap forward. It could not even be compared to the prototype of the pergola which was built for leisure use and for literary discussions, as exemplified in the villas Coricio and Colocci, or with the hunting lodge at Magliana enlarged by Leo X. In its complexity and grandiose conception, the Villa Madama was far superior even to the Farnesina, compared with which it enjoyed the advantage of a raised position on the slopes of Monte Mario, in sight of the city and the curves of the Tiber. Raphael was immersed in the study of classical culture, entirely absorbed in his programme of restoring the city to its past glory, and he took this opportunity to show to what extent the repertory of classicism required a profound change of direction from the tradition it had acquired in the fifteenth century. A typical example of the point at which Florentine classicist culture had arrived was the villa at Poggio a Caiano, with its blocked plan forming a sharp contrast to the natural scenery, and this villa may be taken as the most appropriate term of comparison by which to measure the advance made by Raphael. Instead of standing apart and independently, the Villa Madama was adapted to its geographical position. It interpreted the landscape and made the most of its possibilities. The appropriation of space began from a central core, and continued through a series of amplifications and transformations marked by architectonic signs which, as they move farther from the centre, were qualified by their decreasing volumetric weight. Here, too, there existed a central parallelepiped block, a 'palazzo' standing in its simple geometric affirmation; but its volumetric figure could no longer be isolated, since it was inextricably bound to a series of smaller volumes—wings or terraces—which rooted it to the terrain and formed a harmoni-

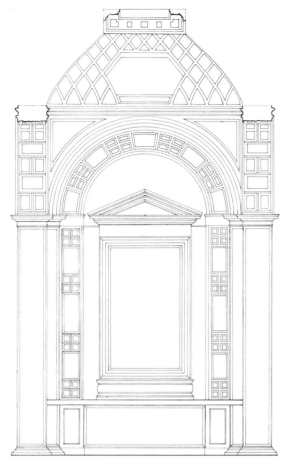

ous connection between its abstract rhythm and the natural undulations of the slope. The large block extended laterally through lower enclosures terminating in minute cylindrical towers (the towers of the artist's youthful landscapes which dissolve in the atmosphere) and presented a different termination on the two sides, while towards the top of the hill it swells into a semi-circular cavity which houses a theatre. Along the axis parallel to the curves of the ground a long terrace on the right led to a concealed garden. In front of the villa a gigantic esplanade was overlooked by stables large enough for four hundred horses. A drawing in the Uffizi which has only recently been correctly interpreted relates to the plan for extending almost to the level of the Tiber the sequence of organized spaces and arranging along the slope three esplanades at an axis, not with the block of the villa, but with the entrance esplanade: the highest to be square, the middle one circular, and the lowest in the shape of a circus.

The composition was intended to be an organization on a grandiose scale of a narrative rich in surprises, where the classical harmony between geometric and natural form was achieved by means of innumerable variations, which rejected any kind of uniaxial structure. Linking elements between the volume of the building and the surrounding space consisted of half-open areas formed by the terraces and enclosures, and those defined by trees, grottoes, geometrically-defined ponds, and the curvilinear shape of the theatre. Compared with the relationship between architecture and nature which could be observed in Roman villas, the rigorous perpendicular character of the plan undoubtedly represented a simplified schematic factor; but Raphael saw antiquity through the eyes of the Renaissance, in relation to the view of perspective: he admitted multi-axiality but rejected the divergence and convergence of axes. Again, his specific attitude towards nature was inspired by the intellectual certainties of humanism, by the 'certain reasons' of Alberti. His method of working, therefore, which he described admirably in verbal terms also, has the full value of a scientific discovery, where the artist avails himself of the possibility of 'recognizing' nature by bringing order to it, in his search for a kind of 'grace' born out of its encounter with man.

The sources which inspired Raphael in planning the villa can easily be identified from his descriptive letter: they are Vitruvius, Alberti, and Pliny. From Alberti and Vitruvius, he derived his very carefully chosen siting of the villa and its surrounding structures, taking account of the prevailing winds to which it was exposed; from Vitruvius he derived the structure of many of the additional buildings, in particular the Ionic porch; and from Pliny, especially from the description of his villas contained in the *Letters* (V, 6; II, 17; IX, 7) he adopted the general concept of the villa-garden relationship, the differentiation between summer and winter quarters, the idea for a hippodrome to extend eastwards, the baths, etc.

Raphael's letter was written with the requirements of his patron in mind and was largely devoted to a description of the various outbuildings and garden areas. From this description, it is possible to reconstruct a sequence of internal areas of space coinciding with the sequence shown in drawing No. 273 in the Uffizi.

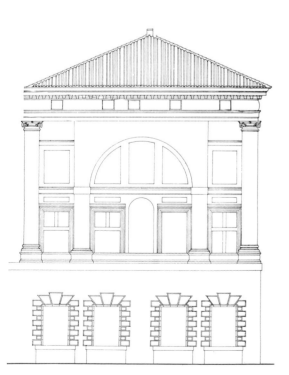

Two large towers dominated the main entrance, overlooking the town, and were explained in the letter as justified on both functional and aesthetic grounds: 'And at first appearance there are on either side of this entrance two large round towers which, apart from the beauty and dignity they impart to the entrance, are of some use also for defence.' The influence of Urbino can be seen in the recollection of the motif by Laurana in the Montefeltro Castle. After passing through the doorway, one reached a rectangular *cortile* (a ratio of one in eight between the sides), then entered a porch 'with six Ionic columns with their antae, and then to the 'Greek style of Porch, similar to what the Tuscans call an *androne* (passageway)', a small rectangular area giving direct access to the central circular courtyard. Around this area were arranged rooms whose form and dimensions were intentionally varied, but always rigorously proportioned on the basis of exact numerical relationships, only in one case with the irrational ratio of 1 : 2. The part of the building

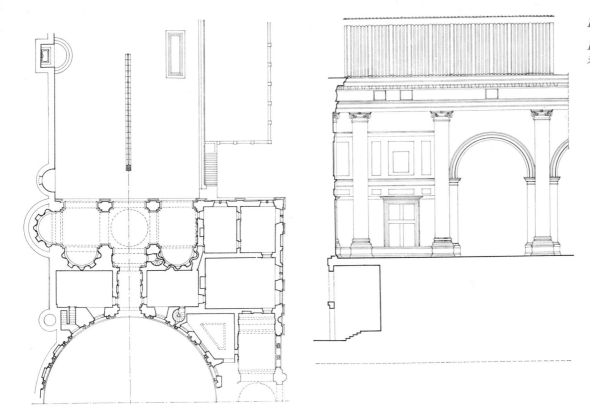

Plan of Villa Madama (1 cm = 6 m).

Exterior of the loggia of Villa Madama (1 cm = 3.6 m).

which is most fully described, in a poetic evocation of its intended atmosphere, is a little circular room in one of the turrets. 'Above the tower which is on the right-hand side of the entrance,' Raphael writes, 'in the corner is placed a very beautiful *dyeta* as the ancients called it. The form of which is round and its diameter 6 rods with a pathway leading from it, as I will explain in its place, protecting the garden from the north-east wind on three sides of the building, and also from the north and north-west winds. As I have said, the *dyeta* is circular and all around has glass windows which now one, now the other, will be lit by the sun from the time of its rising until it sets, and they are transparent so that the room will be very bright as a result both of the continuous sunlight and of the view of the countryside and Rome, for Your Holiness knows that plain glass will not distort any part of it. This place will truly be delightful as a room for conversation with noblemen in winter, which is the use to which a *dyeta* is generally put.' Another *dyeta*, 'made for the hour of extreme heat', was situated in a remote shady position; here the comfort provided was so great that even the baths had to be carefully sited to ensure that a servant could bathe his master without casting a shadow. The theatre was designed in accordance with the rules of Vitruvius, on the basis of equilateral triangles. Raphael described this geometrical construction in the following terms: 'a beautiful theatre made with this mixture and reason', where the analogy of 'mixture' recalls the process of mixing colours and happily evokes the rich colour orchestration he had in mind. The fragments of the villa which have survived can provide only a pale reflection of Raphael's conception and to some extent alter its character, owing to the romantic overtones generally acquired by unfinished constructions which take on the appearance of natural phenomena. One must also remember that much of the work of construction was done after the death of Raphael, by Antonio da

Sangallo, Giulio Romano, and Giovanni da Udine. Once the fact has been established that Raphael was responsible for the original conception of the general structure, it becomes necessary to distinguish what share in the project fell to those who continued his work. The form of the loggia with the asymmetrical rhythm connecting the dividing planes and large niches is without the slightest doubt entirely the responsibility of Raphael and constitutes one of his greatest architectural achievements. Equally certain, the general plan of the decoration was broadly conceived by Raphael, and—in spite of the lack of balance between the vault by Giovanni da Udine and the wall stuccoes of Giulio Romano—it admirably succeeded in modifying the surfaces by means of colour, which Raphael had learnt when he was working on the Vatican loggias and the Chigi Chapel. His collaborators may be held responsible for the glaring incongruities in the design of the external façades, and the unfortunate inclusion of archaic cross-barred windows.

However, these elements are not sufficient to detract from the basic harmony in the overall design of the order, and do not in themselves represent choices of so great an impact that they justify a detailed stylistic examination. Apart from their decoration of the loggia, those who continued the work begun by Raphael in reality did little more than follow the safe lines of a building programme defined in its every detail. It was the most imaginative and coherent programme produced in Rome during those years, and was still inspired by the Renaissance view of architecture as the embodiment of knowledge, or as a philosophy. But though in this respect it was traditional, it already contained the seeds of an interpretation of architecture as a form of rhetoric, and of the relationship between architecture and nature as the mirror of an escape from reality.

ANTONIO DA SANGALLO

In his preface to a new edition of Vitruvius published in 1539, Antonio the Younger recalls that he arrived in Rome at the age of eighteen, at the beginning of Julius II's papacy, and that he immediately started work 'under Bramante the architect'. According to Vasari, in 1512 his master entrusted him with his first independent task: 'the care of the corridor leading to the moats of Castel S. Angelo', left unfinished by Alexander VI. Vasari also stated, however, that during the last years of his life, Bramante was forced by illness to leave to Antonio da Sangallo 'the care of innumerable tasks which he had to perform', and this account seems perfectly credible.

In spite of the undoubted difference in their intellectual stature, the possibility should not be overlooked that the master not only influenced his pupil, but that there was also a reciprocal influence through Antonio's creative participation in the last works of Bramante. It will be seen, in fact, that the first documented independent work of Antonio's, the Palazzo Baldassini, reveals an intellectual maturity and complete emancipation from a passive pupil-teacher relationship of obedience.

There is no evidence to support Benedetti's contention that the architect worked on the church of S. Maria di Loreto in Rome when he was twenty-three years of age, and therefore no justification for his criticism that the façade of the church shows the immaturity of youthful inexperience. The Palazzo Baldassini on Via delle Coppelle has the value of a key document, since it is an authenticated and dated work, revealing the architect's training and personal attitude.

The building was erected between 1514 and 1520, but was probably planned in the years immediately preceding these dates. It represents one of the most interesting and successful attempts to establish a building type on the basis of a rigorous interpretation of a number of requirements viewed at different levels.

The building emerges logically from a simple construction surrounding a little square courtyard, which is open along one side to form a two-storey loggia. The insertion of the staircase on a parallel to the main axis of the site makes possible an annular connection between all the parts, while the position of the bottom ramp at a perpendicular angle to the others and on the same axis as the loggia creates a simple, well-defined relationship of the various levels. When we consider how, by a skilful use of distorted planes, Sangallo succeeded in illuminating extensively those parts of the structure which were half below ground level, while accentuating the height of the ground floor which was intended to house the owner's archaeological collection, we can understand why Vasari described the Palazzo Baldassini as 'disposed in such a way that, small as it is, it is held to be what it is, the most comfortable and foremost dwelling in Rome'. With his technical mastery and profound sense of involvement, Sangallo was able to carry out an up-to-date building programme by creating a type of residential accommodation which was suited to meet the requirements of the rising middle class. The substance of this programme was his desire for simplification, his need for objectivity, and his research into the means of achieving a 'close compliance with the patron's requests for "decorum"'.

Baldassini was not of noble birth, but a much respected jurist, a consistorial lawyer and 'advocate of the poor'. His residence was therefore intended to be remarkable more for its comfort and well designed proportions than for its richness and grandeur. On the other hand, the details inspired by classical architecture, and in particular the Doric doorway which forms a violent contrast to the bare surface of the wall, were incorporated in order to mirror the interests of a great collector of antiquities. Therefore, while the choice of certain stylistic features and the control of the 'tone' of the building to act as a symbol of prestige corresponded to the need for 'social relevance', the demand for objectivity was satisfied by means of two specifically architectonic instruments: the clearly-defined proportions in the divisions of the façade, and the rigorous interconnecting to link in depth the elements belonging to the classical repertory.

In his selection of geometric forms, the criterion of simplification remained valid: the unity of the structure was obtained by superimposing clearly individualized horizontal bands. Between the height and width of each of these bands, there existed a simple numerical ratio. The lowest, comprising the area between the foundations and the upper edge of the band with the frieze of waves, showed a proportion of 3 : 1 between the sides; the second, from the top of the lowest band as far as the upper edge of the second, showed a proportion of 5 : 1 between the sides; and the top one, including the whole of the entablature, had a proportion of 6 : 1. Finally, inside the lowest band, it was possible to distinguish clearly a further one, comprised between the upper edge of the impost of the ground-floor windows and the upper edge of the frieze of waves: this band showed an intermediate ratio of 4 : 1, and in this way completed the progression of simple ratios: 1 : 3, 4, 5, 6.

Similar proportional relationships may be observed also in the ground plan, in the proportions of the individual parts and in the recurrence of the measurement on the courtyard side, as well as in the thickness of the fabric of the façade.

An equally rigorous solution was applied by Sangallo to the problem of syntactic linkage. Here, too, he seemed to proceed by 'horizontal sections', aiming to establish terms of reference which were materialized in structures. These structures then became optical guides leading to the discovery of corresponding proportional relationships, along the path going into the building through the porch and *cortile*. This proportional treatment is especially noticeable in the façade, with its angular rustication by layers of variable height; the ground-floor windows are closely integrated with the cornerstones because their measurements coincide with those of the stones at the same level. Whereas the thickness of the window-sill is equivalent to that of the smaller stones, the corbels supporting it coincide with one of the larger stones, and the same pattern recurs in the case of the upper corbels and the cornice above them; this cornice fits exactly into the space formed by the recession

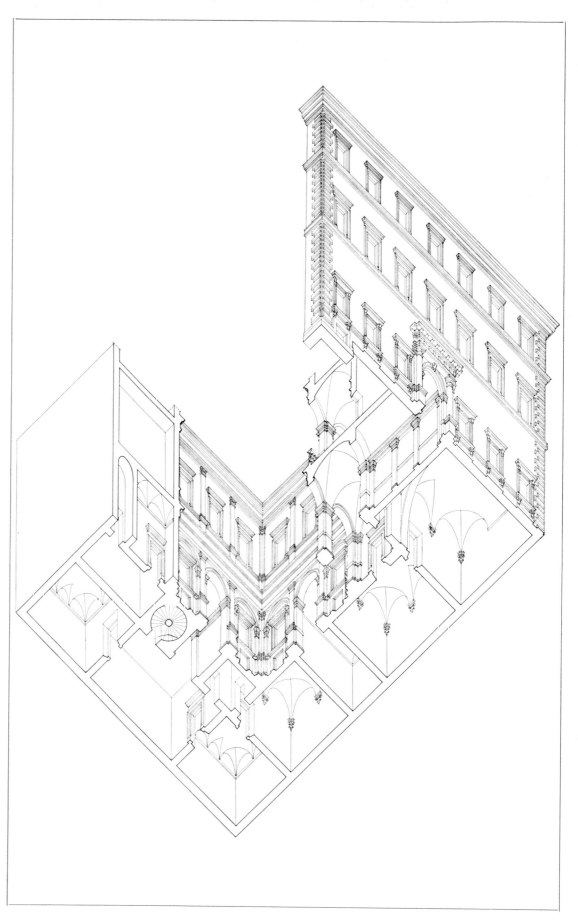

of the stones. These observations reveal the architect's desire to apportion to each element its necessary position, its 'fixed ratio', eliminating from the composition as far as possible any incongruities or elements of chance—or at least any choice which he could not justify—while at the same time simplifying the process of construction.

The pattern of horizontal concatenation reaches its climax, however, in the spatial sequence through which one penetrates into the building. In the porch the pilasters which ornament the walls are of the same dimensions as the pilasters of the courtyard and are placed at the same level, resting on a base corresponding to the base of the loggias. The cornice linking the pilasters at a point half-way up their height corresponds to the terminal moulding of the bases supporting the Doric pilasters which frame the arches of the courtyard. The two levels on which the intersecting orders rest are superimposed without creating a lack of balance, and each structure has imprinted on it a kind of visual memory, making it possible to grasp at all times the relationship existing between the individual parts as well as a global view of the whole organism.

The desire for simplification can be seen both in the inevitable interlocking of the parts and in the emphasis on their plastic quality. Viewed in the light of such models as the Cancelleria, the Palazzo Caprini, or the Farnesina, the Palazzo Baldassini represents a desire for abbreviation and simplicity and may be compared with other contemporary buildings, such as the Palazzo Lante and Palazzo Della Valle, both of which are here ascribed to Andrea Sansovino; but compared to these examples, Sangallo is distinguished by his determination not to allow his desire for simplification to lead him to abandon the regularity and structural unity growing out of the use of the architectural orders, and also to reject firmly every solution in which the serial design of the windows was not clearly determined both proportionally and plastically. The brilliant invention of angular rustication, for which Cronaca's Florentine precedent provided only an embryonic indication, proved wonderfully successful in solving the contradiction between simplification and structural necessity. For although the façade was made up of the addition of separate units, this did not lead to the formation of a cellular structure, as had previously been the case, and the predominant role belonged entirely to the general structure.

At the same time as Antonio da Sangallo was working on the little palazzo on Via delle Coppelle, he came into contact with the Farnese family, who were already becoming interested in the aims of the landed nobility which, after the middle years of the century, became widespread in Latium when the rural nobility recovered its power. The young architect was given the task of restoring or building *ex novo* palaces which were to testify to the family's domination over the soil of Latium. At Capodimonte, Sangallo reproduced in an original manner the polygonal castle which stands above the promontory over Lake Bolsena; at Gradoli, where he built an ancestral residence *ex novo*, he applied the rules of composition used in the Palazzo Baldassini, together with a rhythmical pattern of perforations forming a tangent to the rusticated edges and the unifying horizontal bands on which the coping rests.

Still in Latium, Sangallo designed for the Farnese family the Rocchina on the Isola Bisentina, the church of S. Egidio at Cellere, and the octagonal church at Monte d'Oro. In the little church at Cellere, where one can find anticipations of motifs later used by Palladio, we see today, because of its arbitrary execution, only a rough model, almost like a memory which has been rendered vague and imprecise through being passed from mouth to mouth. About the year 1566, Sangallo altered the Palazzo Del Monte in Piazza Navona, adding to it a slender tower which for more than two centuries formed a background to the view through the length of the square. Here again the structure was divided by superimposed bands, of which the lowest was enclosed by two rusticated corners, the middle one ornamented by wall pilasters placed close together, and the third with a free-standing loggia surmounted by an architrave. This was an up-to-date version of the medieval Roman model of an urban tower, and its unadorned first-floor windows anticipated the later façade of the Zecca. Still in Piazza Navona, the chapel of Cardinal Alborense was constructed in the church of S. Giacomo. The similarity between the stylistic elements in this chapel and in the Chigi Chapel in the church of S. Maria del Popolo may perhaps be due to the architect's collaboration with Raphael, whose assistant he became in 1517 in the building of St. Peter's. If the common element in both chapels is the precision which governs the design of the order, the difference becomes apparent immediately in the functions assigned to the decoration and in the problem of composition which had to be faced. For Raphael the chapel, like his frescoes, was substantiated by a complex iconography which could not be separated from the architectonic image, whereas for Sangallo decoration remained a surface quality enclosed like a precious jewel within the architectural framework. On the other hand, whereas for Raphael the spatial model to which he referred and aimed to 'abbreviate' was the St. Peter's of Bramante, for Sangallo this model corresponded to the internal thickness of a triumphal arch; the background wall against which the altar rests appears in fact like an adjunct to the main structure, since it stands apart from the side walls from which it is separated by a protruding wall pilaster. This concern to treat the area of the chapel as a longitudinal space explains the asymmetrical curve of the pilaster, inspired by the Pazzi Chapel of Brunelleschi. Even in this little work of 'furnishing', Sangallo appeared to be concerned mainly with the problem of the interconnection of the individual elements. This can be seen in the horizontal arrangements of the mouldings on the classical base, which are continued along all the walls and up to the baluster separating the chapel from the body of the church. The same thing can be observed in the impost band of the altar tabernacle, which is continued into the lateral walls and acts as a base for the funerary tablets. The parallelepiping surmounted by a half-drum was one of the geometrical forms most dear to Sangallo; he applied it in the throne room and the Cappella Paolina, and developed the theme of the curved surface with coffer motifs in highly original variations.

Such a roof was a feature also of the church of S. Maria in Monserrato, which was begun by Sangallo in 1518 but finished by others and completely changed by later decoration. Combining his memories of Florentine architecture and of Bramante, Sangallo made a remarkable contribution to the development of the longitudinal type of church, in which he anticipated late sixteenth-century and Baroque styles. This was especially apparent in the area separating the nave from the presbytery, created by four protruding pairs of pilasters and the two archivolts connecting them. These structures were built in the round and stood apart from the walls.

His deliberations concerning the new style for religious buildings occupied Sangallo throughout the second decade of the century. His favourite forms were the structures based on the octagon, the circle, and the longitudinal plan: only exceptionally did he employ the central cruciform plan dear to Bramante, and then always with a sharply divergent emphasis.

The octagonal plan, combined as we have seen in the sanctuary of Monte d'Oro to form a close sequence with the circle, was the basis of the design for the presbytery. This figure recurs later in a series of plans for the church of S. Giacomo at Scossacavalli (Uffizi 1275, 947, 304, 173), in the central church and chapels planned for the Hospital of S. Giacomo (Uffizi 309 and 1349), in S. Maria di Loreto and the designs for San Marco, Florence (Uffizi 807, 871, 873), the Medici Chapel at Montecassino, and the Corpus Domini Chapel at Foligno.

In the church of S. Giacomo degli Incurabili, at Montecassino, Foligno, and in the designs for San Marco, the octagonal area acts as the drum of a circular calotte, while in the other cases the dome takes the form of a pavilion roof. The general tendency evinced in Sangallo's research was that of emphasizing the importance of the larger areas of space by reducing the chapels to independent units and avoiding any dynamic effects. In this connection it is interesting to compare these studies with the series of drawings by Peruzzi which, although produced at about the same time, were all directed towards an exploration of original methods of varying and enriching the classical spatial models. It was only in his plans for San Marco (probably drawn up after the Sack of Rome) that Sangallo made some ingenious attempts to impart a dynamic quality to the octagon by accentuating the diagonal axes and inserting a semicircular choir (Uffizi 1365, 1254, 1363).

In drawing 1364 in the Uffizi, an octagonal drum is superimposed onto a cruciform base; this drawing is therefore related to drawing 706, which certainly refers to S. Maria di Loreto: the cupola appears to be formed from a low octagonal drum onto which a flat dome is placed and connected to it by eight angular volutes. This pattern, which followed the lines of Bramante's models for the bell-towers of St. Peter's, anticipates the treatment of volumes and the breaking up of the structure into different strata which during the years of the Farnese papacy were to lead Sangallo to the goal of St. Peter's.

In his designs for the church of S. Giovanni dei Fiorentini, Sangallo took the Pantheon as his direct source of inspiration and tried to overcome the difficulties caused by putting together the incongruous forms of the colonnade and the rotunda, as well as the lack of homogeneity in the structure of the interior, which was broken up by the entrance and the apse area. In drawing 199 in the Uffizi, the internal area of the rotunda is surrounded by a border of sixteen cells, each surmounted by a small dome. Only the one which lies on an axis with the entrance is differentiated by its circular form, but without breaking the homogeneity of the whole enveloping structure because the communicating arch leading into the central rotunda is identical to all the others. The same central solution is illustrated in drawing 1292, where it is presented as an alternative to a longitudinal design with three aisles and ten minor chapels. The construction of an internal section of the rotunda has made it possible to form a picture of the entire organism, which it is interesting to compare with the later model by Michelangelo. In both cases the point of departure is the Pantheon, and the architect's aim is to develop the structure vertically in conformity with the traditions of the Christian Church; but whereas for Sangallo each individual component remains firmly anchored in the classical method of proportions and a harmonious development is ensured by means of systematic repetition, for Michelangelo the structure is allowed to develop freely, so as to enhance the vertical continuity of the structure without any impediment, and the aesthetic quality arises out of the alternating rhythms and dynamic pulsation. The contradiction which appears in Sangallo's design between the vertical development of space and the rules of classical proportion governing the composition— where the two orders and the dome are superimposed onto each other like two isolated units—is overcome by Michelangelo, who links the ribs of the dome to the protruding columns to form a plastic unity; this led later to a further contradiction between the dynamic role assumed by the order and the proportional composition of its surrounding elements, and this was a problem to be faced at a later stage by Borromini and the masters of the European Baroque. By his compact, plastic structure, again modelled on Alberti's Annunziata, Sangallo referred the legacy of Bramante back to its Florentine sources and provided further evidence of his mature approach to the problem of emphasizing the plastic quality of the structural elements and their constructive and material values.

With regard to the church of S. Maria di Loreto, once it has been established that the work advanced in phases and that Sangallo was not responsible for the original design, it remains to discover what part he had in the execution. On the basis of the reasons given by Benedetti, it seems probable that the faces of the base pedestal represent a simplified version of Sangallo's plan shown in drawing XLIV (Uffizi 786); this design may have been considered too costly, so that a reduction of the measurements was called for. For this reason he might also have abandoned his original intention to articulate the travertine base from which the order rises, so moulding the coupled wall pilasters into a more solid unity, and also sacrificing the classical tabernacles inserted in the intervals between the pilasters. We are therefore forced to the paradoxical conclusion that what was for many

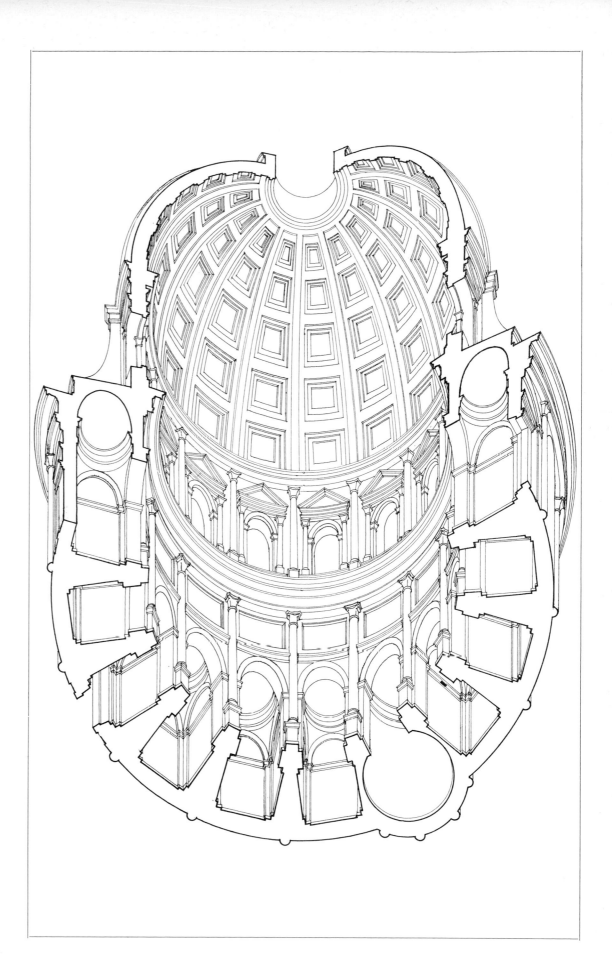

years thought to be the first work of a young novice should be rightly considered a simplified and impoverished version of a design produced when he was at the height of his powers. It is a paradox which leads us to the problem of the unevenness and lack of continuity in Sangallo's stylistic achievements. Apart from the fact that it was impossible for him to carry out personally the enormous number of commissions with which he was entrusted, this unevenness can be explained by his willingness to identify himself with the demands of his patron and to accept the limits imposed on him without reservation. This meant that he accepted also the existence of a hierarchy between minor, 'day-to-day' tasks and prestige works, and if, on the one hand, this attitude denoted an artistic career conditioned by, and subordinated to, economic and practical interests, on the other hand it explains a success which was not only professional but didactic, an unsurpassed ability to create models which could be produced in large quantities and possessed an amazing resistance to obsolescence and wear.

It is in the spirit of the lesser, 'day-to-day' occasion that we should view the chapel of S. Maria Porta Paradisi in the grounds of the hospital of S. Giacomo. The design is octagonal, surmounted by a dome which is broken up by semicircular lunette windows, with tripartite divisions as in the model of Roman baths. The brick terminals of the interior, mentioned in the inscriptions on drawing 1891 in the Uffizi, were intended to provide the same unrelieved surface for the interior (today altered) as in the façade, where the motif of the Roman triumphal arch is given a decidedly anti-heroic interpretation.

Sangallo's contributions to domestic architecture in the 1520s are far more stimulating and original, and confirm his exceptional ability to adapt himself to the aspirations of the ruling class. About the year 1520, he built a house for the Marrano Viacampes; it was a modest building in which the rigid composition of the Palazzo Baldassini was made more flexible in order to conform to the owner's economic and planning requirements. In this exploration of the limits to which a simplified model may be extended so as to fulfil a demand for 'social relevance', everything appears simplified and reduced: the angular rustication is applied only to the ground floor, the small doorway does not differ from other models currently employed—so that Giovannoni has rightly assumed that it was a 'mass-produced' article not by Sangallo's hand—and finally, the windows in the side façade are so arranged that the rule of a constant interaxial area has been abandoned in favour of a regrouping in threes.

The surviving fragment of the contemporary palace built for the Bishop of Cervia in Via dei Banchi Vecchi shows the diversity of approach which could be given to an edifice of this nature, with a prominent position in the town. The main difference from the Palazzo Baldassini is to be seen in the lower part of the building with its mezzanines and shops, as befits the importance of this street, with wide openings shaped on archaeological inspiration. In connection with the linking of the structural elements, Sangallo makes use here of a feature previously employed by Peruzzi in the Farnesina and destined to enjoy great fortune: namely, the distinction between the band dividing the storeys (corresponding almost exactly to the base of the first floor) and the impost band of the windows. A double band is therefore provided which indicates more clearly on the body of the façade a relationship on a human scale, extending also the spatial structure to the outside of the building.

With the Del Pozzo house in Borgo, Sangallo was faced with an entirely different problem, since he was required to build the house on a plot which was long and narrow. Drawing 201 in the Uffizi (drawing L) illustrates a very characteristic first solution. A tall rusticated base encloses the main doorway and two shops with their relative mezzanines, after the example of the shops in Caesar's Forum. The two other storeys repeat a number of earlier experiences: the angular rustication, the double band below the windows, and the intersection of these two features which endows the vertical rusticated column with a function which is almost that of a wall pilaster. The greatest innovations are the corbelled cornice and the coping of the first-floor windows which, apart from their proportions, exactly resemble the windows on the top floor of the Palazzo Farnese. The adoption of this arrangement, freely derived from the entrance doorway of Trajan's Forum facing the Quirinale, shows how Sangallo's style had evolved and become freed from uncertainties and was now directed intentionally towards the reacquisition of those classical modes which were specially suited to emphasize the plastic relationship between the structural elements and the inner walls.

The research undertaken by Wolfgang Lotz, described by Ackermann, makes it possible for us to reconstruct the original appearance of the Palazzo Farnese, which was left unfinished and was later incorporated in the new fabric built for Paul III. The original plan provided for a façade with eleven arch spans and shops on the ground floor, interspersed with twin wall pilasters.

When the building was enlarged, the façade was pulled down and rebuilt about five yards nearer to the new square, but the arches in the courtyard, which originally numberep only three to a side, were preserved. Therefore, it can only be assumed that Sangallo adopted a model similar to Bramante's design for the Palazzo Caprini, with a rusticated base and upper storey ornamented by the order [in this connection a very useful indication is provided by drawing 867 in the Uffizi (drawing XLVI) which, according to a note in Sangallo's own hand, seems to relate to the construction of the Zecca in the Banchi district], whereas it can be established with certainty that in the *cortile*, the design of the arches and of the splendid corner joint, which inspired Michelangelo's design of the Laurentian Library, were prepared not after, but before 1534, and almost certainly around 1529. Postponing our analysis of the Palazzo Farnese to the chapter devoted to Sangallo's late activity, however, it remains to refer, in order to conclude our evaluation of the first period of his activity, to those works produced in his studio in which the contribution of Baldassarre Peruzzi appears a determining factor.

Among the works which can be ascribed to Sangallo's collaboration with Peruzzi, there should be included the plans for the hospital of S. Giacomo and for St. Peter's about which there exists irrefutable documentary evidence, but also two important little palaces: the one known under the name Ossoli, and the one built for the Abbot Tomaso Leroy in the vicinity of the Cancelleria.

Although they differ greatly in the treatment of the surfaces, both these residences are proportioned on the basis of a square. In addition to the 1 : 1 ratio existing between width and height, the same ratio recurs among the three areas corresponding to each storey, as in the Palazzo Baldassini. The Palazzo Ossoli contains features which are typical of both Sangallo and Peruzzi. The ground-floor windows are very similar to those of the Palazzo Baldassini, while these on the first floor resemble the fragment of the palace of the Bishop of Cervia. The arrangement of the rustication around the doorway recalls the doorway of the Castle of Nepi and the small Farnese palazzo at Ronciglione, while the proportions of the first order recall the courtyard of the Palazzo Baldassini. On the other hand, the idea of incorporating a classical frieze with a design of palm-leaves seems more akin to Peruzzi: this same motif was adopted by the Sienese architect in the architrave of the Farnesina doorway and in the trabeation of the Ionic order in the *cortile* of the Palazzo Massimo; a reflection of the Farnesina and an anticipation of the Palazzo Massimo can be found also in the bays, which protrude to a far greater extent than in Sangallo's palace designed for the Bishop of Cervia. The original approach to the handling of the loggia in the *cortile*, where there is a return to the theme of archivolts resting directly on columns and pilasters, reflects the manner of Peruzzi rather than Sangallo. In spite of the limitations inherent in an attribution on stylistic grounds alone, it seems that tradition is justified in ascribing the Palazzetto Leroy to Sangallo also. An ingenious and in some respects fascinating suggestion has been made to the effect that this splendid bourgeois house was

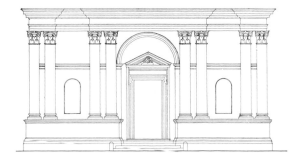

constructed by the same French architect who built the unlucky rotunda of S. Luigi dei Francesi, but on further reflection it seems obvious that a minor architect, who, moreover, was in Rome for only a short time, could not possibly have created so successful a synthesis of such a wide range of technical and stylistic discoveries. The density of this paradoxical composition, this highly calculated spatial organism, can be much better explained as the result of the coming together of two 'specialists' of the level of Peruzzi and Sangallo.

Giovannoni had an easy task in identifying a number of details to be in the manner of Sangallo, but it must be admitted that if the verdict he reached as a result of his analysis is entirely convincing, his failure to take account of the strange, and even exotic, tone of the palazzo as compared with other contemporary adaptations of Roman domestic architecture leads to an oversimplification of the problem. It is true that many of the details bear the imprint of Sangallo, especially the use of the Doric order which occurs here without a projecting cornice; this feature marks a return, in other terms, to the simplified use of the Doric order in the Palazzo Farnese without the frieze in the porch with columns; similarly, the Serliana type of window is another feature in the style of Sangallo and is identical with the window inserted in the temporary partition constructed by him in St. Peter's; the surrounding friezes, the projecting bays, and many other aspects of the building bear the mark of Sangallo. But what was not in his manner was the subtle treatment, the vertical extension of the copings, the raised tympana, and the skilful handling of the rustication which extends beyond the ground floor area to include the band on the bays. The many experiments of Sangallo seem to have been rediscovered by another mind, anxious to round off all the rough corners in his work, but also deeply interested in accentuating the plastic and luministic possibilities of the material.

An autonomous work by Peruzzi, produced without the restrictions imposed by Sangallo's authority, would have used different architectonic terms, and would have taken account of the ideas which had emerged from Raphael's rapid ascent to architectural mastery. We must remember that ten years before, in 1514, Raphael had designed in the church of S. Maria della Pace a fresco depicting the *Presentation at the Temple*, in which he included a palazzo which anticipated the most radical Venetian experiments of Sansovino. In Sangallo's studio, on the other hand, interest may have focussed on the work of filtering, distilling, and at the same time testing, the ideas propounded by the Florentine master. However, the aspect in which Peruzzi's contribution seems most apparent is not so much at the level of the details or the stylistic tone of the work, as in his advancing the type a stage forward by conceiving the courtyard and façade as complementary and closely related structures. Whereas in the type of classical palazzo designed by Sangallo the courtyard —besides the problems of interconnection, illustrated in connection with the Palazzo Baldassini—forms an independent structure, intentionally heterogeneous to the façade, in the Palazzetto Leroy a symbiosis is achieved and the courtyard, ornamented by the same bands although in a pattern of superimposed orders, provides a free and original version of it.

The new hospital of S. Giacomo was to be erected between the Corso and Via Ripetta, in the new area of the city's expansion. A number of drawings in the Uffizi collection document the 'four-handed' planning of this building. All the experience gained by the two architects through their years of research led them to lay stress on one particular geometric priority: that of making rational use of one of the great trapezoid plots created by the intersection of the converging roads of the 'trident', together with their cross-roads. In particular, having from the first selected the plan based on two through-roads, one of which was parallel to the present Via S. Giacomo, it was necessary to mask in some way the irregularity of the areas overlooking the Corso.

Drawings 578, 873, 871, and 870 document three different ways of solving this problem in a progression which reflects the result of the long years of research. At an early stage,

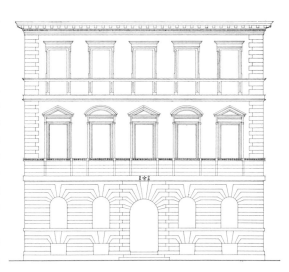

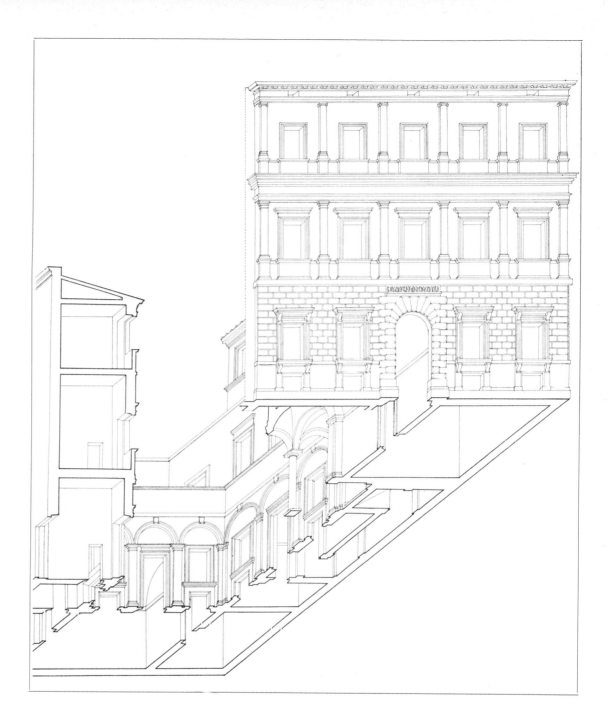

the whole structure followed the direction of Via S. Giacomo with the exception of the round chapel and its porch. Later (in a drawing by the hand of Sangallo), the chapel also was brought into alignment, and the variance from the alignment of the Corso was partially corrected by the modification in the projection of the two bays, corresponding to the through-roads at either side of the façade of columns. In the following stage, there was a return to the idea of siting the church and adjacent buildings parallel to the axis of the Corso, so solving more successfully the conflict between the two opposing lines of orientation, and at the same time demonstrating a rare mastery in the art of compromise. Giovannoni's belief that this design is by the hand of Sangallo is fully borne out by the consummate technical mastery and the lack of preconceived ideas which exemplify this phase of

Antonio da Sangallo: central plan for St. Peter's (1 cm = 28 m).

Antonio da Sangallo: longitudinal plan for St. Peter's (1 cm = 31 m).

the project. Another approach to this problem can be found in drawing 870, by Peruzzi; he solves it theoretically, by placing the principal axis of the building with the entrance to the church on the axis of symmetry of the trapezoid. In this way everything becomes simplified and it is possible to design a structure of impeccable regularity with two small courtyards. The through-roads curve in the shape of a 'C' and the triangular sections in the area are skilfully utilized to contain the stairs and some minor rooms. At either end of the main part of the building running along Via S. Giacomo, there appear two octagonal chapels: one of these was later executed and became known as the church of S. Maria Porta Paradisi.

The possibility of a fruitful collaboration between Sangallo and Peruzzi was threatened by the more arduous challenge of preparing plans for the basilica of St. Peter's. Although we have documentary evidence to show that Sangallo summoned Peruzzi as his assistant a bare four months after his own appointement as architect ot St. Peter's, and that until his death in January 1537 he continued to work as 'coadjutor of the architect', the numerous drawings which have survived by both masters reveal a profound divergence in their views and aspirations. While the inventive activity of Sangallo appears to have been stifled by a number of practical problems—in particular, as we shall see, the problem of the ambulatories—so that in the end his concern with detail caused him to lose his vision of the whole of the great organism, Peruzzi in the best documented stage of his research set himself the problem of the façade and the space of the interior, with the intention of surpassing the limitations of Bramante's idea by striving for a new and more soundly based plastic unity. As we have seen, Sangallo had already worked on St. Peter's, first under Bramante during his adolescence, and later by the side of Raphael, who had summoned him as his assistant on the death of Fra Giocondo. From 1 December 1516, he received for his work as coadjutor a wage of 12½ ducats, exactly half of what Raphael himself received. After the death of Raphael, the project underwent a total change of direction, and from this it may be assumed that Sangallo did not in any way participate in Raphael's decisions and provided his master with a collaboration which was more technical than creative. What is certain is that, before being given the appointment—and perhaps for the very purpose of obtaining it—Sangallo wrote a statement in which, without too many preambles, he spoke as harshly as possible about the work done in St. Peter's by the great artist who had just died.

Sangallo's first basic reaction to the suggestion made by Fra Giocondo and Bramante that the internal space should be extended lengthwise was to return to the central plan, permitting grudgingly a longitudinal development of the exterior only so far as was necessary in order to impart breadth and autonomy to a large porch and benediction gallery. The drawing in the Court Library in Vienna reveals that there was still some hesitation in this choice, since part of the Paleo-Christian nave is preserved and incorporated as a porch in front of the large cruciform area; while in drawing 39 in the Uffizi the right half of the sheet shows a sketch for a longitudinal alternative to the later central solution, and this alternative was developed again in drawing 255, with two different treatments.

The left half of drawing 39 represents the most successful stage in Sangallo's research, before the analytical process began which led him to the 1539 model. Compared with Raphael's designs, this drawing clearly shows an explicit desire to 'return to Bramante'; but it represented something more than a mere nostalgic attachment to the legacy of his master, as is shown by the highly significant and original variants. In the Vienna drawing, the external volume was still based on a cubic structure, from which only the convex apses protruded, and the idea of including four large corner chapels was put into practice without affecting the original form designed by Bramante. In the Uffizi drawing, on the other hand, the diagonal outer chapels, which were probably intended to be the bases for cylindrical towers, are inserted at the edges, thus destroying the original cubic form and creating a curvilinear volumetric block similar to a fortress. The ground plan closely resembles the one ascribed by Serlio to Peruzzi, but departs from it in the cylindrical form of the corner blocks, which would accentuate the plastic dynamism of the structure. At this stage of the planning, it is not easy to imagine how Sangallo intended to develop his project architectonically, but from the direction so far taken in the basic design, it seems that he was aiming at a simplified work of synthesis, in the spirit of the church of Montepulciano which his uncle was building during those same years.

The two surviving elevations in the Uffizi collection (drawings 66 and 259) document another and later phase of the planning, which Giovannoni dates around 1520. The structure appears to be fixed already in the form it was to take in the large 1539 model, with the porch-loggia standing apart from the longitudinal body of the church as a completely separate unit. In the sectional drawing (Uffizi 66), we see Bramante's lines of construction reintegrated and simplified, and only the dome and the crossing depart from the model and testify to a continuous striving for simplification. Although both arms of the crossing are surrounded by the ambulatories, they are no longer intercommunicating; Bramante's transparent colonnades disappear and with the decline of Byzantine-inspired luministic values, there appears that compact wall structure found in classical Roman buildings. The classicist type of test to which Sangallo puts the designs of Bramantean derivation influences the proportions of the nave by burying the bases of the columns below ground level and also influences the lighting by placing in the roof of the nave large lunettes containing tripartite windows of a type found in Roman baths. The dome which for static reasons acquires a sharply pointed profile in the interior—similar to that of Florence Cathedral—loses on the exterior the Bramantean colonnade which would have weakened it statically, and is transformed into a compact structure in low relief, with half-columns backed by a drum, and only eight window openings placed along the principal axes of the building. To compensate for this lack of windows, a wide skylight, similar to the one in the Pantheon, enables light to penetrate from above without obstruction. On the basis of this model Sangallo later designed the cupola for the Steccata church at Parma.

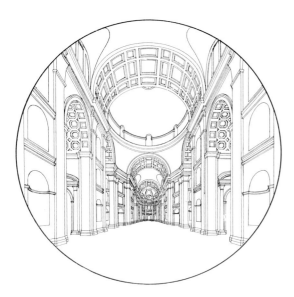

The side view shown in drawing 259 (drawing XLI) clearly reveals the difficulty inherent in this solution. The fact that the ambulatories have been retained means that the large solid block formed by the aisles and dome is surrounded by a much lower structure made up of more minute pieces, so that in both dimensions and rhythm it cannot in any way accord with the upper part, and would determine a continuous obstruction along all the adjoining parts, thus making a grasp of the organism problematical and confused. In this drawing the perimeter wall, unlike its later appearance in the model, has a remarkable quality of its own, but is proportionately entirely inadequate to its role. Its division into two parts, which consisted of a large Doric order surmounted by a very tall upper storey, later served as a model for Michelangelo, though he adapted it to quite a different scale and another context. However, it is interesting to observe that in spite of the great differences between them, both architects treated the upper storey in a similar way, minimizing the terminal effect of the cornice so as to draw the eye upwards to a higher terminal.

Drawing XXXIX undoubtedly belongs to an earlier stage: it is a study for the façade of the church, with a predominantly horizontal development. The rigorous treatment applied to the intersection of the orders continues, but that analytical procedure which caused Sangallo to lose some of his ability to control the organic unity of the form now makes its appearance. His stylistic gifts, his virtuosity in composition, which is demonstrated by the rapid note relating to a joint in the order, are the gilded cage in which Sangallo allows himself to be imprisoned, lured by the bait of Vitruvian orthodoxy.

BALDASSARE PERUZZI, OR EXPERIMENTALISM

In his relief models of classical buildings, Baldassarre Peruzzi examined with endless curiosity the confines of the great kingdom of the classical world, trying to construct an image which would represent it not only diagrammatically, but also with historical accuracy. He followed in this the path laid down by Francesco di Giorgio, Bramante, and Giuliano da Sangallo, but with a new orientation. The erudite and sensitive catalogue of Giuliano da Sangallo, who put on the same plane the detail and the total organism, describing them with equal minuteness and precision, was replaced by Peruzzi's search for a structure capable of expressing through plastic detail the principle of composition from which the entire organism derived, and in this he made use mainly of rapid approximative sketches.

The drawings of Giuliano da Sangallo are narratives, still belonging to the world of fable of the 'mirabilia urbis'. Peruzzi's are synthetic transcriptions, which have no connection with extra-scientific figurative considerations; they are the laboratory instruments of an architect and document his method of designing.

Peruzzi reached Rome when he was twenty-two years of age, when he was probably employed as an assistant to Pietro d'Andrea of Volterra, who executed paintings in the Vatican for Pope Alexander VI. His first pictorial works show close resemblances to the manner of Pinturicchio and so far reveal no evidence of any original gifts. His meeting with Bramante was of vital importance to his development, and he was admitted into Bramante's studio around 1505 at the request of Agostino Chigi. In the words of Vasari: 'Having returned (from Ostia), Baldassarre formed a close friendship with Agostino Chisi of Siena, both because Agostino naturally loved all men of talent and also because Baldassarre was becoming Sienese; so that with the help of this man he could remain in Rome and study Roman things, especially architecture; in these things with the help of Bramante he soon profited wonderfully, and later, as will be said, this gave him great honour and advantage. He still observed perspective, and made himself so great in that science that we have seen few who could equal him therein in our times; as can manifestly be noted in all his works.'

La Farnesina

His friendship with the great banker Chigi, who had become one of the most outstanding figures of Roman high society, provided Peruzzi with two valuable opportunities: he could devote himself to the study of classical architecture without financial worries, and he was commissioned to build a villa to be situated along the straight line of the Lungara.

The building programme put forward by the great Sienese banker was of a kind most likely to arouse enthusiasm in a young architect who was enamoured of classical antiquity: on a site which enjoyed a broad view over the nucleus of the city, a residence was to be constructed which would be suited to the life of society, where cultural meetings and spectacular feasts could be held and all the qualities of a villa, palazzo, and theatre would be found under one roof. This was thus a qualitative rather than a quantitative programme, in sharp contrast to the important building projects of the last fifty years, such as the Palazzo S. Marco and the Cancelleria, which brought into the closely-knit fabric of the medieval city monumental structures which imposed their weight upon it as eloquent symbols of power. The courtly aspirations of the aristocracy were counterposed by Agostino Chigi, the representative of the cultured middle-class who had gained power and prestige through his banking organization, by a building programme which laid no emphasis on ostentation and vastness and was based entirely on an ideal of quiet well-being and refined privacy, modelled on the villas described by the writers of antiquity and by Alberti's praise of 'villa life'. In the central Via dei Banchi, Agostino Chigi possessed a palazzo, now transformed, which housed the offices of his bank, and by constructing a new residence he expressed that incipient awareness of the disadvantages of city life which led in the second half of the century to a sort of doubling of personality, causing the aristocracy and merchants to make extraordinary investments, based on the illusion that their productive potential could be transferred from trading and industrial activities to agriculture. 'In the villa,' Alberti writes in his book *Della Famiglia*, 'you can escape the clamour, the tumult, the tempests, of the town, the square, the palace. In a villa you can hide so as not to see the wickedness, the villainy, and the great quantity of evil men who in a town continuously flutter about in front of your eyes, who never stop buzzing about your ears, who hour by hour keep shouting and roaring throughout the land like most fearsome and horrible beasts. How blessed it is to reside in a villa: an unknown happiness!'

Now that so much of the green space which formerly surrounded the Farnesina has been lost and two noisy streets adjoin it, it no longer creates the impression of a rural villa; but when it was first constructed, its direct access to the shores of the Tiber and the almost suburban character of the site gave it an air of quiet seclusion. Chigi's interest in this aspect of the villa is confirmed by the care lavished on the arrangement of the gardens, and by the inclusion of two smaller constructions in the landscaping: an open loggia overlooking the Tiber, and a building on Via della Lungara intended as a stable on the ground floor and a banqueting hall on the upper storey. Two poems describing the villa, composed by Egidio Gallo and Blosio Palladio, who were typical exponents of the atmosphere in literary circles at the time of Leo X, enable us to reconstruct certain original aspects of the garden, and therefore to appreciate the surviving image of the villa in its rightful context. According to Egidio Gallo, a worthy prelude to the Chigi residence was comprised by the new street built by Julius II: *Vestibulum ante ingens/silicum celeberrima collem/in Vaticanum via fert, ubi Julius arces/templaque inaudite renovat testudinis olim.* As soon as one entered the garden, the eye was drawn not only to the larger building itself (*In medio erecta est sublimibus inclita tectis/parietibusque domus*), but also to its relationship with the surrounding space, created by means of two protruding elements: the bench following the base of the whole perimeter, endowing the entire space around the villa with the quality of an outside porch (*Post ubi progressus patet: ingentisque superbum | Limen adest aditus | subito spaciosa vientur | Atria que ornate circundat undique sedes*), and the space enclosed between the two projecting wings arranged as in a theatre.

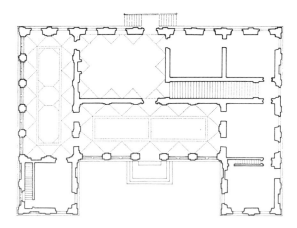

The descriptions give few precise details relating to the gardens, but contain enough information to enable us to evoke its atmosphere, which was still far from the stiff arboreal compositions of the following period. A large central path led to the river bank, where stood two twin colonnades, one intended for use in the hot season, the other for winter. The plants included all species of fruit trees as well as laurels, cypresses, box trees, myrtles, and trimmed hedges.

In his poem *Il Cavallerizzo*, Claudio Corte refers to 'the delightful garden of Agostino Chigi, where people came many times to disport themselves, to joust and break in horses, in its beautiful, charming and shady paths, to escape the discomfort of the heat'.

With regard to the typological ancestry of the Farnesina, there is very little that can be added after the rigorous examination conducted by Luitpold Frommel. Peruzzi selected an 'architectonic genre', in the same way as writers and painters had to select their appropriate genres. By hollowing into the blocked volume on one side and rejecting the inclusion of a *cortile*, the architect was drawing on famous examples, such as the Belvedere Villa which Pope Innocent VIII had built in the Vatican or the villa known as 'alle Volte' in Siena, which Peruzzi himself probably enlarged for the Chigi family. The volume was presented as a demonstrable truth in its unrelieved compact mass; as one passed around the exterior of the building, the modifications introduced by the various façades were revealed: on the side overlooking the Tiber, there originally stood an open loggia with seven arches at ground level, while to the north-west the building extended into an open court, and by its projecting wings and the opening of the central loggia turned towards the image of the nearby city.

Although in his choice of typology, Peruzzi explicitly declared his Tuscan ancestry and his interest in the new Roman tradition inaugurated by Bramante, in the details of his stylistic vocabulary there emerged also—as an intervening factor—an element derived from the style of Urbino, which could be ascribed to the influence exercised over the young architect by the works of Francesco di Giorgio Martini. The most direct references, apart from the treatise by the Sienese architect, were the Cancelleria and Palazzo Rucellai. From Francesco di Giorgio may have been derived the simple form of the windows with downward-facing; from the Cancelleria the coincidence between the slope of the windows and the top of the bases to the wall pilasters, as well as the idea of constructing the base band in a manner corresponding to the coping, distinguishing a sort of potential balcony which was later developed to a plastic dimension in the façade of the Palazzo Massimo. The Cancelleria also provided the most closely allied model as far as the arrangement of the orders was concerned in their relationship to the lateral façades overlooking Corso Vittorio and the garden, where the twin wall pilasters did not appear. The squared windows, on the other hand, derive from Alberti although Peruzzi introduced an original method of incorporating them into the structure, connecting them tangentially to the cornice of the first order, in such a way that they seem attached magnetically, or appended, or immersed in the vibrant rhythm of the frieze band like geometrical pauses in the exuberant pattern of the turrets.

The form of the balusters in the loggia of Psyche derives from Bramante, as does the L–shaped wall pilaster placed between the bays and the receding plane of the loggia. In a more general sense, the composition of the order in the form of a trabeated framework to define and articulate the parts of the volume—but seen at certain points (the two loggias) to be capable of enrichment by the insertion of an arch in its intervals—comprised the specific aspect of this work in which the architect's links with his masters and the emergence of new themes can be observed extremely clearly. Peruzzi faced what might be described as 'the greatest problems' of the contemporary architectonic debate and solved them in the wake of Bramante's open-minded attitude to experimentation, so providing an important contribution to the affirmation of the existence of a 'Roman line'. In the church of S. Maria della Pace, Bramante had associated the system of the arch and the architrave by superimposing one on the other; Peruzzi, however, associated them by interpenetration, as if wishing to demonstrate that the rhythmical division created by the order was a primary gesture and could become enriched by further connotations in the elaboration of the intervals, treated now in a purely two-dimensional way, now spatially. His search for objectivity and universality predominated, but did not yet proceed from an analytical conception of classicity. Already by superimposing two similar orders Peruzzi evinced the tendency, which was so explicit in his drawings, to interpret classical architecture in a pluralistic sense. So, too, the interpretation of the terminal trabeation as an inherent feature of the second order owing to the dimensions of its principal members, although its components presented contradictory characteristics, was a symptom of the rejection of a mechanical structurization of the system of orders and of the direct and significant absorption of the Roman attitude of anti-dogmatism which he had acquired from his personal frequentation of the classical monuments. In the Farnesina everything is clear and demonstrable: every episode is given a 'necessary' position in its context and becomes 'fixed' (a typical example is found in the little squared windows which are attached to the structure and not free-standing, and the same windows solidly anchored in the base band), but the mechanism of the composition was still subordinate to a primary notion (the open volume) and rigorously controlled in order to conform to the clear expression of this idea.

The process of simplification which was so apparent in the choice of architectonic elements—the plain windows, the Doric order in the wall pilasters—was contrasted in the original ornamentation by monochrome frescoes, which filled the plastered wall backgrounds with figures of caryatids and plant decorations. To gain an approximate idea of the original appearance of the façade, we must mentally substitute for the present material consistency of the building planes so vibrant with colour that they recall the architecture painted in the works of Piero della Francesca, Mantegna, and Filippino Lippi.

In the present day, these plastered walls have the violet tinge of volcanic plaster, and form a tenuous contrast to the wall pilasters worked in smooth straw-coloured bricks; the structure of the order thus tends to be reabsorbed in the luminosity of the façade surface. The original chromatic treatment of the corner pilasters, in which the brick texture is interpenetrated by ornamented stonework in peperino, has the appearance of a surface refinement of no clear motivation. If, however, we can imagine the straw-coloured pilasters against greenish backgrounds, and the termination of the grey edges which are connected by the protruding cornice of the same material, then the structure becomes animated and acquires new significance.

The return to the classical models evoked in fifteenth-century painting imbued the building with the joyful atmosphere of the world of fable. Vasari must have been thinking of this when he pronounced his famous judgement ('brought to such beauty and grace that it is not something built, but truly born'), and it was an atmosphere which entirely met the requirements of the humanist patron who had conceived of the house and garden as the home of a precious art collection and a meeting place.

The Interconnecting Internal Spaces
One of the typical characteristics of Peruzzi's work, documented clearly also in the drawings, is his very close attention to the proportioning of the internal parts of the building and their inter-relationship. Numerous designs for buildings which he projected contain notes relating to the proportions selected for the width, height, and length of the rooms, and these dimensions nearly always corresponded to the whole or privileged numbers derived from the theories of Vitruvius. In establishing possible significant sequences of internal spaces for the Farnesina, the iconographic element had to be considered as well as the geometrical proportions. On the ground floor, the basic system of communication derived from the two connected loggias, which were perpendicular to the small entrance porch on the south façade and the frieze room, accessible from the main loggia. The other and smal-

ler spaces were seen as appendices to this arrangement. All the decoration was based on mythological themes, relating mainly to the cult of love. The system of decoration comprised by the loggia of Galatea, the loggia of Psyche, and the Frieze room was connected, so that the individual cycles were enriched through the inter-relationship of the subject matter. The frescoes painted by Peruzzi on the ceiling of the Galatea room have been analysed in a remarkable study by Fritz Saxl, who finally solved the problem of the interpretation of the symbolic elements by referring them to the horoscope of Agostino Chigi. On the basis of the astronomical calculations made by Arturo Beer, it appears that the coming together of constellations and planets depicted in the ceiling frescoes was observed in the sky over Rome on 1 December 1465, the probable date of birth of Chigi.

The framework designed for his paintings by Peruzzi was derived from a rigorous structural interpretation of the geometrical characteristics of the vault with inserted lunettes. The roof shaft, the spaces between the wall pilasters, and the shape of the lunettes, are linked by an unambiguous relationship which makes it possible to join the corner lunettes so that they create a semicircular arch on the diagonal. The three-dimensional lunette motif, the background walls and intervening pendentives thus form a homogeneous band turning at an angle of ninety degrees without any lack of continuity or anomaly. In designing the cornices and the framework for the various scenes, the architect employed perspective rigorously, taking as a privileged viewpoint the entrance door facing the loggia of Psyche. This observation is particularly noticeable in the hexagons inscribed between the lunettes, where the thickness of the cornices varies according to the hypothetical conditions of visibility of a three-dimensional structure with framing in relief.

The most interesting architectonic feature in the pictorial decoration occurs in the surprise effect created by the appearance, as soon as one arrives at the top of the staircase, of the transparent network of the 'perspective room', where the architectonic order suggests a half-real, half-illusory, structure of spatial units which dovetail into each other. Here too, as in the garden loggia, there is a privileged viewpoint—the staircase landing—providing a diagonal view over the whole of the perspective network. This gives rise to a changing spatial effect, so that at times a perfect illusion is created, while at others the subtle artifice is openly revealed. The historical importance of this scenic stratagem has been justly emphasized: it constitutes one of the first experiments in a direct mixture of genres between pictorial space and architectonic space without the intervening element of a flat surface, as found in Bramante. The possibilities of the space are suggested by the perspective and presented to the eye of the viewer not enclosed in a cornice and above ground level, but as an area to be crossed, like a loggia which is rendered measurable and clearly perceived in its dimensional reality through the double line of columns which define it. A parapet which would disrupt the continuity of the floor as a plane of reference would have sufficed to reduce this illusory representation to a mere decorative device, but Peruzzi pursued with determination an aim which was specifically architectonic, and corresponded to what we may take as the central nucleus of the structural invention of the Farnesina: that is, the creation of an original relationship of osmosis between the external and the internal spaces.

The intention of establishing a dialectical relationship between the interior and exterior can be seen even more explicitly in the two loggias, which introduce an element of depth into the expanse of the wall surfaces. The relation between the colonnades and the façades, now that the frescoes have disappeared, presents a sharp contrast, but in their original form it was more gradual and subtle because the wall intervals already introduced into the brickwork of the pilasters the element of infinite continuity, which was in turn contrasted and accentuated by the window openings and terminal frieze. If the loggias introduce into the external composition the motif of filtered and enclosed space, which we may term 'artificial space', in the interior the decorations imitate 'natural' space, both in the sky which acts as a background to the fine, almost metallic, framework of Peruzzi's loggia, and in the Raphaelesque airy bower through which filters the heavenly light.

The relationship between nature and architecture is therefore interpreted as one of dialectical contrast, as an interwoven pattern, or as a continuous metamorphosis. In its geometrical abstraction, architecture projects the world of humanity onto a sensitive object. The perpendicular lines, the Albertian borders which define volumes, represent the primordial gesture of man as he takes possession of nature and measures it with the instruments of his mind; but the object engendered by the mind returns to nature, the common source of every structural conception. Architecture then enters the atmosphere and becomes immersed in it, without fusing together or miming nature, but maintaining a clearcut duality. Man the builder encloses himself in his surroundings, recognizes his individuality by isolating himself from nature, but from within his geometric kingdom, he returns to invoke nature by portraying her and trying to explain her through myths. 'The architecture of the Farnesina', writes Saxl, 'reflects the idea that a brilliant life, as it was conceived by the Chigi generation, could be achieved only in surroundings similar to those in which the great men of the classical era held their feasts. The entire conception of the suburban villa and the ideal of a life spent among the tranquil pleasures of the garden represented to this generation a way of re-living Cicero's Tusculum and Pliny's villa', and he adds, 'the most striking feature in the decorations is their complete lack of any Christian element', an amazing thing when one considers the care with which Agostino Chigi chose for his funeral chapel a scheme of decoration based closely on divine themes. But the distinction between the villa and the chapel corresponds to that between daily life and the time set aside for religious contemplation, and is the key to an understanding of both these works in relation to the ideology which inspired them. Roman classical culture in the first decades of the sixteenth century rested on the certainties of Christianity, but tended to extend the human area to its extreme limits. Through their translation into symbols and myths, human sentiments and actions, though experienced intensely and sensually in their physical reality, may be interpreted as fables and so transcended: life thus becomes an earthly interlude where Eden is again reflected and salvation seems guaranteed merely through man's possession of the Revelation. Eros regains his right of citizenship as a memory, a reminder of the blissful infancy of humanity.

The Farnesina did not have the success that might logically have been expected, and its architect was for many years condemned to a subordinate position as compared with Bramante's more fortunate pupils: Raphael, and especially Antonio da Sangallo with whom he collaborated on several occasions. The death of Agostino Chigi in 1520 deprived Peruzzi of his most influential patron, and made it more difficult for him to take his rightful place in the unwelcoming society of Rome, where he was employed mainly as a decorator of façades. Vasari recalls 'a very fine façade in the city, beyond Campo di Fiore in the direction of Piazza Giudea', and another 'opposite the house of Ulisse da Fano, and similarly the house of the same Ulisse, in which the stories he painted of Ulysses gave him great fame and glory'; but unfortunately none of these buildings have survived. Two of Peruzzi's drawings in the Uffizi provide a probable indication of the development of his ideas in this particular sector. One, which may have had to conform to the necessity of respecting a pre-existing central three-light window, presents two orders of equal height superimposed on a rusticated base. The decoration is inserted in the intervals, and on the top level in which the rhythm of the openings a – b – c – c – c – a – b – a recurs in the simple squared windows. The entrance doorway between two openings linked by a single cornice recalls the feature of the French windows in the Apostolic Palace at Loreto. The interrelationship between painting and architecture emphasizes the plasticity of the structure, which is attenuated and softened by the rhythm of the decoration. Only on the top level does the clearly defined, homogeneous structure yield precedence to the decoration, and above the columns there appear snake-like monsters in a Manneristic style.

The second is the more important of the two drawings. Here the model is Bramante's Palazzo Caprini, translated into more complex terms. On the ground floor, an order of pilasters is flanked by two small bands of equal breadth and encloses architraved windows surmounted by relieving arches. All the elements are jointed and the relief of the stones increases towards the background, so that while the superimposed stones are in such low relief that they can barely be distinguished against the wall pilasters, the windows are surrounded by roughly dressed stone frames in high relief. Whereas statues are placed above the wall pilasters, the bands support twin Corinthian columns designed *en plein air*, as if a fairly deep loggia opened up behind them. In the background to the loggia are unornamented windows, resembling the door to the Palazzo Massimo, and twin wall pilasters which re-echo the order of the columns.

It would be imprudent to ascribe these two drawings to Peruzzi, were it not for the fact that his exceptional spirit of enquiry and interest in stylistic experimentation are amply proved by his relief models of classical architecture, and especially the dated and unanswerable evidence presented by the architectonic background to his *Presentation at the Temple*, painted in S. Maria della Pace about 1516–7. The tower in the background represents one of the most interesting and original interpretations of Vitruvius's theme of the wind tower based on a hexagonal unit, which comprises one of the first architectonic applications of this form; but apart from this innovation, the fresco introduces on the left a perspective view of the wing of a palace incorporating three orders, which in many respects anticipates the Venetian palace of the Zecca (Mint) constructed twenty years later by Jacopo Sansovino. The order of Doric columns with rusticated projections represents a heretical adaptation of Bramante's model with a striving for violent plastic effects reminiscent of Giulio Romano. After his initial experience at the Farnesina, Peruzzi obviously soon gained a keen awareness of the inevitable crisis which was about to overtake the universalistic Utopia; unfortunately, all that remains of this process of self-criticism are a few fragments and indirect evidence. The apse of S. Rocco and the chapels which he built for that church between 1514 and 1520 have been lost, and the same fate has befallen the house 'opposite the Farnese' mentioned by Vasari, which probably stood on the site of the Palazzo Roccagiovine. The Villa Trivulzio at Salone, which is the least known of the few surviving works by Peruzzi, presents more than one point of interest in spite of its unfinished state, and a reconstruction of its original design may be made on the basis of drawing 453 in the Uffizi. The ground plan, characterized by the oval garden to which a longitudinal section of the building is connected at a perpendicular angle to the smaller axis, imbues a modest building project with a monumental vision. Like the stage of a theatre, the villa forms a background to an enclosed space which may have originally been intended for sham water battles and other water games made possible by the presence of a nearby spring. In the ornamentation of the façades, unrelieved bands are used in place of the order, this representing one of the first examples of the 'simplified style' which became highly successful in the succeeding decades. In the external façade over the entrance archway, the introduction of a motif of smooth rusticated surfaces, similar to that employed in the Palazzo Massimo, reveals Peruzzi's precocious interest in this feature.

In 1518 Peruzzi entered the important competition for S. Giovanni dei Fiorentini. The design presented by the Sienese architect has not come down to us, but from the large number of sketches preserved in the Uffizi relating to churches with a central plan, an idea may be obtained of the direction his project might have followed. A group of drawings referring to a church in the vicinity of the Capitol is devoted to the theme of the polylobate rotunda, in which space appears to expand out of a central nucleus towards a surrounding ornamented structure, following the classical example of the Mausoleum of the Orti Liciniani and developed to such an advanced stage that it anticipated eighteenth-century forms (Uffizi, 513 A, drawing XXXVIII).

The method of composition is based on a combination of interwoven and superimposed geometric structures. Drawing 513 shows a central octagonal dome-covered area, around which smaller areas of variable shape gravitate. Along the diagonal axes, the chapels follow

Exterior of Santa Maria in Domnica (1 cm = 3.6 m).

Exterior of Santa Maria dell' Anima (1 cm = 3.9 m).

Exterior of Palazzo Lante (1 cm = 5.8 m).

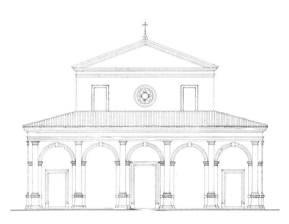

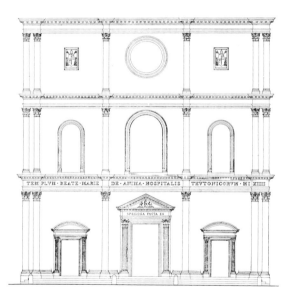

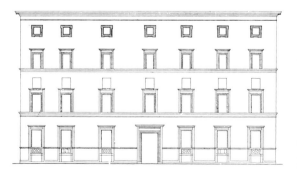

a semicircular design, while along the main axes there are three differently-shaped spaces: one for the presbytery, one for the chapels placed along the transversal axis, and the third for the porch. The complexity of the internal structure is reflected on the exterior by a volume based on an octagonal matrix. In drawing 495, the same method of composition is repeated on the basis of a hexagon, where the variable forms of the entrance and presbytery are preserved but the four lateral chapels are made identical. We have here a critical reappraisal of the centralized structure directed towards the reacquisition of a psychological motivation which, while leaving to the organism its coherent form, would develop it in relation to the requirements of religious worship. The analysis of form is so rigorous that in many of its conclusions it anticipates a debate which was to continue for two centuries. The last Roman work of Peruzzi, which he planned before the catastrophe of 1527, was the monument to Hadrian VI in the church of S. Maria dell'Anima; it was completed in 1529, but Peruzzi had been working on it for the previous five years. In his choice of design, the architect kept to the examples of Sansovino, but in his design of the order, completely bare of ornamentation, and in the robust quality of the structure, the work expresses a change of taste, and a decisive break from the tradition which had established a relationship of symbiosis between architecture and sculpture.

ANDREA SANSOVINO

Andrea Sansovino arrived in Rome in 1505, where he was presented by Giuliano da Sangallo to Julius II, who commissioned him to construct monuments to Ascanio Sforza and Girolamo Basso della Rovere in the apse of S. Maria del Popolo. These monuments show the influence exercised by the new artistic climate of Rome upon a sculptor who was still faithful to the manner of the fifteenth century. Without abandoning the florid style, Sansovino adopted broader proportions based on the square and half-columns which accentuate the plastic quality of the structure. In many works of architecture produced during the papacy of Julius, the name of Sansovino is mentioned without his role being clearly specified. Examples of this are the restoration of S. Maria in Domnica and the construction of S. Maria dell'Anima. In the former case, it is probable that the colonnade once attributed to Raphael was the work of Sansovino. This seems likely owing to the careful design of the mouldings to the order, the taste for geometric abstraction, and at the same time the lack of any clear personal imprint. Similar characteristics recur in the façade of S. Maria dell'Anima, a simple structure which is uncontrolled in its urban setting but is qualified by three doorways which reveal a minute study of ancient sources and a discreet use of polychromy, similar to the layer of marble on the house at Loreto. It seems probable that it was Andrea, not Jacopo, Sansovino who was responsible for the palazzo constructed by Cardinal Giuliano de' Medici in Piazza dei Caprettari, since here, too, the link with classical sources seems to be one of scrupulous and passive analysis, without the ability to transfigure them which characterizes the works of Jacopo. The most outstanding feature in the Palazzo Lante is the framing of the windows and doorway. In view of the early date of this work (1512), we can take this to be the first example of the search for 'absolute' form which is the distinguishing feature of the classical period of the sixteenth century.

The transfer of this type of framing—with supports of double-voluted corbels—from church buildings to domestic architecture is an indication of the importance assumed by the palazzo in Roman culture during those years, and the merit of bringing about this change of emphasis belongs to the architect of the palazzo in Piazza dei Caprettari, whether or not he was Andrea Sansovino. Bramante had already adopted this feature in his Tempietto of S. Pietro in Montorio, taking it from the Temple at Cori, but he did not adapt it to his domestic buildings. In the Palazzo Baldassini, built around 1516, Sangallo still employed windows with downward-turning mouldings in the style of the fifteenth century, but when he discovered the merits of the Palazzo Lante in the third decade of the century, he became its most ardent advocate. The ground-floor windows also, with the delicate ornamentation of the area between the corbels, which is similar in technique to the ornamentation of the monuments in the church of S. Maria del Popolo, have considerable importance in forming a typology where Sangallo's contribution became a determining factor but which probably originated at this point. The archaic treatment of the *cortile*, with the body of the arches resting directly on the capitals, and the design of the first-floor windows, relate the Palazzo Lante to the palazzo built by Cardinal Della Valle and traditionally attributed to Lorenzetto; Vasari refers to this building not in connection with its general construction, but only for its *cortile* and arrangement of decorative fragments and antique statues. Whereas the façade of the now greatly changed palazzo is notable only for the harmonious series of white marble windows resembling those already analysed, in the large courtyard and staircases there appear original touches and a mixture of ingenuous archaisms and intuitions of future developments. Here again the use of polychrome marbles is based on the experience of Andrea Sansovino.

JACOPO SANSOVINO

Born in 1486, Jacopo Sansovino is the youngest of the architects born in the eighth decade of the fifteenth century. His great opportunity came after the Sack of Rome, when he moved to Venice and became the 'reformer' of Venetian architecture. He lived in Rome between 1506 and 1511 and again from 1516 to 1527, employed mainly as a sculptor, first under the direction of his master Andrea and then on his own account. Around 1516, and in any case before the fire of 1518, Jacopo worked on the monument to Cardinal Michiel in the church of S. Marcello. This was a weak replica of the model designed by Andrea Sansovino in S. Maria del Popolo, and the architectural structure was overlaid by an excess of ornamentation. Of a slightly later date was his work on the reconstruction of S. Marcello, which had been destroyed by a fire, and here, together with Sangallo, he brought to fruition one of the most successful typological models produced around that time. In 1518 a competition was held in which all the architects of his generation took part: Baldassarre Peruzzi (b. 1481), Raphael (b. 1483), Antonio da Sangallo the Younger (b. 1483); to everyone's surprise Jacopo Sansovino emerged the winner. The object of the competition was to construct 'the church of the Florentine nation' at a strategic position in relation to the city, that is, at the tip of the wedge formed by the bend of the Tiber in front of the Borghi and the Vatican, at the end of the straight road laid by Julius II. By an irony of fate, the winning design in this competition is also the one about which we know the least. The only information we have is that provided by Vasari, who recalls that 'the Pope praised (the model) of Sansovino as the best one, since apart from other things he had made a pulpit for each of the four corners of the church and in the middle a larger pulpit, similar to that design which Sebastiano Serlio placed in his second book of Architecture.' The interesting theories put forward by Nava and Siebenhuener do not appear convincing, and the plan in Serlio's Fifth Book does not in any way correspond to Vasari's description. At the present stage of our knowledge, therefore, it is not possible to identify the design submitted by Sansovino, and all that can be established is that it fitted into a square area. This was the form of the floor area constructed by Sansovino before he was dismissed, probably as a result of technical inexperience. If one accepts the theory of Siebenhuener which relates both Serlio's plan and drawing 1312 in the Uffizi to this project, Sansovino

would have taken as his basic model the circumscribed octagon which Bramante had already employed in S. Maria di Loreto and which had also greatly interested Antonio da Sangallo the Younger. It is very surprising, however, that a competition of such importance could have been won by the least experienced of the entrants, and for a design based on a form which had been superseded even by Bramante, in S. Celso and S. Biagio della Pagnotta. But this problem, which is the same as the problem of Sansovino's architectural formation, will have to remain unsolved until fresh documentary evidence comes to light. Considerable uncertainty also surrounds the authorship of the palazzo constructed by the Gaddi family on the Canal dei Banchi. Vasari ascribes it to Sansovino, but this is not confirmed in Aretino's famous letter, where he writes of the architectural activity of Jacopo Sansovino; in fact, the only support for such an attribution is to be found in the fact that in 1518 the architect had to arbitrate in a dispute between the Gaddi and Rucellai families (cf. *Lettere romane di Momo*, Rome 1872, p. 54). It is only by dating the palazzo around 1520 that its authorship may be ascribed to Sansovino, but if Pietrangeli's theory that it should be dated to the period 1528–30 is accepted, then this possibility would be excluded. In favour of the attribution to Sansovino, there is the strong argument of the quality of the work and the difficulty of finding anyone who would be capable of it—without having recourse to such great names as Peruzzi or Sangallo. The solution to the restricting feature of the long, narrow site was to insert two successive courtyards, correctly related by Wurm and Tafuri to the Palazzo Corner, and this became the first example of a model which was to find its most successful expression in Peruzzi's Palazzo Massimo, revealing a remarkable mastery of the problems of distribution. From the stylistic point of view, there are no outstanding innovations: in the façade, motifs used by Sangallo and Bramante have been adopted without a strongly marked personal character, and only in the porch with parabolic section and in the first courtyard—resolved in terms of a light chiaroscuro rhythm—can a personal quality be discerned which contains some hint of the intent of purpose manifested by Jacopo Sansovino in his greatest works in Venice.

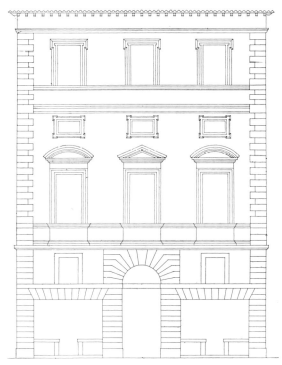

The only authenticated Roman work is the tomb of Cardinal Quinones, executed in 1536, almost ten years after Sansovino's departure for Venice when he already had behind him the experience of S. Geminiano, the School of the Misericordia, and the Palazzo Corner. The distance traversed since he put up the archaic monument in the church of S. Marcello could not be greater; sculpture and architecture have come together without any elements of decoration in a solidly constructed and compact organism. The insertion of the Tempietto of Bramante, uplifted by angels, presents an original and well-defined stratification, and in the context acquires a dynamic and pre-Baroque significance, both through the violent break in the panel and the degree of action in the scene portrayed. In addition, the design of the mouldings and the polychrome decoration which causes the columns to stand out against the background and imparts a strong binary rhythm to the frieze, like a sort of optical echo, indicate that the architect had attained complete maturity and was directing his research along the lines of his great Venetian works.

Vasari mentions also among Jacopo Sansovino's works of architecture 'a very beautiful loggia on the road leading from Rome to Ponte Molle on the Appian Way for Marco Cosci', and 'for Antonio Cardinal Del Monte a large building in his vineyard, outside Rome and above the Virgin Water'. While it is certain that the loggia built for Cosci has disappeared, Sante Bargellini has suggested that the construction in the Villa Del Monte should be identified with a part of the villa on the Via Flaminia later continued by Pirro Ligorio and today the headquarters of the Italian Embassy to the Holy See. The part for which Sansovino was responsible, according to this theory, is the hexagonal courtyard surrounded by Corinthian pilasters which Ammannati used as supports for his fountain.

GIULIO ROMANO, OR THE TIME OF UNREST

Giulio Romano's contribution to the design of the Villa Madama is a critical problem to which there is no easy solution. The most convincing suggestion is the one which attributes to him responsibility for the stucco wall decoration only, leaving to Raphael the design of the structure of the loggia, and to Giovanni da Udine the delicate paintings of the vault. In the wall stucco decorations and in the apses, there is revealed a deep knowledge of classical models and at the same time a subtly destructive and heretical vein which accorded well with Giulio Romano's later works, both in Rome and Mantua. In the apses especially, the addition of large inverted shells to the rectangular coffered ceilings anticipates the taste for geometric distortion and complex structures which later found perfect expression in the ceilings of the Palazzo del Tè.

The first reliable indication of the architectural vocation of Giulio Romano occurred in some of his paintings produced immediately after the death of Raphael, especially *The Stoning of St. Stephen* in Genoa and the *Holy Family* in the church of S. Maria dell'Anima. The architectural importance of the former work lies in its portrayal of Trajan's forum: it is a magical interpretation which transfigures the ruins, with the specially significant feature of the rusticated structure of an imaginary doorway, a clear sign of a developed taste for the intermixture of architecture and nature. In the background to the *Holy Family*, there appears, in an asymmetrical position, the interior of a circular colonnade minutely described in every detail with a degree of technical competence which reveals that the artist was well-grounded in architectural studies.

Simultaneously with these paintings, which reveal a personal luministic interpretation of architecture, Giulio Romano was probably engaged in constructing the villa for Baldassarre Turini of Pescia, later purchased by the Lante family. This little suburban villa, orchestrated in a minor key, was full of stylistic innovations, and provided a foretaste of the architect's future explosive career. On the ground-floor level of the façade, overlooking the city, a varied rhythm with columns, which is far removed from any conventional formula, anticipates the highly complex ornamentation of the internal loggia of the Palazzo del Te.

On the side facing the city, the cubic block of the building opens into a loggia, in which arches alternate with trabeated areas; this motif later enjoyed great success in Northern Italy especially, where Giulio Romano himself introduced it. The *travata ritmica* as employed by Alberti and Bramante has now been simplified and translated into terms of a pure proportional counterpoint, counterposing the slender volumetric forms ornamented by slightly projecting wall pilasters to the two-dimensional pattern of the rhythmic order.

At first the architect felt his way, without making an irrevocable choice of an individual mode of expression, but even in the early stages his predilection for contrasts and audacious mixtures of styles was apparent.

About the year 1523, at the same time as Peruzzi was working on the Villa Trivulzio, Giulio Romano drew up plans for the Palazzo Maccarani in Piazza S. Eustachio, where he introduced the feature of atrophied orders, reduced to the function of simple bands, and utilized the rustication on the doorway in conjunction with the structure of the order. The treatment employed by Bramante in the Palazzo Caprini is adopted here in terms of light chiaroscuro, so that the manifest contrast between the broadly conceived and powerful design and the minute interweaving of the reliefs comes to embody the 'character' of the image. The architect's love of paradox is already present, as well as his intention to resolve the architectonic form in a 'representation'; these characteristics emerged fully in his Mantuan works, but the naturalistic and outrageous elements again appear to have been exorcized by the influence of Raphael.

The last Roman work produced by Giulio Romano was probably his decoration of the bathroom of Clement VII in Castel S. Angelo, a new and almost caricatural version of the hot room made for Cardinal Bibbiena. Here delicacy gave way to a strongly-marked rhythm and rustic tone, similar to that of a hypogeum and very far from the refinement of Raphael. Giulio Romano's violent and ironical manner had not yet burst upon the world but all the preconditions for it were already in existence. The disturbing, paradoxical structures created by one of the few Renaissance artists to have been born in Rome made their first appearance far from his native city and in a very different cultural climate. Rome itself saw only a pale reflection of them, several years later. The only artist whose work reflected the disturbing note evinced in an exceptionally intense form by Giulio Romano in the Mantuan palazzo was another son of Latium: the dilettante Vicino Orsini, who tried in his Bomarzo ravine to exorcize his demons by calling on them magically to populate the 'sacred wood'.

Donato Bramante: Palazzo della Cancelleria (1489–1511).
2. Exterior. | 3. Courtyard, corner pillar. | 4. Entrance. |
5. Loggia.

6. *Donato Bramante: Palazzo della Cancelleria, cortile (1489-1511).*

Donato Bramante and others: Cortile of San Damaso (1489–1511).
7. Upper storeys. / 8. General view.
9. Detail showing windows.

10. *Donato Bramante: Cortile of the Belvedere (1503–13).*

Donato Bramante: Cortile of the Belvedere (1503–13).
11-14. Details.

18. Donato Bramante: Tempietto of San Pietro in Montorio (1508–12), detail of columns.

19. *Donato Bramante: Tempietto of San Pietro in Montorio (1508–12), interior of dome.*

22-24. *Donato Bramante (?): Temple of the Nymphs, Genazzano.*

Palazzo of Cardinal Adriano da Corneto or Giraud Torlonia (1489–1511).
25. Façade. | 26. Cortile.
27. San Lorenzo in Damaso, interior.

28. *San Giacomo degli Spagnoli, interior.*
29. *Santa Maria sopra Minerva, Carafa Chapel.*
30. *Donato Bramante: Loggia, Castel Sant' Angelo (1500–3).*
31. *Palazzo Venezia, hall.*

Donato Bramante, Antonio da Sangallo the Elder, Antonio da Sangallo the Younger: Fortress of Civita Castellana.
32, 33. Details. / 34, 35. Details of the Fortification (Antonio da Sangallo the Younger).
36. General view.

*Baldassarre Peruzzi: Palazzo Farnesina
(1507–11).
37. Aerial view. | 38. Detail.*

*Baldassarre Peruzzi: Palazzo Farnesina
(1507–11).
39, 40. Details.*

41. *Castel Sant' Angelo : Bath of Clement VII.*
Raphael : Rooms of the Vatican.
42. *The Fire of Borgo, detail.*
43. *Heliodorus Hunting, detail (1512–14).*
44. *Logge Vaticane.*
45. *Stables of the Palazzo Farnesina (1514–18).*

46. *Raphael: Church of Sant'Eligio degli Orefici, detail of interior (1516).*

47. *Raphael: Church of Sant'Eligio degli Orefici, detail of interior (1516).*

51. *Raphael: Chigi Chapel, Church of Santa Maria del Popolo, detail (1513–20).*

Raphael and others: Villa Madama (1517–23).
55, 56. Aerial views. / 57. Main façade.

60. *Andrea Sansovino (?): Palazzo Lante (1513).*

61. *Andrea Sansovino (?): Palazzo Lante, perspective view of cortile (1513).*

Antonio da Sangallo the Younger: Palazzo Baldassini (1514–22).
62. Perspective of façade. | 63. Detail of entrance hall. | 64. Loggia.

65. *Antonio da Sangallo the Younger: Palazzo Baldassini, cortile (1514–22).*

Antonio da Sangallo the Younger: Chapel of San Giacomo, Church of San Giacomo degli Spagnoli (c. 1517).
66. Detail of vault. | 67, 68. Details.
69. Palazzo of the Bishop of Cervia.
Santa Maria Portae Paradisi.
70. Detail of exterior. | 71. Interior.
72. Exterior.

73. *Palazzetto Leroy, interior (1523).*

Palazzetto Leroy (1523).
74. Perspective of façade. | 75. Detail of the cortile.
76. Vault of entrance hall.

Palazzo Ossoli (c. 1525).
77. Façade. | 78. Cortile.

83. *Palazzo Senni-Cicciaporci, façade (1521–2).*

84. *Palazzo Senni-Cicciaporci, detail of basement storey (1521–2).*

85. *Giulio Romano: Villa Lante al Gianicolo, exterior (1523-4).*

86. *Giulio Romano: Villa Lante al Gianicolo, interior of gallery (1523–4).*

87. *Jacopo Sansovino (?): Palazzo Nicolini Amici, detail of cortile (1526–7).*

Jacopo Sansovino (?): Palazzo Nicolini Amici (1526–7).
88, 89. Details. | 90. Perspective of façade.

94. *Palazzo Altoviti, façade overlooking the Tiber, before destruction.*
95. *Palazzo in Vicolo Savelli.*
96. *Palazzo in Via Monserrato.*
97. *Palazzetto in Trastevere.*

98. *Palazzo Sora.*
99. *Palazzo della Valle, façade.*
100. *Palazzo Mattei, cortile.*

101. *Palazzo della Valle, detail of entrance to stairway.*
102. *Palazzo della Valle, cortile.*
103. *Palazzo Taverna.*
104. *Palazzo in Vicolo Savelli, cortile.*
105 *Ruins of palazzo in Corso Vittorio.*

112. *Santa Maria dell' Anima, façade.*

113. *Santa Maria in Monserrato, interior.*
114. *Santa Maria dell' Anima, detail of vault.*

112. *Santa Maria dell' Anima, façade.*

113. *Santa Maria in Monserrato, interior.*
114. *Santa Maria dell' Anima, detail of vault.*

Jacopo Sansovino: San Marcello al Corso.
115, 116. Details of interior.
117. Santa Croce in Gerusalemme, monument by Jacopo Sansovino.
118. Santa Maria in Domnica, façade by A. Sansovino (?).
119. Santa Maria in Domnica, detail of pedestals.

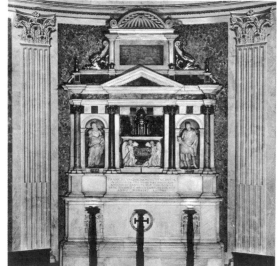

120. *Santa Maria dell'Anima, Tomb of Hadrian VI by Baldassarre Peruzzi (1524–9).*

PART TWO
1527–1564

POLITICS AND CULTURE

The most immediate cause of the Sack of Rome was without doubt the tortuous and hesitant policy of Clement VII, with a number of adverse circumstances contributing to augment its ill-effects. However, it is difficult to avoid the temptation of seeing the symbolic nature of this event as the explosion of an irreconcilable series of contradictions.

The basic contradiction, which came to a head at the time of the Sack, was between the cultural policy and consolidation of temporal power pursued by the church, and its dogmatic attitude. By agreeing to welcome and protect humanist culture and the myth of 'renewal', the church had implicitly collaborated in the process of dismantling the very structures—the old university culture, scholasticism, the mendicant orders—on which its ideological and political power depended. Critical humanism had spread from Italy to Northern Europe where it had inspired the thinking of Erasmus and acted as a catalyst to the revolt of Luther.

Another explosive contradiction could be seen in the threatened status of Italy's economic and cultural supremacy. Her advanced capitalist organization had enabled Italy to draw capital from all Europe; but it had also determined a process of development, as swift as a chain reaction, in those countries where exploitation had been most effective. With the Sack of Rome, at which there were almost as many Spaniards as Lutheran pikemen, Europe took her revenge on Italy for her supremacy and for the parasitical acts of Rome and put a sudden and final end to Italy's illusion that she could protract and consolidate the past golden age. The artistic world, where the seeds of unrest had been germinating for the previous twenty years, suffered the repercussions and defended itself by adopting two contrasting forms of reaction: on the one hand, there was a rigidifying of the academic position, which defended the independence of art against the inroads of time and sought to keep it apart from the course of history in an icy limbo of perfection; on the other hand, there was an attitude of cynicism and rebellion against rules which opened the way to individualism.

From 1527 to 1934, the ambiguous policy of Clement VII continued, influenced by the 'private' interests of his family. He agreed to bow his head unprotestingly to the Emperor in order to gain his protection against the oligarchic republic which had regained power in Florence, and against the Lutherans in Germany. So the Emperor was permitted to be crowned in S. Petronio in Bologna, thus signifying the Pope's unconditional surrender to the imperial authority, with no prospects of future betterment.

Meanwhile Charles assured himself of the support of the powerful Italian families of the houses of Medici, Sforza, Gonzaga, Savoia, and Doria, by a number of concessions and political marriages. As a reward for his coronation, he not only reincorporated Cervia and Ravenna, but also put Alexander, the nephew of Clement VII, in charge of an army which was to attack Florence. Weakened by class conflicts and by the city's exploitation of the countryside, Florence finally surrendered to the siege, so burying for ever the dreams of a generation of intellectuals whose ties with reality had shown themselves more and more weak and precarious.

In the Treaty of Cambrai, signed in 1529, Francis I provisionally gave up his aims of Italian conquest, and in the brief period of peace which ensued, the Pope attempted to reorganize the devasted city. Very little precise information exists regarding the exodus from Rome following the Sack. The figure of eighty-five thousand inhabitants stated by Giovio to have lived in Rome at the time of the papacy of Leo X appears entirely unconvincing. We know for a fact that at the census taken only a few months prior to the Sack, the population numbered about fifty-four thousand. It is probable that after the catastrophe this figure decreased by at least thirty per cent. For about five years, until the election of Paul III, the only work done in Rome was to put right what had been destroyed. Some new urban initiatives were taken—rectifying the line of the Via dell'Orso and starting to lay the Via de' Baullari. The Villa Madama, which was begun by Clement when he was still a cardinal, was burnt during the Sack and remained unfinished.

The papacy of Paul III (1534–49) was one of the longest in the sixteenth century, as mentioned earlier in the Preface, and does not present a historical picture of a period guided by a unified sense of purpose. In spite of his undoubted political stature, Pope Paul Farnese did not succeed in gaining the upper hand over the contradictions which beset him and ended by becoming their interpreter rather than their master. He was brought up in the humanist spirit in the gardens of Lorenzo il Magnifico, and in his youth indulged in a very free life, then found himself invested with the pontifical authority at a moment in history which demanded a very firm hand.

He was closely attached to his family, and might well have become an unscrupulous nepotist, but the interests of the state he ruled were at least as dear to him as the interests of his family. When at the end he was forced to make a choice between the two, he chose the state, so alienating the sympathy of his family and arousing them to revolt against his authority. This grieved him so deeply that it caused his death.

A profound contradiction became manifest also between the first and second periods (after about 1540) of Paul's papacy concerning his attitude towards the biggest problem he was called upon to face: that of defending the church against the schism by instituting reforms in Catholic orthodoxy which would be capable of arresting the movement of disintegration undermining the whole structure of the church.

One of the first important decisions taken by the new pope was to change the composition of the College of Cardinals whose members consisted mainly of favourites of the two Medici popes. He caused a scandal by admitting two of his young nephews, including the famous Alexander, then aged fifteen, who later became the creator of Caprarola, and also admitted to the sacred college such men as Du Bellay, Fischer, and Contarini. The last-named was a Venetian nobleman and pupil of Pomponazzi, and the author of a work on the office of bishop which had put him in evidence as one of the most courageous and well-informed advocates of radical reform in the Catholic church. In August 1535, a 'commission for reform' was appointed, with the task of briefing the Council who were engaged in establishing a moral basis for social customs and eliminating the ecclesiastical abuses of Rome.

A commission to prepare the work of the Council, under the leadership of Contarini, began its deliberations the following year. Besides the Venetian Contarini, it included such men as Pole, Sadoleto, Giberti, and the Neapolitan nobleman Gian Pietro Carafa,

Plan of Piazza Farnese with the palazzo enlarged by Paul III.

who founded the Congregation of Divine Love and later became the fanatical head of the repressive movement.

Sadoleto introduced the discussion. In his speech, he referred to the Sack of Rome as a divine punishment and courageously put the blame for the disintegration of the church onto the sins of the popes. The threatening danger of Turkey was described as the next event to be expected from the unleashing of God's anger and could be avoided only by repentance. In February 1537, the commission had already drawn up a report, later printed under the title *Consilium delectorum cardinalium ... de emendanda Ecclesia ...*; in this document great courage was displayed in exposing fearlessly the many evils of the church.

Practical difficulties led to the postponement of the first meeting of the Council, and the immediate task of reforming the church organization was entrusted to another commission consisting of four members, including Contarini and Carafa. Difficulties arose in relation to the so-called 'compensations', with disagreement over the possibility of collecting a tax instituted by Sextus IV which had to be paid to the Bursar of the Vatican for the granting of favours, even those of a purely spiritual character. Opinions differed as to whether the Pope had the right to turn his spiritual power to economic advantage without incurring the sin of simony. Contarini was intransigent in demanding the total abolition of 'compensations', but Carafa adopted the opposite position. This polarity of views was highly significant, for whereas the former was a convinced advocate of an Erasmian line of evangelical humanism, the latter was destined to become the apostle of the Counter-Reformation movement as such. The choice—rendered inevitable by the revolutionary role of critical humanism—was between the complete renunciation of the economic privileges on which the worldly power of the church rested, and the preservation of these privileges at the cost of compromises in ideology and doctrine, so making it impossible to institute any dialogue with the Protestants. In the statement sent to the Pope by Contarini to justify his firmness, one can feel the undercurrent of the dislike of the humanists for every kind of authority which was not based on reason: 'It is against the law of Christ which is a law of liberty', he writes, 'for Christians to be subject to a pope who governs with absolute authority and merely in accordance with his caprice. The Pope may have received supreme power in the church from Christ, but this is a rule according to reason and exercised over free men.'

The gap between the Erasmians and the 'counter-reformers' was mirrored in the problem of finding a method of bringing heretics back to the orthodox fold. Contarini, Pole, Morone, and Sadoleto believed that heresy could be overcome only by gentle persuasion and love, while Carafa, Alvarez and many others opted for the introduction of the repressive methods of the Inquisition into Italy. Faced with this polarity, Pope Paul III at first maintained a neutral position, but from 1540 he began to move towards the latter method, and in 1542 he appointed as general and head inquisitor respectively Carafa and Toledo. Among those who had spoken in favour of the re-establishment of the institution was Ignatius Loyola, founder of the Company of Jesus (Jesuits) whose order had been approved by Paul III in 1540.

In the international sphere, the papacy of Paul III began badly, at a time when for dynastic reasons England too had withdrawn from Catholicism. At the same time, while Charles V annexed the Duchy of Milan on the death of Duke Francesco Sforza and Francis I formed an alliance with Suleiman the Magnificent, so increasing the seriousness of the Turkish threat to the Mediterranean, the Pope allied himself with the Emperor and with Venice and took advantage of the vicissitudes of the war to act as mediator between France and the Empire, bringing about the meeting of Charles and Francis at Nice, where a truce was made. A Holy League was set up at this time to fight the Turks and it succeeded in preventing the conquest of Corfu. In 1541, the Diet of Regensburg was held, at which Charles V tried to institute a dialogue between Catholics and Protestants; for some days it seemed as if some common ground based on Erasmian humanism might be found to exist between

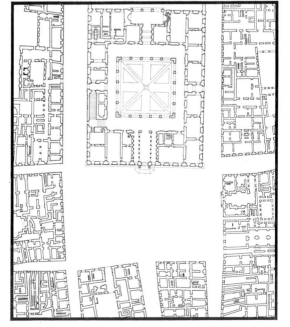

the papal legate Contarini and the Protestant delegates, Melantone and Buzer. At first agreement was reached on the theory of justification, but when the problems relating to the sacraments and papal authority were discussed, the meeting broke up without coming to an agreement. On his return to Rome, Contarini was accused of heresy and his position was considerably weakened, while the rigid orthodoxy of Carafa and of those who believed that lost religious unity could only be recovered by force and repression became firmly established. After the death of Cardinal Contarini, which occurred in Bologna where he was acting as legate to Paul III, the mantle of Erasmian thought was taken up by Reginald Pole, who was employed in Viterbo as legate of the Patrimony. There he formed the centre of a group of intellectuals who were particularly interested in the question of reforming the church and followed the ideas of Contarini relating to justification, including such men as the Venetian Luigi Priuli, Ludovico Beccadelli, the poet Marcantonio Flaminio, Vittoria Colonna, and Carnesecchi. In 1567, Carnesecchi chose to be tortured as a heretic rather than submit to the authority of the church. In Rome, the friends of Cardinal Pole were nicknamed 'the soulful ones' and during the papacy of Paul III were regarded tolerantly.

Meanwhile in 1542 the truce made at Nice was already broken, and Francis I tried to benefit from the failure at Regensburg and the destruction of the Spanish-Genoese fleet by resuming hostilities. He managed to gain England to his side, and on reaching the gates of Paris concluded the Peace of Crépy. Immediately afterwards, he tried to impose on Paul III a Council at which the two divided sections of the Christian church would meet; but the agreement to convoke the meeting in 1545 was countermanded by the Pope, who claimed for himself the right of convocation and direct government. Emboldened by his success in the sphere of religious interests, the Pope turned the occasion to advantage in his customary ambiguous way by removing Piacenza and Parma from the state of the church and making a gift of them to his son Pier Luigi. But Charles V, from whose interference Paul III thought he had freed himself for a long time once hostilities had broken out between the Emperor and the League of Protestant Princes, resulting in the rout of the latter at Mühlberg, immediately stepped in and took control. The Council opened in Trent on 13 December. The papal legate was Cardinal Pole, but by his side the Pope appointed two representatives of the Medicean old guard of the College of Cardinals, Marcello Cervini and Giovanni Maria del Monte, who could neutralize Pole's pacificism. As technical consultants on theological matters, Pole also had at his disposal two men in the trust of Loyola, Laìnez and Salmeròn. Any idea that a possible dialogue with the Protestants might be initiated was immediately discounted, and the Erasmian party became a minority; then with the recognition of the supremacy of the Latin text of the 'Vulgate' over even the Greek and Hebrew original texts of the Bible, critical humanism was rejected and suffered an overwhelming defeat. Pole withdrew, a tired and sick man, while the work of the Council continued in Trent until the outbreak of an epidemic. The greatest causes of contention between Italians and Spaniards centred around the question of the accumulation of ecclesiastical appointments and benefits. The papal legates suggested in 1547 that the Council should be transferred to Bologna, but the Spaniards opposed this move and Charles V refused to agree; Paul III therefore had no other course but to postpone the Council *sine die*. Meanwhile the Pope's son Pier Luigi was killed in a conspiracy, with the possible connivance of Charles V who had laid claim to Piacenza and Parma for his Empire. The last act of Paul III was to draw closer to France, where Henri II had succeeded to the throne. The suggestion that his nephew Ottavio should hand Parma over to Orazio Farnese, the future husband of the king's natural daughter, Diane de Poitiers, was the stratagem by which the old Pope tried once again to play on the antagonism among the great European powers. But his nephew refused to comply with the Pope's wishes, and in this he was supported by Cardinal Alexander. This insubordination by his family inflicted a mortal blow on the Pope, and in early autumn he died amid general grief. His fellow-citizens erected a statue to him in the Capitol.

Principal urban structures in mid sixteenth-century Rome.

The Piazza del Popolo trident—its present appearance.

The little trident formed by the Canal dei Banchi, Via Paola, and Via di Panico—present layout.

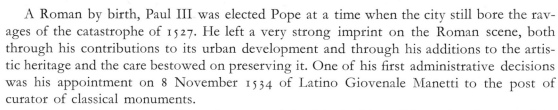

A Roman by birth, Paul III was elected Pope at a time when the city still bore the ravages of the catastrophe of 1527. He left a very strong imprint on the Roman scene, both through his contributions to its urban development and through his additions to the artistic heritage and the care bestowed on preserving it. One of his first administrative decisions was his appointment on 8 November 1534 of Latino Giovenale Manetti to the post of curator of classical monuments.

Unfortunately, the laudable zeal expressed in this decision did not last long, and in 1540 the Pope authorized the builders of St. Peter's to use many of the classical monuments as stone quarries. An opportunity to consider a restructurization of the city, if only as a temporary measure, was provided by the visit of Charles V in 1537, after his victory in Tunis. Sangallo, Peruzzi and many other architects set to work to arrange and decorate the Emperor's triumphal route. The route of the procession was arranged at a meeting of the magistrates of the people held in December 1535 in the Capitol, and was to pass from the Appian Way through a number of ancient and new triumphal arches as far as the Vatican. A curious document lists the churches and other buildings due to be demolished for the occasion: 'Firstly, S. Lorenzo of the Pharmacists, so that the columns on which is written Divine Antoninus and Dive Faustina may be seen. At the palace of M. Aurialo two churches: one named Santa Margherita overlooking the Colosseum and the other named Santa Maria overlooking the Torre de' Conti for the aggrandizement and greater comfort of this palace.' As can be seen, the purpose of these alterations was in nearly every case to make ancient monuments visible or to create space in front of important buildings. It was an anticipation on a small scale of the method, later applied generally by Sextus V, of providing an overall view of the monumental centres, and was inspired by a conception of the city as a spectacle and itinerary route. Rabelais, who was staying in Rome just at the time when these feverish preparations were in hand, referred to the demolition of about two hundred houses and three or four churches. Documentary evidence confirms this statement so far as the churches are concerned, and this makes the figure given for the private houses seem perfectly credible also.

The dread of a Turkish invasion led the Pope to review the defensive position of the city and to undertake a great scheme for the reconstruction and completion of the ancient Aurelian Wall. At the same time, following the example of his immediate predecessors, he concerned himself with the important district of the Pincio, where he straightened the central thoroughfare which thereafter became known as the Corso, and laid the present Via de' Condotti between Tor di Nona and the Trinità de' Monti district. In the area of the bend of the Tiber, the urban developments instituted by the Pope were mainly intended to create space around monumental buildings. In this category could be included the squares created in front of the churches of S. Marco and SS. Apostoli, and in front of his family palace, the Farnesina.

Another important initiative was the straightening of the two streets, Via di Panico and Via Paola, which together with the Canale de' Banchi (the present-day Via di S. Spirito) formed the 'little trident' in front of the Elio Bridge. The roads Via di Torre Argentina, dei Cestari, di S. Maria in Monticelli, della Palombella, and dei Baullari, were either newly formed or improved, and all followed a rectilinear line in conformity with the tradition of the Via Giulia.

During the papacy of the Farnese Popes, the architectural world was dominated until 1546 by the figure of Sangallo, the architect who had gained the trust of Paul III when, in 1517, he was commissioned to construct the Palazzo Farnese. In the development of the personality of Sangallo, there is mirrored the progressive conservatism of the Pope's policy. Even before the death of Sangallo, however, the fact that Michelangelo was commissioned to prepare plans for the reconstruction of the Capitol testifies to the Pope's effort to find an alternative to the archaeological style which had been both supported and eroded by the institution of the Vitruvian Academy.

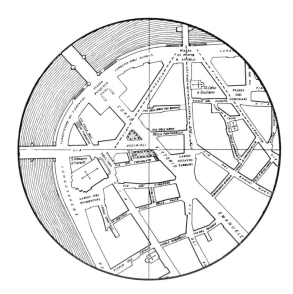

The alternative proposed by Michelangelo matured much later, however—not until his first Roman works were begun. In the fourth decade of the sixteenth century the only concrete alternative to the dominant influence of Sangallo was a decorativism created out of a distorted view of the legacy of Raphael; it was apparent especially in the many examples of façades decorated in sgraffito and fresco, and in such works as the Palazzo Spada and Casa Crivelli, where archaeological taste had led to a disintegration of the artistic language of the Renaissance.

With the election of Ciocchi del Monte as Julius III, papal policy passed through a period of questioning and doubt. The new Pope was elected after one of the lengthiest and most controversial conclaves in the history of the church; four months of wrangling between France and the Empire ended in an improvised and compromise solution. Reginald Pole, supported by the imperialists, needed only one vote to be elected, but failed to obtain it. At that moment, not only the future of the individual was at stake, but the future of the church as a whole. If the Erasmian Pole had been elected, the reform of Catholicism would have taken quite a different direction, and in view of his youth (he was only forty-five), he could have introduced a radical approach to the problem of the Council, who would have been persuaded to reopen the interrupted dialogue with the Protestants. The election of Del Monte was a way of further postponing a decision; although the choice of repression daily became more and more inevitable.

The few attempts made by Julius III to 'enter history' were a complete failure. He wished to bring Parma back to the control of the church, and when Ottavio Farnese formed an alliance with Henri II of France, he was so angered that he declared war on him. Serious lossses ensued, and when Charles V later found himself in difficulties, the Pope was forced to subscribe to an agreement acknowledging the *status quo*. The consistory, which was to ratify the agreement with Farnese, issued a decree which marked another serious defeat for the Pope. The Council which had been reopened in 1551 had to adjourn. In this eleventh session, Charles V had succeeded in compelling the Protestants to send some of their representatives, but the meeting was of a purely formal nature. Requests were made to refer back for discussion everything that had previously been decided upon by the Council, and even to change the constitution of the Council itself, so that the Pope was left in an entirely defensive position. However, the main reason for suspending the session was the grave danger to which the Emperor had been exposed at Innsbruck as the result of a conspiracy against him by the Elector of Saxony.

In the last years of his brief papacy, Julius saw the outbreak of the war of Siena, and the armies of France and the Empire invade the state of the church. His death coincided approximately with the signing of the Treaty of Augsburg in which Charles concurred in the religious division of Germany.

In spite of his choice of the symbolic name Julius, probably inspired by the example of Julius II, Pope Del Monte did not inherit either the firmness or the political talent of his predecessor. He tried to follow in his footsteps as a patron of the arts, as can be seen in what may be considered the happiest achievement of his papacy—the villa built by Vignola and Ammannati at the foot of the Parioli Hills. But whereas for Julius II culture and art had been an integral part of his political design, for Julius III they were only instruments of escape into a pseudo-reality compounded of pleasurable idleness. To travel to his villa from the Vatican, the Pope used to sail down the Tiber on a boat decorated with tapestries and flowers to the accompaniment of music and songs, and he personally followed the progress of the building work with the help of a prelate whom Michelangelo called 'Monsignor this and that'. In the field of urban development, Julius III merely continued the work begun by his predecessor without making any original contribution of his own. During the years of his papacy, Vignola, Ammannati, and Nanni di Baccio Bigio began their work, while Michelangelo produced the Belvedere staircase and prepared plans for the Gesù Church.

Casa Crivelli in Via dei Banchi Vecchi (1 cm = 1.7 m).

Antonio da Sangallo's Palazzetto in Via Giulia (1 cm = 3 m).

House known as that of Paul III's doctor in Via Giulia (1 cm = 1.7 m).

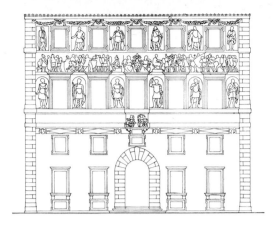

The papacy of Marcellus II lasted only a few short months, and the government of the church then passed to that champion of intransigent repression: Gian Pietro Carafa, the founder of the Congregation of Divine Love. He had remained in the shadow owing to Charles V's opposition to his views, but won his battle at the same time (1554–6) as Charles yielded to fatigue and discouragement and decided to dismember his empire by abdicating. Paul IV, who was of a French line by birth, linked his fate to that of Henri II, offering the king his unconditional support in exchange for the granting to his family of the territory of the Sienese Republic. From then on the Pope's only enemy was Spain, then ruled by Mary who, however, enjoyed the support of England. A Spanish army led by the Duke of Alba reached the gates of Rome, and once again the population was terrorized by the thought of a new sack. Meanwhile Emanuele Filiberto defeated the French at St. Quentin, and Henri II won Calais from the English. Then followed the peace of Cateau-Cambrésis (3 April 1559) which confirmed Spanish dominion over Italy. Again Rome was faced with devastation owing to the Pope's excessive interest in 'private' concerns. But this time the Pope was no longer a humanist who believed in enjoying life, but the intransigent champion of the Counter-Reformation and reorganizer of the Holy Inquisition, who did not fear to expose the church to this fresh humiliation.

The most outstanding example of the anti-reformist intransigence of Carafa, which developed into a real mania, was his persecution of Cardinals Morone and Pole, who were put on trial by the Inquisition. Morone was imprisoned in Castel S. Angelo and although all the evidence was in his favour, was held there until his death by the Pope who—putting scant trust in the divine inspiration of the conclave—feared lest his rival, the leader of the Erasmian movement, might be elected Pope. Pole was in England where he was dismissed from his post as legate and died in 1558 without seeing his name cleared.

In the urban sphere, the name of Paul IV has a sinister link with one of the most repressive of all civil institutions: the creation of the Jewish ghetto. Later revoked by Pius IV but re-established by Pius V, it continued to exist until the last century, forcing a continually growing community to endure a life of segregation in unhygienic and inhuman conditions. The papal bull establishing the ghetto was dated 14 July 1555 and decreed that 'Jews must live apart from Christians both in Rome and in all the other cities of the pontifical state'. In the same period, Sallustio Peruzzi was paid for *fabrica muri pro claudendo Judaeos*.

The most important initiative undertaken by the Pope at civic level was to renew the buildings of the University of Rome, and for this purpose he launched a competition. Towards the end of his papacy, Pirro Ligorio was commissioned to design a small house in the gardens of the Vatican; the house was completed only after the death of the Pope and was named Villa Pia.

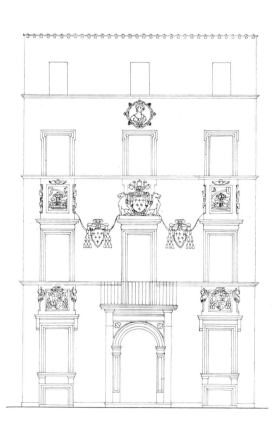

Pius IV, of the Milan branch of the Medici family, was elected in 1559 and immediately summoned Carlo Borromeo to serve as his Secretary of State. The tenacity and political ability of Borromeo, who was one of the fervent champions of the new counter-reformist attitude, rendered possible the early recall of the Council, which opened its doors at the beginning of 1562 and was dissolved finally two years later, after giving the church a new religious constitution.

The current relative calm of the political sphere and his own cultural ambitions enabled the Pope to make a notable contribution to the urban development of the city. To assist him in carrying out his programme, he had summoned to his side Michelangelo, to whom he entrusted not only the continuation of the rebuilding of St. Peter's, but also the construction of Porta Pia and the restoration of the church of S. Maria degli Angeli. The Pope's greatest achievement was to improve the layout of Via Pia, which comprised Via del Quirinale and Via XX Settembre and was intended to indicate the line of the city's expansion eastwards. With the Porta Pia as its background, this road served as an example and influenced the ideas on town planning held by Sextus V. To complete this development in communications, the Pope suggested that Michelangelo should join the Quirinale to Piazza Venezia by means of a monumental staircase. At the meeting of the people's council on 27 August 1558, the Curators proposed: '... since Trajan's column is one of the finest ancient monuments to be found in this city ... it seems fitting that the place where it stands should be adorned and beautified to correspond to its own beauty, and for this purpose a design has been submitted by Michelangelo, as your lordships will see, and in order that so praiseworthy a work should be put into effect, those who live in the vicinity are pleased to contribute half of the cost if the public contribute the other half, it being a public matter.' The cost was approved by eighty-six votes to four, but the work was never carried out.

In the architectural field, a contemplative archaeological style flourished briefly in the work of Pirro Ligorio, who completed the work begun by Bramante in the Belvedere and the little Villa Pia, and built the wonderful Villa Tiburtina for Cardinal Ippolito d'Este.

A clear indication of the future direction to be taken by Sextus V in the field of town planning can be found in the new square in front of St. John Lateran, and in the straightening of Via Merulana which links the churches of S. Maria Maggiore and S. Giovanni. The Borghi region in the neighbourhood of the Vatican was extended by the addition of Borgo Pio, thus completing the scheme conceived by Nicholas V.

FROM PHILOSOPHY TO RHETORIC

Architecture and Culture from 1527 to 1564

The terms of reference employed to describe the evolution of architectural ideas during the years of *plenitudo temporum* are valid for the second period of our story as well. Between 1527 and 1564 History, Nature, and Society continued to change in meaning as great hopes gradually crumbled and the terror of the Sack of Rome had to be overcome.

Now that the first generation of architects, including Giuliano da Sangallo and Bramante, had disappeared, it seemed at first that the important men of the second generation would all have to leave Rome to escape from the tragic economic and political situation created in 1527. Sansovino, Giulio Romano, and Sanmicheli left permanently and took with them to the north the fruits of the research and discoveries produced in the melting-pot of Rome in the 1520s. After a period of difficulty, Baldassarre Peruzzi returned from his wanderings for a time and gave the world his spiritual testament in the house he built for the Massimo family. Sangallo remained the undisputed leader in every great architectural initiative for almost twenty years, preaching the primacy of quantity over quality and developing a rhetorical method of functional architecture to suit the interests of the ruling class.

About halfway through the century, we see simultaneously the re-emergence of Michelangelo, the patriarch of the second generation, and the first appearance of the third: the generation of Vignola, Ammannati, Vasari, Pirro Ligorio, and Palladio, all born between 1507 and 1511. This simultaneity was, however, one of time only, since the meaning of Michelangelo's research was misunderstood by Ammannati, disputed by Ligorio, and substantially ignored by Vignola. It was easier for Michelangelo to strike up a dialogue with the very young architects, such as Tiberio Calcagni, born in 1532 and died prematurely, who was responsible for the execution of the most revolutionary vision conceived by Michelangelo, the Sforza Chapel in the church of S. Maria Maggiore.

The admiring circle of creative minds who had ensured the future of Bramante's ideas did not form around the ageing figure of Michelangelo. His admirers copied his anxiety superficially, while others created around him a void of admiration and reservations.

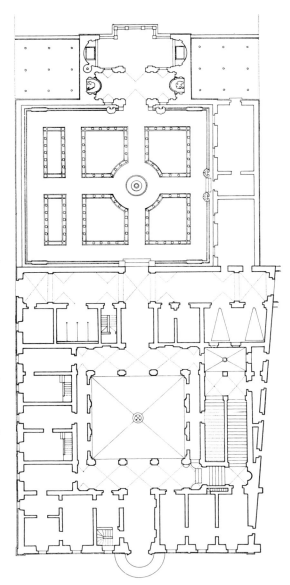

Plan of Palazzo Sacchetti in Via Giulia (1 cm = 5.4 m).

The Catholic Reformation, which was in the process of welding fifteen centuries of religious tradition into a major code of instruction, required artists to abandon critical humanism and devote themselves to the cult of form and correctness. Anxiety became an authorized component, provided it was exorcized at the instant of its appearance by external conformity to rules.

While eloquence attained the highest summits in quality, the role of the architect became more and more degraded as architecture became less an instrument of knowledge and evidence of social reality and more a means of reflecting and enhancing power, understood as an abstract and unchangeable value. There was a strong sense of continuity with the first period of sixteenth-century classicism, and certain problems relating to the universality of the language which had remained questionable became solved in the middle years of the century; but once its ideological basis and profound motivations were lost, classicism was imperceptibly transformed into a movement of revival, a sort of Neoclassicism. The rejection of Mannerism merely postponed the impending crisis, without eliminating its consequences.

We have already remarked on the fairly sharp pause which occurred in the Roman cultural debate at about the beginning of the fourth decade of the sixteenth century, when the defeat of the Erasmians and Paul III's departure from the attitude of benevolent tolerance he had shown towards heretics were ratified by the re-establishment of the Inquisition. The fate of critical humanism and intellectual liberty was then irrevocably sealed.

Of course, not even the Sack, in spite of the decimation of the population, the exodus from Rome, and the climate of frustration and fear, marked a clear break in the world of art. Some of the problems which had been debated in the years of *plenitudo temporum* continued to attract attention and study afterwards, even though an element of optimism no longer prevailed. Paul III's 'great policy' resulted in the recall to Rome of Bembo and Sadoleto, and in the same period, between 1534 and 1550, Claudio Tolomei, Annibal Caro, Vittoria Colonna, Della Casa, Aretino, Berni, and Speroni, all came to live in Rome.

The religious debate had an effect on the world of culture and had an indirect influence on architecture through the programme of reorganizing the church and finding new figurative terms in which to express a different outlook. Michelangelo was the one artist in Rome who was capable of translating into architectural terms the dreams which had erupted out of the contradictions inherent in Christian humanism. In his solitude, he became aware of the precarious and conventional nature of the instruments of the classical language; without abandoning them, he bent them to his own purpose, changing their laws of proportion and composition. Entrenched behind the prestige which had accrued to him through his work, now famous throughout Europe, the great sculptor accepted the terrible responsibility of continuing the work on the fabric of St. Peter's, but laid down the condition that he alone should be answerable for all decisions of an aesthetic nature. Of the new climate of the Counter-Reformation, he rejected both the moralistic functionalism, whereby the artist's role was reduced to that of an interpreter of preordained programmes, and the escapist illusion that architects could hope to continue building in a classical style without being put in the position of specialized, neutral intellectuals. Surrounded by those who chose not to recognize their 'loss of the centre' and those who took account of it only passively, abandoning themselves to current trends, Michelangelo stood alone in trying to recover the centre—which meant also becoming aware of the mobility and historical relativity of every 'centre'.

Through Vittoria Colonna, Michelangelo had come into contact with the followers of Erasmus, and shared with them the fragile hope of Christian intellectuals that the ideals of critical humanism might be preserved and a dialogue re-established with the Protestants. Once even this hope failed, there remained no other course open to him than an escape into mysticism. The vast architectural project which occupied Michelangelo's last years coincided paradoxically with this phase of extreme introversion. Called upon to make a constructive contribution to society, Michelangelo did what many of today's modern artists have done. He constructed by 'destroying', by questioning the dogmas and conventions accepted by a self-contemplative culture, cutting across distinctions of genres (for example, the traditional confines between sculpture and architecture, painting and sculpture) at the very moment when these distinctions were being consecrated by rigorous precepts, and demonstrating that the classical language contained within itself infinite possibilities for change, so that its death as dogma could signify a new and unexpected resurrection.

Through his profound religious experience, the late artistic work of Michelangelo could thus become a symbol of that 'Catholic reform', based on courage, sincerity, and dialogue, which was to flounder as an ephemeral and outmoded 'ideology' before the wave of the Counter-Reformation, where caution, hypocrisy, and the refusal to participate in a dialogue found a fertile soil.

The misfortune suffered by the figurative arts in the period of the Counter-Reformation as a result of the 'moralizing', anti-pagan crusade, had only a marginal effect on the world of architecture. For example, nothing similar to the famous dispute regarding the Last Judgement can be cited in relation to any building or church, while an event such as Ammannati's attempt to destroy his own works of pagan inspiration could not even be contemplated in the field of architecture, where no one thought of demolishing churches because they were too similar to pagan temples. The deviations in doctrine, historical inexactitude, offences against decorum and decency, for which Michelangelo was blamed by his critics— even such sensitive critics as Gilio who appreciated his original artistic gifts—related to the aspect of content insofar as figurative works were concerned, while the semantic content of architecture was obviously considered by the spokesmen for the new culture to be too slight, and in any case inoffensive. Just as architects did not reject the technical and formal advances made in Renaissance painting, so too they did not desire to return to the forms of medieval architecture by abandoning the laws of classicism. The most authoritative spokesman on the subject of architectural precepts was Cardinal Carlo Borromeo; in his *Instructiones Fabbricae Ecclesiasticae*, he gave official sanction in the words of the typical formula *non vetatur* to the permanent validity of the system of orders. In Chapter 34, he declares: *Non vetatur tamen pro fabbricae firmitudine, si ita architectonica ratio aliquando postulat, aliqua structura generis vel dorici, vel ionici, vel corinthii, vel alterius huiusmodi operis.* Even the arguments submitted by Borromeo against the central type of composition were not based on compulsion and were motivated by historical considerations (*Illa porro aedificii rotundi species olim idolorum templis in usu fuit, sed minus usitata in populo christiano*, Inst. II). In fact, it was just at the time of the Counter-Reformation that Cataneo and Palladio declared in their treatises that the central plan was particularly well-suited to the Christian church for symbolic reasons, and their opinions were not challenged or censured.

However, the privileged position which architects seemed to enjoy as a result of the liberty conceded to them and the official recognition of their artistic autonomy was only illusory, because it was impossible to continue the process of research, which had flourished under the Renaissance, in the sphere of the problems set by patrons and the role of architecture in its cultural context.

Confining ourselves to the situation in Rome, the change which had occurred in papal policy radically altered the function of architecture in the process of developing the urban nucleus. From the ambitious plan to raise the state to a position of political power, based on an alliance with European high finance, to the reality of submission to feudal Spain, the transition was sudden and alarming. From an affirmation of the universal role of the church through her achievements in culture and through the myth of renewal, artists were now engaged in exalting her power and prestige.

Architecture was no longer required to represent the universalist ideology in abstract form or to perpetuate the myth of renewal; but to participate with all the technical means and stylistic discoveries at its command in aiding the reorganization of the church.

The interpretation of the classical language in relation to Christian civilization also changed gradually, with the result that architects came to find instruments in their hands which were identical in form but changed in meaning. Classical terms ceased to be abstract instruments of philosophical cognition, and became the rhetorical means of concrete application. Ancient architecture thus no longer appeared as a totality and philosophy, as it had done to Alberti, but as a technique; this enabled Vignola to isolate the orders from their religious context and illustrate them systematically in their autonomous reality.

Between the classicism of the first decades of the century and the Neoclassicism of the mid-century, there was reproduced the antinomy between philosophy and rhetoric to which Pico referred in his letter to Ermolao Barbaro in 1485: 'O my Ermolao,' wrote Pico, 'I am not sure that I have understood you. Your style is sublime. I and our Poliziano often read those of your letters which we can have sent to us or to others, and the new ones must fight to cast out the old. You draw the mind of the reader where you will. And now I am here thinking about one of your recent letters where you pour scorn on those barbarous philosophers who because of their rough, uncultured, and squalid style, neither lived when alive nor will live when they are dead. Or else will live condemned and vilified. How affected I became, and ashamed, and repentant of my studies! I begin to think that the sixty years spent on them would have been better spent doing nothing. What can be done? It seems that by studying Thomas (Aquinas), Duns Scotus, Alberto, Averroes, I have lost my best years and many sleepless nights when I might perhaps have achieved something in good literature. Yet, to find consolation, I asked myself: but, suppose one of them returned to the world, would he not find something to set against such arguments? And then it seemed to me that one of the not least eloquent of them would thus have defended the least barbarously possible his barbarisms: "We, O Ermolao, were famous when we were alive and after our deaths will live not in the schools of grammarians and in colleges, but in the circles of philosophers, in the meeting places of learned men, where the discussion does not centre on the mother of Andromache and the sons of Niobe or other such anecdotes. But centres on the debate *de humanarum divinarumque rerum rationibus*."

'In considering, discussing, and explaining these matters, we were so subtle, penetrating, shrewd, that if anything our sin was to absorb knowledge too eagerly. But can one sin by seeking too hard for the truth? If someone were to accuse us of lassitude or slackness, let him make enquiries and he will see that if we barbarians lacked eloquence, we did not lack wisdom. Not having the latter joined to the former is as much exempt from blame as perhaps it is blameworthy to have them joined. For who would not condemn in an honest virgin coquetry and adornment? The contrast between the orator and the philosopher is such that it could not be greater. For what is the office of the rhetorician but to lie, deceive, cheat, embroil? What in short is eloquence if not pure mendacity, imposture, deceit?'

The reduction of the role of architecture from a form of philosophy to rhetoric, which characterizes the middle years of the century, coincides in the literary sphere with the questioning of the validity of Platonism and of the new Scholasticism and Aristotelianism. Aristotle's *Poetics*, a text which had met with scant favour in humanist circles and was criticized by Ludovico Vives as being 'entirely devoted to the consideration of old poems and those ineptitudes in which the Greeks are so tiresome', suddenly became a 'best-seller', and between 1540 and 1550 ran into five editions: one printed in Basle, one in Paris, one in Lyons, one in Florence, and a fifth edited by Francesco Robertello, which was destined to exert a great influence on Italian culture.

Robertello viewed the text of Aristotle as a cultural instrument which was able to direct the arts towards 'a certain reason and norm'—a sort of scientific theory of literature which would make it possible to pass from the imitation of ancient texts to the definition of method. But the reason why great interest was aroused in the book just at that time should be sought in Aristotle's discussion of the morality of art and its relationship to the passions. His consideration of the problem of catharsis and the effect of the work of art upon those who experience it moved the analysis of artistic creation away from a search for perfection based on the relationship between the work of art and its creator to a consideration of its social function and usefulness.

Together with the *Poetics*, the *Rhetoric* of Aristotle was at the centre of literary discussion in the second half of the sixteenth century. By the side of the courageous attitude of Patrizi, who in his ten dialogues *Della Retorica* (Venice, 1562) stated the view that the rhetoric of classical writers was unsuited to modern times because of the different social and political situation, we find a number of works in which a comparison is made between the Greek and Roman traditions, praising Aristotle to the detriment of Cicero. Speroni's *Dialogo delle Lingue* is particularly interesting for the lively and full discussion which takes place between his two masters: Bembo and Pomponazzi. Whereas the former reaffirms the ideals of classicism, introducing the clear distinction between the physical quality of language and style as a literary and poetical factor, Pomponazzi open-mindedly espouses the cause of 'anti-classicism'. 'I am firmly of the opinion,' Speroni makes him say, 'that the study of the Latin and Greek tongues is a cause of ignorance. We lose countless years in miserably learning those two languages, not because of their intrinsic greatness, but simply because we turn ourselves to the study of words against the natural inclination of our human intellect, which is desirous of pausing in the cognition of those things through which it becomes perfect, not content with being bent in another direction, and therefore by adorning the tongue with pretty words and trifles, our mind remains empty.'

Manifestations of an independent viewpoint and opposition to academic classicism appeared in architecture also—we need only consider the passage in Alvise Cornaro's treatise where he makes a claim for the merits of comfort as opposed to courtly magnificence—but the exceptional career of Michelangelo and the courageous experimentation of Ammannati in Palazzo Firenze so far had only a very slight effect on the Roman climate.

The most pertinent aspects of the dispute concerning rhetoric were therefore not related to polemics or innovation, but to technique, and were directed to a re-evaluation of metaphor and symbol and a complete return to classical formative methods. The opposition revealed in the dialogues by Tomitano, *Della lingua toscana*, between Paolo Manuzio who defends Cicero, and his interlocutor who regards him as a pygmy against the Hercules Aristotle, represents the contrast between two generations who have formed from the classical language two radically diverse instruments. The new generation valued technical refinement more highly than ingenuity, just as Vignola might have contrasted his elegant staircase at Caprarola with the unresolved contradictions in Bramante's spiral staircase in the Belvedere.

The validity of the comparison between the methods of rhetoric and those of the architectonic language is attested in a very revealing passage in Tomitano's dialogues: 'These are', he writes, 'the foundations of the rhetorical fabric and the doors as I have described. After these follow the walls above ground which have as their stones works, broad and narrow, illustrious and vulgar, pure and elegant, severe and pleasing, free and tamed, tardy and swift. And like marble which accompanies stones to make the palace more illustrious and magnificent, so, too, by adding adornment to words does discourse become magnified and illustrious. Such are figures, lights, colours, and other similar things.

'The building is given various apartments for different purposes and uses; so too is discourse, by means of its arangement, varying its parts, members, examples, and artifices. Style is the text formed by the words, conceits and aphorisms are the beams which support the structure of the roof. Number is the harmony which is perceived there. But Diligence is that trusted negotiator to whose alertness the governing of all matters is committed. She makes impossible things possible, difficult things easy, hard things soft, obscure things luminous, doubtful things manifest, confused things distinct...

'The fourth Idea, or column of the fabric of the discourse, will be Beauty of speech. Here it would be necessary to have beauty in eloquence itself, so as to express its ornaments one by one. This is a matter for diligent study, bringing due proportion and beauty to all our compositions. Discourse receives from her those instruments which make it appear so pleasing and refined to our ears; in the judgement of men of understanding there is discovered in her a precise and graceful manner, so that in the presence of the listeners every term of gentle gladness takes its place. She tempers bombast of speech, removing the foul impurity of vulgar, plebeian words, and correcting every effect of ugliness in discourse. Her conceits and aphorisms are those which were given to the other Ideas, but with a wonderful beauty arranged; wherefore the discourse with its own essence and colour appears to be filled and uncoloured. She glows with her own light and by her beauty the other forms of speech are made beautiful and admirable. To her are referred those words which contain exquisite grace, intelligible brevity, frank sincerity and comely charm.'

The man of letters who best exemplified the newly-created encounter between literary and artistic culture was Claudio Tolomei. In completely new terms he approached, not the Pope as his predecessors had done, but an aristocrat, Agostino de' Landi, and suggested that he should commission a cultural project directed to the divulgation and systematization of the heritage of classical architecture. The analogy with the programme suggested to Pope Leo X by Castiglione and Raphael is evident but it is an analogy in form only. The political motivations and optimism which had inspired the earlier generation had now gone, and had been replaced by an attitude of rigorous, almost bureaucratic detachment, led by deductive arguments to the absurd suggestion that the text of Vitruvius should be translated into Ciceronian Latin. However, there was nothing surprising in such an idea, since it was held by a man who was determined to seize an opportunity to graft a quantitative metre of classical origin onto the vulgar tongue. In Rome, Tolomei founded after 1540 the Academy of Virtue, or Vitruvian Academy, about which unfortunately we know very little except that it was certainly the meeting place for all the most important Roman architects of the time, among them Jacopo Barozzi da Vignola, who though still young had already distinguished himself. The plan to work together as a team described in the letter of 14 November 1542 was probably the original idea behind the founding of the academy and is summarized here in Tolomei's own words.

'Firstly, therefore, a Latin book will be made, where by means of full notes all the difficult parts of Vitruvius which it is possible to understand will be clarified; and those in particular appertaining to the rules of architecture, drawing diagrams where it might be necessary for the greater clarity of those places. And since the writings of Vitruvius are very varied, both printed books and written manuscripts, this often gives rise to confusion and obscurity: therefore a work of annotation will be made of the various texts, which are remarkably divergent and of some importance, with the decisions as to which reading has been found most pleasing and for what reasons; intending later to print an edition of Vitruvius based on those texts which will be rightly approved. It is certain that Vitruvius made numerous diagrams, so that certain parts of his work might be better understood, and placed them at the end of each book; as he testifies many times. But just as countless other ancient books have been lost, so these too have not come to light. With this in mind, they intend to renew all the diagrams, drawing them with the utmost beauty and refinement possible, correcting those parts where Giocondo erred, and adding many others to them in places that are not now there; which things greatly assist our understanding of this author.

'Vitruvius used numerous Greek and Latin expressions, which to other ears appear new and rarely heard. Therefore for the benefit of those who study this book, a very plain Latin vocabulary will be made, listing in alphabetical order all the Latin expressions, especially those containing some doubt and obscurity. And since this author is full of Greek expressions, especially those relating to the orders and rules of Greek architecture, another list of Greek expressions will be made, expounding them later in Latin words; then countless expressions of Vitruvius which now appear obscure will become clear, and the explanations will also include their derivations and etymologies.

'To some people the manner of speaking of Vitruvius often appears strange; being very far from that used by Caesar and Cicero, and other good Roman writers; therefore a Latin work will be made of the modes of speech of Vitruvius; there it will be seen whether the many harsh expressions of which he is accused can be defended from the example of other good writers, and those which will not have this defence will be noted as personal and peculiar to his own mode of speech.

'This question has aroused the desire to see whether Vitruvius could be translated into a clearer and more purified Latin, coming as close as possible to the words, the fluency, and the texture of those other good Latin writers: which thing if successful will be most beautiful, seeing Vitruvius cease to be harsh and rough, and become pleasing and well-rounded.

'Matters relating to architecture are greatly desired, and practised today by men who have not much knowledge of the Latin tongue, such as sculptors, painters, master wood-carvers, and ordinary architects. For this reason Vitruvius has so far been translated at least three times from Latin into the vernacular, but so strangely, and with such rough and involved words and expressions, that without a doubt he can much less easily be understood in the vernacular than in Latin. This has occurred because those translators did not know the correct rules, and the right method of transferring one language into another; apart from the fact that many passages, being difficult, were not understood by them. Therefore this useful work will be done again, translating Vitruvius into the beautiful Tuscan language, and trying to do it in such a way that if he is so difficult because of the subtlety of his thought, at least he should not be coarse because of the roughness and complexity of his words.

'In addition, another useful task will be done, making a Tuscan vocabulary in alphabetical order of architectural terms, so that all parts should be given their common and true name: and where in the vernacular anything does not have a name, it will be added and will be formed by common agreement, taking care to derive it from good sources, and in correct form. Such a thing is permissible to all authors in the expressions which relate to the art itself. And in this way it will be seen widely how Greek and Latin architectural terms can comfortably fit into the Tuscan tongue. This labour will be very useful to those who may desire to speak or write about this art in the vernacular. And for greater clarity and usefulness another vocabulary will be made in the vernacular in the order of instruments or parts, as for example, taking the column together with its base and its capital; illustrating it as a figure each one of its members should be described separately; like the base, the cornice, the taurus, the fillet, and so on. In this way, by looking at the diagram, one will immediately know the name of each of its parts.

'Then follows the task of connecting the words of Vitruvius with examples of works; this book will be very useful and fine, because where Vitruvius states a rule, or an order of architecture, in this book it will be shown where such an order may be observed in ancient buildings; and finding that the architect has departed from it in some other building, it will warn him of it, explaining why the rules given by Vitruvius have not been observed in that place: so in a sense practice will be joined to theory, and one will be led to beautiful and useful contemplation.

'In viewing the buildings of Rome with respect to their architecture, another no less useful or beautiful study will be made, to consider and understand the antiquities in the light of their history; there the original square form of Rome will be clearly shown, and the addition made to it from time to time, looking for those doors and roads about which information may be obtained, and also the temples, porticos, theatres and amphitheatres, the courts, basilicas, arches, circuses, bridges, and every other kind of building of which any vestige remains; throwing light also on many others which have entirely disappeared, and pointing out where they used to be. And in short omitting no part where history can elucidate truth. Explaining in which periods they were made, and for what use they served;

stated and expounded in the work in good order, these matters will bring pleasure to our understanding and usefulness to our knowledge of them: when apart from adding to our knowledge of these respected relics, they will clarify many obscure passages in the works of Greek and Latin poets and historians and orators. There will be added to the aforementioned books a most beautiful and useful work, containing drawings of all the Roman antiquities, as well as some which are outside Rome, about which we possess some knowledge through their fragments. There they will show diagrammatically all the plans, the outlines and perspectives, in many other parts, as necessary, adding their correct and true measurements according to the length of the Roman foot, with a note on its proportion in relation to the measurements of our own times. And close to the said diagrams two explanations will be given: one by way of history, showing what building it was, and by whom and for whom it was made. And the other by way of architecture, expounding the laws and the rules and the orders of that building; if done diligently, apart from its usefulness to all architects, this thing will in a sense draw out of the grave the Rome which is now dead and bring her to a new life, if not so beautiful as before, at least with some semblance or image of beauty.

'To some it will appear that such an undertaking is too vast and too difficult, and that it embraces too many things, which could never be brought to a conclusion, besides the fact that some parts will be obscure, so that it will be impossible to illustrate them in any way.

'But when he knows that not one, but several fine minds have been directed to this noble task, and that each one has his own particular duty assigned to him, then he will be no more amazed, I believe, than one is amazed at seeing work going on in a big city at a hundred or more arts at one and the same time. When every heavy weight is divided into many parts it becomes light also. Therefore by dividing these tasks among so many learned men, there is no doubt that in less than three years the whole work will be brought to a conclusion. And let no one think that they are so bold as to imagine they can illustrate those things in which no spark or seed of life remains; but they think that those things which still preserve some breath of life should not be allowed to be buried by the injuries of time or the darkness of ignorance.'

Most of Giulio Romano's mature works were produced in Mantua, far from the society of Rome, and impinged on Roman culture only indirectly. This left a significant gap, to be shared between the generation of Vignola (1507), Ligorio (1510), Ammannati and Vasari (1511), and the ageless Michelangelo, who brought his disturbing presence and the rebellious gestures of a great man who had outlived the period of humanism to the lives of these 'young sages'. Vignola and Ligorio represent the two opposing forces in the continuation of the culture of classicism. The former deliberately attached himself to Bramante through the pragmatism of Sangallo, while the latter did not conceal his predilection for Raphael and Peruzzi. But this continuity was in any case a matter of deliberate choice, since the requirements of patrons and the very function of architecture had changed so profoundly that any connection in form or taste were rendered illusory.

Vignola grew up in the climate of the Vitruvian academy: with different methods he faced a task similar to the one Raphael had set himself, but at a purely artistic level and without political overtones. The result was neither an archaeological *corpus* nor a humanistic compendium in the manner of Alberti, but simply *La Regola* (The Rule): this was the most successful and elementary of all the treatises, and became the catechism of architectonic doctrine, reducing all the contradictory theoretical and practical heritage of classical architecture to a closed and immutable system. The pivot of Vignola's system of construction was the module, a relational and therefore universal unit of measurement as compared with such conventional units as the foot or arm which varied from region to region. By entirely ignoring any reference to local traditions and putting forward proportional systems based on the recurrence of multiples of a value related to, and coinciding with, a real element in the same system—the half-diameter of a column—Vignola succeeded in writing the most universal of the books on architecture. This work became the handbook of correct form, and was destined to fulfil a function which continuously evolved as it was adapted to the outlook of the Mannerist, Baroque, Neoclassical, and Academic architects.

The distance between Vignola and Alberti is great, and only partly to be explained through the point of view of the different aims of the two authors. The return to a didactic type of artistic literature, in which particular rules or notions seemed to require the context of a generalized framework, defined the level of weariness into which the humanist debate had declined. Architecture—in this debate—had figured as the model of a structural order analogous to that of philosophical thought; it had a part in that generalized intellectual movement for clarity and logical systematization. Yet it would be entirely wrong to think that Vignola wanted to reduce architectural design to a flat assembly of the types of composition minutely described in his book. The key to an understanding of Vignola's theory is to be found in Vasari's definition of the rule contained in the prologue to the third part of his *Lives*. 'The rule in architecture was thus the method of measuring the antiquities in a search for absolute values', he wrote, adding, 'to attain perfection a licence will be necessary, which though not being of the rule, would be governed by the rule and could stand without causing confusion and spoiling the order.' It is clear that, however it may be interpreted, the programme of 'manner' presupposes a secure grasp of the rule as being indispensable to that subtle transgression which enlivens but does not subvert the order, in which such a programme is effected. In the architecture of Vignola there are frequent cases of licence and no lack of stylistic inventions, but the rule is always present in the manifest correctness of the fundamental principles.

In the work of Pirro Ligorio the presence of the classical tradition is almost overwhelming. As an antiquarian by profession, every decision he made was conditioned by his knowledge of the classical world, and this gave him the assurance that he could make new discoveries and develop the classical forms in an original way. Nurtured in a literary and mythological culture, he fought for a programme of the correct codification and decodification of images. He was fascinated by the possibility that decoration could be used to add an allegorical dimension to a building and transform it into a parable, rich in allusions and ambiguities; so he became the poet of lyrical escapism. But the most important aspect of Ligorio's contribution to architecture concerns his relationship to nature. In this sphere, the 'architectonic' waters of the Villa d'Este represented the antiquarian's artistic consecration of a taste which had grown more widespread in Rome ever since the first half of the century, as we learn from letters by illustrious writers.

Caro wrote to Monsignor Guidiccione in 1538: 'I shall not describe to Your Holiness the artifice of making the water rise, although it appears to me the most remarkable thing that exists, since (as you write) you have water with the fall and with its natural course; and the arrangement of the remainder derives from this in every detail. At the head of a large pergola, Monsignore has made a rugged wall of a certain stone which in Rome is named *asprone*, a kind of black, porous tufa; and certain masses are placed one above the other haphazardly, or more precisely, with a kind of disordered order, which make projections in one place and cavities in another where plants are to be placed; and the whole wall together has the appearance of a rugged and bevelled antiquity. A door is let into the middle of this wall, leading to a passage containing a few rooms; it is also rusticated on the sides and has overhanging stones above, so that it is more like the entrance to a grotto than anything else; and on either side of the door in each corner is a fountain; and the appearance of the one on the right is as follows. It is cast at one time of the same stones between the two walls which form the angle, with rocks protruding beyond the angle around two arms, and beneath it is a niche made also with protruding stones, as if it were a piece of hollowed mountainside. Inside this niche is placed an antique basin, upon two plinths, with heads of lions, which acts as the basin of the fountain. Above the basin, between its inner edge and the wall of the niche, extends a river of marble with an urn under the arm; and below the basin another receptacle of water, like those in the Belvedere, but round to serve as a recess. The other fountain on the left side has the surface, the niche, the basin, the receptacle below the basin, and the whole almost identical to the other, except that where the former has the river above the basin, this one has an expanse of water almost an arm and a half in diameter, with a background of shingle clearly outlined, and along the banks certain small caverns as if they were hollowed out by the water: and in this guise appear both fountains. Now I will relate how the water comes to each one, and the effects it creates. Inside the wall described, more than a rod in height, is a tank or reservoir full of water, serving both these fountains; and from here, through lead pipes which can be opened and closed, the water is brought and taken away in each one, and to the one on the right side this is done as follows. Its pipe is divided in two, and the one which is larger leads a great source of water inside, right up to the edge of the river described; thence, issuing forth, it meets the obstacle of certain small rocks, which breaking it, make it create a greater noise and splash over a wider area, and one part falls straight down to the ground, while the other runs along the bed of the river, and in running overflows in many places, and tumbling noisily through all of them flows into the basin, and from the basin (full as it is) circles right round the edge and falls into the lower receptacle. The other part of this pipe, which is a small pipe, carries the water over the surface of the niche, where there is a basin which is perforated in several places, and through these holes, through certain small channels, are sent only drops of water over the surface, and from here in drops, like rain, they fall into the basin, and in falling pass through some white patches of congealed water, which are found in the Tivoli fall, which are adapted to it in such a way that it seems that the drops of water have naturally congealed there. And so between the noise of rushing from above and the running in all directions a beautiful sight and loud murmur are created. The fountain on the left side has the pipe divided into two parts also; and the smaller part, just as has been said of the other, leads the water above to make the same rain through the same patches, and fall into the basin in the same way. But the other larger part of this pipe leads it into the expanse of water described, and here it separates into several branches: whence gushing impetuously, it finds the basin of the expanse of water which obstructs it, and breaking it makes a very beautiful gurgling and splashing entirely similar to the rising of a source of natural water. When the sea is full, the water falls in a thousand places into the basin, and from the basin through a thousand others into the last receptacle. And thus between the raining, the gurgling, and the pouring of one and the other, apart from the seeing, a very pleasing and almost harmonious feeling is created, since to the murmuring of both there is joined another sound, which is heard but one does not notice from where it comes; because inside between the reservoir and the niches over each of them are artfully placed some clay pots, large and slender with a wide belly and narrow mouth in guise of cauldrons, or rather storage jars. The water from the reservoir pouring into these pots, before it reaches the aforesaid basins, falls into them from above, restricted and with such an impetus that it makes a great noise on its own and by its multiple echo it becomes much louder still. The reason is that the pots have holes in the middle so fill up only as far as the middle, and being placed with their bottom in balance, they do not touch at almost any point. So that between their suspension and their concavity they make the thunderous noise I have described; which is prolonged and deep, and carries farther than those outside, and joins itself to them in the manner of a double-bass, replying to them in the same proportion as the crumhorn replies to the bagpipes. So much for the sound.

'But a no less beautiful effect is created for the sight; because as well as the site being spacious and well-proportioned, it has on the sides espaliers of ivy and jasmine, and above some pilasters adorned with other greenery, a vine pergola, so splendid and dense, that by its height it has a noble air; and by its thickness it has an opaque and dread quality, which contains something of the elements of privacy and dignity together. One then sees around the water fountains little fish, corals, rocks; in the cavities, little crabs, mother-of-pearl, snails; on the shores, shells, millepedes, moss and other water grasses. I have forgotten to speak of the lowest receptacles under each of the two fountains; when they are full, in order that they should not overflow, there is an open water-pipe a finger's breadth below the top edge through which it flows out and enters a small sluice which carries it to the river. And in this guise the fountains of my Monsignore are made. Regarding the one by the Sienese in Via del Popolo, if I do not see it, I cannot trust myself to write of it. The more so since I have never seen it play, and do not know the ways of the water.'

Ligorio added to the gardens recalled by Caro and Tolomei an allegorical dimension and a geometrical structure adapted to the natural form of the landscape. He drew his inspiration from Hadrian's Villa, although without changing the very free composition, based on continuously varied axes and a free assembly of autonomous symmetrical units. A number of preconceived ideas prevented him from fully realizing the possibilities of Roman naturalism, which strangely enough occurs in those years only in the work of a brilliant dilettante, in the sacred wood of Bomarzo. The ecstasy of movement and light created in the water spectacles of the Roman villas, even though in a rigid and inhibited form, anticipates the emergence of the naturalistic movement. The animistic view of nature, stated in *De rerum Natura iuxta propria principia* by Bernardino Telesio (1509-88), almost a contemporary of Pirro Ligorio, may perhaps be the hidden source of inspiration for the Villa d'Este.

THE MATURE WORKS OF PERUZZI

'Then came the year 1527, in the cruel Sack of Rome, and Baldassarre was taken prisoner by the Spaniards and not only lost all his possessions, but was also greatly tormented and tortured, because having a grave, noble, and gracious appearance, they took him for some great prelate in disguise or some other man who could pay a large ransom. But finally when those impious barbarians found that he was a painter, one of them, who was a great favourite of Bourbon, made him paint a portrait of that evil captain, the enemy of God and men ... After this, Baldassarre being released from their hands he embarked for Porto Ercole and thence to Siena. But on the way he was robbed and despoiled of all his belongings, and had to go to Siena in his shirt.'

More than for the other architects of his generation, for Peruzzi the Sack constituted a traumatic experience, destined to have a profound effect on his whole outlook. As early as 1530, however, after a period of travelling in Tuscany and Emilia, we find Peruzzi engaged in the construction of the castle of Rocca Sinibalda outside Rome; two years later he began work on the Palazzo Massimi, and in 1534 Paul III confirmed his appointment as architect to St. Peter's, together with Antonio da Sangallo the Younger. Peruzzi died in 1536, possibly poisoned, in precarious financial circumstances at the age of fifty-five; he left unfinished an illustrated edition of Vitruvius and a work on the ancient buildings of Rome.

The palazzo built for the Massimi family, constructed probably in the last two years of Peruzzi's life, may for its poetic intensity and extraordinary wealth of ideas be considered his spiritual testament. It represented his attempt to incorporate in one work the result of long and intense periods of meditation into the forms and meanings of classical antiquity and into the possibility of a new kind of architecture which would be profoundly imbued with the ideals of classicism but rooted in a spirit of 'courtesy' and restless curiosity, in a series of values which could be termed 'historical' insofar as they appertained to his own time—the time, that is, of that generation of intellectuals who were heirs to the great hopes of humanism and had been affected by the 'great fear' aroused by the break in the political balance of power and the religious unity of Europe.

The new palazzo was built on the same site and conformed to the same spirit as the old 'palace of the portico' built around the mid-fifteenth century. The site was longitudinal in form, with an average width of about 23 metres, so that it was not possible to build on a monumental scale; it was even difficult to adopt the much-favoured 'palazzetto' with central *cortile* surrounded by the plain blocks of the building. From the first, Peruzzi aimed to imbue his subject with a monumental spirit by introducing a qualitative density to compensate for the modest dimensions of the site.

After trying to treat the façade as a flat surface and to accept for the courtyard the form imposed by the irregular shape of the plot, the architect evolved a highly original solution. The façade is gently curved, bringing together two lateral lines, the corridor giving access is no longer axially placed, but is connected tangentially to the area of the *cortile*, and in the irregular area of the remainder of the plot a staircase is arranged longitudinally. This ingenious arrangement corresponds to a spatial organism which is full of novelty and surprise. The continuing alteration in the predominant axes of the individual sections, arranged in sequence, induces the effect of an uninterrupted narration, maintained at a virtuoso level of intensity. Viewed from afar, either lengthwise or at a tangent, the colonnade takes on the function of a symbolic anticipation of this spatial effect; in fact, since it is illuminated in a way which is homogeneous with the courtyard, it represents a connecting element at the centre of the façade between the interior and exterior, and through its convexity and 'unfolding' motion expresses the dialectical relationship between private space and urban space.

Having passed through the colonnade, its transversal development in relation to the axis of penetration creates a visual, bilateral expansion (*diastole*). The long corridor leading to the *cortile* introduces an interval of suspension (*systole*) into the sequence, and this in turn is subtly modified by the decoration of the barrel-vaulting towards which the bare walls seem to lead the eye of the viewer. Once in the courtyard, the view again broadens and arouses a new interest, like an unexpected dramatic happening.

But immediately below the colonnade, there appears the complex and intimately dialectical nature of the courtyard, where the terminal effect of the first order is counterbalanced by the lateral recession of the upper levels, and the closure of the upper levels in the background wall is counterbalanced by the opening of the large loggias on the opposite side. This extremely complex image would appear to be dominated by a series of firm structural references, but absorbs the attention of the viewer to such an extent that he is unable to grasp them. The architect is at one time the author and the 'executant' in a musical sense, both the constructor and producer of his work. In this programme light plays a dominant role. Architecture has to become transparent, as permeable to the view as to light; the difficulty represented by the confined space has to be overcome, or even reversed, by means of artifice. The basic expedient implicit in the design consists of the use of rays of light to accentuate the chiaroscuro effect. The columns are perpetually half immersed in shadow and half in light, except where the rays of the sun fall on them directly. In addition to these beams of light, dazzling light effects are introduced elsewhere also: the barrel-vaults over the two ground-floor loggias contain perforations which are similar to those found in Roman *crypto-portici*, so that the stucco decorations stand out in relief and allow the light to penetrate. This magical light, that of the *crypto-portici*, throws the vault into relief, giving it the appearance of a plastic mass, and has been re-evoked by that ardent student of ruins, Peruzzi, to bring to the heart of the city an 'emotion' of antiquity.

The exciting journey continues, past the entrance to the courtyard, and on towards the second small courtyard or the staircase, with its landings projecting onto the loggias.

The choice of the stylistic features and methods of composition found in classical repertory is handled by Peruzzi with a sureness and independence of judgement which reflect not only his familiarity with the ancient world, but also a 'modern' sensibility. His classical studies resulted in the free and 'critical' use of the knowledge he had acquired. The architect seems less concerned with achieving an abstract coherence of style than with the exciting possibilities of the individual project, and the unrepeatable individuality of every spatial situation. In the colonnade, he employs an anomalous Doric order without metopes or triglyphs, and this problem is resolved in the entablature in a highly calculated linear continuity. In this context of a Doric ornamentation, he then inserts the carefully contrived Ionic doorway, which closely resembles the model of Vitruvius.

In the courtyard, the Doric columns are treated more massively while the entablature is simplified by the abolition of the frieze to convey an anomalous impression of the triglyph in its subtly rhythmed guttae. The rejection of the archway framed by the order syntagma and the choice of trabeated orders forms a contrast with the barrel-vault of the colonnade at ground level, so creating a proportional hiatus which is successfully resolved by the spaces created by the perforations. All the stylistic choices are subordinated to the exigencies of the general transparent structure, and whether they are based on the rules or the exceptions to the classical norms, they are always directly motivated, without any element of artistic caprice. Even the little staircase windows, which like those of the façade mezzanines are cut into a rimless plaster cartouche, seem to have been created with spontaneous irony out of the difficulty of this situation.

The most radical innovations in the Palazzo Massimo are to be found in the façade. It is here, in fact, that the typological discoveries of the first three decades of the century, which had contributed so greatly to spreading a knowledge of classical culture, were radically re-examined. Against Sangallo's model of continuous superimposed bands terminated by a frame (cornices + rusticated quoins) and Bramante's model of a rhythmical order rest-

Transversal section of Palazzo Massimo (1 cm = 2.5 m).

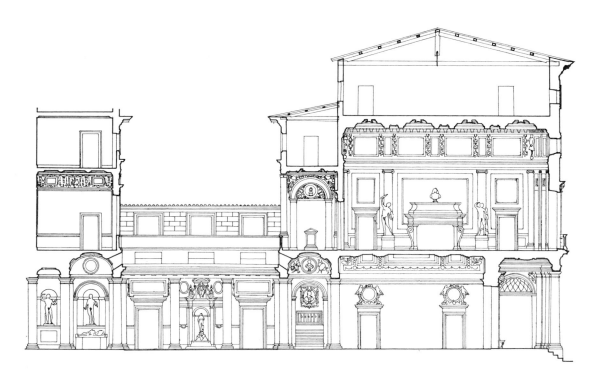

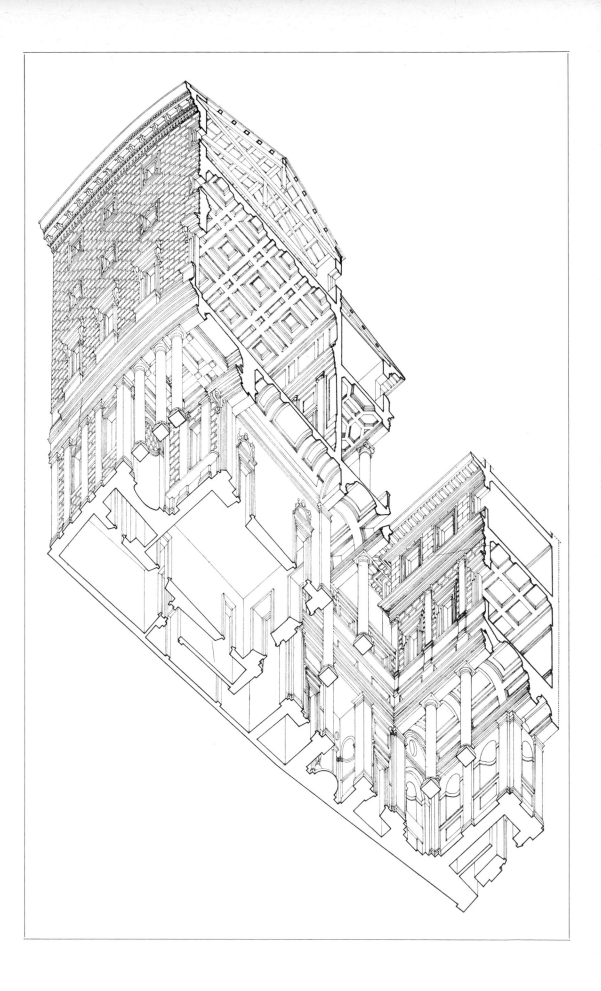

ing on a continuous base, Peruzzi took a third course: that of rejecting a perspective closure and choosing open continuity. Viewed from the street, at an axis with the palazzo, the façade has the appearance of a continuous ribbon endowed with an aesthetic character which is perfectly successful even though the entire length of the building cannot be apprehended at one glance. At the end of the façade, the protruding curve, observed from the original viewpoint, gives the palazzo the semblance of an isolated cylinder.

In view of the fact that two of Peruzzi's pupils, Serlio and Cataneo, both wrote in favour of the cylindrical palazzo, it may be supposed that it was Peruzzi who inspired this model and that he wished to suggest it in perspective in the Palazzo Massimo. In its original position in the town, it was much less visible than it is now and the best points from which to view it were then on the axis and tangentially. There was no point at which it was possible to view comfortably the whole extent of the façade. Once an immediate visual contact with the palazzo had been formed, the impression of a continuous convex building must in any case have been predominant. The fact that the curvature was not based on the arc of a circle but on a mixture of two right-angles and an arc was dictated by the need to avoid angular joins with the sides of the street, which would have resulted in both a waste of space and a break in the continuity of the street.

Having established the principle of the indefinite continuity of the rhythmical sequence, Peruzzi concentrated his whole attention on the vertical accentuation of superimposed plastic elements. The windows of the *piano nobile* acquire a primary structural function by being placed with their protruding bases onto the Doric cornice, while the windows of the other floors suggest this same rhythm in a less marked form, being almost reabsorbed in the uniform rhythm of the rustication. The cornices of the two mezzanines acquire in this context the quality of variations on a single theme, stated plainly, expanded, and taken up again in a simplified and compressed form below the cornice. After the harmonic experiments of the first decades of the century, this return to a melodic treatment in the Palazzo Massimo indicated Peruzzi's distance from the path initiated by Sangallo and suggested that classical culture could be developed in an anti-academic and anti-rigorous sense— although diverging sharply from northern and Manneristic developments. This method became a point of reference for the following generation, especially for Pirro Ligorio and Vignola; but no one else was capable of deciphering in all its complexity and richness the art of Peruzzi, that unrepeatable harmony in which 'staging' is accorded with structure, courtesy with decorum, research with invention, anxiety with hope.

CLASSICISM AS MANNER

The Works of Antonio da Sangallo's Maturity

In the years 1527–30, Antonio da Sangallo was employed mainly as a military architect outside Rome: at Ancona, at Orvieto where he built the famous Well of S. Patrizio, and at Loreto where he continued the work of Bramante and Sansovino. In 1530 he built the Cesi Chapel in the church of S. Maria della Pace—one of the few cases where he set himself the problem of the relationship between sculpture and architecture. The basic feature, chosen in order to dominate the rhythm of the ornamentation, was the triumphal arch. At the sides of the intervening space the walls are treated in an ambiguous manner, and may be interpreted either as unified structures or as the result of the coupling of candelabrae or wall pilasters separated by a niche. Typical elements of the Sangallo repertory such as the band with Greek-style frieze, and the attic base developed horizontally, appear here in a new context, influenced by the exciting plastic quality of the surfaces, which is no longer obtained naturalistically but as the result of the entirely artificial texture of the ceiling dec-

Plan of Palazzo Massimo in its original surroundings compared with its present position (the area marked with a dotted line indicates the width of the old street, while the continuous line marks the width of Corso Vittorio Emanuele II).

Exterior of Palazzo Massimo (1 cm = 4 m).

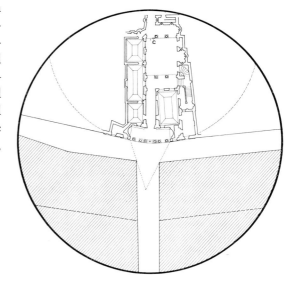

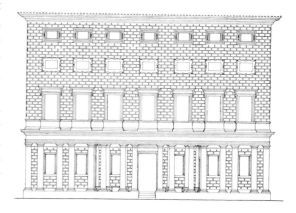

orations. A similar experiment, though on a much vaster scale, may be seen in the Fortezza da Basso in Florence, where the geometrical treatment of the rustication imbues the wall mass with a crystalline vibration and at the same time, through the hemisphere incorporated in the pyramid, introduces a semantic allusion (the cannon ball against which the wall has to be a defence) which is made absolutely clear and yet is also denied by infinite repetition.

The election of Pope Paul III Farnese in 1534 brought Antonio da Sangallo to the forefront and made him the most important figure in the cultural movement out of which the Academy of Claudio Tolomei was born in 1542. In 1536 Sangallo was engaged in preparing the triumphal welcome for Charles V on his return from his victorious campaign in Tunisia. The programme established by Giovenale Manetti envisaged an allegorical route past the ancient Roman monuments, which was intended to re-create a heroic image of the city; a new road was laid which led from the Appian Way, along the present Via dei Trionfi, and on to the Vatican, passing through the great classical triumphal arches as well as the modern imitations put up for the occasion by a team of architects, including Baldassarre Peruzzi, Raffaele da Montelupo, Aristotile da Sangallo, and Marten van

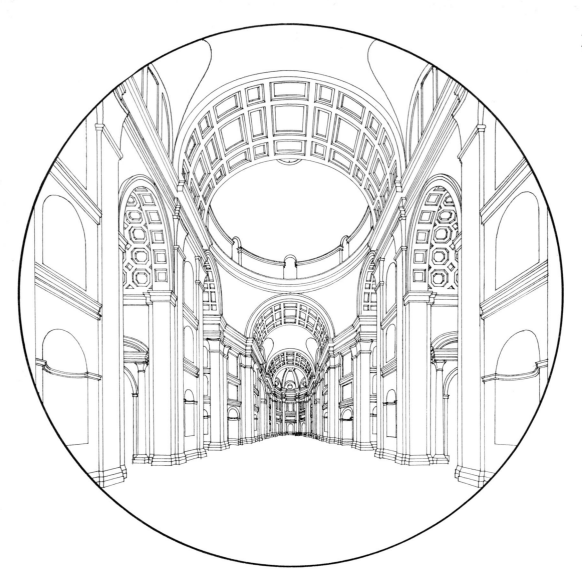

Antonio da Sangallo: first design for St. Peter's, perspective view of the interior.

Heemskerck. The few surviving drawings by Sangallo and Peruzzi reveal two clearly differentiated tendencies: Sangallo's, which was closely linked to classical themes and typological research, and Peruzzi's, directed towards an experimentation in new harmonies of composition based on elongated proportions. In Uffizi drawing 1087, the most interesting of the authenticated drawings by Sangallo, the model was derived from the Arch of Titus and treated in a simplified form; it was compared with an alternative consisting of a rusticated arch, surmounted by a large attic and enormous heraldic devices, an anticipation of a rhetorical interpretation of the classical repertory which became typical of pre-Baroque culture. Sangallo's broad interests and technical skill are especially apparent in the plans shown in drawings 330 and 331 in the Uffizi, where he first experimented with an original form of cruciform arch surmounted by a cupola, recalling Bramante's construction in the background to the *School of Athens*, and later tried out a curved arch with two façades, one being concave and angular, the other rectilinear.

In 1538 Paul III decided to start work again on the new St. Peter's. Sangallo was asked to revise his plan, and together with Antonio Labacco to make a complete model

of the building. In the same period, important work was undertaken in the Vatican Palace around the Sistine Chapel.

The modifications made to the 1520 plan seem to indicate that the Pope's intention was to put the building programme into operation without taking heed of economic considerations. Taking up his work again after a pause of twenty years, Sangallo did not have the courage to introduce substantial modifications into his plan. No alteration was made to the ground plan with its marked autonomy of the porch-façade structure and completely detached bell-towers—like those of the church of the Madonna di S. Biagio at Montepulciano—and similarly the form of the exterior was not altered, although the interior reverted to the original centralized plan. The most important variant relates to the sharp distinction which had existed in the 1520 plan between the monumental block formed by the two aisles with dome and the lower section comprising the ambulatories. In order to eliminate this double structure and its resultant contrast in scale, there were two possible solutions: the one, later adopted by Michelangelo, which consisted of completely abolishing the ambulatories, and the other, of raising them to a higher level by adding a second gallery.

Sangallo chose the latter course, and so set the seal on any possibility of solving the contradictions and lack of balance in his work. By raising the continuous ring of the ambulatories, the dome becomes submerged and appears to float on the surface of its gigantic base without any clear plastic or geometrical relationship between base and dome being established. To compensate for this effect, the happy solution applied to the drum in the 1520 plan has been sacrificed in favour of a return to Bramante's idea of a circular gallery; but whereas for Bramante this gallery—by fallacious reasoning—was to act as a support, for Sangallo its function was to be decorative, and he developed it on two levels and removed it from the thrust and weight of the drum by making it protrude beyond it. In this way the extrados of the dome barely emerges, and seems stifled by the drum as well as weighed down by a gigantic lantern.

Compared with the 1520 plan, a serious degree of complexity has been introduced. Everything has become complicated and fragmented, without any general idea or structure of immediate figurative significance emerging to create a unified composition out of this amazingly complex organism. The laboriously superimposed external orders seem only an inadequate parody when viewed in relation to the gigantic internal order; in addition, the height of the gap between the two orders—similar to Michelangelo's conception for the façade of S. Lorenzo—makes it even more difficult to apprehend the surfaces as a unified whole. The problem of lighting, which had already caused difficulty in the original plan where it was only partially resolved by means of light conductors, was made very much more acute by the presence of the second perimetrical gallery. Because of this gallery, light reached the interior only in reflected form, as filtered through the open galleries. It is difficult to see the intention behind this design, in which many of the firm achievements of Bramante—whose direct heir was in fact Sangallo—seem to have been lost. An inscription in Sangallo's hand, contained in Uffizi drawing 267, is the only objective and direct evidence we possess concerning his attitude towards problems of style. 'The cupola', he writes, 'must be arched according to the rule, shaping a semicircular piece of wood 98 long with diameter 14, and with the compass drawing a circle on a half-sheet of paper on the same body a half circle by half-diameter, that is, the opening of the compass should be $9\frac{8}{9}$; later, flattening this paper, an oval is made of which half will be eleven and if it were whole it would be 22 by $19\frac{7}{9}$, this being more graceful than the sharply pointed arch and a good ancient form that is made with mastery; the pointed arch is German, and this does not reach as high as the pointed arch ...' The dilemma between 'good ancient form' and 'German' did not in theory cause Sangallo any doubts, yet it is just for this 'Gothic' element that his plan for St. Peter's was criticized; it seems to contain a confused aspiration to employ the instruments of classicism in order to create anew the development of a medieval cathedral. In fact, many of the contradictions in Sangallo's work did not derive from aesthetic questions but implied a vaster horizon. To use the language of Latin civilization in order to create the largest church of a religion with a history of fifteen hundred years behind it implied a new ideological awareness and an ability to distinguish indications of method extending far beyond the specific discipline of architecture. Bramante had tried to find a middle way through the use of late classical models and had left a heritage of doubts and contradictions. Sangallo was faced by a range of problems which extended beyond technique and architectural autonomy. Neither Vitruvius nor the classical monuments could assist him in such an arduous task, while Bramante's principle of spatial structures was already being questioned in the external treatment of volumes.

The composite and abnormal nature of the organism planned for St. Peter's should rightly be interpreted not as a type of 'Manneristic' Gothicism, but as the result of the difficulty of adapting archaeological classicism to a scale which was uncontrollable in terms of a syntactic 'assembly' of conventional stylistic elements.

Michelangelo, by adopting the 'heroic' scale inspired by his individualistic and introvert nature, swept the field clear of every direct reference to the classical monuments and invented a new language. Sangallo, who was the heir to the Florentine tradition and the universalistic aspirations of Bramante, was unable to reconcile its contradictions, and he bent his efforts towards distinguishing rules for assembling features which were already known; he took arches from the Colosseum, aediculae from the Pantheon, plastic sequences from the Roman baths, and put these elements together most effectively; but the content appeared to escape him. Behind the gigantic protruding apses, there seem to be concealed improbable amphitheatres; behind the octagonal towers placed over four edges of a die, batteries of cannons seem to peer as in a fortress; the large open passageway between the porch and the basilica acquires the quality of a town gate; splendid fragments emerge at random from their context like the wreckage of a ship. A study of the large model renders the plastic density of the image even more paradoxical; this 'concentrated' architecture acquires a monstrous, nightmarish fascination. We find before us a most disturbing testament: the skilful builder, the man entrusted by a dominant class which has successfully absorbed revolutionary cultural experiments, the man who by his pragmatic vision and cultural interests was better able than any of his contemporaries to acquire unprecedented social prestige for the profession of architect, this man, when he met his greatest professional opportunity, was unable to do more than give expression to a profound sense of inadequacy between style and content. In the same way, Pirro Ligorio and Piranesi at a later date show the crisis of classicism as a foreshadowing of nineteenth-century historical eclecticism after the seizure of power by the middle-class.

However, it would be unjust not to acknowledge that the huge wooden model contained some very fine ideas which show that the architect's research was not purely formalistic. Such ideas occur mainly in the structure of the porch-façade, the part of the work which was completely original. The structure of the façade simulates a process of gradual advancing of two wall surfaces in relation to a plane of reference in recession. In view of the isolation of the bell-towers, an optical impression is created of an advance not on two, but on three, distinct fronts, whose plane of reference is the actual volume of the church, which is visible through the gaps between the bell-towers and the façade. The section farthest forward is that of the central bay containing the entrance and benediction loggia, two arches of equal measurement repeating the preferred relationship 1 : 1 so frequently employed by this architect. The five plastic sub-units which can be distinguished at volumetric level create an original composition, which might be algebraically expressed as follows:

I				I
T	T	T	T	T
U	U	O	U	U
M	M		M	M
o	o	O	o	o

The relationship between the sub-units is established on the basis of a series of analogies which suggest centrifugal and centripetal movements in relation to the central axis. The centripetal tension is achieved between the two smaller lateral arches which extend to the central arch and two large tabernacles, marked by the letter 'u' surrounding the curve of the benediction loggia. The centrifugal tension is achieved by analogy, since the bases of the bell-towers are entirely similar to the spans which contain the smaller arches but with the openings terminated by an aedicule.

These two tensions are balanced in the unifying attic and in the second order, where the groups indicated in the diagram by the letters U and M are repeated; these groups are entirely similar to each other and occur now in the central body where they surround the loggia, now in the bell-towers beyond the opening which separates them from the central body. The final unifying factor comprises the five tympana, where apart from a slight variation in the size of the central tympanum, a continuous series is created as follows:

T   T - T - T   T

Such a complex formal organization reveals a great effort to develop new forms and anticipates a possible synthetic aim as well as analytic separation. In particular, the clear demonstration of functions, so evident in the assembly of portal and loggia as well as in the detached bell-towers, constitutes a determining contribution to the foundation of an 'architectonic rhetoric'.

While much of his energy was devoted to his model of St. Peter's, Sangallo made two interesting experiments in the qualification of internal space: the Sala Regia and Cappella Paolina in the Vatican. Today the impression created by the former is completely distorted by Vasari's decorations, but it once contained an explicit reference to Giuliano da Sangallo and in particular to the central reception room of the villa at Poggio a Caiano. The idea of modifying a parallelepiped area by means of a large barrel vault indicates a puristic intention effectively expressed by the impeccable design of the large marble doorways giving access to the various adjoining rooms. However, the beams of light which fall unobstructed from the large lunette window counter this purist choice by imposing the personal mark of plastic violence which distinguishes the most important of Sangallo's works of architecture. The same striving for a chosen and impeccable form recurs in the external windows of the ducal room, where the prototype of the windows of the Temple of the Sibyl at Tivoli was for the first time reconstructed in strict conformity to the original. In the effort to obtain absolute accuracy in the definition of a type, one can observe the influence of the study of Vitruvius which occupied Sangallo at this time, when he was engaged in completing the first 'professional' translation of the obscure text of this author. The search for a concrete, tactile form which would yet possess all the authority and rigour of a type, found its most complete expression in the doors to the throne room and the windows mentioned, without for this reason losing any of the personal imprint of the artist which was lacking in the dogmatic exercises of the academicians.

In the Cappella Paolina, Sangallo employed again the composite order of fluted wall pilasters which he had incorporated in his youthful Chapel of S. Giacomo, but now the longitudinal area is ornamented not only along the larger axis but also along the smaller, so indicating a possibility for expansion in a cruciform shape, enhanced by the opening of large lunettes in the pavilion roof. The pattern of large square mirrorings perfects this ambiguous illusion of centrality, inaugurating a series of experiments into the mixture of types which engaged Roman artists during the latter part of the century.

Sangallo's most important contributions to church architecture in the last period of his activity were represented by his plans for S. Tolomeo at Nepi and the façade of S. Spirito in Sassia. These were related on the one hand to the tradition of Alberti, and on the other to the image of the four-sided arch of the Forum Boarium, and on the basis of these two models Sangallo established in an embryonic form the type of the façade with two orders of varying widths which three generations of architects adapted to their individual needs. However, the type which became the model for a suggested perspective depth was created at S. Spirito in the form of a hollowed block, where autonomy as an isolated slab was acquired only at the level of the tympanum.

For the façade of the church of S. Tolomeo at Nepi, Sangallo reverted to the tradition of the plans for St. Mark's church in Florence, some of whose results have been referred to above; he examined the question of superimposed orders but seemed to be ensnared by the difficulty of assembling autonomous units in a meaningful way. He was more successful in his research into a typology for the structure as a whole. In two alternatives shown

in Uffizi drawings 551 and 865, this appears as the assembly of a number of interconnecting spatial units. In both cases, the key to the composition is an octagon surmounted by a dome, to which is juxtaposed a three-nave structure with side lateral chapels on a square matrix. A different treatment was envisaged for the remaining smaller areas of space which merge in the octagon. Drawing 865 shows three apses with a diameter which is much larger than that of the intervening archways, while drawing 551 indicates two rectangular aisles and a circular presbytery cut down by a third by the connecting arches. A motif common to all these designs, derived from the plan for St. Peter's, consists of the two chapels, octagonal or square in shape, placed at the sides of the presbytery. There is no fluidity in the space, which has been crystallized into pure geometrical blocks: at a number of points breaks occur to ensure that the sequence of structures does not flow without interruption. It seems as if Sangallo feared that he might lose control of each of his 'arguments' and wished to break up his composition so as to express its logical analysis in a didactic manner by isolating each individual proposition.

It is interesting to observe how Michelangelo handled the same problem of connecting a central area to apses having a diameter larger than that of the intervening space. In the Sforza Chapel in S. Maria Maggiore, he aimed to achieve an effect which was the exact opposite of the one desired by Sangallo, cutting across every geometric distinction in a dynamic movement which brought a radical innovation to the traditional relationship of perspective between the outer wall mass and the inner wall—a relationship to which Sangallo remained faithful even when, as in his late works, he himself contributed to creating an awareness that it had become obsolete and no longer valid.

Sangallo's Work for the Farnese Family

The most important achievements of the last period of Sangallo's activity are to be seen in the field of domestic architecture. The power-seeking programme of the Farnese family found in him a ready ally, who was already able to anticipate the utilization of the image created by architecture in its urban setting in order to symbolize an acknowledged and indisputable hierarchy, a solidly based, transcendent power structure, as expressed in Vignola's Palazzo Caprarola, where Sangallo himself had a hand in the design of the volumetry and urban siting.

The little we know concerning the city of Castro, which was reconstructed by Sangallo after 1537 and razed to the ground by Pope Innocent X in the seventeenth century, indicates that it was an urban organism entirely conditioned by court life. The main square was dominated by the Zecca and a kind of inn probably intended for the guests of the Farnese household. The extant drawings relating to this building show that Sangallo had experimented with the design of an order above a colonnade, as did Sanmicheli and Sansovino. Drawing 1684 may perhaps relate to the Ducal Palace, where many of the features found in the Farnese palace in Rome reappear in a less severe context, characterized by the large apertures at ground floor level and a small terminal gallery.

During this period, Sangallo approached the problem of the palazzo from two standpoints, oscillating between closed, compact forms, symbolizing a defensive attitude, and attempts, always conditioned by the demands of the volumetry, to open out the building to meet the urban surroundings. In each case, however, the programme of suggesting the power of his patron was reconciled with an ideal of forming a harmonious relationship to the urban environment. Significant examples of this trend are the plans for a house to be built for himself in Florence (Uffizi 767) and the design, later executed by Nanni di Baccio Bigio, for the façade of the Palazzo Salviati on the Lungara. In the former, the vaunted aristocratic compactness is tempered by the subtle elegance 'in the Greek manner' of the cornices above the windows and doorway, while in the latter the ornamentation in the central section and two smaller wings indicates the desire to provide a unified perspective view for the very long wing.

The casuistry of Sangallo's research into the theme of the palazzo does not stop here: sketches for the palace for Cardinal Sanseverino and a series of anonymous drawings show that if the architect's name has remained linked especially to the model of the early Palazzo Baldassini, in reality he experimented with a whole series of different forms, and manifested a tireless inventiveness in the face of which even Serlio's theoretical propositions appear schematic and over-simplified.

Further evidence of Sangallo's interest in the design of the palazzo—an interest partly due to psychological factors—can be seen in what amounted to a mania for acquiring property. In addition to his houses in Florence, Sangallo possessed a residence in Via Giulia in Rome and was thinking of building another, and larger, house in the same street; of this house he probably executed only the ground floor and it was later completed by Annibale Lippi and known as the Palazzo Sacchetti. If the tone of the first building was modest and simple, though enriched by a hierarchical differentiation of the central axis, the latter, judging by its magnificent windows, seemed intended to bear the appearance of an ancestral hall.

When Cardinal Farnese was elected to the papacy in 1534, his palace was unfinished, but work had already begun on the reconstruction of its urban surroundings in order to provide a background suited to its importance. The decision to extend the palace by increasing the number of spans from 11 to 13 and bringing the façade about five metres forward was taken in order to endow the building with a more massive dimension in its urban setting, as befitted the new role assumed by the Farnese family. In actual fact, the increase in dimensions was much greater than might be thought from the addition of only two spans, when one considers that the spans in the courtyard increased from three to five. The width of the façade increased from about 24 metres to 38, and although these dimensions were much smaller than those of the early Renaissance palaces such as Palazzo Venezia or la Cancelleria, Sangallo was able to turn them to advantage so as to convey a pre-eminent monumentality which could not be denied.

We have seen that the first palazzo was ornamented with twin wall pilasters on the façade; the process which led to the model tested in the Palazzo Baldassini came about in stages, one of which is documented in Uffizi drawing 998 where, while it appears that the choice of the windows for the two upper floors was already made, the final formulation of the organism as a whole was still far off. In the sketch on the right margin of the sheet, there appears a corner wall pilaster placed so as to enclose the two series of windows. If we imagine that the drawing relates only to the upper floors, it is possible that at an early stage Sangallo had envisaged a rusticated ground floor with the plane of the façade enclosed by an order at the corners. The development of a tendency towards simplification and volumetric compactness may be observed in this return to rusticated quoins interrupted by dividing bands and decreasing in size from floor to floor in the same way as an architectural order, as well as in the increase in the distances between the floors. The same features as are found in the Palazzo Baldassini—the connection by tangency between the rusticated quoins and far windows and between the doorway and central windows—create in this new dimension and very different conditions of visibility a much more distinct impact; this is partly due also to the coping, where every archaic element has been abandoned and the relationship between it and the inner wall is that of a modelled unit having an autonomous perspective spatialism. Looking back on the Palazzo Baldassini over a distance of more than twenty years, Sangallo might well have made the same comment on it that he applied to the doorway of the garden of Giovanni Choritio, in his note to Uffizi drawing 77: 'It is not good: it was one of the first I made; I did not yet properly understand Vitruvius.'

Sangallo's youthful experience was lived through again in the Palazzo Farnese, but from the height of an intellectual maturity and with the knowledge of how to control the optical properties of form, so that the extreme simplicity of his statement could now convey an admirable precision and strength. More even than in the main façade, his ability to design

Design for the Ducal Palace of Castro.

Plan of Palazzo Farnese (2 cm = 4.8 m).

Axonometric of the cortile of Palazzo Farnese.

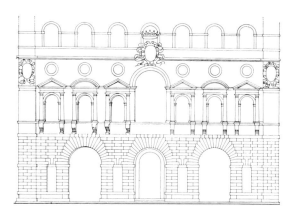

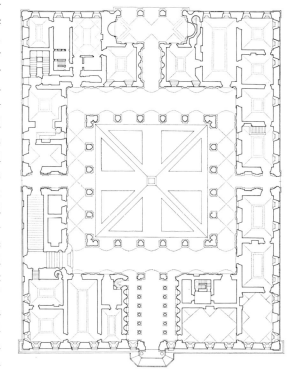

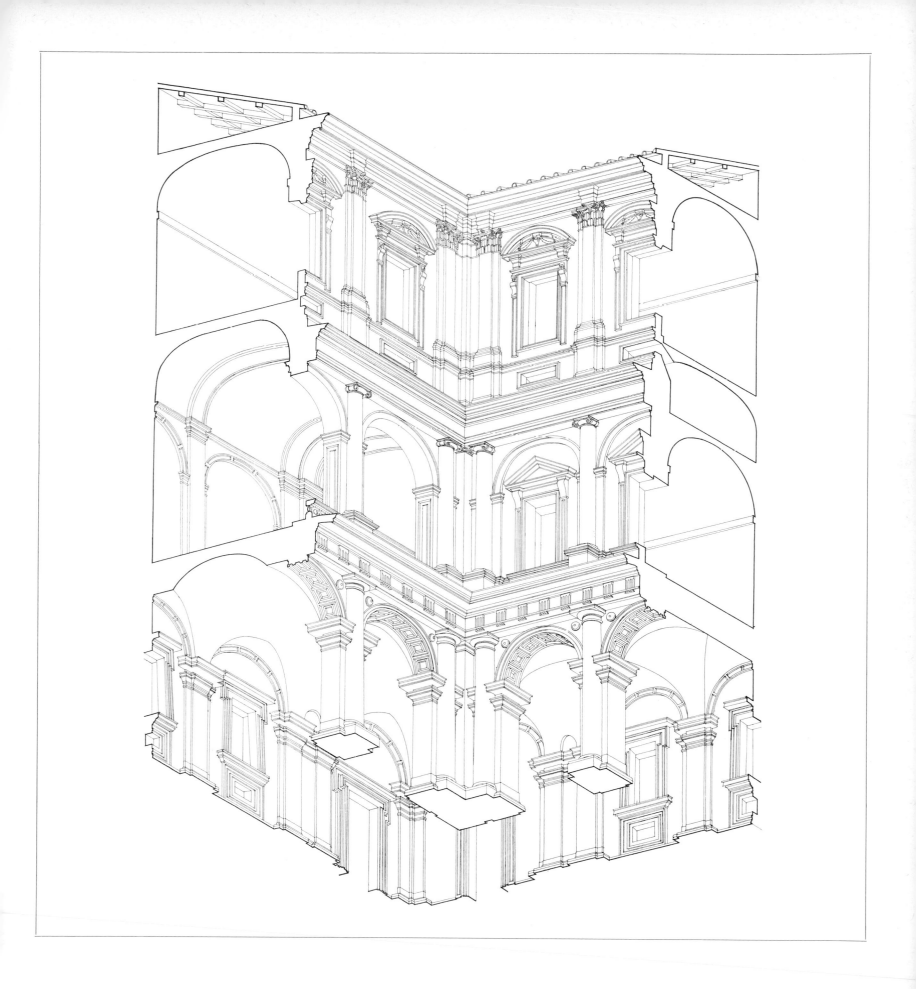

on a grand scale can be appreciated in the lateral façades, where by interrupting the series of window openings at two points he has made it possible to view the cavity of the great courtyard from the exterior. Again, the arrangement of the distributive functions of the palazzo is full of technical and stylistic innovations. But the most important factor is that for the first time the structure of an urban palazzo has been given the form of a homogeneous parallelepiped. In view of the fact that the loggia overlooking the Tiber was added by Della Porta as a simplification of the plan proposed by Michelangelo, it may, in fact, be possible that Sangallo intended to construct four homogeneous façades, and this hypothesis is confirmed by the numerous plans preserved in the Uffizi. In this way the Palazzo Farnese was to express fully an ideal which its great predecessors—the Palazzo Strozzi, the Palazzo Medici in Florence, the Palazzo Piccolomini in Pienza, etc.—had only touched on, while remaining firmly anchored in their urban network and having to compromise with binding distributive exigencies, at least in some of their façades. In contrast, the Palazzo Farnese stands like a rural villa in complete isolation as an absolutely autonomous unit: it is situated in the town, but refuses to come to terms with its urban surroundings. It represents the triumph of pure form whose law of coherence is imposed as an imperative to which all else must remain subordinate. Observe, for example, the arrangement of the grand staircase: it occupies the entire depth of the fabric, and in order to correspond with the façade, the closure of two windows was rendered necessary. To illuminate the inter-

Section of the gallery and first ramp of the staircase of Palazzo Farnese (1 cm = 2 m).

Longitudinal section of Palazzo Farnese (1 cm = 6 m).

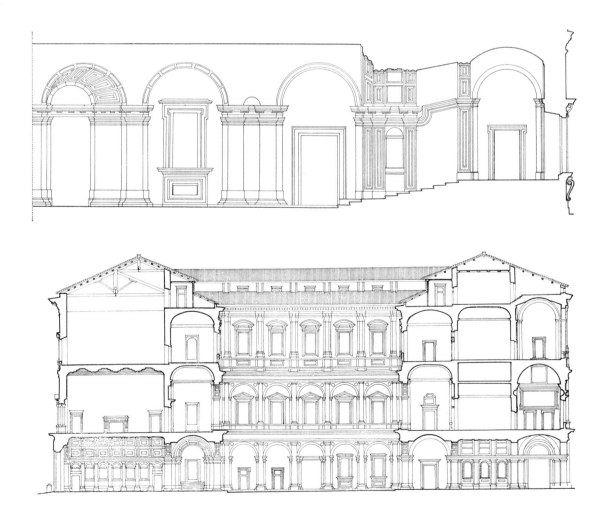

mediate landing parallel to the façade, a small courtyard was inserted into which light flowed from above and through a pair of windows which were left unframed.

As in the Palazzo Baldassini, the greatest stylistic achievement of the Palazzo Farnese is to be seen in the sequence porch-courtyard, completed in this case by the monumental staircase. Here, too, the dominant idea is that of interconnection. As in a film sequence, the various sections are linked by analogies and repetitions, with certain themes acting as a unifying accompaniment. In the entrance to the staircase and in the perspective apertures which relate the porch and loggia, there may be seen one of the most original stylistic innovations of Roman classical architecture. The principle of bevelling corners yields here to a relationship of interaction between space and mass. In this detail, one can identify the first appearance of a form which was adopted by Michelangelo for the upper storey to St. Peter's and later in the false perspective framing in the Palazzo Barberini by Bernini and Borromini. The latter is indebted to Sangallo also for the variants of the splendid curve of the impost cornice to the barrel-vault of the Farnese staircase.

In the porch, the theme of the 'serliana' (where an arch is framed by two smaller architraved sections) is extended in depth and halted as it becomes narrower, forming a kind of stage setting where, after areas of filtered light, the figure of the arch reappears three further times in the same dimensions but with differentiated intervals. The form of a rectangular barrel-vaulted area is here shown at its most complete and refined expression, and this is partly due to the cross-pattern of light and shadow created by the illumination from the two far windows. The effect of gradations of shadows, vibrant with reflected light, as applied to the rugged surface of the travertine and the shiny granite columns, endows this area with an unmistakable quality. When we try to explain how so elemental a structure could impart a harmonious quality of this nature, we discover that one of the main factors is that the dimensions of the columns are adapted to a human scale, while the column bases serve an optical function by creating a visually opaque band below them and so limiting the spatial transparency to the zone of the column shafts which are situated in a central position in relation to the viewer's field of vision. In compensating for the protrusion of the impost cornice of the vault, the bases determine an equilibrium based on plastic values. A similar feature recurs in the order of pilasters in the *cortile*, where at the same level as the porch column bases an apparently inexplicable broadening can be observed; this serves on the one hand to 'recall' the structure of the porch, on the other to balance the shortened cornice which surmounts these same pilasters.

When later in the courtyard we come to the order of Doric half-columns framed by the arches resting on pilasters, we gain a complete picture of the complex problem of composition which Sangallo had to face. His task was to relate closely three orders of varying heights, emerging from a single predominant plane. And it was this broadening of the pilasters just mentioned which made the relationship possible, since it corresponded at the same time to the curve at the starting point of the shaft of the little columns in the porch, and also to the moulding of the Doric columns of the gallery whose proportions were much larger and which were moreover set on a stylobate.

In the same spirit of a lucid conclusion to a 'scientific' dispute, Sangallo approached the problem of the courtyard. Bramante's solution of the corner wall pilaster immersed in the pillars, as well as the solution based on the distancing of the supports from the corner applied by Laurana at Urbino, were rejected in favour of a synthesis which consisted of separating the terminal elements of the order away from the corner and placing an intervening pilaster to protrude from the concave corner and so provide the abstract line of its edge as a term of reference. This solution, as well as the shell-like cover surmounting the Doric cornice of the pilasters, reveals a strange convergence of views between Antonio da Sangallo and Michelangelo. This was all the more significant in that almost certainly the colonnade of the Farnese *cortile* was designed by Sangallo in the first phase of construction, and in any case before 1527. Sangallo's contribution to the Roman 'forma urbis'

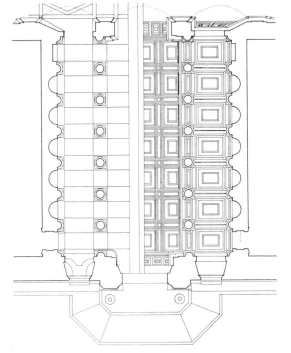

concludes with an unfinished work which in its picturesque appearance of a ruin is endowed with a plastic violence. The S. Spirito gate, curved and animated by the protruding columns which are almost detached from the massive inner wall, represents Sangallo's last grand architectural gesture, anticipating a theme which was taken up by Alessi and developed fully only a century later by the masters of the Baroque.

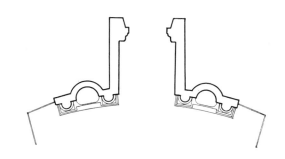

Porta Santo Spirito, plan (1 cm = 4 m).

BE A FRIEND TO THE COLD STONE AND THE INNER FIRE

The Roman Architectural Works of Michelangelo
Michelangelo's presence on the architectural scene in Rome began to be felt at the time of the death of Sangallo or, more precisely, with the preparation of the first plans for the Capitol in 1536. His architectural contributions previous to the Sack, at the time when 'sweet liberty' reigned, were either of slight importance or were inextricably linked to his own figurative works, such as the sculpture for the tomb of Julius II or the paintings on the ceiling of the Sistine Chapel.

An isolated instance of an early work without originality or verifiable influence on Roman culture was the façade to the little chapel known as the chapel of Leo X in Castel S. Angelo, executed in 1514. This was a very early example of Michelangelo's architecture, preceding the Florentine works, and produced at a time when architecture represented only a minor facet of his activity. In fact, his acceptance of the commission may have been due to a desire to try his hand at a form which until then had remained extraneous to his work, except as a background to his figurative inventions.

A first design for this chapel is known to us through a drawing by Giovan Battista da Sangallo in the Lille Museum. Bearing in mind the appearance of the chapel prior to the unfortunate reconstruction carried out by Borgatti, we see that the solution applied by Michelangelo represented an advance on this first idea, even though the quality of the details is such as to preclude his direct participation in the execution. The interest of the chapel lies in its anticipation of a future programme of research which was carried out by Michelangelo only several years later. Of particular interest are the characteristics of the selected features—a classical aedicule, surmounted by a triangular tympanum and framed by two wings so as to suggest the possibility of lateral expansion. The same feature re-appears, in varying proportions, in the façade to S. Lorenzo, in many designs for tombs, in the architectural background to the *cortile* of the Palazzo dei Conservatori, and in the façade to the Sforza Chapel in the church of S. Maria Maggiore. Taking the classical model of the aedicule of the Pantheon as a starting point, the ground plan of this chapel is obtained through a process of systematic dilation. In particular, the aedicule is expanded laterally by means of two narrower intervals at the sides, ensuring complete autonomy and distinct-ness to these intervals by the protrusion of the cornices. This method of construction is equivalent to an interpretation of the façade in terms of perspective depth, since the re-lationship between the aedicule and wings is the same as that between a figure and the back-ground arranged 'behind' it, at a vague distance. The second process of transformation relates to the interpretation of its proportions. A comparison with the Pantheon reveals the absence of preconceived ideas in this approach: the rectangle comprised between the shafts of the columns has been decreased in size from approximately 1 : 2.5 to 1 : 0.8 so far as the relation between base and height is concerned, while the intercolumniation of five diameters in the classical example has been increased to eleven diameters.

The large spaces between the columns are thus out of proportion to the entablature: this is the problem of araeostyle intercolumniations (where the space between the columns exceeds three diameters) about which Vitruvius wrote that in church buildings it was necessary in such cases to replace stone by wood in the entablature.

The problem was solved by Michelangelo by means of a prop which crossed over the cornice to create a structure similar to that of windows made in the form of a Latin cross. But the origin of this composition was entirely different and may be found in the architect's wish to adopt the classical model and extend it as far as 'breaking point', under the critical conditions provoked by an extensive proportional interpretation.

In addition to the vastly increased proportions and to a desire to make the structure reveal the forces to which it was subjected, one may also observe in the façade of this little chapel a taste for intricate ornamentation, for composition built up in several stages wherein it is possible to isolate various formative phases. In the original feature of the strengthening beam inserted at the centre of the window, entirely similar to wooden scaffolding which would be employed in order to strengthen an unsound structure, we already have in a nutshell the problem of intersecting orders and 'temporal' structures found in the Capitol.

In 1518 Piero Soderini asked Michelangelo to design 'an altar and ornament' and two tombs in 'half-relief', to be placed in the Roman church of S. Silvestro in Capite. Drawing 114 in Casa Buonarroti, identified by Popp, enables us to know some of the ideas Michelangelo considered for the wall tombs—which he indicated on a diagram of the church. The most interesting ideas relate to an abstract problem of composition. The insertion of a circle into a square framework was researched in an exceptionally rigorous manner, while the placing of a fifteenth-century type of marble urn inside the circle—for symbolic reasons connected with Neoplatonism—demonstrated a tendency to justify the exceptional form of the composition from a symbolic viewpoint, imbuing the tomb with the sense of a restatement in figurative terms of the cosmic relationship between earth and sky, life and death.

The Capitol

The need for a radical urban reconstruction of the Capitoline area became clearly apparent in 1535, when the welcome was prepared for Charles V. The first tangible proof of Paul III's intention to transform the piazza was provided only in 1537, when he decided to move some sculptural groups from the Lateran; at the same time, the civic administration decided to undertake the restoration of the Palazzo dei Conservatori.

The first document confirming Michelangelo's responsibility for directing the Capitoline works is dated 1539 (he had already been consulted about the removal of the statue of Marcus Aurelius). In this document, explicit reference is made both to the siting of the statue of Marcus Aurelius and to 'muros fiendos in dicta platea'—a clear indication that as early as this stage the statue and piazza were considered as parts of an organic unit. The later phases of execution cover the staircase to the Palazzo dei Senatori, built after 1544 under the direction of Michelangelo, and the Palazzo dei Conservatori, which was begun in 1563 by Guidetti who scrupulously followed the lines indicated by Michelangelo, and by 1565 was at the stage of the roofing of the first section overlooking the city. Knowing Michelangelo's method of planning—admirably documented in the series of drawings relating to the Laurentian Library—we can exclude the possibility that he prepared a final draft at the initial stage of the building operation (1537–9) and later adhered to it faithfully throughout the various phases of execution. The famous engravings by Lafréry and the preparatory drawing for them are therefore to be considered as the end result of a planning process which lasted almost twenty years. One cannot accept either the argument put forward by certain historians that the entire project should be dated to the fourth decade of the sixteenth century on the basis of a so-called disparity of style between the Capitol and such late works as the Porta Pia and the Sforza Chapel, since the attempt to fit the 'style' of Michelangelo into cut-and-dried periods contradicts the reality of the actual works.

It seems most likely that the design illustrated in the sixteenth-century engravings corresponds exactly to the last design of Michelangelo's, and since it is impossible to make even a tentative reconstruction of the vicissitudes of the planning process, an attempt will be made here to analyse the finished work under the headings of the problems which had to be overcome and through the corrective filter of the architect's plan.

Plan of the Campidoglio.

The Iconological Problem

The studies undertaken by Saxl, De Tolnay, De Angelis d'Ossat, and especially Ackerman, contain many points of great interest regarding the iconological interpretation of the Capitol. These findings will be used here to advance the hypothesis of an organic conceptual structure. The key to the iconological structure may be distinguished in the two dedicatory inscriptions inscribed in the walls at the entrance to the Palazzo dei Conservatori:

<table>
<tr><td align="center">S.P.Q.R.</td><td align="center">S.P.Q.R.</td></tr>
<tr><td align="center">MAIORUM SUORUM PRAESTANTIAM</td><td align="center">CAPITOLIUM PRAECIPUE IOVI</td></tr>
<tr><td align="center">UT ANIMO SIC RE</td><td align="center">OLIM COMMENDATUM</td></tr>
<tr><td align="center">QUANTUM LICUIT IMITATUS</td><td align="center">NUNC DEO VERO</td></tr>
<tr><td align="center">DEFORMATUM INIURIA TEMPORUM</td><td align="center">CUNCTORUM BONORUM AUCTOR</td></tr>
<tr><td align="center">CAPITOLIUM RESTITUIT</td><td align="center">IESU CRISTO</td></tr>
<tr><td align="center">PROSPERO BUCCAPADULIO</td><td align="center">CUM SALUTE COMMUNI SUPPLEX</td></tr>
<tr><td align="center">TOMA CAVALERIO</td><td align="center">TUENDUM TRADIT</td></tr>
<tr><td align="center">ANNUM POST URBEM CONDITAM</td><td align="center">ANNUM POST SALUTIS INITIUM</td></tr>
<tr><td align="center">MMCCCXX</td><td align="center">MDLXVIII</td></tr>
</table>

The first inscription, dated after the year of the foundation of Rome, records the restitution to the Capitol of its ancient historical dignity, and the second, dated after the birth of Christ, substitutes a consecration to Christ to the original consecration to Jupiter.

The interpretation of the meaning of these two inscriptions (the antithesis and equivalence between the ancient consecration to Jupiter and the new consecration to Christ) may be viewed from two fundamental aspects: the relationship between the piazza and the city (heteronomy of the monument) and the symbolic significance of the spatial organism (where the monument has an autonomous value). Concerning the relationship between piazza and city, one should take note of two important features: the double line of vision towards the old city (the ruins of the Forum) and the modern town, and the contrast between the fortress and the city in the direction of both the Forum and the low Piazza dell'Aracoeli. The Capitoline hill, symbolically crystallized into a completely artificial structure, acts in a mediatory and unifying capacity between the old and the modern city, the former (the past) at its rear, and the latter in front (the present). The fact that Dupérac's engravings were drawn from a very high viewpoint, almost level with the top of the baluster of the Palazzo dei Senatori and thus presenting a 'bird's-eye-view', may probably be explained by the impossibility of seeing the landscape and ruins of the Forum beyond the line of the buildings from any other point.

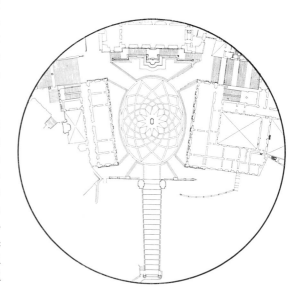

As an urban feature, therefore, the Capitoline serves a function which is similar to that of a miracle play, or a historical pageant: a 'speculum doctrinale' like Raphael's paintings in the Stanza della Segnatura. As in a pilgrimage, the visitor ascends to a platform which provides a view of the city from which an edifying moral has already been extracted. The new Capitol is the reverse of the old (literally the reverse, since its access has been inverted), but at the same time it represents a continuity of the old building, lying open towards the city and having as its plane of reference the dome of St. Peter's. If we look towards the background, beyond the bulk of the castle-palazzo dei Senatori we see stretching before us a dead, funereal majesty: in the forum and Palatine ruins, nature and history have become inextricably interwoven. In contrast, the spectacle from the other side is brimful with life. The majesty of the past lives once more in the Capitoline monuments which stand as a demonstration of continuity, where public authority and its alliance with the church are celebrated together.

The same type of unity, with a distinction between secular and religious themes, may be observed in the architectural organization. The floor pattern has been rightly shown to contain a cosmological significance, and its convex shape may be interpreted as both a shield and a cosmic symbol. The Capitol, therefore, like the 'umbilicus mundi' presided over by the Emperor, Antoninus Pius, (the correct attribution of the statue to Marcus Aurelius did not become known until much later) towers over the city like a symbolic 'Kosmokrator'; but also at the same time, like a Sacred Mountain, 'Mons Salvationis', traversed by the cross which is clearly recognizable in the group formed by the ramp and piazza together with the lateral staircases. Each of the elements in this symbolic structure is capable of a double connotation—secular and Christian. The twelve-sided cosmological floor pattern corresponds to the symbolic portrayal of the church through the twelve apostles and the twelve pillars of the tribes erected by Moses at the foot of Sinai. The crown with twelve rays around the statue of Marcus Aurelius may be an allusion to the ancient Capitoline cult of the sun, but is also a symbol of Christ. The staircase, which accentuates the distance from the city and imbues the piazza with the sense of an enclosed area, is a triumphal route and at the same time may be interpreted as an essential element in defining the hill in a Biblical sense as a mediation between earth and sky (Sinai) and as a citadel (Zion). In the words of Psalm 47: 'Beautiful for situation, the joy of the whole earth, is Mount Zion, on the sides of the north, the city of the great King. God is known in her palaces for a refuge.'

The cult of antiquity in the sense of an anticipation and allegorical equivalent of the revealed truth informs the image of the Capitol in accordance with the historical outlook of humanism. Although conceived in the climate of the Council of Trent, its ideological roots were still those of the Renaissance. And it cannot be said that the spirit of the Counter-Reformation was gratifyingly mirrored in the new urban image. Once Michelangelo was dead, the implementation of his ideas proceeded so slowly that it was not until the height of the Baroque period, when the museum building was erected, that the spatial entity of the whole urban complex was complete and imbued with unforeseeable potentialities.

The Problem of Syntax

In Michelangelo's design for the Capitol, the neo-humanist iconology corresponded to a revolutionary formal structure. He proposed to insert a statue to Jupiter in the recess of the staircase but refused to accept passively any of the traditional forms of classical architecture; he did not erect temple columns or structures derived from the Roman classical tradition, preserving only the conceptual structure of the order, and creating buildings without any precedent in the sphere of formal construction.

The thread of Michelangelo's innovations can be followed by analysing three predominant aspects of the complex: the themes of variations in level, intersecting structures, and optical rectification.

In Renaissance architecture staircases were for a long time only of secondary importance. Alberti considered them a necessary evil which could interfere with the method of composition based on superimposed cubic structures typical of his time. In the Belvedere, perhaps for the first time, Bramante used the staircase as an axial motif, and the source of Bramante's inspiration—the Temple of Fortuna Virilis in Palestrina—served also to suggest to Michelangelo the use of ramps in the stairway to the Palazzo dei Senatori; but he interpreted this feature in a very different light.

In the Capitol, the inclined planes and the oblique line of the parapets have become a primary structural element which has an influence on the perception at each stage of viewing the piazza. From below, following the line of Via dell'Aracoeli, the winding access ramp appeared in the original plan like a sharp wedge isolated in space and forming a violent contrast to the sheer wall which was to transform the hill into an artificial geometric block. The long, unstable route across the sloping plane contrasted with the absolute equilibrium experienced on arrival at the piazza. Here, the double staircase of the Palazzo dei Senatori has become a dominant feature, but in the gaps between the buildings two descending paths can be distinguished which were probably also intended to be geometrically defined. After crossing over the centre of the piazza, one becomes aware of the other stairways rising in the opposite direction along the sides of the lateral palazzi. Continuously ascending perspectives enable the eye to expand, in reaction to the spatial compression exercised by the centripetal volumes of the buildings.

The theme of the intersection of architectonic orders has precedents in Roman classical architecture and appeared in the designs for St. Peter's prepared by Bramante and Sangallo. In the Capitol, Michelangelo employed it in a more radical version, to suggest the impression that the final form of the buildings was the result of a stratification of successive phases of construction, which were perfectly accorded among themselves, but clearly distinguishable in the final image. By denuding the Capitol of all secondary structures, it can be seen that it may be reduced to three large temple structures, one of which (the Palazzo dei Senatori) is raised on a podium and preceded by a baldacchino. However, these primary structures also contain other structures which are supported by the larger framework, like excrescences on ancient ruins whose minor scale forms a contrast to their epic grandeur. This interweaving of orders is carried out with the utmost rigour in the Palazzo dei Conservatori, where the large pilasters are flanked by columns, and the crowning entablature is echoed by a minor entablature supporting the walls which are pierced by the first-floor windows. Each element is made fully autonomous and recognizable throughout its extension, as can be seen clearly in the interior of the colonnade, where the smaller columns, arranged in groups of four, support a baldacchino system consisting of free-standing architraves and small pavilion vaults. That Michelangelo intended to suggest continuity of the order extending into depth also, beyond the terminal walls which were considered as temporary screens, is demonstrated by the column connection affected by a niche, or by the soffit of the architrave cut brutally to stress the antithesis between the walls and the more noble structure of the order.

On the plane of stylistic elaboration, the staircase to the Palazzo dei Senatori and the Palazzo dei Conservatori contain many radical innovations in spite of the apparent 'correctness' of their design. In the staircase, Michelangelo obeyed a need for simplifying and consolidating forms; but behind this need, which seems to have been dictated by tactical considerations in relation to Roman society, one can sense the mature experience of the architect of the Laurentian Library, where every so-called 'absolute truth' in the classical repertory was referred back for discussion. The idea of having two steps turning round the whole length of the staircase as well as along the flat façade, and of enhancing its value as a horizontal link by means of the splendid hollowed seat, imbued the image with a dynamic value which was further accentuated by the ornamentation of the ramps. The most significant and revealing detail of the staircase can be seen in the design of the parapet, where each of the balusters rests, not on a conventional plinth, but on a 'C'-shaped curve of the steps.

The stratification of the steps, which is visible from the exterior of the staircase also, thus remains the primary structure which governs the composition and produces in the interior an interacting dynamic effect in all parts of the structure, anticipating the analytical method applied to the Laurentian staircase, described later in Michelangelo's vision of 'ovate boxes'.

In the Palazzo dei Conservatori, Michelangelo's control extends only as far as the impost of the second cornice. Up to this level, each part is characterized in an original manner without the 'Florentine' acrimony aroused in the Laurentian Library, but with no less a critical attitude towards classical models. In the capitals to the columns, Michelangelo's

Detail of the ceiling, part of the colonnade in Palazzo dei Conservatori (1 cm = 90 cm).

Perspective reconstruction of Michelangelo's design for the Capitol Piazza.

criticism of the Ionic model hinges mainly upon its compactness, its 'frontal' nature, which, as is known, does not permit of a homogeneous solution between perpendicular façades except by having recourse to anomalous angular capitals. Although Michelangelo did not have to deal with the problem of the angle, he reduced the frontality of the capital by forcing the volutes into an almost diagonal direction through the action of their constraining bonds. The very elegant entablature of the smaller order is animated by the chiaroscuro effects of the dentils, which protrude from the shadow only at the points at which the pilasters are attached, so creating a musical effect by not ornamenting the cornice proper in the same way as in the sub-cornice. The large central window of the Palazzo dei Conservatori cannot be ascribed to Della Porta, who in the execution of the Palazzo dei Senatori and later in his original work always followed the course of simplifying the complexities in Michelangelo's designs and conforming to classical orthodoxy. In fact, none of the followers of Michelangelo ever showed a sufficient degree of originality to justify an attribution on stylistic grounds, while the radical criticism of classical models implied in it fully authorizes its attribution to Michelangelo. The processes of interpenetration and sectioning, and the creation of perspective depth by means of slight irregularities are typical elements of Michelangelo's style which did not find any followers among Roman architects.

In the smaller windows of the Palazzo dei Conservatori, the point of departure is the aedicule of the Pantheon which had served as a model for Sangallo in the Palazzo Farnese. Michelangelo criticized the aedicule on the grounds of its self-sufficiency and absoluteness, and the fact that it did not form an organic entity with the wall. This connection was obtained by dividing the entablature above the columns and making it follow the background wall, with the projections reduced to pure outlines: the aedicule is thus incorporated into the wall and becomes an organic projection from it. Here again the method of compotion employed is dialectical, based on the opposition of two irreducible forces—the forward projection of the columns of the tympanum and little balcony, and the centripetal recession of the cornice and coping which is echoed in the large inverted shell.

Optic Problems

Of the characteristic features of the Capitol, the one which should be considered as fundamental is the optical ararngement of the composition which governs and justifies many of Michelangelo's choices. To analyse the geometric structure of the ground plan first of all, it is based on a central trapezium (the piazza), in which is inscribed an oval combined with a second trapezium (the access staircase) and two irregular rectangles (the lateral staircases). If we also break down to its elemental forms the staircase of Palazzo dei Senatori, we find again a series of trapezia (the ramps) combined with rectangles (the landings). There is no need to point out that this represents an entirely new departure for Renaissance architecture. The trapezium is found only in Pienza, while the oval, which enjoyed a great vogue in the following decades, had previously been applied only by Michelangelo, in the mausoleum of Julius II, and by Peruzzi in the villa at Salone.

The basic choice of the trapezium arose from a chance factor, the non-perpendicularity between the façades of the old Senatori and Conservatori palazzi; yet it is true that, while preserving the linc of the large ancient building which contained the Tabularium, Michelangelo could very easily have slightly altered the orientation of the façade of the Palazzo dei Conservatori when he made a radical reconstruction of the building. The decision to preserve the alignment would not have been taken unless it had been considered advantageous from the spatial point of view. It should not be forgotten, moreoever, that at the time of Michelangelo a piazza, in the true meaning of the term, did not exist: there existed only the two old buildings forming with their façades a slightly acute angle, and the monastery of S. Maria d'Aracoeli appeared in the far distance. It would therefore be wrong to think that Michelangelo was working on a space which was already formed. On the contrary, in a disorderly and haphazard situation, he envisaged the possibility of finding a new order by creating a symmetrical irregularity in an already existent wing.

What could have been the source of Michelangelo's interest in the trapezium? In the urban sphere, we have already observed his interest in tangential views along the sides of the Palazzo dei Senatori, but on the optical plane also, certain relevant aspects should be noted. Following the access line of the ramp, the trapezoid form of the spatial model may be termed 'anti-perspective': that is to say, it tends to reduce the impression of depth. If we compare the frontal view of the Capitol to a fifteenth-century form of central perspective, we observe immediately that the horizontal lines of the two lateral buildings are not parallel but diverge considerably. From a psychological viewpoint, the divergence in the wings produces the effect of a closure at the rear and so accentuates the impression of an enclosed space, like an open-air room. At the same time, the fact that the distance increases between them as we look towards the background produces an effect of far greater parallelism than would have been the case if the wings really were parallel. A possible explanation is that Michelangelo was following Vitruvius in wishing to adapt the principle of optical rectification to an urban scale, resisting the effect of perspective diminution, and aiming to induce in the perception of the viewer the Platonic conception of rectangular space, freed from every empirical distortion.

Another, more realistic suggestion is that Michelangelo wished to lessen the rigidity of a perpendicular composition and, through the divergence of planes and the complexity of relationships among the three volumetric elements, to create a greater spatial dynamism and a sense of progressively expanding vistas as the eye follows the privileged line of visibility. This hypothesis seems borne out by the repetition of the divergence in the wings, both in the access staircase and in the stairs leading to the Palazzo dei Senatori. In this way the same broadening of the perspective as the eye moves towards the objective to be attained would be repeated four times between the outskirts of the city and the papal-imperial baldacchino, so creating an exciting route which is not conceived in abstract

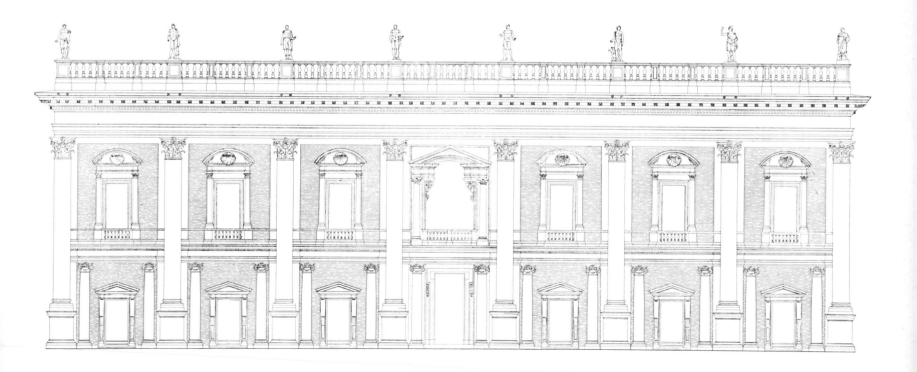

form but is continually affected by the presence of man. When we consider that the policy pursued by Paul III was aimed at achieving an organic alliance between the papacy and empire so as to recover the religious unity of Europe and defeat the enemies of Christendom, then it can be seen that the Capitol represents the symbolic expression of this profound aspiration towards unity whose roots go back to Dante's *De Monarchia*.

The Palazzo Farnese

On the death of Sangallo in 1546, Michelangelo inherited together with the responsibility for St. Peter's another unfinished work: the Palazzo Farnese. The first phases of its construction have been described in the chapter on Antonio da Sangallo and there is no need to refer to them again here. Michelangelo drew up a second plan for the façade, in which he respected Sangallo's design for the windows but modified their proportions by constructing a taller and protruding cornice and slightly raising its impost base. In the work as a whole, in spite of the greater dynamic tension produced in the organism through adjustments to the dimensions, Michelangelo showed a great respect for the work of his rival, which was improved but not distorted by his intervention.

On the *piano nobile*, the only variant he introduced was the abolition of the double arch which was to connect pilasters and columns in the large central window; this was replaced by a rectilinear trabeation on which he placed the large Farnese coat of arms.

On the second floor, he put in hand the windows designed by Sangallo, which were probably already carved. The small variant in the two far windows on the right of the main façade, which are without the interior connecting cornice to the tympanum, indicates a minor correction intended by Sangallo himself. A variant of fundamental importance, however, occurs in the cornice which, compared with Sangallo's manner, has acquired a density of vibration which imparts a new vitality to the entire block.

In the *cortile*, Michelangelo's contribution is to be seen especially in the third order, because the second was executed by Vignola with only slight departures from earlier designs. Here the arcade was abandoned in favour of an architraved order of Corinthian wall pilasters protruding far out of the wall and extended laterally by two small wings. As in the smaller order of the Capitol, where the architrave and sub-cornice are treated in the same way as each wall pilaster, the cornice itself remains rectilinear and encloses the sky over the courtyard in a perfect square. In contrast to the simplified capitals, the design of the entablature and windows is very rich and fanciful, imitating the style of grotesques, so that we are reminded of a passage in the dialogues of Francisco de Hollanda in which the following words are put into the mouth of Michelangelo: 'And so there grew the insatiable human desire to prefer to a building with its columns, and doors, and windows, a chimerical, grotesque edifice, whose columns are made from cherubs issuing form the calixes of flowers, and the pediments and architraves from branches of myrtle, the doors from rods or other things which seem impossible and unreasonable, but can become beautiful when executed by someone very knowledgeable.'

Not even in St. Peter's are the mouldings and the elements composing the order, the mutules, and triglyphs, treated with such a high degree of freedom. The hollowed finial, for example, which marks an advance on the Laurentian Library, stands out sharply from the level of the guttae and the shadow created by its deep recession is countered by two slender listels which capture the light.

The one variant of those proposed by Michelangelo which would have profoundly altered Sangallo's construction was not put into effect. It would have entailed an optic recession of the *cortile* and the linking of the palazzo to the former Chigi Villa by a bridge across the Tiber. Vasari writes of this proposed project: 'then Michelangelo directed that a bridge should be made across the river Tiber, so that one could go from that palazzo in Trastevere to another garden and palazzo belonging to them, and looking out of the front door which faces the Campo di Fiore, one could see at a glance the *cortile*, the fountain, Via Giulia,

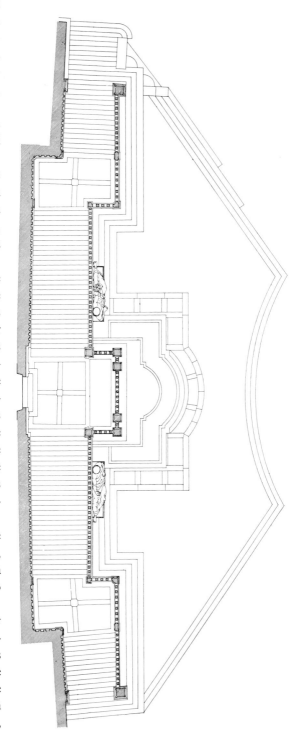

Staircase of Palazzo dei Senatori (1 cm = 3 m).

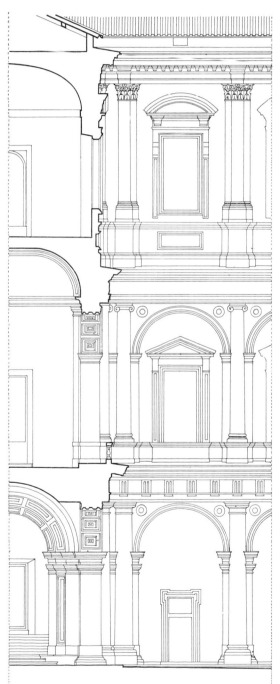

and the bridge, and the beauty of the other garden, up to the far door leading out to the Via Trastevere.'

Two contemporary engravings show how the courtyard would have appeared with the opening of the first-floor loggia. As Ackerman has rightly pointed out, the opening of this loggia—once the whole of the palazzo side on the Via del Mascherone was completed, at least to ground-floor level—would have resulted in the apparent recession of the central part of the façade overlooking the Tiber, thus producing a similar volumetry to that of the Farnesina and anticipating the Palazzo Barberini.

The diagram on page 214 represents an attempt to show how the palazzo would have appeared if this exciting idea of Michelangelo's had been realized.

St. Peter's

When Michelangelo was invested with the supreme responsibility of his lifetime, the task of continuing the construction of St. Peter's, the successive alterations made to Bramante's original plan by Fra Giocondo, Raphael, Peruzzi, and Sangallo, had combined to reveal all ist inherent contradictions. Bramante began with a brilliant idea for creating internal space by an organic combination of classical motifs co-ordinated into spatial units, but was unable to find an equally simple and clearcut solution for the external mass of the building. This problem created doubts which were reflected in Bramante's last plans, and emerged fully in Sangallo's work where the crisis of classicist culture was expressed dramatically.

Michelangelo's opinion of Sangallo's model is well known, but it is worth reminding ourselves of it because it contains the seeds of the great innovations he introduced when he freed himself from the unsolvable problems arising out of the liturgical programme laid down by his patron. 'And it cannot be denied', Michelangelo wrote to Bartolomeo Ferratino in 1555, 'that Bramante was as excellent an architect as any who has existed from ancient times onwards. He prepared the first plan for St. Peter's, not full of confusion, but clear and distinct, luminous and isolated all round, so that it did not interfere with any part of the palazzo; and it was considered a beautiful thing, as can still be seen; so that whoever has departed from the design of Bramante, as Sangallo has done, has departed from the truth; and that this is the case anyone with unimpassioned eyes can see in his model. By that circle which he makes outside it, he firstly takes away all light from the building of Bramante, and not only this, but in itself it has not yet any light at all: and there are so many dark hiding places between the top and bottom that they provide great opportunity for countless crimes: such as hiding outlaws, making false coins, imprisoning nuns, and other crimes, so that in the evening when the church was closed, twenty-five men would be needed to seek out those who remained hidden inside it, and they would have a hard task to find them. Then there would be this other difficulty, that by encircling Bramante's building with the projection shown in the model, it would be necessary to level to the ground the chapel of Paolo, the rooms of Piombo, the Ruota, and many others: not even the Sistine Chapel would, I think, remain untouched. Concerning the part made from the outside circle, which they say cost a hundred thousand crowns, this is not true, since it could be made for sixteen thousand, and by destroying it little would be lost, because the stones used there and the foundations could not become available at a more appropriate time, and the building would be improved by two hundred thousand crowns and three hundred years of time. This is how it seems to me and without passion; since to win would be a very great loss to me. And if you can make this clear to the Pope, you will do me pleasure, for I do not feel at ease.'

Michelangelo does not show himself to be well informed about the various stages of the planning and wrongs Sangallo by attributing to him the initiative of surrounding the apses with ambulatories. Bramante's original plan on parchment (Uffizi, No. 1) contains no ambulatories, but they appear distinctly in all successive designs and were clearly motivated by Bramante's need to fulfil the requirements of the church, especially in connection with Holy Week services when processions had to pass round the apses. But it is true that

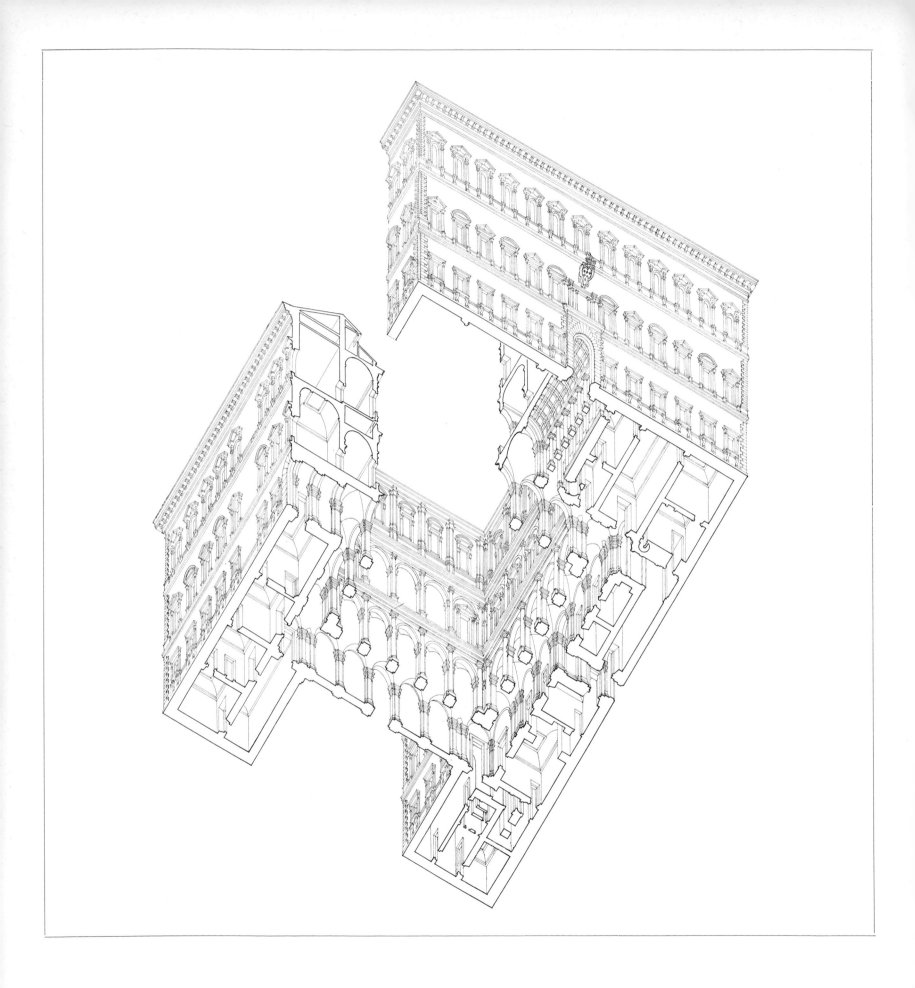

whereas Bramante had turned this feature to aesthetic advantage by opening the ambulatories to the exterior and illuminating the apses with a filtered light, Sangallo completely separated the ambulatory spaces from those of the naves, thus considerably reducing the degree of illumination in the interior as a whole. As for the danger to the Sistine Chapel referred to by Michelangelo, it may be noted that Sangallo's model would have respected its integrity even though the gigantic bell-towers placed only a few yards away from it might easily have endangered its stability.

However, the letter to Ferratino clearly shows that the question of doing away with the ambulatories, and so drastically reducing the volume of St. Peter's, represented a vital battle in which, as Vasari has pointed out, Michelangelo implicitly upheld the superiority of quality over quantity and the belief that a grandiose concept could be realized independently of the actual dimensions of a building. The success of his proposal, which meant that sections endowed with a precise liturgical significance could be omitted, was due not only to the great esteem in which the aged architect was held, but also to the fact which he pointed out in the letter that this would enable costs to be drastically reduced and the building time shortened.

In his treatment of Sangallo's scheme, Michelangelo behaved like a gardener who prunes a plant so drastically that he removes its leaves and branches and leaves only the bare stalk intact. He retained, as he could not fail to do, the central structure of the internal space with the four piers and the arms of the cross—in which the theme of the triumphal arch was repeated eight times—but sacrificed all the articulation which tended to integrate the space of the central crossing with other volumes which had been endowed with their own autonomy. Of particular significance was the abolition of the chapels which formed a static conclusion to the four large intersecting aisles arranged round the central space. The general design of the internal space, based on a cross intertwined with a network of four intersecting elements, was thus finally replaced by the design of a cross intersected by a kind of ring which formed an unbroken link through the remaining sections of the aisles. However, Michelangelo's contribution to the design of the interior does not stop here, but extends also to the form of the apsidal terminations. Here, the plasticity of the wall had become dulled in the flat modelling of the wings and was re-created by Michelangelo to enter fully into the 'awesomeness' of his late-period works. Behind each of the wall pilasters, the wall was articulated by the insertion of deep sockets to contain the huge windows, which were extended to the point of destroying the original tabernacle-type of structure and reducing it to a few disjointed fragments: broken tympanum parts fitted into the sockets, membratures reabsorbed into the wall, bits of the structure, now transformed, bathed in the even light. Originally the ends of the cross were all worked in travertine, including the caisson sockets. The very careful design of the cornices, the subtle distinction between the neutral wall background and the window sockets, characterized by a continuous horizontal rustication, show the importance accorded to these spatial terminations; Bramante's conception of an indirect, filtered illumination, obtained by means of the ambulatories, was now replaced by a view against the light, so that the depth of the wall became accentuated and it acquired the quality not of an inert mass, but of a 'body', a resistant muscular fibre.

With regard to the treatment of the external volume, Michelangelo adopted a more radical position. The parts already completed comprised only a central nucleus which did not protrude at any point beyond the enveloping structure except for Sangallo's semicircular extension to the north apse which had just been started. It was therefore possible to bring a completely fresh approach to the problem without having to make serious adjustments to work already begun, and Michelangelo did so by dissociating himself from every previous suggestion. Bramante and his successors had always viewed the organism as a system of spatial cells endowed with a relative autonomy, and their method of handling the exterior had always been to endeavour to translate this aggregation of cells into volumetric terms in a way that would be recognizable from outside. The two solutions of Bramante which we have examined employ the same technique of assembling more or less organically connected sub-units. In the hope of solving the contradiction in Bramante's work, Sangallo had employed the serial motifs of the *consecutio temporum* of the classical period.

Michelangelo took over the shapeless and confused mass which the unfinished building must have presented in his time. He considered the internal organism as an accomplished fact, complete in itself: it would have been useless to project its fragmented volume on the exterior. In order to make its essence comprehensible, it was necessary to renounce any attempt at descriptiveness or at creating a mechanical relationship between the interior and exterior; the external mass of the building had to reveal the simple idea which governed the organism, and at the same time it had to be a self-sufficient and completely unitary structure. The relationship between the interior and exterior was not mechanical but dialectical, and entrusted to the expansion of the convex apses (centrifugal force) and to the braking action performed by the diagonal piers on the exterior which corresponded to the square grouping of the minor volumes counterbalancing the apse protrusions (a chain to contain the centrifugal thrust).

The outer wall appears a homogeneous enclosure in which, as a result of the oscillating rhythm of the intervals between the wall pilasters, there is a constant alternation between contraction and expansion.

The rhythmical arrangement of the order, which is very similar to that of the ends of the crossing in the interior, is based on a hierarchical distinction of the various wall 'strata', revealing a very high degree of complexity as well as of clarity. We must first of all identify the primary structure, consisting of a pair of Corinthian pilasters, coupled by a continuous entablature; this group recurs throughout in both the rectilinear and the curved sections, and alternates with an interval also of constant dimensions, but associated with an alternately protruding and receding cornice. We thus have a distinction among the intervals which is not confined to the varying distances between the supports but informs the whole plastic treatment. We might say that in relation to the wall as a whole the pairs of adjacent wall pilasters constitute a buttressing system similar to the one employed for a far different effect in the dome. In this way, two pairs of contradictions underline and confirm each other: that between wide and narrow, and that between receding and protruding. The latter recurs again in the interior in both the narrower and wider intervals, since in both cases the wall pilaster is echoed by a counter-pilaster endowed with a crypto-capital and a simplified Tuscan type of base. Whereas in the narrow intervals a plain wall appears beyond the counter-pilaster, possessing no other ornamentation than the simplified base, in the larger intervals at the second order the wall recedes farther and the large windows appear inserted in a framing traversed by a series of horizontal mouldings. This recession is later further countered by the protrusion of the moulding supporting the aedicule.

In addition to the stylistic features observed in the organization of the order, there are some exceptional points which should not be overlooked. In particular, the alternating series of large and small interaxial areas dies away to correspond to the angular buttressing, in which the pattern of the smaller interaxial area is repeated between the two sides, so confirming its primary and structural function. In this case the two angular wall pilasters merge into a single pilaster which stands fully apart from the wall. A further plastic modification to this angular feature derives from a remarkable anomaly: namely, the fact that in relation to the wall surface it protrudes farther than the normal pair which is repeated along the whole circuit, the reason for this being that the wall pilaster recedes deeper into the wall and so makes it appear to protrude to a greater extent. To this pilaster there corresponds, on the opposite side, a single curved wall pilaster placed between the angular piers and the sloping bevelled linking sections to the apses. These sections are not conceived as simple linking elements, but as protruding blocks which contain the apsidal protrusions and at the same time appear to be pulled forward by them to take up the anomalous position of an inclined angle which is not forty-five degrees, as might be supposed, but is free of every preconceived geometric definition.

This rapid analysis of the structure makes clear Michelangelo's intention to create a whole series of opposing and contrasting forces without resolving them into a synthesis. Observed from below, the gigantic outer wall has the appearance of a band made up of vertical sections which appear to be held together by a kind of magnetic attraction instead

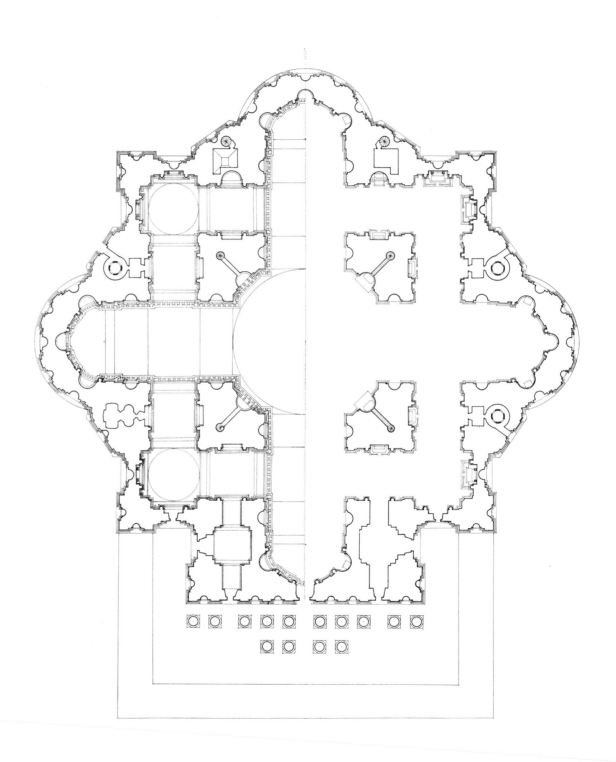

of being solidly welded. The large entablature, which traditionally served to relate together the elements of the structure, has been made responsive to every minute irregularity in the wall, forming countless angles and protruding so slightly that it barely interrupts the vertical flow of the edges. Then the attic storey with its very slender cornice leads the viewer even more clearly, in a harmonious conclusion to the architectural discourse, to the huge volume of the dome above, which in the plans was to be introduced by four smaller domes. We know that at an early stage Michelangelo provided a far simpler version of the attic storey, and a recent study by H. Millon has shown that this simplicity was not due to incompleteness but was decided upon deliberately. Although it is difficult to believe that the final version which was already present in a drawing made in 1565 could be the work of Pirro Ligorio, it should not be forgotten that the only solution to the problem proposed by Michelangelo about which we have documentary evidence (even though later contradicted) is the one illustrated in Luchino's engraving. In this engraving, the attic storey appears as a perfectly smooth band surmounted by a small cornice similar to the one in the final version, and interrupted only by groups of large windows corresponding to the internal volume of the apses. These large windows are framed by large splayed arches, which are shaped so as to admit as much light as possible. The most interesting aspect of the attic storey in this first version is its sinusoidal curvilinear form; it envelops the convex volumes, the apses, and the cylindrical shapes of the large spiral ramps, and gently brings them together by counter-curves. Above the large cornice a flat section began, without

Exterior of the apse of St. Peter's (1 cm = 4 m).

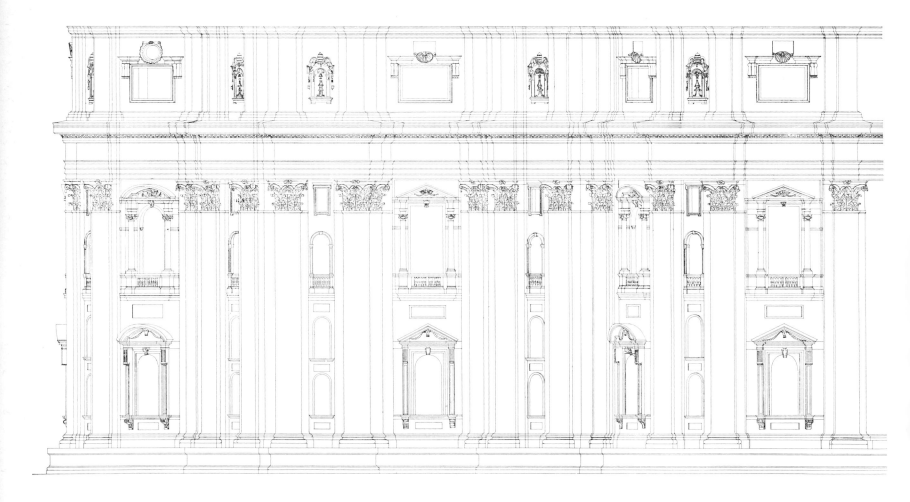

any ornamentation or relief and moulded as flexibly as if it were clay. In the first idea its function was to introduce at first sight the dome, and before that the extrados of the large vaults of the crossing and apsidal terminations—all spherical surfaces which anticipated the theme of the dome.

The flexible modelling of the curvilinear band served to introduce the cupola which is supported by a completely smooth base resting on an elaborate cornice. Over the cornice, after a further interval, the decorations on the wall of the apse, in low relief, are repeated in fully-rounded form. The pairs of wall pilasters are replaced by pairs of free-standing columns linked up to three-quarters of their height to the cylindrical drum, by means of a receding wall section. On this drum there are inserted windows in which the theme of the tabernacle is given a highly original interpretation. Whereas the tympani protrude considerably, the cornicing of the windows appears to be drawn inwards and merges in the body of the wall.

Viewed from below, the cupola forms a relationship of necessity with the apse wall: the tumultuous and unresolved tensions reappear, at first reconciled in the monodic rhythm of the drum, then channelled into the convergent band of the ribs of the vault, to be resolved in the vibrant nodal point of the lantern. The problem of whether or not it was Michelangelo who made the decision to raise the curve of the cupola finds modern critics still divided; in the absence of documentary evidence they have been drawn into a debate as subtle as it is unproductive, revealing nothing so much as the divergent tastes of those taking part in it.

Without entering the fray, one can view the problem in the light of the urban value of the dome. The façade, as designed by Michelangelo and known to us only indirectly through the modifications introduced by his successors, apparently permitted an optic connection, although in view of the closeness of the viewpoint an optic rectification of the semicircular profile would have been required. The choice of a higher dome—if Ackerman's argument is accepted—would indicate that Michelangelo considered that the long view of the building in its urban setting was more important than the more strictly architectonic view obtained at close range.

The Church of S. Giovanni dei Fiorentini

'Most illustrious lord Duke of Florence,' wrote Michelangelo to Cosimo de' Medici in 1559, 'the Florentines have many times had a great desire to build here in Rome a church to S. Giovanni. Now hoping to have a more favourable opportunity to do so in the time of your Lordship, they have decided upon it, and have put five men in charge who have several times asked and begged me to make a design for that church. I, knowing that Pope Leo had already given a start to that church, answered that I would not undertake it without the permission and patronage of the Duke of Florence. Since then I have received a very cordial and gracious letter from your Illustrious Lordship, which I take as an express command to attend to this church of the Florentines and which gives me very great pleasure. I have already made several designs adapted to the site which the above committee have set aside for this work. They, as men of great talent and judgement, have selected one of them, which in truth appeared to me as the most praiseworthy; it will be drawn and designed more precisely than I myself could do on account of age, and will be sent to your Illustrious Lordship: and whatever will seem best to you will be carried out.' Vasari specified that five plans were prepared out of which the choice was made, and he added that Michelangelo, usually modest when speaking about his work, declared that, 'if they carried that design to its conclusion ... neither the Romans nor the Greeks in their times ever made such a thing.' In all probability, four of the five designs submitted were those contained in drawings 121, 124, 120, and 123 in Casa Buonarroti; the fifth, which has been lost, is the direct precedent of the final design known to us through the engraving by Le Mercierw here the wooden model executed by Tiberio Calcagni is reproduced. Michelangelo's point of departure, or at least the most autonomous of the designs submitted, can be seen in drawing 121, in which features reminiscent of the church of S. Stefano Rotondo and the baptistery of St. John Lateran may be recognized. The ground plan is seen as the product of two constant aspirations: the desire for a centralized structure, and the desire to make a hierarchical distinction by accentuating two preferential axes. It was probably due to an iconological motivation that the architect inscribed the cross in the circle, but at the same time he must have envisaged the dynamic interest created by circular sections hollowed out by the projecting area of the chapels.

An alternative to this circular solution is provided in drawing 123, which owing to the massive size of the columns would seem to relate to a building of smaller proportions, although still closely connected to the S. Giovanni series through the central structures referable to a baptismal font. The organism consists of a large square hall, divided into nine sections by an internal arrangement of arches, and enclosed on three sides by semi-circular apses. The model seems remotely derived from the church of S. Maria delle Grazie at Pistoia, built by Michelozzo and Ventura Vitoni. The third drawing represents the most elaborate and contradictory stage of the planning. In a single design there are recollections of 'beautiful S. Giovanni', the temple of Minerva Medica, St. Peter's, and S. Stefano Rotondo. The octagonal design and the cruciform are intertwined with the square, and out of the intersecting points hexagonal chapels and blocked semicircular areas of space are created. Diagonal structures projected onto the floor recall the design made by intertwined arches, similar to those in the church of S. Evasio in Casale Monferrato. The work of synthesis undertaken on Bramante's St. Peter's appears here in a more complex and indirect form. The square exterior has been made octagonal, while the arms of the cross have lost their continuity and become pulsating spaces; the roof then becomes the dominant feature, while the arms are reduced to limp terminal spaces. Each problem gives rise to another, and no immediate solution appears possible. This design provides final proof of Michelangelo's originality, and his ability to remain outside the conventional ideas of his contemporaries; it is at one and the same time unresolved and prophetic.

Drawing 123 is closer to the final solution although still connected to drawing 124. The central space has become a rotunda, intersected by two pairs of perpendicular figures with varying development in depth. The accentuation of the axes, which suggests the image of a radiant cross, recalls a shallow drum with lunette or even a starry sky, but the ambiguity of the pattern is not conducive to well-grounded deductions. This design is undoubtedly the most convincing of the four analysed, yet the idea of englobing the four elliptical chapels into a single large cubic block with rounded edges reflects an earlier stage of the treatment of the volumetric problem, which, however, appears to be entirely resolved in the wooden model. This model differs from drawing 123 in the form of the smaller chapels, the centrifugal arrangement of the columns on the wall, and the abolition of the baptismal baldacchino.

The model appears to provide a solution to many of the problems which had emerged in the other designs, and represents the most mature and rigorous approach to the theme of the centralized church evolved during the period of the Renaissance, especially so far as creating an organic relationship between the interior and exterior was concerned. In order to understand completely the considerations which determined the direction of Michelangelo's research, we must refer to the opinion he expressed of a classical building which was taken as a model by Renaissance architects: the Pantheon, with which the church of S. Giovanni forms a precise dialectical relationship. We know that Michelangelo greatly criticized the Pantheon and believed it to be the work of several architects since the connection between the church structure and the Rotunda was, in his view, not resolved. The church of S. Giovanni, like the Palladian church at Maser, probably represented an explicit attempt to overcome this lack of continuity in the structure. In the interior, the relationship between the dome and drum, which in the classical model relies purely on

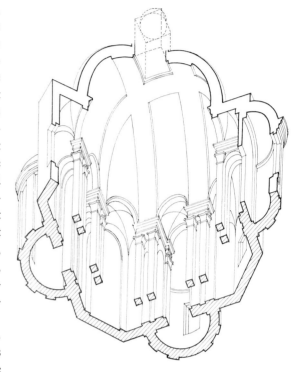

Axonometric of Michelangelo's design for San Giovanni dei Fiorentini, after drawing No. 120 A in Casa Buonarroti.

Axonometric of Michelangelo's design for San Giovanni dei Fiorentini, after drawing No. 124 A in Casa Buonarroti.

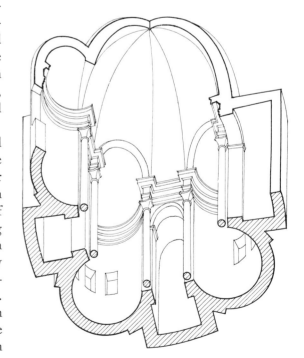

View of Michelangelo's final design for San Giovanni dei Fiorentini.

superimposition, now becomes one of organic interconnection. The insertion of the chapels, which in the Pantheon is disguised by the colonnaded triforia, is now clearly revealed through the arched openings. On the exterior, the smaller sections surrounding the dome do not impede the view, but at the same time accentuate its importance by a process of interconnection which is made apparent through the linked concavities.

In relation to this design, some critics have spoken of a desire by Michelangelo to adopt a classical style as an alternative to the designs containing a more explicit search for dynamic tension and an articulated, open spatialism. In fact, Michelangelo adopted a highly critical attitude towards the classical tradition and expressed the proud certainty that he was able to 'supersede' it. Those who see S. Giovanni as an anticipation of Neo-classicism are basing this view on an incorrect interpretation of the graphic evidence, and a failure to perceive the dynamic and structuralist nature of the organism. By analysing the interior, one can see that the principal radio-centric structure is made up of pairs of superimposed free-standing columns, linked by radial ribs and horizontal connecting bands. This creates a circular structure composed of dynamic lines which transcends the classical type of coffering and contrasts with the inert flatness of the enveloping structure.

The last example of Michelangelo's attitude of rebellion against the tendency, generally accepted by his contemporaries, to worship abstract rules and classical orthodoxy, was provided in the Porta Pia. In the finished work, as in the many preparatory drawings, two only partly converging tendencies may be discerned: the constructive one by which the urban problem was to be treated in a new way with the gate acting as a visual pole to draw together the urban image, and the destructive one by which the models accredited by tradition were exposed to irony and even sarcasm in order to show their state of dissolution and crisis.

From the urban viewpoint, the Porta Pia marks a new departure and establishes a method which was to remain valid for the visual reorganization of the city structure carried out twenty years later by Sixtus V. The gate stands at the end of a long urban perspective, the Via Paola; but as a background feature, it does not act as a perspective terminal. Whereas in the base section the wall screen connects the two perspective wings (originally consisting of boundary walls with only a few buildings), at the top the aedicule which continues the motif of the gateway appears to float in the sky. Seen from afar, the vertical group comprised by the gate and aedicule fills the portion of sky contained between the two wings, although not completely; bathed in light, it appears as a cipher, an emblem imbued with symbolic meanings. A hypothesis which appears entirely valid has been put forward by De Angelis d'Ossat, according to whom the medal coined by Federico Bonsagni represents the outer façade of the gate; this is confirmed by the small apertures on the sides, which are almost like arrow-slits, and its direct link with the town walls; and it is probable also that Michelangelo intended to construct the outer façade to back onto the side facing the city and to connect it to the town walls by means of diagonal linking sections. It is known that in his *Dizionario*, Pirro Ligorio accused Michelangelo of misusing emblems and decorations in the gate and failing to give them a symbolic meaning. It is very unlikely that this judgement is correct and that Michelangelo explicitly rejected an iconological content for this work.

It should not be forgotten that in the Christian tradition the door is a symbol for Christ: *Ego sum ostium; per me si quis introierit, salvabitur*, we read in Chapter 10 of St. John (I am the door: by me if any man enter in, he shall be saved). In the part facing the city, the door indicates the collapse of security, of defence built upon faith, and the loss of salvation. The demons entwined in the structure indicate the danger of perdition for those who depart from the truth.

The external façade was intended to imply the opposite meaning, but unfortunately all that we know of this façade with any degree of certainty is contained in the unreliable image shown on the medal. However, the festoon over the entrance, which is similar to those in the attic storey of the dome of St. Peter's, could well be a symbol for salvation, while the large shell is certainly a reference to the eternal nature of both the city and the church. Drawing 102 in Casa Buonarroti certainly relates to the exterior; one can recognize the protruding central section with the two small windows that could still be seen in the eighteenth century behind the constructed façade, as shown in an engraving by Vasi. Here, in a framework which is more solid but no less endowed with the quality of 'awesomeness', there appears a vessel at the top which might be a symbolic reference to baptism, and thus to salvation.

The Sforza Chapel

'It is rough, because whereas all other chapels in Rome are made of fine marble, and in most cases of noble ancient marble, this one is made entirely of travertine, except for the altar and two tombs placed on the sides; but as for the design it is a proof of the genius of Buonarroti, because it contains a magnificent simplicity, a novelty which though bizarre is very orderly, and a great and awesome quality which amazes those who see it, and in such a form that it does not seem as if you are seeing a real thing, but an abstract idea, either invented by the mind or seen in a dream, of the most singular and magnificent building surpassing the forces of human thought.' In these words Monsignor Bottari described the Sforza Chapel in a letter written in 1743. And in truth, this small unadorned appendage to the great Roman basilica, like a palimpsest inlaid with gold and marble, is together with the wall of the apse of St. Peter's the greatest evidence of the point at which Michelangelo's architectural research has arrived.

In the Sforza Chapel, the structural invention is concentrated upon a nodal composition of an exceptional plastic force, a diagonal band which connects the wall panels. On entering, one has the impression that the rectilinear walls at the sides of the rear chapel project towards the viewer as far as the head of the diagonal, where the movement is roueatd into two directions, one centripetal, the other centrifugal in relation to the transversal axis. The latter ends in the taut arch of the apses which link the piers and bring about the suppression of the contrasting forces.

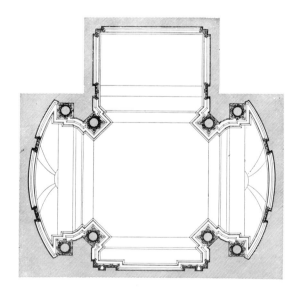

The area of space is submitted to the influence of several lines of direction simultaneously: it deepens with the development of the longitudinal axis, contracts at the sides in contact with the broad curve of the walls, and in the centre it is held in by the angular buttresses and adopts a vertical movement. The innovations in method found in Michelangelo's Florentine architecture have undergone a change in scale. The effects he once aimed to achieve through the articulation of the enveloping structure, the intertwining of latent structures, the creation of several simultaneously possible viewpoints, and the temporal dimension of the dynamic action, have now been sought and obtained by employing simplified instruments to act directly upon the space. The wall regains its continuity, and through its curving produces a sense of fluidity, and the plastic effects are concentrated round a few elements only in an alternate series of vibrations and contractions. The roof no longer has the function of a terminal or contrasting feature, as in the Medici Chapel or St. Peter's itself. Between the roof and wall, there exists an absolute continuity in which all dynamic forces are reconciled. The lines of tension in the base are prolonged until they meet and are resolved, without the dialectical anomaly of the drum, in a continuous pattern where movement becomes an intimate attribute of the organism: it is no longer expressed through projections which are extraneous to the main structure but forms part of the continuous design like an intimate circulation of energies. Michelangelo's anthropomorphism thus attains its most intimate and intense form of expression, after making the wall permeable to space and uncovering its muscular structure; following the same route which led to the last of his *Pietà*, Michelangelo wished to imbue his architectural works with an inner incorporeal energy connected with the most vague and fugitive aspect of experience— space itself.

The geometrical means by which the organism is created are extremely clear; at the sides of the central area measuring 10.20 m. a side on which stands the canopy supported by the diagonal order, the shallow apses are inserted, measuring barely 6.20 m. To the entrance there corresponds a small nave only 1.70 m. deep, while the chapel of the altar is 6.20 m. deep. The total width is therefore slightly greater than the length and the centres of the two apses do not correspond with the centre of the canopy: the curves are more sweeping: 10.20 instead of 9.80, which is a sufficient difference to remove the impression that the curved walls are part of a single cylinder, and at the same time by employing an identical measurement (the curve of the apse is equal to a side of the impost square) an impression of regularity and harmony is produced which is reinforced by the slight difference between the total height and length, about 20 centimetres.

The final example of Michelangelo's architectural activity is the church of S. Maria degli Angeli. The church was hollowed out of the ruins of the Baths of Diocletian, with the addition of a few wall partitions to mark off the church from its surrounding structure, and represents a solemn act of humility and renunciation of form. In order to appropriate the area of the church all that was needed was a gesture both utilitarian and religious—that of fixing boundaries and enclosing the site. Architecture and existence have become reunified and equal.

VIGNOLA, OR 'APPEASEMENT'

Of the third generation of sixteenth-century architects—the generation which included Palladio (1508), Pirro Ligorio (1510), Vasari and Ammannati (1511)—Jacopo Barozzi da Vignola (1507) was the first to make a solemn impact on the Roman cultural scene.

His opportunity came with the death of Paul III, when his work in S. Petronio Bologna on the high altar baldacchino was arraigned by the church overseers. The election of Julius III and Vasari's vaunted good offices resulted in his appointment as papal architect, and at the same time he was commissioned to erect the Tempietto of S. Andrea on the Via Flaminia and to participate in the construction of the neighbouring suburban villa situated in a valley lying between the Parioli and Pincio hills.

Among the several directions followed by Roman architects around the middle years of the century: the academic followers of Sangallo, the anti-dogmatic revolt of Michelangelo, and the uneasy classicism of the now vanquished Raphael-Peruzzi line, Vignola did not have to make an irrevocable choice. He took what he required from all the traditional methods, seeing no conflict between them, using the various contributions to form a synthesis which would reconcile all differences. However, the choice which he refused to make in the sphere of style was introduced in the ideology, and in spite of his early experience as a painter and the variety of work he had undertaken in the north, the choice he made was to accept Sangallo's definition of architecture as an autonomous discipline and technique, an instrument of organization and power, and a direct expression of the authority and ideals of the dominant class.

Vignola fully adhered to the ideals of the Vitruvian Academy, according to which architecture possessed a universalistic and instrumental function, and he set himself the task of constructing a logical system out of the discoveries of the two preceding generations, seen from a distant perspective which disguised their differences and 'appeased' them. But the attitude of the new generation saved the architect from a work of pure conservation and enabled him to fulfil a creative role, even though it was within that process of impoverishing the architect's function which corresponded to the instrumental programme of the Counter-Reformation. Vignola's first modest opportunity for architectural work in

Axonometric of the Sforza Chapel.

Detail of the corner node of the Sforza Chapel (1 cm = 40 cm).

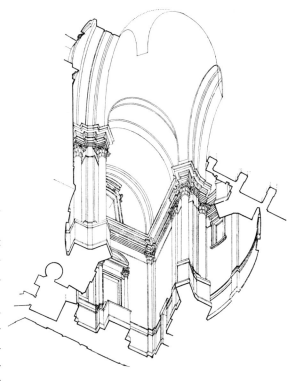

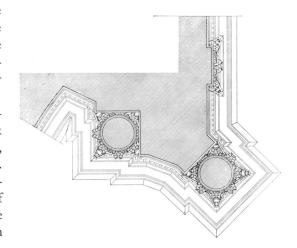

Rome was probably to assist in the construction of the Palazzetto Torres in Piazza Navona; this building was not destroyed, as is believed in error, but relegated to a dark little courtyard among some buildings at the concave end of Piazza Navona which were reconstructed after the Corso Rinascimento was built. The theme of the Banchi loggias in Bologna recurs here, but in a freer development and a more elegant form as a result of the overall system of proportions. The building was partly unfinished, and in a reconstruction sketched by Letarouilly, it can be seen from the arrangement of the orders and the subtle handling of plastic effects that Vignola was interested in the works of Peruzzi. Especially noteworthy is the panelling which echoes the outlines of the order; this motif gained rapid popularity and relates this building to the Palazzetto Spada in Via Capo di Ferro, where at least in the second order it is more than likely that Vignola had a direct hand in the work.

The church of S. Andrea on the Via Flaminia represents Vignola's first decisive project, and shows how important his Roman experience was to the architect. As in Michelangelo's church of S. Giovanni dei Fiorentini, this little church is based on a critical approach to its obvious structural anomalies, which were unacceptable to a man of the Renaissance. In the Pantheon the brutal interpenetration of the porch, the rectangular bay, and the Rotunda created a lack of harmony between the organism and the façade. Michelangelo had solved this problem by doing away with the façade as a frontal plane, thus making S. Giovanni the product of solidly interpenetrating volumetric units all visible at one time, and in a relationship of reciprocal advantage. Vignola, on the other hand, preserved the façade because his interest in frontality was in direct relationship to his adherence to the ideology of 'decorum', but in his volumetric definition of the organism, he already established conditions. In the first place, the basic geometric design excluded the circle in favour of the oval, so expressing a preference for a directional and longitudinal form, rather than a symmetrical figure without intrinsic frontality. In the second place, the oval cupola was supported not by a cylindrical drum, but by a cubic block whose stereometric characteristics extended into the interior. Bramante's principle of 'growing together' was abandoned and replaced by the assembling of pure volumes.

In the interior, skill and an experimental approach were well balanced. The whole of the building was subjected to the laws of the order, which demanded respect for a rigid distinction between the shaft and entablature, divisible in their turn into base-shaft-capital, and architrave-frieze-cornice proper. On close observation of the building; the meticulous interpretation of the rule suggested to the architect that he should include the whole of the pendentive area in the interval reserved for the frieze. It is only when this point has been clarified that it becomes possible to explain the apparent anomaly of the simple, low architrave placed above the capitals and lacking the upper elements of the trabeation, and at the same time the complex design of the impost cornice of the cupola, rigorously proportioned to the height of the pilasters. This stylistic stratagem is resolved in the luminous quality assumed by the whole of the cresting area: a blinding light striking between the two solid structures of the base and shallow dome.

The novelty of this little church—with its double casing of the internal walls, its window niches in the façade, the original rhythmical pattern of the external order, and even its actual preference for effects of silvery chiaroscuro created by slight protrusions—are already expressive of an attitude which set a rigorous observance of rules against a modest desire for experimentation in new forms of composition.

The same freedom in composition together with observance of rules guided Vignola in his work on the Villa Giulia; the section for which he was responsible comprised the principal villa opening in a concave shape onto Ammannati's garden theatre. Following a longitudinal direction along a privileged axis, the villa built for Pope Julius was so well adapted to the form of the landscape that the image of nature entered it from above, framing the vast enclosed space. The idea behind the design was probably worked out by the patron and the architect together, with the additional advice of Vasari, and perhaps also of Michelangelo. It appears to grow out of a focal point: the horseshoe loggia which the villa adjoins but does not envelop, leaving its final spans uncovered. Compared with this loggia, the façades looking onto the city appear notably severe, as if they wished to conceal and atone for the 'frivolity' of the internal space. This aspect becomes even more apparent in the plan, where the uneasy marriage between the semicircle and the perpendicular surround produces a series of dead spaces and useless wall depths.

The double-edged programme which was common to many of the architectural ventures of Julius III can be clearly perceived. The leisures and delights of court life had to be hidden behind a façade of 'decorum'. The opening out of the building towards space, and the subtle treatment of the enclosure had to be countered by a grave note and a sense of sullen defensiveness. The extrovert and pleasing appearance of the Farnesina and Villa Madama were replaced by the principle of absolute introversion and the *hortus conclusus*.

On the exterior, Vignola's ambition to achieve a synthesis is too much in evidence. The edges are marked by angular wall pilasters, articulated in such a way that they offer a symbiosis between the angular rustication employed by Sangallo and the system of orders found in Peruzzi and Bramante. The same pattern is found in the large doorway, where the form of the rustication is derived from Sangallo while the columns are taken from Serlio. Even the ornamented windows of the Banchi loggias in Bologna have been remodelled in a more robust form after the example of the most accredited classical models. The elements derived from northern architecture, such as the violent, even brutal, central motif with radiating beams and friezes curving out into the void, play only a modest part in a composition in which full account is taken of local tradition. It was originally planned that little cupolas should be placed above the staircases so as to impart greater weight to the structural elements, and the fact that these were omitted in the final version detracts from the success of the composition as a whole. The main importance of this work of Vignola's lies in its tendency to accumulate plastic values at a well-defined 'focal point' of the composition.

In the structure of the semicircle the influence of northern architects, especially Giulio Romano, proved a far more decisive factor. The frequency of the apertures and the complex rhythm according to which they are grouped marked an innovation, as did the variety of architectural features employed—tall pilasters, slender free-standing columns, small curved wall areas, and large arches marking the two far ends and centre of the sequence. When analysed as it appears in the two superimposed planes, the rhythmical sequence may be expressed in the following algebraic terms:

$$a \quad a \quad b\,b\,b\,b\,b \quad a \quad C \quad a \quad b\,b\,b\,b\,b \quad a \quad a$$
$$A \quad a \quad b\,b\,b\,b\,b \quad a \quad A \quad a \quad b\,b\,b\,b\,b \quad a \quad A$$

The method of connecting arches and colonnades with their corresponding entablatures to the impost cornice of the arcades occurs frequently in the drawings of Peruzzi and also in Sangallo's design for the church of S. Giovanni dei Fiorentini (*cf.* Uffizi drawing 233), but in the form in which it was employed by Vignola it results in an anomalous rhythm recalling Giulio Romano's treatment of the Palazzo del Te in Mantua.

The technical and professional assurance which Vignola demonstrated, and his ideological adaptability made him the natural heir to Sangallo, whom he had probably come to know among the circle of the Roman academy. It is therefore no matter for surprise if his meeting with the Farnese family led to a 'love match' which lasted until the architect's death in 1573. The Farnese family was one of the most solid and conservative among the Roman nobility, and for a long time had been interested in the exploitation of their estates. The ideological basis for all their activities was the cult of authority and decorum, and the perpetuation of these values as absolutes, untouched by time.

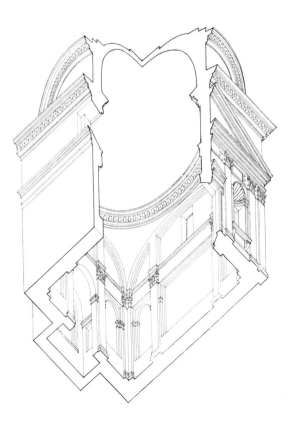

Axonometric of the church of Sant'Andrea on the Via Flaminia.

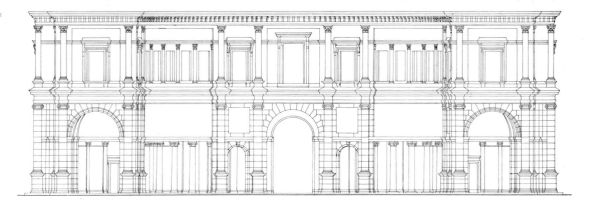

View of the internal façade of Villa Giulia (1 cm = 3.3 m).

Plan of the Farnese palace of Caprarola.

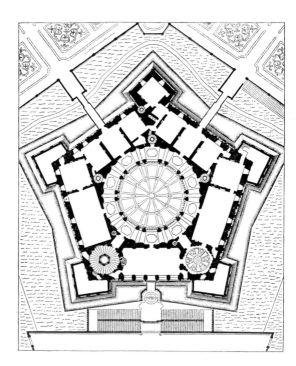

Alessandro was born in 1520 and appointed cardinal at the age of fifteen. Even after the death of his uncle, he remained one of the most influential personalities in the College of Cardinals. His refined humanist education and his love of art made him not only an enthusiastic collector of works of art, but also an extremely knowledgeable patron, able to collaborate at every level in the planning of his building and decorative ventures. The construction of the villa-castle of Caprarola had been decided upon much before his time, and we have seen how Sangallo and Peruzzi drew up plans for its position and pentagonal volume. Vignola inherited from his predecessors only the foundations, so that he could not be held to their intentions and was able to enjoy the utmost liberty in developing the structure. But this liberty was of a strictly technical nature only, since the cardinal's ideological aspirations were so clearly defined that they not only dictated the purpose of the work, but actually suggested the 'tone' he desired it to convey.

Vignola's task was not confined to the erection of a building in isolation and the layout of the gardens; as Lotz has shown, his task extended to a complete redevelopment of the medieval quarter in which it was situated. The extension of the theme of the palace to include the surrounding district was essential moreover in order to stress the precise significance that the residence was intended to represent, so that far from being in an isolated situation, it was placed frontally in relation to an axis acting as a counterpart to the long lines of roads stretching beneath it. The district was reconstructed by Vignola on a capillary basis, arranged around an axial route closely in line with the axis of the castle and lying on the watershed of a steep hill. The district was thus divided into two sections, so sharply distinguished one from the other that the inhabitants nicknamed them 'Corsica' and 'Sardinia'. As Gerard Labrot has rightly observed (*Le Palais Farnese de Caprarola*, Paris 1970), the entire spatial structure of the Villa Caprarola is based on the double symbolic contrast between high and low, fore and rear, which in both the architecture and the great pictorial decoration serves to reinforce the principle of authority and majesty, creating an unbridgeable gulf between the powerful and the weak, nobles and plebeians, friends and strangers.

The Farnesina and Villa Madama were erected in rural surroundings, and enclosed by gardens, so that they had no structural relationship with the city, while in spite of its isolation the Villa Giulia had presented a two-sided image. Caprarola, on the other hand, acquired meaning and value through its structural relationship with the populated district lying at its feet. But this relationship did not express, as did a feudal settlement, the kind of social pact whereby the feudal lord guaranteed the protection of his subjects in exchange for their loyalty; in connection with the Villa Caprarola it would be less accurate to speak of 'feudalism' than of 'rural nobility', that is to say, a system in which submission is an external and indisputable fact which cannot be questioned, and the link between the ruling power and the community brought no other factors into play but existed purely as a static ritual.

After his work on the Villa Giulia, Vignola was the architect who could best be relied upon to carry out his patron's designs with wholehearted personal participation. The programme of enhancing the power structure represented by the Farnese family was based on a fundamental ambiguity. Contemporaries were united in praising the ingenuity of a building which was at one time both a castle and a villa, a fortress and palace, and clearly understood the intentions of the patron, for whom the forms of architecture were more important as vehicles for his message than for their own essential qualities as constructive or functional elements. The palace had to present the appearance of a fortress, not so as to fight off improbable assailants (the large number and width of the apertures would have enabled any such assailants to conquer and destroy it without difficulty), but to demonstrate the power of the Farnese family.

The large esplanade with its ramps and complicated system of entrances combined the qualities of an urban piazza and a military parade ground, and it was here that the building entered into a dialogue with the city as a whole; but this was merely at a surface level, since in reality a moat separates the square from the building, while a narrow doorway emphasizes its unattainable majesty. The ramps appear to wish to embrace the city, in the manner of a Palladian building, but the villa itself, far from opening out towards the city in a welcoming gesture, seems firmly held in the grip of a vice, while the differences in level accentuate the impression of cold, aristocratic detachment which was still far from the theory of 'popular persuasion' propounded a century later by Tesauro.

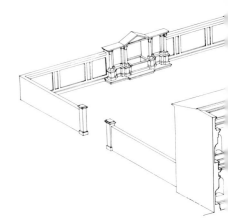

If the Villa Giulia was a double-sided structure, introverted in its façade and extroverted in the courtyard, the Villa Caprarola presents an even more complex and ambiguous relationship between the architecture and its surroundings. The pentagonal block has five almost identical façades, the most ornate and open of which is the one looking onto the landscape. The gardens projecting onto the hill from the two rear façades of the pentagon are situated at first-floor level but have no direct connection with the building, which remains unaffected by their presence. But in the interior, in the suite of frescoed rooms, the circular courtyard, and the amazing spiral staircase, the severe atmosphere and solemn rhythm are interrupted and a sense of vibrant euphoria is created, although a feeling of cold melancholy intrudes now and again. From the stylistic viewpoint, the features selected by Vignola confirm his ability to take what he found most suited to his needs from whatever source was at hand—the 'well-regulated mixture' recommended by Gilio in his *Trattato sugli errori dei pittori* (Treatise on the errors of painters) dedicated to Cardinal Alessandro Farnese in 1561.

The base section and the curvature of the vaults are treated in the manner of Sangallo, with the window copings contrasted to the wall surfaces. The whole of the central area of the façades, however, is ornamented by an order of wall pilasters with a line of arcades in the style of Peruzzi. The two top floors, which were for the servants' quarters, are vertically linked in a single order. In the sequence of large doorways with columns occupying various levels, the lesson of Serlio has been absorbed and adapted in an original and personal form on the basis of a calculated optical progression. The whole composition of the terracing at different levels responds to the logic of an axial function; this is true even though, just as in Cellini's sculpture, there is created a plurality of viewpoints from which the spatial organism may be perceived equally clearly in all its complexity.

The parts of the building which are architecturally most significant are the spiral staircase and circular courtyard; the theme of centralization is developed in both these parts with absolute rigour, and the ceiling decorations create in both of them resonances of colour which penetrate the shadows and cause them to vibrate, evoking the unreal world of a dream. Bramante's Belvedere staircase was the prototype from which Vignola was enabled to give proof of his technical superiority and impeccable style, thus emphasizing the distance which had been traversed between two epochs. Bramante employed progressions of orders which he subtly harmonized so that, when viewed from below, the illusory impression would be created of a spiral in a series of superimposed circles; Vignola, in contrast, re-solved all possible contradictions inherent in a spiral form by reducing it to an absolute continuity. Then he concluded the structure in a virtuoso manner, adding a dome section over the staircase to terminate the spiral without creating a sudden break. The use of twin supports, the choice of the Doric order so as to reinforce the spiral rhythm by means of the triglyphs, the design of the baluster in which openings alternate rhythmically with closed sections, the ordered pattern of the wall pilasters which gently repeat the rhythm of the columns on the perimeter, the impeccable technique and subtle handling of the patches of light to connect the landscape with the windows—all these features indicate that one of the high peaks in the classical Renaissance has been attained. Formal perfection, which is the counterpart of the fall in value of theoretical concepts, here reaches so high and per-suasive a quality that it appears to develop in a substantial form the research which was undertaken in the early years of the century, so marking a second rebirth of the ideal *con-cinnitas*.

The same perfection of form characterizes the courtyard area, in its circular enclosure surrounded by high grey stone walls. Its slender proportions, the delicate, taut design of its rustication, and its highly calculated rhythm of sistoles and diastoles in the order, trans-form the model of Bramante, which was still full of rough edges and sudden breaks in rhythm, into a Petrarchan flowing harmony.

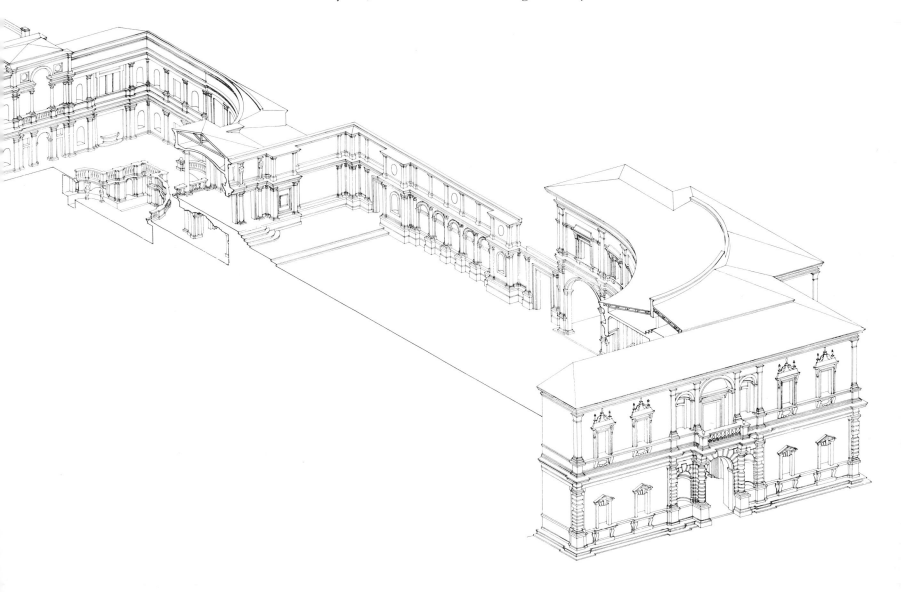

The works of Vignola bear the same relationship to classical sources, perceived now through the medium of an abstract theoretical system, as did those of the painters who were summoned by Cardinal Alessandro to compose the great decorative cycles. In the paintings, mythology is introduced to point an allegorical meaning, reflecting a clearly-defined system through which the revealed truths of Christianity could be expressed in the light of a concept whereby history was viewed as a static structure, where every event, however it might be clothed, is always identical; in the same way, Vignola adopted the forms of antiquity, simplified, polished, and sublimated them in order to relate them to a form of objectivity so high and absolute that it would take them outside the course of evolution and history, and project them beyond the limits of time itself.

BARTOLOMEO AMMANNATI, OR THE UNQUIET CONSCIENCE

Of the third generation of architects—if we except Vasari, whose only finished work consists of the modest chapel of S. Pietro in Montorio and the chapel built for Pius V which falls outside the chronological limits of this study—the only one who was educated in the Florentine school was Bartolomeo Ammannati. He came to Rome in 1550 with the firm intention of devoting himself to the study of 'ancient architecture'. By 1552 his studies were already rewarded when he was granted a commission to design a fountain on the Via Flaminia to mark the entrance to the site on which Julius III had intended to construct his villa. The simple structure, to which Pirro Ligorio later added a storey, was made to curve slightly after the example of Sangallo's Zecca. The very careful design of the orders marked a desire to conform to classical models which allowed very little room for originality, but by making the large aedicule a dominant motif he created an image of an illusory perspective depth, so opening the way to a new orientation in architectural research. This was confirmed by the work done to the interior of the villa, covering the whole structure at various levels viewed as a background to the courtyard. The link with the parts of the palace built by Vignola was established with great subtlety, so that the two parts are integrated without being fettered. However, the stylistic features selected by Ammannati can be clearly distinguished from those of Vignola: they are more subtle in tone and their derivation from the antique is less formalistic and more literary. The internal details of the loggia show that Ammannati had a far from superficial interest in the Florentine works of Michelangelo, and they are evoked here very prudently in an ambition to 'redesign' in an individual manner the orders and minor constituent elements of the architectural discourse.

In the courtyard the main impression is one of pulsating rhythms and silvery chiaroscuro effects, and we become aware of the architect's desire to re-create the form of classical peristyles enlivened by transparent openings. However, the semicircular area comprising the nymphaeum is segregated from its surroundings by unbroken walls, and developed at the lower level where a highly complex ornamentation creates scenographic effects.

The complicated rhythmical orchestration of the second courtyard, which unfortunately was drastically reconstructed in the eighteenth century, was a consequence of the architect's stay in Venice; Ammannati was one of the first architects to bring to Rome some of the innovations discovered by Giulio Romano. Ammannati's most original contribution can be seen not so much in the details as in the overall arrangement of the itinerary which leads the observer from the majestic stage-setting of the first courtyard, animated with transparent effects, to the intimate, secret tone of the nymphaeum and to the luminous atmosphere of the loggias, from which he is surprised to perceive the varying levels and superimposed architectural motifs.

Bartolomeo Ammannati: fountain in Via Flaminia (1 cm = 2 m).

A different and more disturbing orientation characterizes Ammannati's intervention in the Palazzo Firenze, which may be recognized in the rearrangement of the original courtyard and in particular in the additional section inserted between the courtyard and garden. Whereas the design of the loggia overlooking the garden remains faithful to the classicism of Sangallo, the façade onto the courtyard is composed in a dramatic atonal mode, employing terms which are entirely extraneous to the Roman ambience. The frame of the two superimposed orders is reinforced laterally by openings which break up the even rhythm. The assembly at one place of the most disparate elements produces an effect of instability and conflicting tensions which are entirely new in Roman architecture and are already completely imbued with the spirit of Mannerism.

Many features have been taken from Michelangelo's repertory but appear here in a different logical context. For example, the little windows of the Laurentian Library have been incorporated at the very top of the ground-floor niches in what appears to be an ironical and mocking evocation, while the laborious triple repetition of the cornicing on the first-floor niches looks like a strange confused version of the large windows of the courtyard of S. Lorenzo transferred to a different setting with little sympathy or understanding.

The spiritual crisis which later led Ammannati to denounce the pagan and lascivious nature of his youthful production is foreshadowed by this mannered and clumsy work, already so far removed from the joyous sunlit architecture of the Villa Giulia. In place of the crisis in content which affected his works of sculpture, what we have here is a crisis of faith—faith in the myths of correctness and stylistic coherence, and faith in syntactic rules as the only means of overcoming the rigid and therefore opaque nature of architectural language. The pagan nature of architecture, which had to be fought and overcome, was identified in the acquired body of clearcut rules handed down by the preceding generation; opposed to these rules was the ambition to create a 'different' architecture, which must be allowed to shake off its debt to the classical world.

Of the other works generally ascribed to Ammannati, there is no doubt that the Palazzo Caetani in Via delle Botteghe Oscure is to be exluded, since it is one of the buildings which owes most to a strict adherence to the lines laid down by Sangallo. Many doubts remain concerning the attribution of the Palazzo Rucellai on the Corso, now Palazzo Ruspoli, in which the example of Sangallo is developed in an original manner with an unusual emphasis on proportions. The feature which came closest to the style of Ammannati was the large window inserted inside the doorway on the Corso; unfortunately, this window has since been removed, but we know that it was very similar to those later built into the ground floor of the Pitti Palace in Florence.

PIRRO LIGORIO, OR 'THE FRUITS OF THE INTELLECT'

The new man of the third generation of sixteenth-century architects was not a 'professional' like Sangallo and Vignola, nor a painter like Vasari or a sculptor like Ammannati; he was an 'antiquarian', a man of letters and a painter, to whom the classical tradition represented not only a world of self-sufficient forms to be created anew in their structural values, but above all a world of symbols, of myths and legends which lent substance to forms that would otherwise be silent and meaningless.

A hundred years earlier, Leon Battista Alberti's antiquarian interests represented merely one aspect of the general non-specialist orientation of critical humanism; in Pirro Ligorio they represented a vocation so specialized that it became a veritable monomania and thus a means of escape. Yet this did not prevent him from fighting his own cultural battle with dignity. It was a battle for the recodification of the figurative repertory of architecture and decoration and for the conquest of a freedom which would be inseparable from the rule. It led to the creation of the gardens of the Villa d'Este, one of the most extraordinary and fascinating examples of sixteenth-century architecture, and in the Villa Pia it made him the prophet of a form of relationship between architecture and nature which was destined to come fully into its own in the two following centuries. It is a paradoxical fact that Ligorio, who was a classicist and an enemy of the licence that Michelangelo permitted himself, was himself a precursor of the Baroque through the contradictions he displayed (all of them, however, internal to the classical system) between obedience to the rule and transgression of the rule which was subservient to the example of antiquity.

Pirro Ligorio was educated in Naples but his archaeological interests soon brought him to Rome. His first work in Rome was in the field of façade decoration, an art which had continued to be very popular since the early sixteenth century. He invented a new style, which fell outside the categories of pearly monochromes, graffiti, and highly coloured frescoes: it was an imitation of metal relief work in various shadings of yellow, probably derived from the figures of painted sovereigns on the dado of the Stanza dell'Incendio in the Vatican.

By 1549, through his façade and ceiling decorations and his designs of 'antiquities', Ligorio had already become sufficiently well known to be admitted to the Congregazione dei Virtuosi in the Pantheon and to the 'family' of Cardinal Ippolito d'Este, who on his return from France had been appointed governor of Tivoli by Julius III.

Villa d'Este

His meeting with Cardinal Ippolito marked the beginning of a radical change in the life of Ligorio. At last the exceptional erudition he had acquired through years of study found a field of application where it could be displayed, and his artistic ability could be put to use under the protection of a learned patron. And this was not just any patron, but Ippolito, the son of Lucrezia Borgia and Ercole d'Este, one of the most influential members of the College of Cardinals, and together with Alessandro Farnese the most learned and 'magnificent' of the cardinals and one of those who most openly aspired to the papal throne. During the time when he had been a papal legate in Paris, he had asked Sebastiano Serlio to build him a residence which is described minutely in Serlio's Seventh Book. On his arrival in Rome, he chose for his town residence the Palazzo di Monte Giordano, and as a suburban residence the villa that later became the papal villa on the Quirinale. However the Tivoli estate, granted to him by the new Pope as a reward for supporting him in the conclave, was so dear to Ippolito that soon after his triumphal entry into the city, he decided to extend the old monastery intended as his residence, and to make a garden along the lower slope, which already possessed the prophetic topographical features of a 'happy valley' from where a splendid view over the distant city could be enjoyed.

Problems connected with the plots of land, houses and churches which had to be destroyed in order to make way for the villa occupied the cardinal's administrators for more than a decade, and the layout of the gardens and palace was still unfinished when Ippolito died in 1572. However, at the beginning of the work the architect planned his programme of construction and iconological intent, much of which is known to us through a detailed description of which two copies have been preserved, one in Paris and one in Vienna. From this description, those who succeeded Ippolito were able to have the work carried to a coherent conclusion.

Pirro Ligorio, who was in charge of the work until 1568, was the inspirer and director of the great enterprise, and it is interesting to recall that his frequent visits to the site at Tivoli made it possible for him to initiate for the first time a systematic programme of research, including excavations, into Hadrian's Villa. Ligorio's contact with this extraordinary villa in its romantic landscape, where Hadrian had given his architects the reverential

Plan of Palazzo Firenze (1 cm = 11 m).

Palazzo Firenze, external façade overlooking the garden.

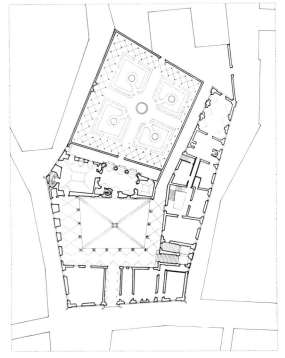

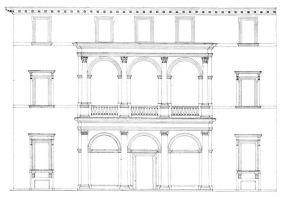

232

task of preserving intact the memory of his voyages and so reconstructing metaphorically the visual experiences of a lifetime, undoubtedly caused him to visualize the Villa d'Este also as the image of a remote mythical garden, as the unfolding of a narrative—or rather, of many interwoven narratives—and as a topographical synthesis of a much wider landscape.

By following the architect's description, Coffin and Lamb have reconstructed the iconological programme, though without interpreting it fully. We shall therefore add to their important findings some suggestions of our own, particularly where they throw light on the specific contribution of Ligorio.

There are at least four significant strata which may be identified in the villa, all of which, as we shall see, bear closely upon the personality of the cardinal and his past and future life:

a) the villa as 'the garden of the Hesperides';

b) the villa as a sacred wood, posing the problem of a choice to be made between vice and virtue (myth of Hercules);

c) the villa as a site consecrated to the memory of Hippolytus (Virbius), son of Theseus; and

d) the villa as a topographical image of the extent of the territory of Rome, from Tivoli to the sea.

The Garden of the Hesperides

An emblem painted on the bedroom of the Cardinal's palace provides a key to the enigma. It contains a garland of golden apples with the inscription *Ab insomni non custodita dracone*. Together with the garland, there appears the eagle of the Este family, so that the image can be interpreted in the sense that the apples are no longer guarded by the dragon who protected the garden of the Hesperides but are now under the care of the Este eagle. The reference to the myth of Hercules is thus made explicit and becomes charged with several symbolic meanings.

The eleventh labour, imposed on Hercules by Eurystheus, was to obtain the golden apples which were held safe in the garden of the Hesperides. The apples were a marriage gift from the Earth Mother to Hera, who had entrusted them to the care of the daughters of Atlas guarded by the hundred-headed dragon Ladon. After he had completed this labour, Hercules was tormented by thirst and by stamping on the ground he caused a river to gush forth (*cf.* Igino, *Astronomia poetica* II, 3).

Greek sources concur in naming the geographical location of the garden of the Hesperides as the slopes of Mt. Atlas; indeed, the same name refers to the sunset, for it is at the sunset hour that the sky becomes tinged with shades of green, yellow and red, calling to mind an apple tree laden with fruit; then after the sun has been cut off from the horizon as an apple is cut from a tree, it disappears towards the west and as soon as it has set, the evening star, Hesperis, appears in the sky.

In the villa at Tivoli there are numerous references to this myth: the image of Gaea, the Earth Mother, placed at the centre of the Organ Fountain; the statue of Hercules, which was to stand at the centre of the gardens; the dragon, to which a fountain is dedicated; and the continually recurring theme of garlands of apples found throughout the decoration. But the most important reference is the general one by which the whole of the garden enclosure becomes bathed in a mythological transfiguring light through a number of highly evocative analogies—its position on the slopes of the mountain, its exposure to the west, and the presence of water and grottoes.

'Thus,' wrote Pirro Ligorio (*Dizionario*, book XII), 'villas attract men to a solitary abode far from the affairs of the town, enticing them like clear waters.' Tivoli is one of the few places where the pedantic scholar allows his feelings free rein, introducing a note of immediacy and spontaneity. The same sentiment seems to have inspired the serene image of the terraced gardens, traversed and rendered vibrant by the waters, animated by the shades of mythical beings, who seem literally to dwell amongst them, they are a fragment of a golden age cherished and reincarnated through the intellect.

The Myth of Hippolytus

In the myth of the garden of the Hesperides, the personal reference to the cardinal is to be found in the interpretation of the myth which Fulgenzio has given. He sees in the three apples three fundamental virtues: serenity, generosity, and chastity, the last of which is the connecting link with the myth of Hippolytus. References to this myth are found in certain parts of the gardens, and it was also the subject of a series of reliefs designed by Ligorio which have survived in the form of illustrations to a biography of Hippolytus-Virbius based on classical sources. The connection between the two themes appears also in the dedicatory epigrams written by the cardinal's poet friend Marc-Antoine Muret and mentioned by Coffin.

Hippolytus, the son of Theseus and Antiope, is the hero of the tragedy of that title by Euripides, the subject of which is his chaste resistance to the advances of his stepmother Phaedra. Hippolytus was killed by Poseidon and according to Latin mythology was later brought back to life through the intervention of Artemis, when he acquired the name Virbius, that is, Vir Bis, or man twice over. Artemis hid him in the wood of Ariccia on the Alban hills. It is interesting to note that in taking the story of Hippolytus-Virbius from classical sources, Ligorio carefully avoided any reference to his supposed marriage to Artemis and to the nymph Egeria. In order to make the legend appear apposite to the cardinal, he obviously thought it necessary to dwell on the aspect of chastity. It is also possible that the reference to the rebirth of Hippolytus under another name may have been intended as an allegory of the cardinal's election to the papacy, since he never attempted to hide the fact that his ambitions lay in this direction.

All the central area of the gardens is devoted to the theme of chastity, which is expressed in the polarity between the grotto of Venus, dedicated to 'voluptuous pleasure', and the grotto of Diana and Hippolytus, dedicated to 'honest pleasure and chastity'. The two grottoes are connected to other areas in which there are statues of characters symbolizing either vice and its dangers (Helen, Clytemnestra, Castor, Pollux, Leda) or the virtues (Lucretia, Penthesilea, etc.). Coffin explains that an allegorical reference was intended by the relative position of the two grottoes and the statue of Hercules. From the centre of the gardens, where according to the description the statue of Hercules was to stand, the road leading to the grotto of Diana is rugged and bare, while the road to the grotto of Venus is pleasant and decorated with beautiful fountains.

The Topographical Image of the Villa

The end of the adventures of Hippolytus in the wood of Ariccia, which was clearly visible from the Villa d'Este, forms the link between the second and fourth strata of the iconological programme. As we have seen, the latter relates to the sacred associations of the site; the villa becomes a cosmic image, since the water gushing out of the lap of mother earth (Organ fountain) passes through a series of channels and ends its journey in the fountain of the Sea; but it is more especially an image of the territory of Rome. The two most important fountains are dedicated to Tivoli and Rome and the channel which links them represents the Aniene. Tivoli, the city of waters, is represented by a portico and large cascade; Rome is evoked in her ancient splendour through a series of minute structures and symbols (most of which have now unfortunately been destroyed).

As in the Japanese gardens of the Zen cult, but in a far less abstract manner, the area of the gardens acquires an unexpected density, as an image of something much vaster which lies outside itself and is 'represented', or described by synthetic means.

The topographical image indicates a possible connection with the person, or at least the aspirations, of Ippolito d'Este, since the route from Tivoli to Rome, represented in the gardens by the roaring waters, may have been intended as a symbol for the cardinal's coveted transition from the purple to the pope's tiara.

The Landscaping of the Gardens

This richly developed iconological structure had its counterpart in an extremely clear and rational arrangement of distributive functions. This must have created an open, joyful atmosphere in the gardens, especially at the time when the trees were newly planted and had had not yet conferred on the villa the wild and romantic appearance it possesses today. The most interesting aspect of the design is the dynamic interaction of the two alignments presented by the building and the lower garden. The divergence of a few degrees is resolved by making the esplanade, with the avenue named 'the cardinal's walk' subordinate to the palace and creating a common perpendicular relationship among all the other paths depending on the central avenue situated on the axis of the two-storeyed loggia in the centre of the building. The paths are connected by sloping diagonal links, and without in any way impairing the clarity of the composition, this arrangement increases its pictorial and dynamic interest. The network of paths is made up of thirteen longitudinal and eight transversal avenues, which generally link symmetrical or equivalent poles. A clearly defined hierarchy exists among the thirteen longitudinal paths which makes the central route predominant, so repeating the pattern of the Villa Caprarola, where the palazzo was enclosed from below so that its importance became accentuated.

Among the transversal avenues, however, there are three which have been given more importance than the others on the basis of the principle of bipolarity. The first (the cardinal's walk) has at one end the fountain of Aesculapius and at the other the grotto of Diana; the second, the fountains of Tivoli and Rome; and the third, consisting of two adjacent roads, the Organ and Mother Earth fountains and the fountain of Neptune (not executed). The central area lying between the two roads is occupied by the ponds which at one time were enlivened by criss-crossing sprays of water which Montaigne remembered for the splendour of their rainbow effects.

The Architectural Innovations

Pirro Ligorio's architectural contribution can be particularly observed in the Tivoli fountain. The choice of the oval as the basic form and of the minor axis as the most important one, though it may be derived from Peruzzi's Villa Trivulzio at Salone, is here exploited in an original way to create an impression of broad vistas and open expanses. The basic architectural rhythm is created through the contrast between the semi-oval concavities of the portico with loggia, and the convex form of the great fountain basin from which the water descends to form a sort of luminous cone trunk. The gentle flowing lines of these elements, designed in a subtle manner with barely defined contours, reverberate in the natural setting in which they are placed.

Pirro Ligorio here shows himself to be a great director, not only in a theatrical sense as the organizer of a spectacle to be enjoyed from a fixed viewpoint, but also, and to a greater extent, in a 'cinematographic' sense, since everything conspires to lead the observer onto the stage so that he too becomes an actor and protagonist. We need think only of the passage cut out under the dark gallery, where the water forms reflections against the light, or of the fact that it is possible to walk behind the cascade and to see its transparent and continuously changing motion and listen to its roaring waters. The importance accorded to water as pure form and dynamic force, which became so much in evidence in the art of the Baroque age, is already completely expressed in these gardens. Although they had many imitators, and may have been superseded in richness of orchestration and structural complexity, they have never been surpassed in the intensity of the impressions they convey through their subtle analytical description of water.

The fountain of Rome, now reduced to a sorry fragment, was to be a plaything for the architect in his capacity of archaeologist, where contrasts of scale were to be pursued to the point of improbability. However, the happiest inventions are to be found in the ponds and in the Organ and Screech-owl fountains. Montaigne has given us a description of these fountains as they appeared in his day. 'The gushing of infinite spurts of water,' we read in his *Voyage en Italie*, 'either held back or thrown from a single valve operated from a great distance away, I had seen before elsewhere on my journey, at Florence and Augsburg, as previously descibed. The organ music—the real music of a real organ which, however, always plays the same notes—is obtained as a result of the water falling with great violence into a round grotto, where it whips up the air and forces it out through the reeds of the organ so providing them with wind. Another rivulet moving a cogged wheel plays in a pre-established order on the keyboard of the organ; and one also hears what appear to be the notes of trumpets. Elsewhere one hears the singing of birds: there are certain small bronze flutes such as are seen in a nympheum, which—by the same artifice as the organ—produce a sound similar to that made by children blowing through little earthenware vessels filled with water; then from other valves an owl is set in motion, which appears at the top of the rock and immediately causes this music to cease, frightening the birds by its presence, then again it yields them the place, and so on alternately, whenever desired. From one point it emerges like a rattle of cannon shot; from another it comes as a denser and weaker sound, like that of an harquebus: a sudden fall of water into the conduits causes these noises when the air is forced to emerge at the same time. All these inventions and other similar ones, founded on the same natural principles, I have seen elsewhere.

'There are basins or fishponds, surrounded by stone parapets, and above, many stone pilasters with sharp edges at a short distance away; from the top of these the water pours out with great force, not upwards, but in the direction of the fishpond. The mouths are turned inwards, one facing the other, so that they throw out the water and scatter it into the bowl with such violence that the jets cross each other and meet in mid-air, causing a dense and continuous rain to fall onto the water; and the sun, casting its rays on the bottom of the basin and in the air and all round that place, produces so clear and distinct a rainbow that it has no need to envy those we see in the sky. Never had I seen anything like it elsewhere.'

It was probably Pirro Ligorio who was responsible for rediscovering the technique of fountain effects invented by Heron of Alexandria, and he used these effects with the assistance of a few skilled craftsmen to make both the Organ and Screech-owl fountains function. Heron's insistence on the element of surprise, his enjoyment of pleasure as an end in itself and his belief that technique should be put to the service of entertainment, found a sympathetic interpreter in the Neapolitan antiquarian.

All that has survived of the Screech-owl fountain is the enclosure with the background inlaid with multicoloured scales. In his design for the walls of the hollowed niches, Ligorio employed the current fashion of simplifying and reducing the order to the form of simple unmoulded bands, and indicated the distinction between structural elements and intervening areas through the texture of the design.

In the Organ fountain, the violent tensions conveyed through the surfaces were certainly motivated by considerations of content connected with the orgiastic cult of Mother Nature, the figure which occupied the large central niche before the little dome-covered temple was constructed (in the early seventeenth century). The complex design, with its extreme accentuation of the chiaroscuro reliefs, produces a grotesque and orgiastic effect on the form of the fountain. Although the broken tympanum was not executed until the time of Cardinal Alessandro, after the death of Ligorio, it is not improbable that it was Ligorio who designed it. It is true that he severely criticized Michelangelo and the Mannerists for making bad use of this same feature, but in this case at least he might have felt able to accept it as the symbol of a death divinity, such as Gaea, the great Mother from whom all

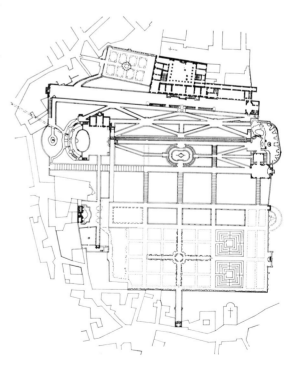

Plan of Villa d'Este, Tivoli (1 cm = 40 m).

is born and to whom all must return. As we read in Ligorio's *Dizionario*: 'Those also seem worthy of praise, who in architecture have made many sections one inside the other, some broken and some whole, and place in the churches of God, in private houses and in great palaces such features as the ancients used in tombs; they force themselves to produce such trivialities and besides this have gone so far as to vary the forms of the surmounting cornices, and the epistyles of these buildings which have symmetrical outlines, and have made them overhand and fall beyond the outer perpendicular, which is against the nature of squaring and the breaking up of things which are firm and stable.'

The most important architectural features of the Villa d'Este, the palace, the banqueting or Belvedere loggia, and the grandiose design of the terracing, are imbued with a monumentality and classicism which are far from being conventional and academic. His daily frequentation of the ruins and his awareness of the least widely known aspects of Roman classical architecture enabled Pirro Ligorio to stand apart from the current Sangallesque trend and approach the refined stylism of Vignola. The palazzo is treated with extreme simplicity, the mass of the building being modelled by the angular pavilions which, in an engraving by Dupérac, appear to be raised in the way of turrets. The only outstanding accent, which announces the presence of the garden and leads the eye towards the great tree-lined avenue, is the two-storeyed pavilion; this was undoubtedly derived from the loggia which Michelangelo designed for the Capitol, but is here treated very differently in terms of violent chiaroscuro effects and an illusory accentuation of perspective depth. In the design of the serliana window enclosed in the framework of the order, the columns are almost completely detached, thus articulating the cornice, while at the centre the coupling of the column by means of the entablature represents a return to the theme of the aedicule as an autonomous feature. We have here a clear foretaste of the allusive interplay of recessions and protrusions which was to dominate the handling of the façade throughout the whole of the seventeenth century.

The banqueting loggia was completed after Ligorio's departure from Rome in 1569, but was certainly begun earlier, since the finishing touches in travertine were already in hand at the beginning of that year. This loggia is the most important part of the villa from an architectural point of view. The motif of the triumphal arch occurs in a simplified form, and great technical skill is shown in the treatment of the linking sections between the structural elements. The progressively increasing depth of the reliefs in the openings surrounding the niches reveal an interest in subtle plays of light, as though the architect wished to create for each vertical element an answering echo which grew more and more tenuous. In the interior, in the relationship between the framework and the vast space beyond the luminous zone, we may observe a desire to introduce a psychological factor to reconcile the rhetorical solemnity of the building with the search for forms which welcome the outside world as well as forms enclosed within themselves.

At the same time as he was engaged on the Villa d'Este, Pirro Ligorio constructed a little palace of a 'severe style' Lodovico Torres of Malaga (1552). The palace was situated in the Piazza Navona, by the side of the tower designed by Sangallo for the Del Monte family, and is characterized by the rustication which covers its entire surface in a decreasing relief. A reference to Sangallo is apparent in the rusticated quoins in the doorway, and in the ground-floor corbelled windows, but is contradicted by the continuous rhythm of the wall which seems to indicate a greater interest in Peruzzi's line of research. The refusal to force the theme onto a monumental plane, and the decidedly modest and discreet approach, were probably to some extent the result of the attitude of contrariness so often evinced by Ligorio. The only innovation, which cannot be said to be attributable to binding structural considerations, was the variability in the distances between the windows of the façade facing onto the Piazza Navona. The fact that the distance tends to increase at an even rate proceeding from the Vicolo della Cuccagna towards the Via della Posta Vecchia might indicate that the architect wished to create the optical impression of a curving façade when viewed from afar, as if to re-echo the curvilinear termination at the opposite side of the square. But this would have been contrary to the ancient form of the Roman circus which Ligorio had been studying during that same period, and which interested him so much that he made it the subject of his book, *Libro di Pyrro Ligorio Napolitano delle Antichità di Roma, nel quale si tratta di Circhi Teatri e Anfiteatri*, (Book of Pirro Ligorio Neapolitan on the Antiquities of Rome, describing Circuses, Theatres and Amphitheatres), published by Nicola Tramezzino in 1553).

Villa Pia

Another favourable opportunity to express his poetic world was presented to Ligorio by his compatriot, the fanatical Pope Paul IV Carafa, who in 1558 had the idea of building for himself a *buen retiro* in the Vatican gardens, just beside the Belvedere courtyard. This building was completed by his successor Pius IV, and then became known as Villa Pia; it was described by Burckhardt as 'the finest abode for spending the afternoon hours that modern architecture has devised'. Paul IV probably wished to introduce a more modest note into this little construction to counterbalance the rich ornamentation of the Villa Giulia, built by his predecessor. But the spirit which pervades this building is certainly not that of an unbending grand inquisitor, and the taste of the antiquarian together with the dynamic inspiration of the architect reign supreme.

As in the Villa d'Este, the ground plan follows the slopes of a hill and interprets its topography architecturally, not in the rigid manner of an enclosed composition like the Belvedere, where the inspiration Bramante drew from Roman villas was bookish and based entirely on texts, but with the loose and free approach which was traditionally accorded to buildings situated in a panoramic position. Ligorio was one of the first to rediscover this classical tradition and to incorporate it in his own concrete experience, even though he did so only schematically.

The new factor in the organization of the villa consists in the arrangement by which Ligorio took as his primary structure not an architectural volume, but a cavity, an open space. The connection with the landscape, which in the Villa Giulia was achieved by cutting down hillocks and trees at the background to the courtyard, is here created by means of a complete fusion between the architectural image and the landscape, made possible by the insertion of a low partition which circumscribes the site without segregating it and permits the images of the neighbouring architectural monuments, dense clumps of trees, and distant profiles of hills, to penetrate and play their part in the composition. It is not unlikely that at least in an early stage of the planning, the oval area was intended as a lake for the staging of sham sea-battles, as in Salone, and that the loggia and large seat would be used as platforms from which to look out onto the spectacle.

The choice of the oval, which Ligorio also employed in the Tivoli fountain, enabled him to create an entirely new biaxial composition, for which Peruzzi's Villa Trivulzio provided a conscious term of reference. The dimensional hierarchy of the main axis is mirrored and accentuated in the volumetric masses which were placed around the enclosure: four iso-orientated parallelepipeds differing greatly in height. The two gates, in the form of little temples, act as optical guidelines to give a broader vision and 'appropriate' the area of the site; while in contrast the little palace is given a strongly-marked vertical development at the rear.

To this precise and highly calculated organization of space, which with very different instruments provides a not unworthy answer to Michelangelo's design for the Capitol, there corresponds a manner of treating volumes which has always left critics perplexed. The restless and uninterrupted rhythm of the surfaces with their over-rich ornamentation of stuccos and marble fragments has caused them to speak of *orror vacui*, of a 'false pictorialism', of confusion, of meaningless decorativism, and an uncontrolled dispersion of plastic effects. But on a close analysis it can be seen that none of these accusations can be

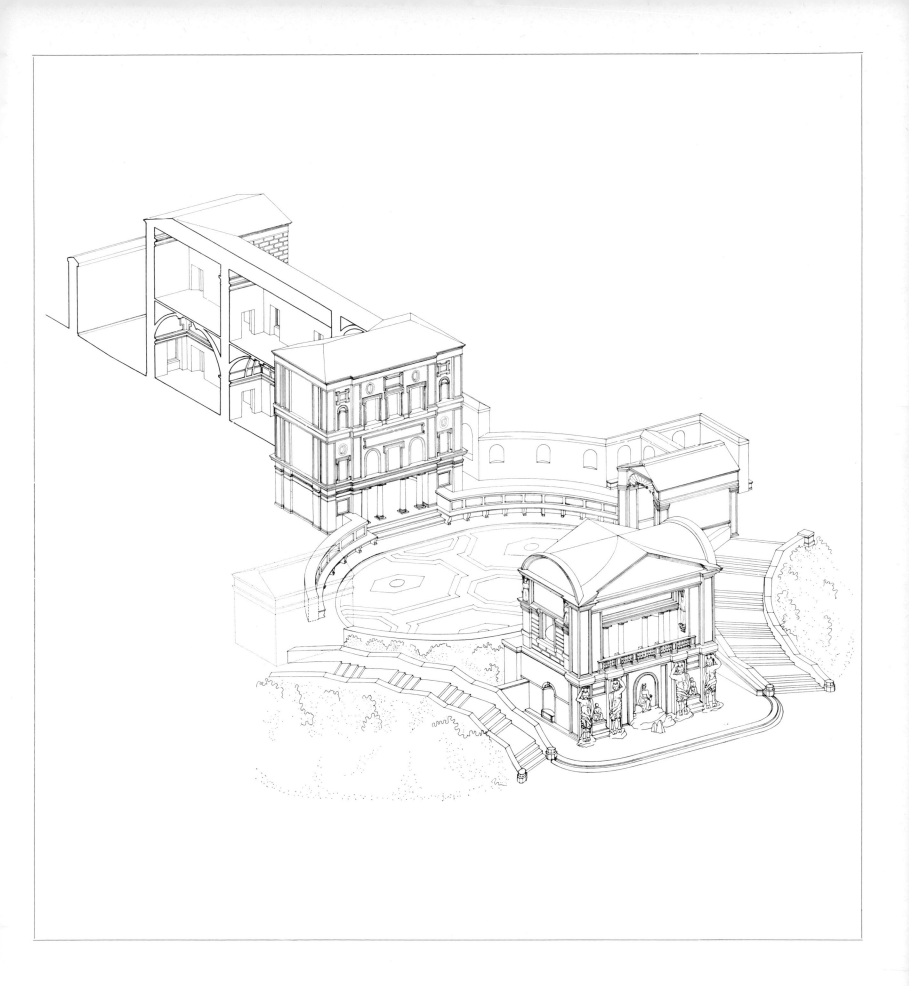

substantiated. With regard to the accusation of meaningless formalism, it must be said that in the absence of a thorough investigation of the iconology the accusation is, to say the least, rash. Certain features which can readily be deciphered, such as the presence at the opposite sides of the loggia of the figures of Faith and Flora, the obvious classical inspiration behind the sea-battles, and the reference to Peter's boat, indicate that a whole complex system of symbolism is waiting to be discovered, based on a metaphorical use of classical mythology, in order to express a Christian meaning. This was in accordance with the tradition of the early Renaissance, which was soon to be severely condemned by the church, but can easily be explained by Ligorio's neo-humanist outlook.

The accusation concerning the dissolution of the plastic structure of the order may be answered by saying that this was the result of an explicit intention supported by rigorous research, and led to two important effects: the enhancing of pure volume, not fragmented by chiaroscuro, and the establishing of an equivalent density of colour vibration between figure and background, architecture and landscape. Like the architects of the fifteenth century, but with a different sensibility, Ligorio took as his model the florid architecture of the time of Augustus which had survived in the form of bas-reliefs and fragments. And it is perhaps the fascination and dream-like unreality of certain classical architecture as seen in a simplified form in reliefs or paintings which inspired Ligorio in this building, representing the homage of a third-generation architect to the ideals which had been held by Raphael and Peruzzi and at the same time providing an uncertain forestaste of the disturbing images of Piranesi.

To match the colourful exterior with an even greater degree of intensity, it was intended that most of the interior wall space should be covered with tapestries so as to provide a suitable background to the sculptural antiquities. To fit in with this scheme of decoration, ceilings were designed to amplify the pattern of high reliefs in an original composition of close-knit architectural features. The rear section of the villa is half-hidden among trees, and with its slightly rusticated surface, it returns to the 'minor tone' of the Palazzo Torres, and through its surface rhythm acquires the immaterial and diaphanous quality of a painted background.

From 1561 Pirro Ligorio was active in the Vatican Palace also; here he altered Bramante's setting for the Belvedere and gave the whole complex a scenographic and pictorial interpretation. He elevated the walls and added a fine rustication which accentuated the wall backgrounds, contrasting with the architectural orders, and so profoundly altered the original image by decreasing the degree of rhythmical intensity. In compensation, the large niche has been given dimensions in keeping with the gigantic area of space before it and becomes its primary structure, able to create an effect of unity out of the disparate elements in Bramante's inadequate structure. However, the connection between the various strata superimposed on the sides of the great cavity is too weak, and the large horseshoe loggia is not sufficient to consolidate the fragile organism.

Among the works of Ligorio, mention must also be made of the courtyard in the University of Rome. The original idea of enclosing this area within two semi-oval porticos (partially executed by Della Porta) accords fully with Ligorio's architectural outlook, and he had already employed the feature of the biapsidal hall in the banqueting loggia of Tivoli and at the Villa Pia inside the Belvedere. Before withdrawing into an aggrieved silence as a misunderstood antiquarian, Ligorio left this last work as a precious legacy to Francesco Borromini, who seventy years later erected the dome of S. Ivo against the concave background of the courtyard. The last years of Ligorio's stay in Rome were dominated by his obstinate quarrel with Michelangelo. This passage taken from his treatise clearly relates to the Porta Pia and exemplifies his attitude: 'If they make a gate to the city,' he writes, 'they set a mask at its centre as if it were a temple to Bacchus or a Theatre, and the more fearful they feign it, the more they repute it to be a fine and laudable thing; instead of carving on it fine deeds, Bishops, and some fine thing which would show us Justice, Equity, or the

Plan of Villa Pia, Vatican (1 cm = 7 m).

Exterior of the Palazzetto of Angelo Massimi (1 cm = 3.3 m).

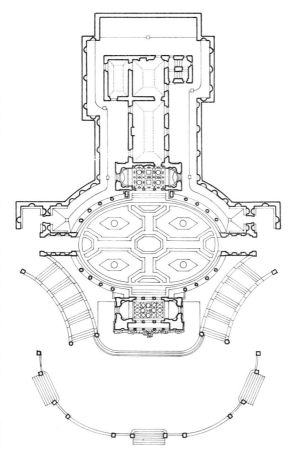

memory of the founder, or the image of the one who created the heavens and earth, or some other thing worthy of divine glory; we place there certain frivolities, certain disjointed things apt to arouse discord, and the uncertainty of life, things which are truly questionable.

'Those men live by evil speaking and sophistry but we shall wait to do well, when we can by good means, those things which they do not understand and which they blame, not being ashamed to say that he who in architecture follows the method of Vitruvius is a trivial man, and he who follows the style of Raphael of Urbino in painting Parmigiano, Correggio, Giorgione, is a person lacking judgement and displeasing, and those who imitate the ancients are without intellect, so senseless are their criticisms that they think it an ordinary matter to imitate the style of those who were the best. What they would like is for people to follow exaggerated and displeasing things, as if they were possessed.' Pirro Ligorio does not know and does not wish to understand his contemporaries, and feels out of touch with his time, which he describes with profound melancholy 'as an era of lost hope, a tormented sea without salvation ... a garden of thorns full of springs out of which strange tempests are born.'

THE SANGALLO SCHOOL

We possess very little information about the group of architects to whom Michelangelo referred as the 'Sangallo school', that is, the circle of architects who collaborated with Antonio da Sangallo the Younger and continued his work after his death; Vasari, who as a self-styled pupil of Michelangelo, represented the opposing faction, did not think it worthwhile to collect information about them, and none of his successors considered it necessary to give posterity detailed facts concerning the mediocre followers of the great Florentine master. The few architects who can be said to validate the term applied by Michelangelo include Sangallo's brother, Giovanni Battista, also known as Francesco, the author of a poor translation of Vitruvius, his cousin Aristotile, also called Bastiano, Giovanni Mangone, Pietro Rosselli, Baronino, Nardo de' Rossi, Nanni di Baccio Bigio, Annibale Lippi, and Antonio Labacco. Of these the only ones who are distinguished by known works of an individual character are Rosselli, Mangone, Nanni, and Annibale Lippi, and Labacco who wrote *Libro appartenente all'architettura* (The Book of Architecture) published in 1552.

The only known work by Pietro Rosselli is the house built for Prospero de Mochis in Via dei Coronari. This is a typical example of the 'artisan' production of the first decades of the sixteenth century and still closely connected to the manner of the last years of the previous century, when Roman culture was of a distinctly provincial nature.

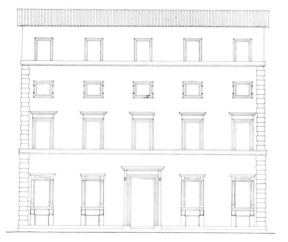

Giovanni Mangone, on the other hand, was an intelligent successor to Sangallo. His only documented work, the little palace built for Angelo Massimo next to Peruzzi's masterpiece, testifies to a tendency to translate Sangallo's model in terms of a proportional equilibrium, abandoning the plastic stresses employed by the master. In the concave background to the courtyard, where the irregularity of the plot is skilfully exploited, and in the selection of the feature of architraved loggias, Mangone shows an individual approach as well as an interest in the works of Peruzzi. A building which is very similar to this house, though designed with greater academic rigour, is the Palazzo Caetani in Via delle Botteghe Oscure; this is a version in a minor key of the Palazzo Farnese, where the plastic accents are evenly distributed according to a rhythm which is impeccable in its monotony. Giovannoni attributes to Mangone also the Palazzetto degli Alicorni, which was destroyed and has been poorly reconstructed in recent times. This building is of interest because of the few stylistic innovations which were introduced into it, but it is without the formal qualities of the Palazzetto Massimi. It is difficult to determine the extent of Mangone's participation in the construction of the church of San Luigi dei Francesi, evidence for which is provided in Uffizi drawing 1892.

Nanni di Baccio Bigio is known mainly as a sculptor and a personal enemy of Michelangelo. His authenticated works of architecture are the Porta del Popolo, the construction of the Palazzo Salviati on the Lungara designed by Sangallo, and the wing of the Palazzo Mattei overlooking Piazza delle Tartarughe.

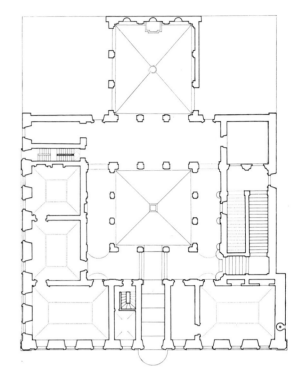

All these three works reveal the architect's archaeological interests. In the Palazzo Salviati he actually resurrected the *opus reticulatum* to provide a neutral background for the heavy articulation of the ground-floor cornices. In the doorway, the style of Sangallo appears in a simplified form, denuded of its characteristic horizontal interconnecting sections. The free-standing columns, set completely away from the background wall, without even the corresponding wall pilasters, have been reduced to decorative elements which even on a formal plane are extraneous to the structure. A simplified style, containing many archaic and ambiguous features, has been employed in the Palazzetto dei Mattei to add to an unusual building type of medieval origin a courtyard surrounded by low buildings.

A less insignificant contribution to Roman architecture was made by Nanni's son, Annibale Lippi, who completed with delicate workmanship the large house which Sangallo had begun for his own use in Via Giulia and which had been acquired by Cardinal Ricci di Montepulciano. He placed over the powerful windows designed by Sangallo a fragile coping with trapezoid opening derived from the Temple of the Sibyl at Tivoli which had been one of Sangallo's favourite sources, but the proportions in which he employed this feature here were totally inadequate to the building as a whole.

Lippi's great professional opportunity came with the villa which Cardinal Ricci had built on the Pincio and which was later acquired by the Medici. It is not impossible that, at least at an early stage, Lippi worked together with his father Nanni on this villa. The only documented reference mentioned by Lanciani refers to *magistro Nanne Architetto*. Here, following a series of examples extending from Raphael's Palazzo dell'Aquila to the Palazzo Spada and the works of Pirro Ligorio, there was put into effect (perhaps at a later stage with the assistance of Bartolomeo Ammannati) the most radical attempt so far known to reduce the type of the suburban villa to a pattern of pure volumes, ornamented by a dense coating of reliefs and niches. Although the central part still retains a distinct structure, built upon a series of superimposed elements co-ordinated by the great serliana window, in the wings the niche windows and bas-reliefs are arranged in such a way that the tradition of 'exhibiting' archaeological fragments is upheld, a tradition which had existed since the first period of the Renaissance during which archaeological fragments were displayed in courtyards.

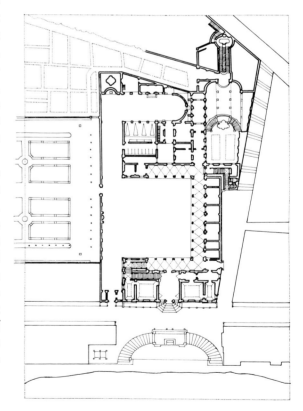

Viewed in the light of the traditional forms of Renaissance composition, what we have here is a complete reversal. The technique seems to be borrowed from the embossing used in silverwork or bookbinding, and no longer conforms to any of the architectural rules. Certain not very precise copies of architectural plans made by medal designers have the same fascination and the same quality of approximations in which only the volumetry can be clearly grasped. The shifting of the towers and vistas is the most original aspect and the one which best responds to the nature of the site. The walk which has been made on the roof, between the towers, enables the viewer to follow an aerial panoramic route which serves a 'narrative' function, endowing the villa with a bold appearance and making it stand as a term of reference on an urban scale. It is interesting to note that the design of the corbels on the inner doorway to the loggia is close to that on the main doorway to the Palazzo Orsini in Bomarzo: according to Calveri, this would seem to indicate that Ammannati, or more probably Lippi, took part in the work at Bomarzo.

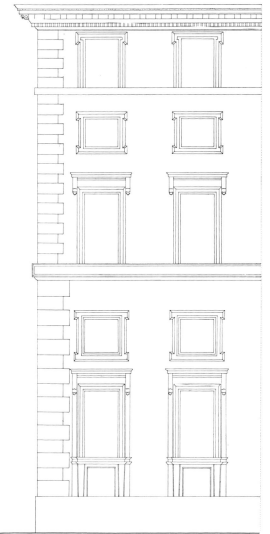

Plan of Palazzo Caetani (1 cm = 5.6 m).

Plan of Palazzo Salviati in Via della Lungara (1 cm = 24 m).

Detail of the exterior of Palazzo Caetani (1 cm = 1.6 m).

The phenomenon of a culture which came into being to serve the economic structure of the 'rural nobility', especially in Upper Latium, cannot be understood without at least some reference to Vicino Orsini, the duke of Bomarzo, who for thirty years after 1550 became the creator, the director, the worshipper, and the victim, of an invention which was partly architectural, partly literary: the Sacred Wood of Bomarzo.

The Sacred Wood was founded earlier than the gardens of Caprarola, Tivoli and Bagnaia, and provides a useful term of comparison; even though its artistic paternity cannot be proved, it is at all events one of the most impressive manifestations of the anxiety and anti-urban tendencies of those who wished to escape the pressures of city life and seek a contemplative existence in rural surroundings in the second half of the sixteenth century.

Orsini was a dilettante, a man of letters and an avid reader of all kinds of books; he was acquainted with the best-known exponents of Roman culture and had numerous friends in all parts of Italy. There is documentary evidence of his connections with Annibal Caro, Bernardo Tasso, Francesco Molza, Claudio Tolomei, Francesco Sansovino, Capello, and with Betussi who dedicated to Orsini his dialogue *Raverta* in which 'love and its effects are discussed'. Cardinal Alessandro Farnese, for whom the Villa Caprarola was built, Cardinal Gambara, who owned Bagnaia, and Cardinal Madruzzo who possessed a villa at Soriano on the Cimino, were his friends and visitors, and even Gregory XIII Boncompagni expressed the intention to visit the garden of Bomarzo.

Whereas for Farnese, Gambara, and Ippolito d'Este, escape from city life to the pleasures of the villa was indicative of a dichotomy typical of the period of the Counter-Reformation, when the contemplative life represented one side of a coin whose reverse consisted of an intense whirl of political and social activity, for Vicino Orsini the Sacred Wood represented the absolute denial of the city as an institution, as a complex social structure which it was impossible to reduce to so elemental and archaic a model as the patriarchal institution of Bomarzo.

Right up to the present day, any attempt to discover an inherent iconological intent in the villa of Bomarzo has failed. By the side of mythological figures whose significance can easily be deciphered, there are certain exotic animals in which there appears to be an obscure reference to eastern traditions. In some of his letters, Orsini speaks of 'castles of Atlas', but an interpretation of the complex as an allegory of the story of Atlas is substantiated by only a few features, such as the elephant and dragon, while many others appear to invalidate it. From the point of view of both the general composition and the stylistic features, the wood conveys an impression of a collection of fragments, interrelated only through a chance and empirical route which bears no connection to the arrangement of the architectural objects. The technical origin of the sculptures lay in the main in the transformation of irregular masses of peperino into naturalistic and anti-geometric shapes, and Orsini did not wish to influence this arrangement, but preserved the chance factor to create interest and surprise.

Orsini's aversion for city life is expressed in his correspondence with Drouet published by Bruschi. In a letter written in 1577, he declares, 'I do not know what has brought me here (to Rome) because my affairs do not force me to come nor am I drawn by pleasure', and in another, 'it would be better to imitate me, for every inhabited place is the mortal enemy of my sight. I spend all my time in the mud in my little wood ... Yet I am determined to remain with my troubles in Bomarzo.' Elsewhere he asks Drouet to forgive the fact that his letters 'stink of pig as I do', and adds, 'if I were conversing with a (different) person ... I should be ashamed to say such disgusting things; but I know that you (who) are not shocked at having left the Pope's palace, will surely not be shocked by any other thing which may happen.'

For Orsini everything that came from the town was depraved and without interest; the only exception were his books, especially those from which he learned about strange and remote events. '... I should be glad if you would give me some information concerning all parts of the world, the Occident, Australia, etc., both in general and in detail, and in a long letter let me have a detailed report *in omnibus et per omnia*.' Of the life of his own time, Orsini took only the aspects relating to culture, which could help him to withdraw from society into a sort of pagan, hedonistic asceticism. The fascination of Bomarzo lies in its immediacy as a stark rejection of reality and history, though these factors played so large a part in artistic culture also. Orsini states plainly those things which Giulio Romano, Pirro Ligorio, and Vignola express ambiguously in a subtle play of the intellect. The eccentric country squire, however, rejects this ambiguity, cuts down his bridges with good taste and 'manner', and lays bare his heart. 'Only to open one's heart', reads the earliest of the inscriptions in the Sacred Wood, while on the terrace of the villa, which lies open towards the untamed panorama of the ravines of the Roman countryside, the most conflicting statements appear side by side: *Ede bibe et lude | post mortem nulla voluptas* reads one inscription, and on the opposite side, *Sperne terrestria | post mortem vera voluptas*; the third inscription suggests a solution: *Medium tenuere beati*, which casts doubt even upon doubt itself—but does not for this reason represent a certainty.

121. *Baldassarre Peruzzi: Presentation in the Temple (c. 1514). Santa Maria della Pace.*

122. *Baldassarre Peruzzi: Palazzo Massimo alle Colonne, façade (1532–6).*

124. *Baldassarre Peruzzi: Palazzo Massimo alle Colonne, central part of façade (1532–6).*

129. *Baldassarre Peruzzi: Palazzo Massimo alle Colonne, detail of portico (1532–6).*

Baldassarre Peruzzi: Palazzo Massimo alle Colonne (1532-6).
130. Cortile. | 131. Loggia. | 132. Interior of loggia.
133. Baldassarre Peruzzi: Villa Trivulzio, entrance (1525). Hall (Tivoli).
134. Baldassarre Peruzzi: Palazzo Massimo alle Colonne, detail of vault of entrance hall (1532-6).
135. Baldassarre Peruzzi: Villa Trivulzio, entrance hall (1532-6).

Antonio da Sangallo the Younger: Model for the
reconstruction of St. Peter's (1539).
136. Detail of the façade with the two bell-towers.
137. Detail of porch. | 138. Interior.

Antonio da Sangallo the Younger: Santa Maria di Loreto (1531 – c. 1550).
145. Façade. | 146. Interior. | 147. Detail of niche. | 148. Interior of dome.

158. Cappella Paolina in the Vatican.

162. *Antonio da Sangallo the Younger: Santo Spirito in Sassia, façade (1538–44).*
163. *Vatican buildings, corbel of a balcony.*

Antonio da Sangallo the Younger: Palazzo Farnese (1534–46).
171. Entrance. | 172. Barrel vaulting of entrance. | 173. Gallery.

176. *Antonio da Sangallo the Younger: Palazzo Farnese, staircase (1534–46).*

177. *Antonio da Sangallo the Younger: Palazzo Farnese, detail (1534–46)*.

Antonio da Sangallo the Younger, Michelangelo:
Palazzo Farnese (1534–46).
178. Cortile. | 179. Cortile, detail of second
and third storeys.

Michelangelo: Piazza del Campidoglio (1537–64).
180. Aerial view. | 181. Palazzo Nuovo.

182. Michelangelo: Piazza del Campidoglio, Palazzo dei Conservatori (1537-64).

187. Michelangelo: Piazza del Campidoglio (1537–64). Palazzo dei Senatori, stairway.

188. *Michelangelo: St. Peter's, apse (1555–64).*

190. *Michelangelo: St. Peter's, apse (1555–64).*

Michelangelo: St. Peter's (1555–64).
191. Detail of apse. | 192. Interior, window
of apse.

*Michelangelo, Giacomo della Porta: Model of
the dome of St. Peter's (1558–86).
193. General view. | 194. Section.*

195. *Michelangelo: St. Peter's, detail of drum (1555–7).*
196. *Michelangelo: St. Peter's, window in drum (1555–7).*

197. *Michelangelo: Santa Maria degli Angeli, aerial view (1563–4).*

198. *Michelangelo: Santa Maria degli Angeli, interior (1563–4).*

Michelangelo: Cappella Sforza in the Church of Santa Maria Maggiore (1564).
199. Detail of vault. | 200. Detail of pillars. | 201. Vault.

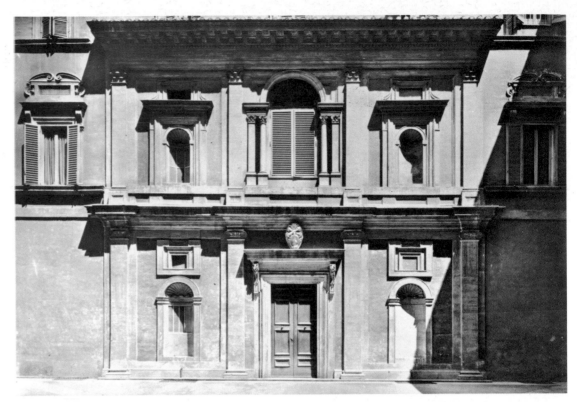

Bartolomeo Ammannati: Palazzo Firenze (1552–4).
206. Façade. | 207. Exterior overlooking the cortile. | 208. Detail of doorway. | 209. Detail of niche.
210. Bartolomeo Ammannati: Palazzo Caetani, window (1564).

211. *Giorgio Vasari: La Conversione di San Paolo Chapel in San Pietro in Montorio (1550–3).*
212. *Giorgio Vasari: Room of the Hundred Days in the Palazzo della Cancelleria (1489–95).*
213. *Giorgio Vasari: La Conversione di San Paolo Chapel in San Pietro in Montorio, detail of balustrade (1550–3).*

214. *Jacopo Vignola: Palazzo Farnese, aerial view (1559–73). Caprarola (Viterbo).*

215. *Jacopo Vignola: Palazzo Farnese, stairway and façade (1550–9). Caprarola (Viterbo).*

Jacopo Vignola: Palazzo Farnese (1550–9). Caprarola (Viterbo).
216, 217. Details of exterior stairway. | 218, 219. Doorways.

Jacopo Vignola: Palazzo Farnese (1559–73).
Caprarola (Viterbo).
220. Cortile. | 221. Loggia over the cortile.
222. Antonio da Sangallo the Younger:
Foundations of the Palazzo Farnese (c. 1540).
Caprarola (Viterbo).

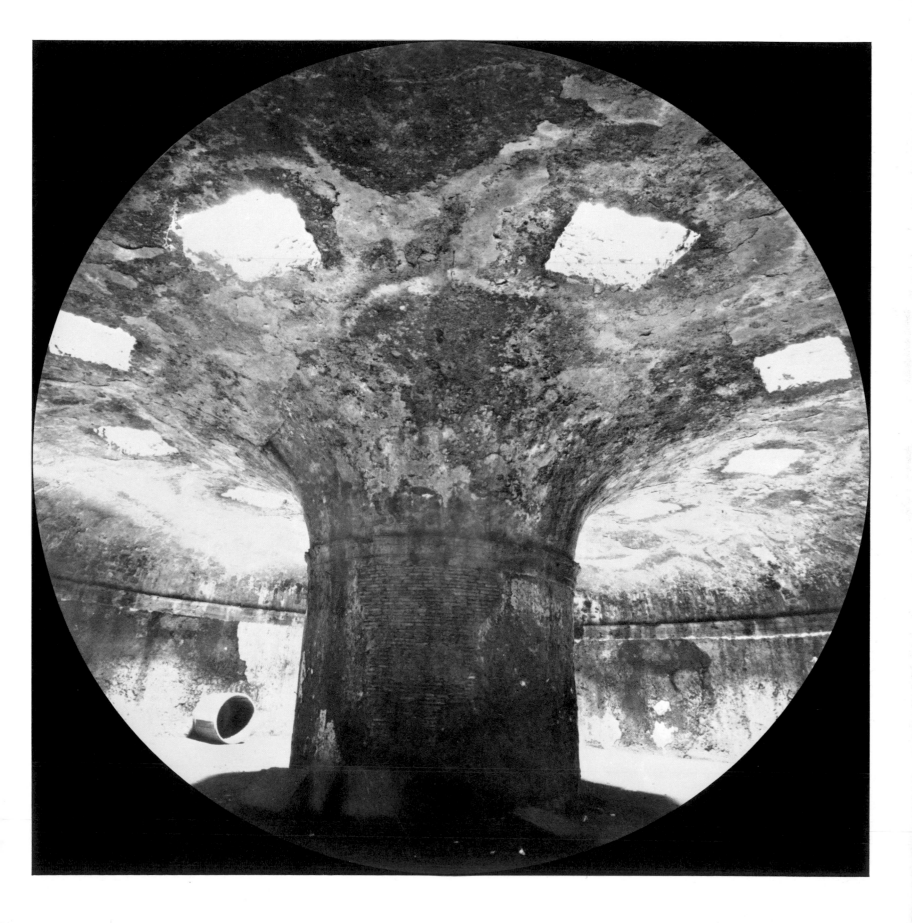

223. *Jacopo Vignola: Palazzo Farnese, scala regia (1550–9). Caprarola (Viterbo).*

224. *Jacopo Vignola: Palazzo Farnese, scala regia (1550–9). Caprarola (Viterbo).*

226. *Jacopo Vignola: Palazzo Farnese, scala regia (1550–9). Caprarola (Viterbo).*

227. *Jacopo Vignola: Palazzo Farnese, vault of round chapel (1550–9). Caprarola (Viterbo).*

Jacopo Vignola: Palazzo Farnese (1550–9). Caprarola (Viterbo).
228. Map of the World Room, ceiling depicting the constellations.
229. Round chapel, detail. | 230. Room of the Deeds of Taddeo Zuccari.
231. Antechamber of the Council Room, ceiling.

Jacopo Vignola: Villa Giulia (1551–5).
232. Aerial view. | 233. Main façade.
234. Doorway.

235. *Jacopo Vignola: Villa Giulia, façade overlooking the cortile (1551–5).*
236, 237. *Bartolomeo Ammannati: Temple of the Nymphs in the Villa Giulia (1553–5).*
238. *Jacopo Vignola: Villa Giulia, detail of ambulatory around the cortile (1551–5).*

239, 240. Bartolomeo Ammannati: Temple of the Nymphs in the Villa Giulia (1553–5).

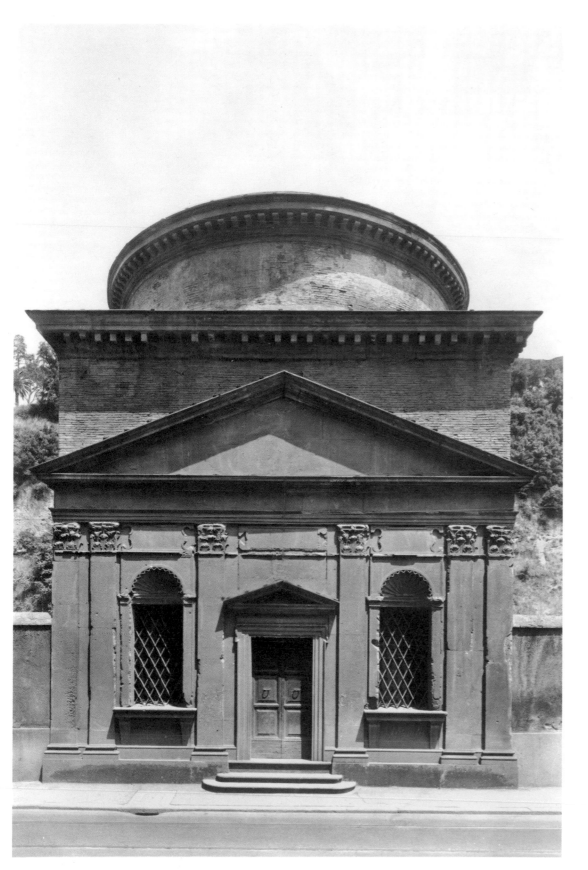

248, 249. *Pirro Ligorio: Frescoes in the oratory of San Giovanni Decollato.*
250. *Pirro Ligorio: Tomb of Pope Carafa in Santa Maria sopra Minerva.*

248, 249. *Pirro Ligorio: Frescoes in the oratory of San Giovanni Decollato.*
250. *Pirro Ligorio: Tomb of Pope Carafa in Santa Maria sopra Minerva.*

Examples of small palazzi and houses of the period 1527–64.

251. *House in Via Monserrato.*
252. *Palazzo in Piazza Aracoeli.*
253. *Palazzo Cadilhac in Via Monserrato.*
254. *Perspective view of Via Monserrato.*
255. *House in Via della Guardiola.*
256. *Palazzetto Crivelli in Via dei Banchi Vecchi.*
257. *Palazzo Cesi in Via della Maschera d'Oro.*
258. *Façade attributed to Vignola in a courtyard near Piazza Navona.*

264. *House in Via del Governo Vecchio.*

265. *House in Via del Governo Vecchio.*
266. *House in Via Montevecchio, façade.*
267. *Palazzo Cesi, façade.*
268. *House in Via del Governo Vecchio, detail of façade.*
269. *House in Via Montevecchio, detail.*

Palazzo Spada.
270. Façade. | 271-273. Interiors.

Pirro Ligorio: Villa d'Este at Tivoli (1550–72).
282. Loggia. | 283, 284. Temples in the garden.

Pirro Ligorio: Villa d'Este at Tivoli (1550–72).
285. Organ Fountain. | 286-289. Details of Organ Fountain.

Pirro Ligorio: Villa Pia (1558–61). 290. Aerial view. | 291. Terrace.

Jacopo Vignola: Giulio Farnese temple at Bomarzo near Viterbo (1565).
296. Façade. | 297. Apse.
298. Santa Maria della Valle. Bomarzo (Viterbo).
299. Villa Orsini, rock sculpture. Bomarzo (Viterbo).
300. Villa Orsini at Bomarzo near Viterbo (1565).

301. Villa Orsini, rock sculpture. Bomarzo (Viterbo).

PART THREE

THE LANGUAGE OF ROMAN CLASSICISM

Now that our analytical itinerary has been concluded, the overall picture which has emerged from the phenomena studied is that of a structure which is endowed with its own internal logic and which cannot be reduced to a cut-and-dried system.

Historical evidence provided by theoretical documents and practical examples shows that the ideas which gave rise to the most intense controversy were those centring round the concepts of 'universality' and 'correctness' in the language of architecture, and that the basic term of comparison for every attempt related to the attainment of these objectives remained the classical heritage, as presented in its double reality of the Vitruvian theory and the direct evidence provided by the Roman ruins. But it cannot be denied that within the context of this programme there were various phases, and that among these phases a dialectical relationship can be established.

The first of these phases occurred when the validity of the Florentine system was shown to be founded on a mistaken conception concerning the 'antiquity' of the Romanesque monuments. Just as the scientific method of Valla had threatened the basis of the temporal power of the church, so too Alberti and Bramante by their scientific study of classical monuments cast doubt on the theory of perspective as it had been originally formulated. It is true that the spatial cell based on the dynamic continuity in four columns connected by four archivolts was based on the rules of proportions governing the orders, but this cell had no counterpart in the verifiable heritage of the ancient world. However—and this is where we recognize Bramante's great intuition—it could not be replaced either by a return to the effects of plasticity and mass employed by the ancients, or by an episodic rediscovery of values in the classical heritage which had remained free; it was necessary to replace the old language by a new one which would be applicable to an equal degree.

Bramante came to Rome in order to rest and study, but was soon called in by Julius II to seek a solution to this problem. He did so, after the example of Alberti, by connecting the order and wall so closely that they became fused into a single unit.

The technique of rubble masonry in a form of shuttering gave him the idea of discarding the skeletal cell which was marked by lines of force in favour of the 'bodily' cell, enclosed by the wall and defined plastically through the effects of light. The system of dovetailing superimposed units was replaced by the organic system of 'growing together', by which the organism and its parts were interpenetrated and had a reciprocal interaction.

This proved to be a fundamental advance because it solved the inherent contradiction between optical reality and formal structure which had impeded the development of fifteenth-century architecture; however, in its turn it gave rise to new contradictions which Bramante left unsolved—for example, the problem of the relationship between the interior and exterior.

For the pupils of Bramante, the viewpoint had already altered; the demands they were called upon to fulfil were no longer the noble ones indicated by Julius II. Apart from the work of continuing St. Peter's, the central need, which was closely related to the interests of the aristocracy of bankers and merchants, was for the construction of urban 'palazzi' and villas. The ideal of architectural 'correctness' followed with some ingenuity by Bramante, who to a large extent had failed to complete his programme of preserving intact the 'tone' of ancient architecture, now became the dominant theme among his followers and corresponded to a renewed interest in social codes of behaviour. Castiglione's *Courtier* was written at about the same time as interest in the palazzo began to become widespread in the 1520s, and it is not surprising that he religiously preserved a letter in which Raphael described the comforts of the Villa Madama in some detail.

The richness and variety of building production in this sector attained an unprecedented level; we need only remind ourselves of some of the buildings erected in this short period of years: the austere Palazzo Baldassini, the grandiose Palazzetto Caprini, the florid Palazzo Branconio, the Farnesina with its decoration of monochrome paintings, the palazzi Maccarani, Ossoli, Leroy, while at the same time in S. Maria della Pace Peruzzi painted a building which foreshadowed the most mature domestic architecture of Sansovino, and Raphael in *The Fire in Borgo* anticipated Palladio's design of the Basilica (Vicenza).

The new importance accorded to the residential theme produced a mixture of styles between domestic and religious architecture through which it was possible to solve the problem posed by the scarcity in classical antiquity of residential models which could be adapted to the requirements of the new urban situation.

Between the time of the death of Bramante and the Sack of Rome, the reacquisition of the restrained tone of classical architecture seems complete, largely thanks to the decisive contribution of Raphael; this was true not only at a structural level, but also in the treatment of surfaces and the complex pattern of spatial and chromatic effects. In contrast to the cultures of the other Italian centres, Roman culture was able to find standards of judgement which could yield choices very close to unanimity, so that what remained of the fifteenth-century culture could be purged of a whole series of barbarisms which had still been present in the style of Bramante.

Antonio da Sangallo mastered this rigorous language and enlarged his area of research, demonstrating that it could be applied to a wide range of subjects and situations. But when he set himself the task of planning St. Peter's, he found that he had unwittingly acquired an explosive problem. In seeking to adapt his methods to the vast scale and the revolutionary organism created by Bramante, he discovered that the orthodox classical forms for the temple system were inadequate to the purpose of structuring the gigantic exterior of the cathedral. Nor could this problem be solved simply by incorporating pinnacles and towers of a Gothic type. Michelangelo found a solution—at the expense of correctness—by drawing upon Gothic tradition to make the ribs of the dome perform a structural function and to create a dense rhythm of apsidal wall pilasters.

In Michelangelo's late works, he rejected the over-simplified and illusory theory that the classical heritage should necessarily be equated with the orthodoxy of the temple system based on the assembly of elements whose forms were firmly established by a fixed body of rules. In exposing the weakness of this theory, he oscillated between the ironical, destructive spirit of the Porta Pia, the revolutionary Sforza Chapel, abdication of direct intervention in the church of S. Maria degli Angeli, and a confident attitude to the construction of the Capitol and St. Peter's. In each of these works, the myth of correctness was challenged and discarded in favour of the ideals of rediscovery and 'free examination'. The window cornicing in the Capitol and St. Peter's marked a return to a conception which viewed the type as an empty canvas to be transformed, or a theme around which to weave variations in a musical sense.

Both Vignola and Ligorio adopted a rigorous academic approach, though their manner differed. In contrast, Ammannati in the Palazzo Farnese was seen to be the only architect besides Michelangelo who could provide Rome with direct evidence of the Mannerist revolt in all its contradictory aspects.

Ligorio advocated reliance on archaeological method, but at the same time, like the rest of his generation, responded to the appeal of the naturalism and irrationalism of the Mannerists. His method was two-sided—the severe style appropriate to urban architecture (in Palazzo Lancellotti) being contrasted to the leisured richness and spectacular licence permissible in the rural villa. Vignola, on the other hand, brought into the academic tradition

Rows of houses in Borgo, with graffiti decorations (1 cm = 2.3 m).

House in Vicolo del Governo Vecchio. Example of a painted house of the early sixteenth century (1 cm = 4.25 m).

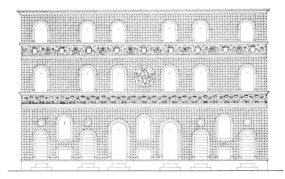

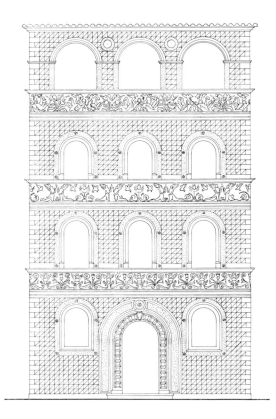

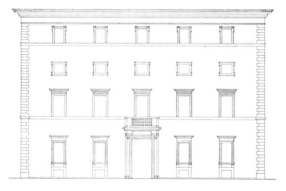

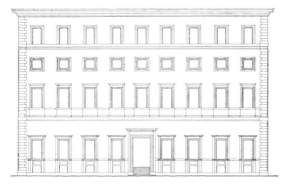

a few of the stylistic innovations which had come from the centres of northern Italy. He applied his archaeological interests, which he knew how to exploit with greater cunning than did the previous generation, to the same formal problems, and inaugurated a 'revival', or more precisely a 'survival', of classicism. This was followed, though not passively, by Giacomo della Porta (who at the start of his career built the Oratory of the Crucifix in 1564) and Domenico Fontana, who put into effect the ambitious designs of Sixtus V.

The evolution of Roman architecture during the chronological period 1503–64 seems therefore to have been sinusoidal in form, although the degree of oscillation tends to become progressively smaller, so that the 'result' greatly resembles a parabola. The recovery of the central plan at first represented a tendency to be followed enthusiastically, then an object which appeared to slip out of its captor's hands just when it came close to being grasped, then an illusion to be dispelled, and finally a myth to be 'preserved'—with rather a guilty conscience, since it was related to the political designs of the Counter-Reformation.

Neither from the point of view of their aesthetic qualities, nor from that of their influence on European culture in general, did the products of Roman culture correspond to the progressive or involutive nature of the architectural product. Nevertheless, at a time when the ideological foundations of classicism were being eroded, Vignola was successful in attaining a degree of intensity and creative power in Caprarola of which none of his contemporaries was capable. This will in no way amaze those who reject the temptations of moralistic criticism and adopt the method of historical materialism so as to arrive at a correct interpretation of the relationship between structure and superstructure and between ideology and artistic production. The historical importance of Roman culture in the late sixteenth century consists partly in the very difficulty it presents to anyone attempting to reduce it to a mechanical system; this is due to the philosophical overtones associated with architectural activity and to the complexity of the economic and political forces to which it was exposed at a time when the ideological debate was becoming arid.

In the gap between what could be foreseen and allowed for, and between what could be deduced from given premises and that which existed in reality, it is possible to recognize the significance and value of the individual contributions made by certain personalities and tendencies towards the development of the discipline in which they were engaged and to study the specific nature of this contribution. This in our view is the correct scientific method to be adopted by history when it is put to an analysis of the territory of architecture. These conclusions may be usefully exemplified by making a horizontal classification of categories, based on the points that have already been considered in connection with individual personalities, and at the same time examining the influence of architecture on the fabric of the city and the social situation.

The Orders and their Syntactic Connection

Architects who worked in Rome during the period under discussion attempted to formulate standards of judgement sufficiently exact to ensure that all non-idiomatic expressions and mixtures of style could be expunged from the language of architecture. The refined instruments of linguistics, and in particular those relating to Chomsky's transformational theory, are highly applicable to a study of the processes which were employed in testing the grammatical validity of the expressions which inspired the Roman architectural reformation, as codified by Serlio and Vignola; but in order to avoid the introduction of too many technical terms, we shall attempt to sum up the results of this research on traditional lines. From Bramante to Sangallo, and later to Vignola, the strategy selected for the process of purifying and universalizing the architectural language advanced on two fronts: the admission into the repertory of new elements taken from classical architecture, which had remained extraneous to the architecture of the fifteenth century, and the exclusion of a much wider range of features which had come into current usage. The criterion for selection was on the one hand the Vitruvian legacy, and on the other—and it is here that the original and specific aspect of Roman classicism becomes apparent—a desire for rationalization which led architects to interpret the classical heritage in a systematic and synthetic manner, refusing to accept its contradictory elements and its pluralism.

In this desire for standardization and simplification, the orders became the main elements of the structure, governing every detail of the composition. The most notable rediscovery was that of the Doric, while what was excluded covered all such features as wall pilasters with openings, candelabra, polistyle pilasters, octagons, etc., which had enriched and given greater flexibility to the style of the fifteenth century. The five orders became the primary structural elements in the repertory, and an exclusive judgement had to be applied to them. The same intent to establish a norm regulated the definition of the proportions and the design of the individual elements of the order; innovations were no longer admitted, but only a rigorous attitude of objectivity in referring to sources. However, in order to allow some margin of flexibility in the assembly of the superimposed elements, it was permissible to eliminate some of them completely (for example, the frieze inside the entablature, the pedestal, or the stylobate).

Certain of the rules of proportion—the rule, for example, according to which the level of the first moulding of the architrave and that of the top of the column had to coincide—were studiously observed, even by Michelangelo; only Giulio Romano, in the *cortile* of the Palazzo del Tè, dared to transgress this rule by placing the cornice farther back, in a gesture of obvious pride at his intentional defiance of a well-known rule. With regard to the method of superimposing orders, the hesitation evinced by Bramante (or his successors) in the context of the Belvedere could no longer be conceived by the men of the next generation, who imitated the models of the Colosseum and Theatre of Marcellus to achieve highly refined and impeccable effects in this sphere.

The most interesting term of comparison by which to judge the classicist reformation and its evolution (the sinusoidal model previously mentioned) relates to the repetition of the architectonic orders in a series. In the drawings which illustrate these pages, an attempt has been made to classify the various solutions brought to this problem by arranging them according to groups. When they are compared, two fundamental facts emerge: the linguistic creativity of classical culture, which once the instrument by which the grammatical correctness of expressions could be tested was distinguished, did not hesitate to invent new ones; and the tendency gradually to expunge those features which occurred with greatest frequency in the fifteenth-century tradition.

The model A.1., a homogenous sequence of trabeated supports, is the type which by its elemental and basic character is best able to resist obsolescence and change in fashion. We find it only rarely entirely in the round in colonnades, but it appears very frequently in the form of a rhythmical pattern outlined on a wall in low relief.

Models A.2. and A.3. occur in the same way. We find A.2. completely in the round only rarely (examples are the two Massimo palaces); but it ofter occurs in combination with the wall, after the pattern of Bramante's Palazzo Caprini and Raphael's Chigi stables.

Absent from this catalogue are the models obtainable by ornamenting the cornice in the same way as the columns. In the case of A.1., A.1.1. is obtained by extending the trabeation to each of the columns, and A.1.2. by employing it so as to link the supports in groups of two, so generating a sequence of aediculae. In the case of A.2., A.2.1. is obtained by extending the trabeation to each pair of twin supports (this is the form Michelangelo adopted for the drum of the dome of St. Peter's), or A.2.2., a sequence of aediculae with twin supports which has not yet appeared in Roman classicism.

A.3., on the other hand, enjoyed a vogue in the first decade of the century in the wake of the Cancelleria and Palazzo of Cardinal Adriano, but now lost ground and was employed only exceptionally, in Palazzo Ossoli and Villa Giulia.

B.1. and B.2. are forms typical of the Brunelleschi and Lombard tradition; they were very widespread in the first decade of the century but then disappeared almost entirely apart from some minor cases. The only exception was Peruzzi's refined variant of this model in the courtyard of Palazzo Ossoli.

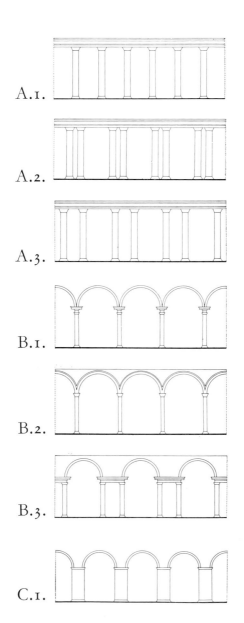

A.1.

A.2.

A.3.

B.1.

B.2.

B.3.

C.1.

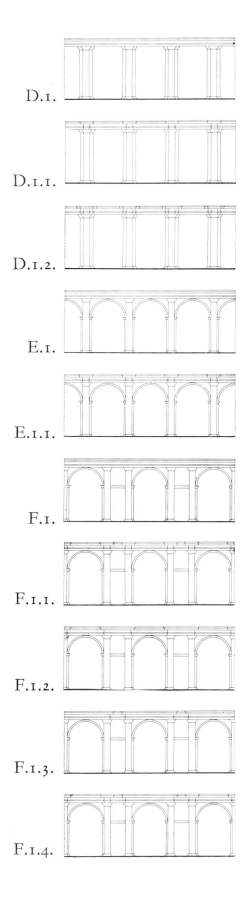

D.1.

D.1.1.

D.1.2.

E.1.

E.1.1.

F.1.

F.1.1.

F.1.2.

F.1.3.

F.1.4.

B.3. was a highly original invention of Giulio Romano's. He introduced a more advanced version of it in a monochrome decoration in the room of Constantine, where the entablature was curved in the manner of the temple of Tarmassus. It appeared first in the second decade of the century but did not make a great impact on Rome, although it met with great success when transplanted into northern Italy, from where it was brought back to Rome in the fifties and sixties. In its contracted version, as a window consisting of an arch with two lateral architraved sections, this form had previously appeared in a window in the Vatican throne room, constructed in the time of Julius II, and in the mullioned windows of S. Maria del Popolo.

C.1. is a form of classical derivation, employed to great effect by Alberti in the wings of the Tempio Malatestiano, but was seldom found in Rome and then only in the first period, in the courtyard of the palace built for Cardinal Adriano da Corneto and in the courtyard of Palazzo Vidoni, as well as in some minor works.

The series D.1., D.1.1., D.1.2. represents merely an elaboration of A.1. through wing sections which echo the form of the support of the order at its sides. This form was first applied in the Belvedere courtyard, and it is important for creating a hierarchical distinction between the pier and the pilaster, obtainable by the process of eliminating the base from the pier. This led to the introduction of neutral wall membratures which were endowed with certain characteristics of the order without being assimilated into it. The variants D.1.1., D.1.2. relate only to the ornamentation of the cornice, which may reflect only the wall pilaster or else the pier together with the pilasters.

The series E. and F. represent the fundamental and typical instruments of Roman classicism. E.1. created through a synthesis between A.1. and B.1., is the specific stylistic discovery of Roman architecture, and had been reintroduced into fifteenth-century building in an episodic manner. The most coherent examples were those in Rome, such as the courtyard of Palazzo Venezia, the Vatican Loggia, the portico of S. Marco, and those for which Leon Battista Alberti was responsible in Rimini and Mantua. In sixteenth-century Rome this form was carefully studied in all its manifold possibilities. The design of the cornice was such that the supports could either be detached from the wall or interconnected so as to form embryonic aediculae, and the intercolumniations could be distinguished into positives and negatives.

The series F., or 'rhythmic frame' (*travata ritmica*), was created from the non-functional arch and its intertwined sequence. From the rhythm a - b - a, there grew not a pure repetition a - b - a a - b - a, but a related sequence a - b - a - b - a, in which the motif lost its autonomy to the extent that the intervals 'a' belonged to both contiguous groups a - b - a. At Mantua Alberti had carried out his first experiment in this direction, and it had served Bramante also for the upper part of the Belvedere courtyard. Sangallo used it mainly for doorways, while Vignola transformed it into a continuous ring in the courtyard of Caprarola, and in Villa Giulia combined it with A.1. and E.1. The design of the various parts of the trabeation made it possible in this case also to isolate the supports or to group them in two different ways (F.1.2., F.1.3.) or, in the case of doorways, to isolate the far supports and join the central ones (F.1.4.).

There should be added to the models illustrated in this catalogue those obtained by the methods of superimposing and intertwining. For example, the phased superimposing of D.1. onto A.1. results in a mixed form (D.1. + A.1.) used by Bramante in the second order of the cloister of S. Maria della Pace, while the grafting of an element B.3. into the form E.1. results in the form employed in Palladio's Basilica (A.1. + B.3.), anticipated by Raphael in the palace depicted in the *Fire in Borgo*. Then the insertion inside the arches E.1. of a trabeated system A.1. of a height corresponding to the impost plane of the arches determines the model of the large window in Villa Madama (E.1. + A.1.).

The system employed by Michelangelo in the Palazzo dei Conservatori, on the other hand, may be considered to be the product of the intersection of D.1. with A.3., where the height of A.3. is equal to half the height of D.1.

From the second decade of the sixteenth century, Peruzzi and Giulio Romano, in the Villa Trivulzio in Salone and the Palazzo Maccarani, began to reduce the order to a system of bands, which were treated in a manner analogous to that employed by Bramante in the wing sections, losing some of the qualifying elements of the order (capitals, for example in the first order of Palazzo Maccarani) or through a further simplification as pure rusticated surfaces. The band system was already present in the mysterious Palazzo Cicciaporci, which was once ascribed to Giulio Romano by analogy with the Palazzo Maccarani, but was certainly of too early a date to make such a hypothesis acceptable. The fact that a recently discovered engraving in the Lafréry series attributes the palazzo to Bramante poses the question of its possible function as a prototype both for the band system and for the arrangement of smooth rustication in the shop area.

Already, in a series of drawings by Peruzzi, a simplified system of an unornamented order was applied to various models, such as A.3. and F.1., but this system was not fully developed until after the fifth decade and then mainly in the climate of Mannerism, in Umbria, Tuscany, and the region of Padua. In Rome it was handled with great refinement by Giacomo della Porta, who in this way stored up a precious legacy for the masters of the Baroque.

Subordinate Features

The constituent elements of the order proper (pedestal, column, trabeation, and tympanum) do not exhaust the architectural repertory. Where they are joined to the wall—which happens constantly, with the sole exception of partitions, ciboria, or free-standing columns— the demand arises to create a relationship between the interior and exterior by means of doors and windows, and to relieve the bareness of the wall by the inclusion of bands, cornices, or such features as accentuate the constructive technique, for example rustication and brick screens. The coupling of the order and wall determines several methods of grafting, such as the cell, interpenetration, or 're-echoing' through the wall pilasters. The wall as such may instead be modified by reliefs or openings, or else hollowed by niches.

The only feature which was prescribed by Vitruvius in accordance with the temple system was the doorway, for which he established firm rules governing the particular types to be used in connection with each one of the orders.

The buildings currently produced in the first years of the century incorporate various types of openings based on models derived from the tradition of classicism, although the criteria for their acceptance were empirical, and without the support of theoretical verification.

The window model employed in the Cancelleria, for example, was derived from the Arco dei Borsari in Verona and repeated in many versions as a means of graduating the interrelationship between the structural elements and the decoration (for example, the palazzo of Cardinal Adriano, the Palazzetto Turci in Via del Governo Vecchio, the Palazzo Ricci, etc.). Alongside this model there appears a type of simplified cornicing derived from the type of the architrave; it is usually curved and turned inwards over the side pilasters. In the interior of this cornicing there frequently appears a cross-shaped partition of late-Gothic inspiration. Other models were derived from the insertion of an arch supported by moulded articulated pilasters within an aedicule designed in low relief and surmounted by a tympanum. The same episodic pluralism is found in the doorways, where the very frequent use of wall pilasters with ornamentations of openings and the low relief decoration of the membratures demonstrate a conception of the type as an empty canvas to be enriched and characterized by means of decoration.

Between 1515 and 1525, an opposite tendency was manifested in this sector, where the type was set up as an absolute norm, and variations in the handling of a theme were significant only insofar as they approached ever more closely to a clearcut effect which could be rationally demonstrated. Under the influence of the Vitruvian theory and on the basis of a scientific study of the classical monuments, the task of severely expunging all extraneous

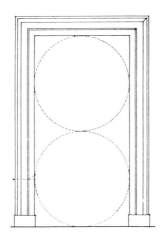

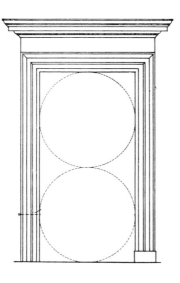

Cornicing suitable for doors or windows of the type M.1.1.

Cornicing suitable for doors or windows of the type M.1.2.

Cornicing suitable for doors or windows of the type M.I.3.

Cornicing suitable for doors or windows of the type M.A.I.

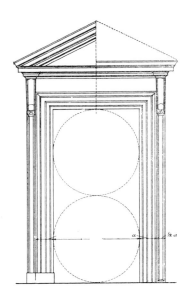

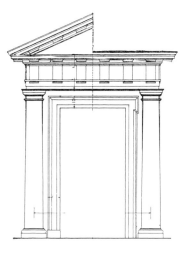

elements was undertaken. The models for window framing—at a time when building activity was expanding—were reduced to two only: the rectangular form in which the architrave moulding ran all round the framework, but without fifteenth-century edging (M.I.), often surmounted by a smooth frieze and a cornice (M.I.2.) which may be supported by double-voluted corbels (M.I.3.); and the type derived from the tabernacle of the Pantheon (M.A.I.). Both these forms appeared as coherent fragments of the temple system; they were subject to the rules of the orders and were therefore variable only within a well-defined range of possible proportions.

In the thirties, on the initiative of Sangallo, the repertory of window models was enriched by a type derived from a synthesis of the arch and the aedicule, while Peruzzi invented the cartouche window in the mezzanine of Palazzo Massimo.

The motif of the aedicule, an elemental unit of the temple system, provided an object of research and study for nearly all the architects of the sixteenth century. Bramante did not yet incorporate it into any of his Roman works (unless one accepts the view that he collaborated in the design of the Palazzo Sora, although here the motif was developed in an archaic manner and in low relief). The rediscovery of this feature was probably due to Raphael, who suggested it for the altars of St. Peter's, the windows of Villa Pandolfini, and Palazzo Branconio, as well as in the circular courtyard of Palazzo Madama, where it appeared without a tympanum. In the same period, Sangallo adopted it in his *imago Pontis* and in his first design for Palazzo Farnese.

Michelangelo developed the aedicule theme in St. Peter's and the Capitol with variations of an extraordinarily powerful plasticity. He intervened critically in the structure of this feature and, as Sangallo had done timidly before him, he challenged the rules of composition to which it was subservient. The lower cornice of the tympanum became a non-functional feature; in the Palazzo dei Conservatori it was made to recede into the wall and was then fragmented; in St. Peter's it was submerged by the void, and finally, in the Porta Pia it was abolished. In the large central window of Palazzo dei Conservatori one aedicule and a curved tympanum interpenetrate, as do another aedicule with a triangular tympanum, as if to embody in the finished work an element of hesitation together with a refusal to make an exclusive choice. The stylistic innovation which developed into a type and entered the visual habits of the man in the street became the indispensable support for a lucid process of decomposition and free heretical recomposition, through a sort of contradictory process to that of referring to classical sources.

In the years of his maturity and after a close study of Vitruvius, Antonio da Sangallo devoted a great deal of research to the question of windows and doorways. In the second floor of Palazzo Farnese, he experimented freely in methods of integrating the motifs of the arch and the aedicule, interrupting the lower cornice below the tympanum, while in the ducal room and throne room of the Vatican he designed with impeccable elegance windows and doorways which were among the most beautiful produced during the whole period of the Renaissance. The Temple of the Sibyl at Tivoli and the Temple of Cori provided him with prototypes which he adapted according to his own taste, finding a perfect equilibrium between the need for a plastic reinforcement of the structure and the desire for elegant proportioning. The models represented by an architrave surrounding a rectangular area and by a cornice or tympanum resting on corbels were valid for both windows and doorways (M.I.3.) and coincided with the instructions given by Vitruvius relating to doors of the Ionic order. This feature was already present in the tradition of Alberti, but in a version derived from the late-classical period example of Spoleto, in which the proportions of the corbels were exaggerated in an expressionist manner. The quite different example of the archaic Temple of Cori, in which the corbels are tall and very slender, provided Roman sixteenth-century architects with a fruitful term of comparison and an inducement to find a compromise solution.

From the time of Michelangelo the rigorous approach to this theme, which had acquired the character of a learned disputation into the 'quintessence' of the type, gave way to the process of weaving variations around a theme. In the drum of the dome of St. Peter's, the corbels are doubled, while the cornice of the intervening area is drawn back into a deep hollow. Vignola, however, returned to the academic form in the Villa Giulia, confining himself to crowning the entablature with a florid decoration of classical origin.

The type of the 'kneeling window' is the version of types M.1.2. and M.1.3. adapted to the requirements of ground floors, and is therefore provided with a protruding sill supported by corbels among which a second window was usually inserted for the cellars. Interest became concentrated more and more on corbels, until the splendid example provided by Sangallo in Palazzo Sacchetti and Vignola's version in the Villa Giulia, where for the first time we find the volutes hinged at an angle of ninety degrees.

The 'Rustic Mode', Rustication, and Horizontal Bands

Within the classical system, the wall too became modified in a novel way by making the constructive process apparent, either in its 'real' form or in its figurative 'representation'. The most amorphous and elemental solution to the problem was to employ plasterwork, which tended to reduce the wall to a neutral surface, to which were contrasted without intervening structures the parts of the order or the subordinate constituent features which were nearly always executed in stone. On the other hand, an autonomous structure was that of the brick screen which appeared in the sixteenth century in two distinct versions: the 'rustic' version in which brick served a constructive function and where the additions of mortar in medium thickness usually appeared in stylized form; and the 'smoothed' version, that is, smoothed after being put in hand and composed of very thin bricks (flat broken tiles or similar elements), derived from Roman architecture of the Imperial Age and from tombs especially.

The technique of smooth brick inlay had already been completely reintegrated by Sangallo in Palazzo Baldassini, and determined a relationship between wall and structural elements which was not one of pure contrast but of a 'reduced' plastic and linear connection. In fact, the surface was modified by the texture and grain of the brickwork and by the horizontal strips added to it, so that it did not appear as a simple background but as part of the structure, in a similar way to a muscular texture. Whereas Roman classical architecture was satisfied with unifying walls and membratures through the texture of the brick, sixteenth-century architects preferred to achieve effects of contrast by using straw-coloured travertine or greyish peperino, reproducing in an attenuated and 'desublimated' form, in a new demand for solidity, the Florentine colour dichotomy between bright stone and pale backgrounds.

The last method of modifying the wall surface was to employ rustication. This was a typical instrument of perspective 'gradation' in its various metamorphoses—from the *aggressive and naturalistic rustic* style to the *geometrically controlled rustic* and finally the *smooth* style, employing the textures of *stone*, *brick conglomerate*, and *brick plasterwork*. In Roman fifteenth-century architecture, smooth rustication reached its climax in the Cancelleria, where the form of its ornamentation was derived—as the Palazzo Massimo was later—from the temple of Mars Ultor. With the Julia gate of the Belvedere and the base storey of Palazzo Caprini, however, Bramante introduced an entirely different version of rustication, derived from the encircling wall of the Forum of Augustus—although with some reference to the medieval and Florentine traditions. In this way the 'rustic mode' was created; it was substantiated by the works of Sangallo, who made it possible in doorways and rusticated quoins to impart greater solidity to the mass of the façades. Compared with Bramante's Tribunali, for example, Sangallo's manner tended to accentuate the geometrical nature of the rustication by reducing the roughness of the plastic treatment and employing bands to induce effects of luminous vibration. With Giulio Romano, however, there came into being an intermixture between rustication and the membratures of the order, and a desire to change the 'rustic' into the 'polished', the formless into the formed, and so to portray form at its nascent stage when it is in the process of acquiring definition. The earliest signs

Palazzo of Cardinal Adriano (1 cm = 6 m).

Palazzo Cicciaporci in Via di S. Spirito (1 cm = 6 m).

Façade of the Zecca.

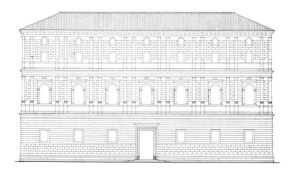

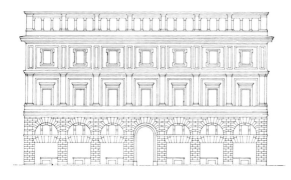

Palazzo Chiovenda in Piazza Montevecchio created by doubling a terraced house (1 cm = 2.5 m).

House known as Raphael's house in Via Giulia (1 cm = 2 m).

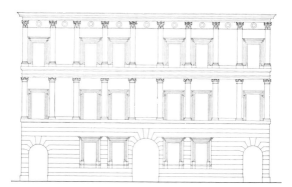

of this research into mixed forms can be seen in the doorway of Palazzo Maccarani, where the tympanum is fragmented by the eruption of a halo of shells, and again in the windows of Palazzo Vidoni, certainly by the same hand, where the shells fill the empty spaces of the tympani and transform them into incumbent masses pervaded by the half-shadow. The same theme was later adopted by Vignola in the Villa Giulia, where he applied the method of Serlio and erected an order consisting of an assembly of moulded rusticated rocks. An example closely resembling the manner of Giulio Romano occurs in the doorway of Casa Crivelli, which is encrusted with rustication.

The version of the theme provided by Pirro Ligorio in the sphere of domestic architecture remained close to Peruzzi's model of Palazzo Massimo, while in the fountain of the Screech-owl in the Villa d'Este and in other nymphaea the technique of stuccowork was introduced to ornament the rustication and cause the edges to acquire greater relief. In the Organ Fountain the theme was reversed in the wall of the large niche, divided by bands into protruding smooth membratures alternating with neutral zones inlaid with chips of grey stone. Ligorio's transformation of the rhythmic truss of Bramante's Belvedere into a form of smooth rustication expresses the complete triumph of a fashion and the 'loss of discernment' resulting from its indiscriminate use. The 'certain reasons' to which Ligorio referred in relation to the symbolic significance of the ceiling decorations actually corresponded to the 'uncertain reason' of his stylistic choices.

Considerable importance was given in the language of Roman classicism to horizontal bands which were extraneous to the repertory of the order proper, such as mouldings marking the division into storeys and decorated fillets. The archetypal form is that of the protruding listel which in military architecture became a convex moulding band. On the basis of classical precedents, the fillet usually appears decorated by a Greek fret or with a spiral wave pattern (*chien courant*). Sangallo employed this feature so frequently that it became to some extent his personal mark, but there was no lack of examples of original variations on this theme. Strips and cornices were adopted in order to unify the impost plane of the windows, and in this case they absorbed their sills also. However, the 'storey-dividers' quite frequently corresponded to the impost plane of the ceiling and in such cases a second fillet was introduced at the level of the window-sills.

Domestic Architecture

Under the auspices of the Institute of Humanities, Milan Polytechnic, a research project has been in progress for several years into the appearance that certain Italian cities must have presented during the sixteenth century. Recently, the architects Fregna and Polito have taken as a sample the area around Via Giulia, and have uncovered certain typical characteristics of the sixteenth-century city which are to be the subject of a future publication. From the information they have so far released some interesting facts have emerged.

The smallest constituent element, the rows of one-family houses, continued to be in very general use throughout the sixteenth century, even in new and reconstructed districts. The average width of the plot for such types of houses varied between 18 ft (414 cm) and 24 ft (552 cm) while the average depth was about 15 metres. These dimensions were conditioned by such technical factors as the standard length of the wooden beams employed for the ceilings and by traditional forms of very ancient origin. The position of the staircase, following a longitudinal direction along one of the boundary walls, made it almost obligatory to subdivide the available space on the two floors, and this model permitted only a limited number of variants. We have previously observed that until the mid-fifteenth century the popes were constantly concerned with the question of bringing together adjoining groups of one-family houses to form broader units which could house greater numbers of people and so meet the needs of the growing population.

In the sixteenth century, this type of housing was still erected for the artisan class of the population, while the rising middle class aspired to more substantial residences standing in their own grounds. The type of the 'palazzetto' with its innumerable variants was therefore developed, usually out of the aggregation of several plots originally occupied by rows of houses (recurring dimensions were 36, 48, 100, 136, 150 feet and multiples of these units).

The palazzetti usually extended in depth to about thirty metres, so that they completely covered the narrower blocks or occupied half the depth of the larger blocks. The structure of the palazzetto was entirely similar to that of the large palazzi, and consisted of simple blocks which partially or completely surrounded a central court. There are extremely rare examples of 'T' and 'H' structures containing two smaller courtyards.

From the most elemental type, in which the courtyard contains no loggias and is adjacent to other building plots on two or three of its sides, we come to the more complex forms in which the courtyards have loggias on four sides, simple blocks at the side edges of the plot, and double blocks on the façades (Palazzo Farnese). The width of the blocks varies from seven to twelve metres and that of the loggias from two to four metres; in the Palazzo Farnese one even finds the exceptional dimension of six metres. Movement in and around the various areas was mainly across the uncovered loggias; it was only towards the mid-century that enclosed corridors came into use, or ante-rooms arranged parallel to the main rooms through which people could pass without being exposed to inclement weather. A typical example is the Palazzo Capodiferro, where there are no loggias on the upper floors of the courtyard. The staircases almost always have a spine wall and the first standard ramp at an axis to the loggia parallel to the façade, but then follow a longitudinal direction in relation to the plot, at an angle of ninety degrees.

With regard to the sequence of internal rooms, the distinctive character imprinted on them comes principally through the interaction among the three dimensions of the enveloping structure, and through their pictorial decoration. Flat roofs and wooden ceilings were more generally employed than vaulting, especially in the first decades of the century, since vaulting was usually reserved for the loggias. The technique of inlay consequently developed and architects experimented with types of lacunaria, employing all possible combinations of polygonal forms. As in medieval times, the main structural element remained the fireplace; it was made to conform to the traditions relating to the order, with the theme of the doorway and aedicule being adapted to its different proportions and functions, although with a very free relationship between the membratures which permitted brilliant variations on the theme of the corbel and console bracket.

In contrast to the monotonous treatment of space and highly simple arrangement of the various sections of the building, we are struck by the complexity and variety of the treatment of façades, where in only a few decades architects exhausted a whole gamut of forms which were to exert an influence on the course of European architecture for the next three centuries. With regard to the sources for models of façades which could be applied to domestic architecture, it was found that the classical heritage provided very few examples and theoretical precepts, and Renaissance architects had to compensate for the lack of sources and for the fact that it was difficult to adapt classical types to the new residential demands; they did so by introducing an admixture of various types, such as religious buildings, or by adapting medieval models to the classical forms.

Even Alberti had not avoided this artifice in spite of his archeological culture, and had superimposed the texture of the orders onto the ground plan of the palace-fortress which was part of the Florentine tradition.

The Cancelleria represents the first of a series of sixteenth-century experiments into the superimposing of a rhythmical pattern of bands ornamented by smooth rustication and—on the upper levels—by a twin order.

This type was adapted to various proportions: from the minute Palazzetto Turci to the palazzo built for Cardinal Adriano in Borgo. But even before 1510 an alternative form was provided by Peruzzi's Farnesina, in which he rejected the dialectical method of superimposing contrasting strata in favour of unifying the complete organism by means of a continuous pattern built on the basic unit of the order. Soon afterwards Bramante brought about a sudden change of direction from research into the Tabularium system, and he

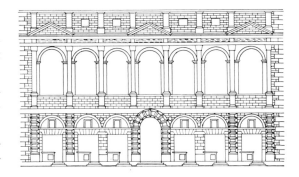

Design by Fra Giocondo for a palazzo in Via del Pantheon (1 cm = 4 m).

Palazzo in Via del Governo Vecchio, 14-17 (1 cm = 2.5 m).

Palazzo in Vicolo Montevecchio (1 cm = 2.5 m.)

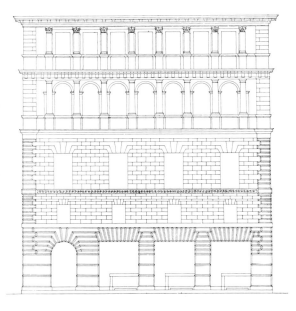

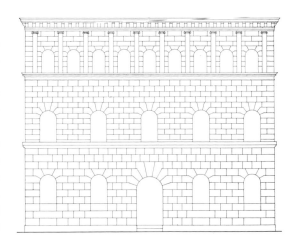

Façade of Palazzo Ossoli (1 cm = 2.5 m).

Façade of the palazzo of Giacomo Bresciano (1 cm = 3 m).

Palazzetto Spada (1 m = 3 m).

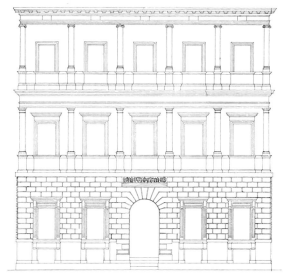

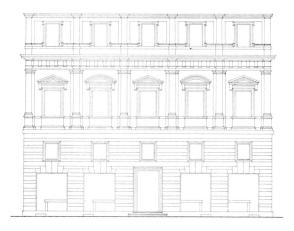

superimposed a group of twin columns in high relief onto a rusticated base, designed in a vigorous and uncompromising manner. In this way he expressed in terms of perspective depth a method which had become exhausted in harmonious proportional design. Rustication connected with the technique of pre-cast masonry marked a return to the naturalism expressed in the Roman monuments of the Age of Claudius, but seen now in illusionistic terms and from an intellectual standpoint. It inaugurated a series of powerful pictorial effects which were most outstanding in the Palazzo dei Tribunali.

At about the same time, Fra Giocondo probably drew up plans for a palazzo in Via del Pantheon, of which only the foundations and the still intact ground floor with shops were completed; however, a sketch for the plan of the complete building remains, although it has been related in error to Bramante's Palazzo dei Tribunali until quite recently. Over a line of shops arranged as arched openings following the example of the Forum of Caesar, there was erected a series of arches framed by the order, similar in both appearance and proportions to the arches in the Tabularium. The building was to be surmounted by an attic storey, of a form closely derived from antiquity, and three tympanums. It was exceptional among the buildings constructed in this time in that its close reference to Roman classical monuments imbued it with a heroic tone, far different from that of the other palaces which were being erected during the same period of years. This anomalous example may be related to two palazzetti which showed equal originality: 14-17 Via del Governo Vecchio, and 3 Vicolo di Montevecchio. The former has three bands and is characterized by smooth rustication and windows cut directly into the wall without cornices, and with two ornamented storeys superimposed and relieved by an order of lower proportions. By superimposing contrasting zones there was the danger of creating a sense of fragmentation, but in spite of its proportional values, an impression of unity is achieved through the chromatic effects obtained from the continuous pattern created by the reliefs. The same motif of the order recurs in the house in the Vicolo di Montevecchio, but here it is inserted on a plinth at the top floor and introduces an even more archaic note, as an ingenuous recapture of an ancient form still perceived in the spirit of the *Mirabilia Urbis*.

The papacy of Leo X coincided with the fashion for superimposing orders onto a rusticated base. After the Palazzo Caprini, the theme was taken up again in the Palazzo Cicciaporci Senni, the Palazzo Caffarelli Vidoni, the house of Giacomo Bresciano, and the Palazzo Ossoli, and variations were introduced into the reliefs and rhythms by diminishing or exaggerating the effects of chiaroscuro. This was the period when the middle class attached to the Vatican, the class of merchants and bankers, and the nobility, could still find some common ground through architecture adapted to the scale of the urban network. The Palazzetto Bresciano, which was barbarously destroyed in recent times and reconstructed with little regard for coherence, is a typical example of a bourgeois residence in which a subtle and harmonious balance is achieved between quantity and quality.

Almost simultaneously, before the 1520s, two new types were created, which were equal in originality but otherwise poles apart: the Palazzo Palma Baldassini and the Palazzo Branconio dell'Aquila. While Sangallo emphasized the isolation of the building and the sharp delimitation of the property through the use of rusticated quoins, Raphael conceived of an open system which could enter into a reciprocal relationship with the neighbouring buildings. The area of the street became unexpectedly filled with a colourful decorative scheme which complemented the lucid composition of the colonnades and aediculae with tympanum.

Like Bramante, Sangallo too was a firm advocate of the order resting on a rusticated base, and incorporated the feature both in plans which were never put into effect, and in such works as the inn at Castro, the Zecca in Castro, and the Zecca in Rome. The Rome Zecca (Mint) was erected around 1524 as a background to the typical triangular widenings formed by the convergence of two road axes.

The idea of curving the façade level to centre on the point at which the two lateral façades converged represented a revolutionary innovation, especially from the urban viewpoint, since it established a clearly-defined relationship between the environment and the form of the architecture, thus anticipating the approach adopted by Peruzzi to this problem in the Palazzo Massimi and also the experimental methods of Baroque town planning. Moreover, the architecture of the Zecca implied a criticism of the Palazzo Caprini, and in contrast to the latter the classic function of the base was restored—that is, it again became a subordinate element, 'cast out' from the weight of the order.

The type represented by the Palazzo Branconio would not be comprehensible were it not for the reigning fashion for painted façades, which came into being largely through the works of Maturino and Polidoro da Caravaggio, Baldassarre Peruzzi, and later Pirro Ligorio and the Zuccari brothers. In this field fifteenth-century forms persisted for a long time, although they were transformed by the complexity of the iconological decorations which were nearly always inspired by the glorification of Rome. In the Palazzo Ricci and Palazzo Massimo, the continuous narration eventually absorbs and annuls the architectural structure, reducing the flanking streets to the role of pure colour vibration.

The impact which this fashion must have had on the urban scene cannot easily be re-created in the city of today, since the great height of the buildings obstructs the flow of light into the streets, while the few surviving examples of graffiti and frescoes have seriously deteriorated. However, we may easily imagine the colourful effect created by these involved decorations, which transformed the area of the streets into a place of contemplation, where one could follow a 'narrative' as one walked through them. The Counter-Reformation inherited from the Renaissance a city whose central districts must have been very strongly marked by the extrovert spirit and pomp of the first decades of the century. And much time was to elapse before these traces disappeared beneath the red and earth-coloured plasterwork of the Baroque city.

After the Sack of Rome, there was a period of stagnation when inventiveness declined. We have the finest examples of the work of Sangallo and Peruzzi in the Palazzo Farnese and Palazzo Massimo, two unsurpassable examples which mark the end of a great period of activity and leave a void behind them. After the example of Raphael, Mazzoni created the Palazzo Spada, with a façade containing two floors superimposed onto a rusticated base, where in a flat and clumsy form the motifs employed in the Palazzo Branconio reappear. In the courtyard and interior decoration, however, the building attains a far superior level, and brings to Rome a breath of Mannerism originating in northern Italy and France.

On the other hand, we may consider the Palazzetto Spada and the house known as 'Raphael's house' in Via Giulia to be derived from Peruzzi. The subtle gradation of the rustication resembles that employed by Pirro Ligorio for the Palazzo Lancellotti, constructed at a later date.

In the fifth and sixth decades of the sixteenth century, building activity diminished both in quantity and quality; houses constructed for the middle classes were no longer representative of a universal ambition, while noblemen's palaces repeated wearily models which had already been tested elsewhere. The architectural interests of the powerful families became concentrated on villas, which represented to them an expression of faith in the myth of feudal nobility as well as an escape from everyday reality.

One of the last examples on the theme of the one-family house was the Palazzetto in Piazza Navona by Vignola, where he returned to his early work in the Bologna loggias and transcribed it delicately and brilliantly into a minor key. Its appearance more or less set the seal on Roman bourgeois architecture as a terrain for stylistic experimention. In the first decades of the century conditions had existed which had enabled the intellectuals attached to the papal court to make a contribution through their building initiatives to defining the form of the city; in this way they were able to assume a role no less important than that fulfilled by the aristocracy in advancing the development of an avant-garde culture. These conditions no longer prevailed and were never again to be repeated, not even in the Baroque period when for a short time Rome once more became the 'city of architecture'.

The Re-planning of Rome.

302. *Via della Lungara, a link road between the Vatican and Trastevere.* | *303. Via Monserrato, while retaining its winding shape, is entirely rebuilt along its sides.* | *304-306. Via Giulia, the first straight thoroughfare, linking Ponte S. Angelo to Ponte Sisto.* | *307. Via dei Banchi, co-axial with S. Angelo, is the central line of the first 'trident', a radial structure which became typical of Baroque town planning.*

The street space.
The street façades, articulated by a more spacious rhythm than the tightly packed medieval ones, acquired a continuity of development due to the recurrence of horizontal lines and the even spacing of the windows in the sixteenth century. | 308. A typical example of a sixteenth-century street: Via de' Monteroni. | 309. Via de' Delfini, a side street whose upper cornices illustrate the appearance of the top of the buildings of the period. | 310. The persistence of irregular corners of medieval origin is turned to good account by a new architectonic interpretation. | 311. The side of Via Giulia leading to the Tiber, composed of a succession of parallelepiped blocks placed in a straight line.

The rhythm of proportions in façades of the first period (1500–27).

In the first years of the sixteenth century façades conformed to one of three basic types: one in which the orders of architecture were used to construct a rigid proportional framework in which doors and windows were an intrinsic element; one where the prominent feature was a continuous surface of wall broken only by cornices and horizontal bands; and lastly a combination of the two preceding types over a rusticated podium at the ground floor level.

312. Palazzo della Cancelleria (1489). | 313. Palazzo del Cardinale Adriano (1496–1504). | 314. Palazzo Ricci (c. 1550). | 315. Palazzo Lante (c. 1500). | 316. La Farnesina (1508–11). | 317. Palazzo Ossoli (c. 1520). | 318. A house in Via del Governo Vecchio. | 319. Palazzo Vidoni (1516).

The rhythm of proportions in the second period (1527–64).
Both the columnar framework and the window framing underwent a progressive plastic enrichment in the second period of sixteenth-century Roman architecture. Wall pilasters were echoed by counter-pilasters or by fillets, tympana formed an articulated or broken pattern, and in some cases the functional elements (doors, windows, galleries) were absorbed into a single plastic and decorative formal structure.
320. Michelangelo: Third-floor windows overlooking the courtyard in the Palazzo Farnese (1546). | 321. Palazzetto Spada (1540). | 322. Giulio Mazzoni: A house in Piazza dei Caprettari. | 323. House on the Via Giulia belonging to Paul III's doctor. | 324. Windows of the Villa Medici (1564). | 325. Palazzo dei Conservatori (1568). | 326. Palazzo Farnese (1514–50).

Painted façades.

327, 328. At the end of the fifteenth century it became fashionable in Rome to paint the exteriors of buildings in fresco or sgraffito. This treatment became so popular in the early years of the sixteenth century that a note of gaiety characterized the replanned town, while at the same time it was reminded of its origins by the choice of predominantly mythological subjects for these paintings.

Rusticated Quoins

The fashion for rusticating the cornerstones of buildings began in Florence (Cronaca's is one of the earliest examples) and spread rapidly in Rome in the early years of the sixteenth century until it became one of the typical features of the urban scene. As well as indicating the social prestige of the owners of the house, this fashion had an important effect on the visual appearance of the city as a whole, where the innumerable rusticated corners on the buildings of sixteenth-century Rome formed a close-knit pattern which fulfilled a unifying function.

329. *Florentine-style corner on the Palazzo Taverna, Via della Vetrina.* | 330. *Antonio da Sangallo the Younger: Corner of the Palazzo Farnese.* 331. *Bramante: Base of the unfinished Palazzo dei Tribunali.* | 332. *Corner of an unfinished palazzo, Via dei Banchi Vecchi.* | 333. *Corner of a sixteenth-century building, Via de' Funari.*

The luministic and plastic values of the rusticated method.
Two examples of the growing importance of rusticated walls.
334. Base of the Palazzo Vidoni, attributed to Raphael. | 335. Corner of the Palazzo degli Accetti, Via dei Banchi Vecchi.

Architectural solutions to the problem of corners.
An overriding problem in sixteenth-century Roman architecture was that of making organic link sections between perpendicular planes. Several solutions had been tested in the classical school of architecture. In St. Peter's, Bramante solved the problem by cutting the four central pillars at forty-five degrees; in this way he combined an octagonal structure with the square which had become the standard norm for dealing with the concave dihedron, while articulated wall pilasters were used for convex corners. After 1570 in the Jesuit Collegio Romano Ammannati carried the theme of the rounded corner to the exterior of the building, thus opening the way to the variations of Baroque architecture.

  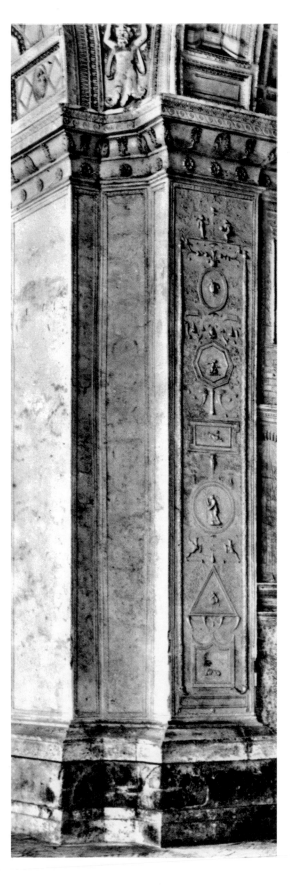

336. *Link section of the pilasters at the entrance to the Pantheon.* | 337. *Corner of the façade of Santa Maria di Loreto (1507).* | 338. *Corner pilaster of the Villa Madama (1515–17).* | 339. *La Farnesina (1508–11).* | 340. *Treatment of corners in the house of Bartolomeo da Brescia.* 341. *Corner pilaster of the Villa Giulia (1551–3).*

The orders in the treatment of corners.

From the restrained treatment of the cloister of Santa Maria della Pace to the extremely elaborate courtyard of the Palazzo Farnese— which in Michelangelo's handling of the third storey acquired an unprecedented complexity and rigour—there lay an area of research which utilized the pilaster as an element of continuity or separation between contiguous perpendicular planes.

342. Bramante: Corner pilaster in the cloister of Santa Maria della Pace (1500–4).

343. Antonio da Sangallo the Younger: Palazzo Farnese, cortile (1514–46). | 344. Baldassarre Peruzzi: La Farnesina (1523). | 345. Palazzetto Leroy (1523). | 346, 347. Antonio da Sangallo the Younger: Palazzo Baldassini (1510–15). | 348. Bartolomeo Ammannati: Villa Giulia, nymphaeum (1551–3).

349. Jacopo Vignola: Villa Giulia, corner pilaster (1551–3).

The orders and the treatment of the architrave.
The rediscovery of the Doric order, a typical feature of early sixteenth-century architecture, inaugurated a period of ever-increasing interest in the compositional values of pillars. After the original 'philological' interest had become exhausted, Michelangelo set himself to 'redesign' freely the architectural orders by modifying the rules of composition which governed them.
350. Donato Bramante: The Doric architrave on the Tempietto of San Pietro in Montorio (1502). | 351. Donato Bramante: The Corinthian architrave in the interior of St. Peter's (c. 1518). | 352. Antonio da Sangallo the Younger: The Doric architrave of the courtyard of Palazzo Farnese (1514–46). | 353. Michelangelo: The cornice of the apse of St. Peter's. | 354. Jacopo Vignola: The cornice of the Villa Giulia (1551–3).

Horizontal bands as elements of continuity. *Starting as a functional element to link the window-sills and as a linear break in the surface of walls, the band came to assume a growing importance for its plastic and luminous qualities. Antonio da Sangallo was the most noteworthy exponent of the expressive qualities of this feature.*
355. Palazzo della Valle (1517). | 356. Painted house in Vicolo del Governo Vecchio.
357. Palazzo in Via de' Delfini. | 358. Palazzo Farnese (1514–46). | 359. Unfinished palazzo in Via dei Banchi Vecchi. | 360. Palazzetto Leroy (1523).

Elements of composition. The serliana.
The accentuation of the central portion of the mullioned window by contrasting the arch and the trabeated three-lights began with Bramante's Sala Regia in the Vatican, and in Giulio Romano's Villa Lante the theme of the arcade was applied extensively. Roman sixteenth-century architecture thus developed in a way which was to become typical of the Po valley style after the dispersion of Roman artists following the Sack of Rome in 1527.
361. Window of the present-day Sala Regia in the Vatican (1540). | 362. Cortile of Palazzetto Leroy (1523). | 363. Cortile of Palazzo Cenci.
364. Villa of Pope Julius, nymphaeum. | 365. Loggia of the Villa d'Este at Tivoli. | 366. Villa Medici (1544).

The stylistic problem of doorways.
In the early sixteenth century, architects worked from clumsy provincial models derived from the classical aedicule translated into bas-relief and intended merely as decoration. With the rediscovery around the year 1520 of Roman prototypes of doors and windows—first in importance the door of the Temple of the Sibyl at Tivoli—there grew up a repertory which was destined to have a lasting influence on the whole of European culture.

367. *Entrance to a single-family house in Via della Lungaretta.* | *368. Doorway in Via della Lungaretta* | *369. Doorway in Via Capodiferro.* *370. Doorway in Via dei Coronari.* | *371. Doorway of the Palazzo De Cupis in Via dell'Anima.* | *372. Doorway of Palazzo Pichi.* | *373. Door in Palazzo Sacchetti (c. 1543).* | *374. Entrance to Palazzo Cadilhac in Via Monserrato.* *375. Doorway of Palazzo Lante (c. 1500).*

The role of rustication in defining the doorway as an autonomous structure.
376. Doorway of the Villa Giulia looking towards Monti Parioli. | 377. Palazzo of the Bishop of Cervia in Via Monserrato. | 378. Palazzo in Via della Maschera d'Oro. | 379. Palazzo Crivelli in Via dei Banchi Vecchi. | 380. Casa dei Fiorentini, in Via Giulia. | 381. Palazzo in Piazza Sant'Egidio in Trastevere. | 382. Palazzo Conti at Poli. | 383. Palazzo Ossoli in Piazza Capodiferro (c. 1525). | 384. Palazzetto Leroy in Via dei Baullari (1523).

The treatment of windows.

The late fifteenth-century predilection for window cornices decorated in low relief, derived from the Arco dei Borsari in Verona, where the arch is placed within a rectangular structure, was replaced in the sixteenth century by two basic types: a type derived from the classical aedicule, and another where above the rectangular window frame (which echoes the modenature of the cornice) there was placed a projecting cornice or tympanum; double-volute corbels were often used.

385. Palazzo della Cancelleria (1483).
386. Casa de Mochis, in Via dei Coronari (1516).
387. Palazzo in Vicolo Savelli. | 388. Palazzo del Drago, in Via dei Coronari. | 389. Coupled windows in Via de' Cimatori. | 390. Villa Medici (1544). | 391. Palazzetto Leroy (1523).

The classical aedicule as model and as a type.
While early sixteenth-century architects had been content to copy the Pantheon aedicules faithfully, or at the most to change to an order different from the original Corinthian, Michelangelo later began to develop new variations on this theme by the processes of sectioning, displacing and breaking up surfaces.
392. The temple of the Pantheon. | 393. Model for St. Peter's by Antonio da Sangallo the Younger. | 394. Window of the Palazzo dei Conservatori. | 395. Window of the apse of St. Peter's. | 396. Villa Madama. | 397. Dome of St. Peter's. | 398. Central window of the Palazzo dei Conservatori.

The classical corbel and its interpretations.
399. Andrea Sansovino: Doorway of the Palazzo Lante (c. 1500). | 400. Antonio da Sangallo the Younger: Doorway of Santa Maria di Loreto (1507). | 401. Doorway of the Villa Orsini at Bomarzo. | 402. Antonio da Sangallo the Younger: Doorway of the Palazzo Sacchetti (c. 1555). 403. Annibale Lippi: Doorway of the Villa Medici onto the garden (1544). | 404. Michelangelo: Monument to Cecchino Bracci in the church of Santa Maria in Aracoeli (1544–5). | 405. Michelangelo: Window of the drum of the dome of St. Peter's (c. 1560).

Window Corbels.

406. Antonio da Sangallo the Younger: Palazzo del Console di Firenze, Via Giulia. | 407. Antonio da Sangallo the Younger: Palazzo Farnese. 408. Antonio da Sangallo the Younger: Palazzo Sacchetti (1543). | 409. Andrea Sansovino (?): Palazzo Lante (c. 1500). | 410. Antonio da Sangallo the Younger: Palazzo Farnese (1514–46). | 411. Michelangelo: Apse of St. Peter's (1564). | 412. Jacopo Vignola: Villa Giulia (1551–3). | 413. Bartolomeo Ammannati: Palazzo Caetani, detail of the corbel. | 414. Raphael: Palazzo Caffarelli-Vidoni (1515).

Reticulated and interwoven patterns.
In the decorated coffering of wooden ceilings geometric structures of great complexity were employed in which the elements belonging to the classical tradition were elaborated with new dynamic and symbolic motifs.
415. Palazzo Spada. | 416. Sala Regia in the Vatican. | 417. Palazzo Farnese. | 418. Palazzo Spada. | 419, 420. Palazzo Farnese.
421, 422. Palazzo Massimo.

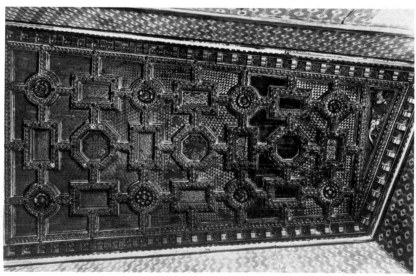

The return to the Antique. Forms derived directly or through the intermediary of Roman prototypes.
423, 424. Interior of the ground-floor gallery in the cortile of the Palazzo Massimo, with openings of a type inspired by the Roman cryptoportici. | 425, 426. The octagonal ceiling coffering in the chapel of San Giacomo degli Spagnoli by Antonio da Sangallo the Younger, compared with the vault of the Basilica of Maxentius. | 427, 428. Stucco decoration on the Villa Madama and fragment of the Ara Pacis. | 429, 430. Windows of the Palazzo della Can-
celleria and their prototype in the Arco dei Borsari, Verona. | 431, 432. The interior of the Tempietto of San Pietro in Montorio compared with a

reconstruction of the Monument to the Alps in Nice. | 433, 434. Column in Michelangelo's doorway to the Palazzo dei Conservatori and octagonal pillars in the so-called burial place of Annia Regilla. | 435, 436. Window by Michelangelo in the apse of St. Peter's and Roman prototype at Todi. | 437, 438. Windows of the piano nobile of the Palazzo Farnese and the Pantheon. | 439, 440. Sectional wall divisions in the Palazzo Farnese and in the outer wall of the Forum of Augustus.

The interest in archaeology and the placing of classical fragments in new contexts.
In the second half of the sixteenth century there was a widespread interest in collecting archaeological fragments. This produced a decorative style which transformed the façades of buildings into showcases presenting continuous contrasts in scale.
441. House decorated with archaeological fragments in the Roman Compagna. | 442. Cortile of the Palazzo Corsetti in Via Monserrato. | 443. House in Vicolo delle Grotte. | 444. Villa Medici. | 445. Courtyard of the Palazzo Corsetti in Via Monserrato.

ORIGINAL DRAWINGS

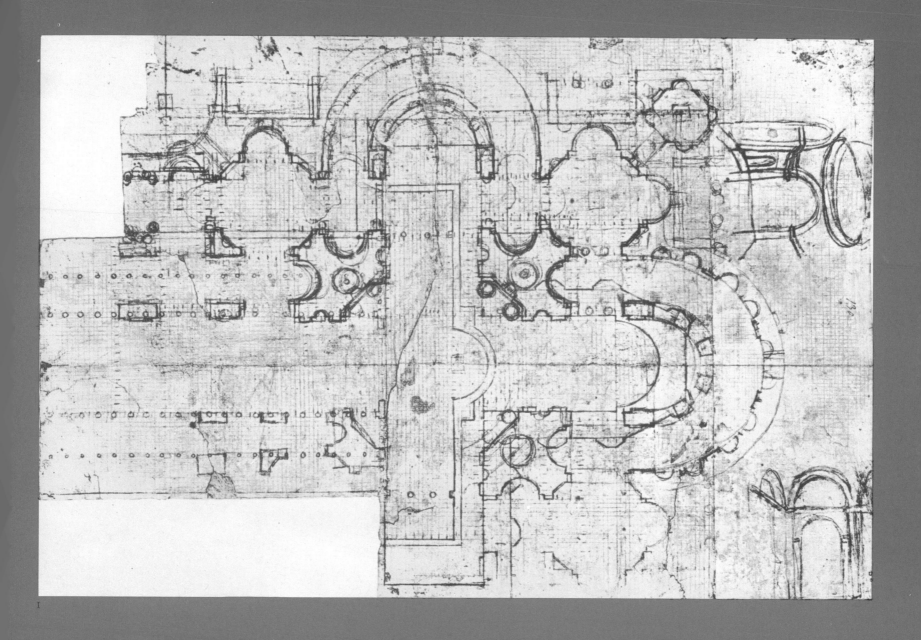

II

IV

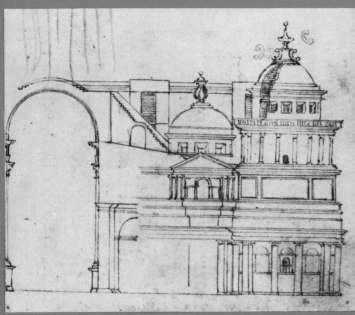

III

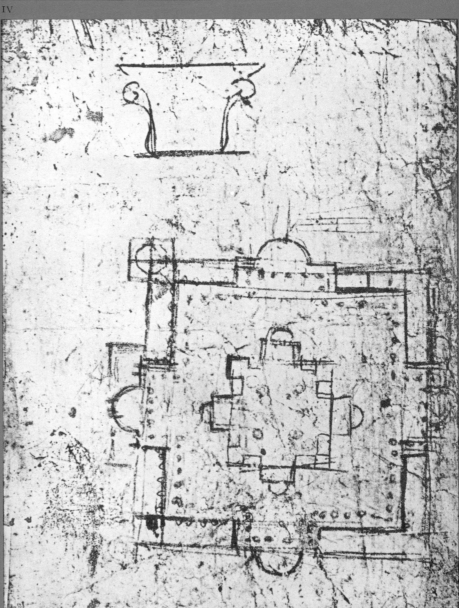

V

VII. *Marten van Heemskerck: view of the interior of the old basilica of St. Peter's, with the new incomplete construction in the background. Berlin, Kupferstichkabinett, Skb. II, f. 52.*
VIII. *Marten van Heemskerck: view of a detail of Bramante's fabric of St. Peter's. Berlin, Kupferstichkabinett, Skb. II, f. 8.*

VII

VIII

ERRATA

PLATES

Plate 69	Palazzo of the Bishop of Cervia	Palazzo Accetti
Plates 243-246	(1544)	(1564)
Plate 281	Room in Palazzo Sacchetti	Room in Palazzo della Cancelleria
Plates 296-297	Jacopo Vignola: Giulio Farnese temple at Bomarzo	Giulia Farnese temple at Bomarzo
Plate 304	Via Giulia	Via di Ripetta
Plate 344	(1523)	(1508-1511)
Plate 350	(1502)	(1508-1512)
Plate 351	(1518 c.)	(1514 c.)
Plate 366	(1544)	(1564)
Plate 369	Doorway in via Capodiferro	Doorway in vicolo dei Venti
Plate 373	Door in palazzo Sacchetti	Door in palazzo del Console di Firenze
Plate 377	Palazzo of the Bishop of Cervia, in via Monserrato	Palazzo Accetti, in via dei Banchi Vecchi
Plate 380	Casa dei Fiorentini, in via Giulia	Palazzo del Console di Firenze
Plate 388	Palazzo Del Drago, in via dei Coronari	Palazzo Massimo alle Colonne
Plate 390	(1544)	(1564)
Plate 402	(1555)	(1543)

IX

X

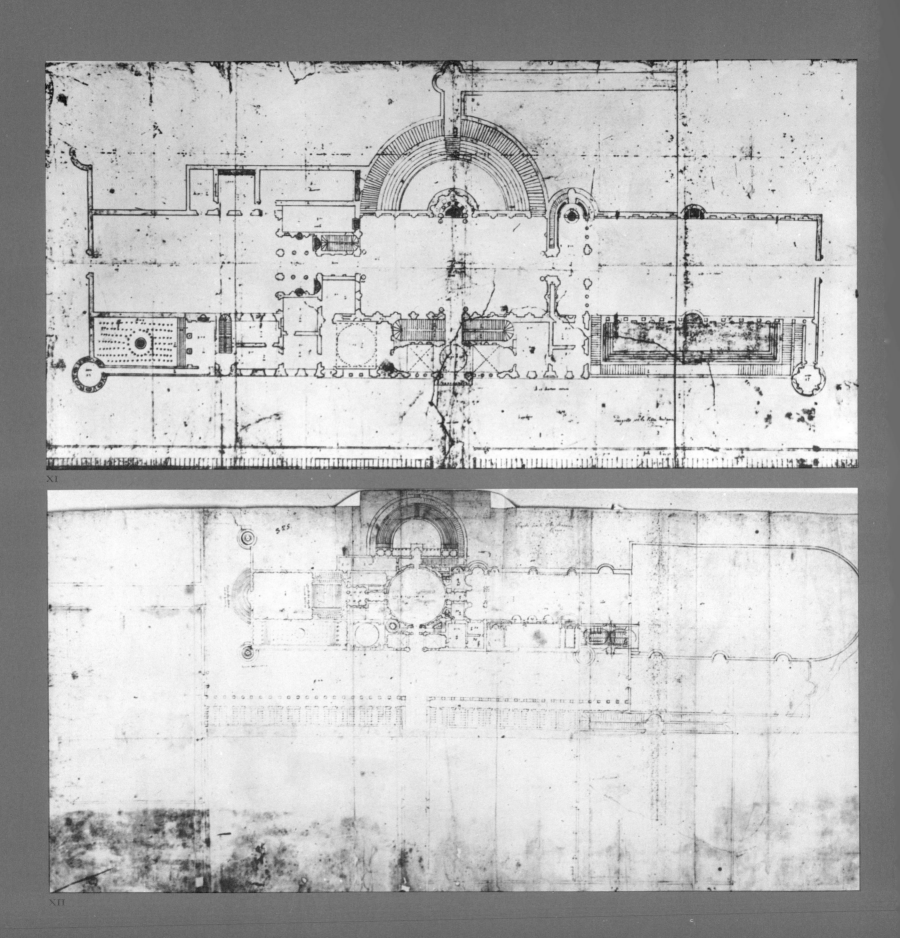

XI

XII

XIII

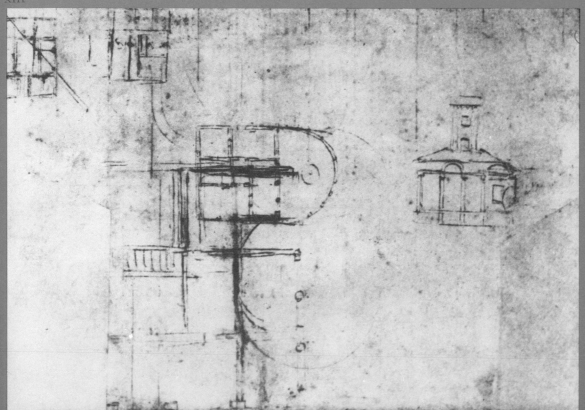

XIV

XV

XVI

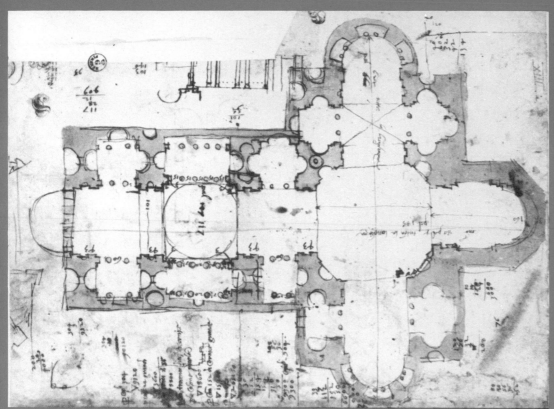

XVII

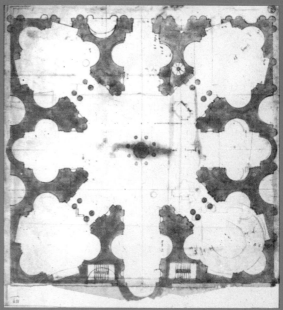

XIX

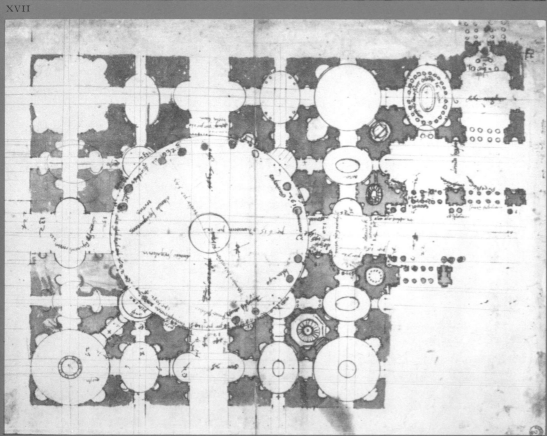

XVIII

XX. *Baldassarre Peruzzi: architectural drawing. Uffizi, 149 A.*
XXI. *Baldassarre Peruzzi: architectural drawing. Uffizi, 176 A.*

XXII. *Baldassarre Peruzzi: design for a dam (eighth mode). Uffizi, 587 A.*
XXIII. *Baldassarre Peruzzi: design for an oval church. Uffizi, 4137 A.*

XX

XXII

XXI

XXIII

XXIV. *Baldassarre Peruzzi: architectural drawing. Uffizi, 321.*

XXV. *Baldassarre Peruzzi: architectural drawing. Uffizi, 553 A v.*

XXVI. *Baldassarre Peruzzi: architectural drawing. Uffizi, 424 A.*

XXVII. *Baldassarre Peruzzi: architectural drawing. Uffizi, 143 A.*

XXIV

XXV

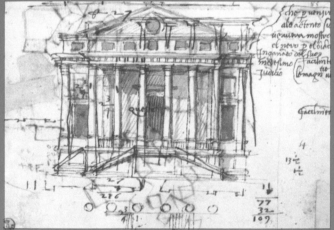

XXVI

XXVII

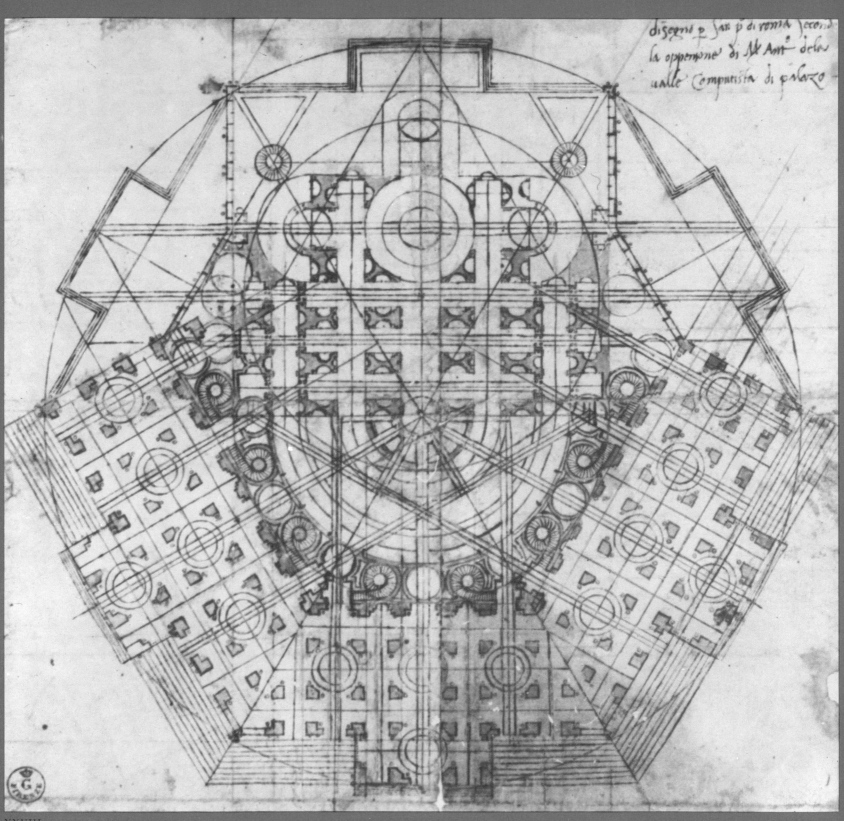

disegnio p̄ San p̄ di roma second
la oppemone di M̄ Ant̄ dela
uall Comptista di palazo

XXVIII

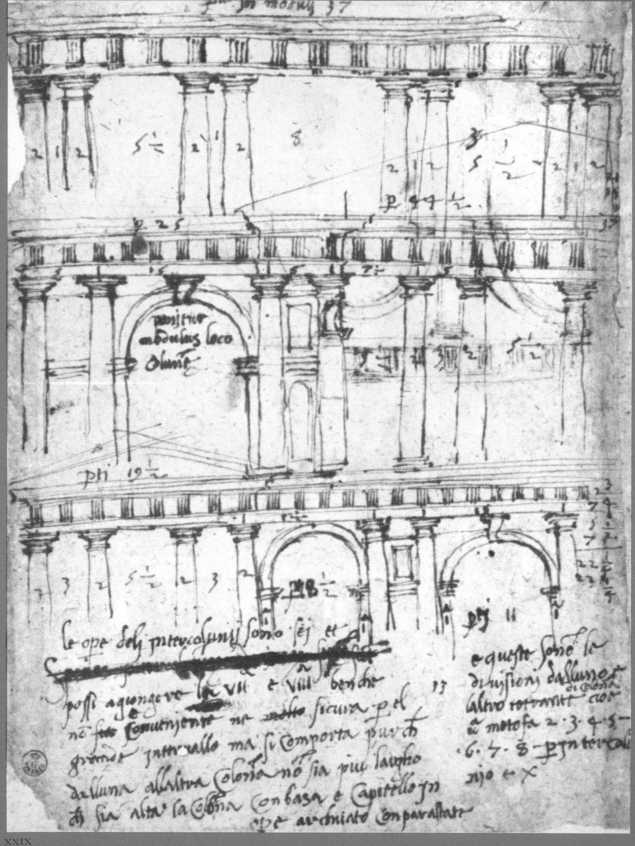

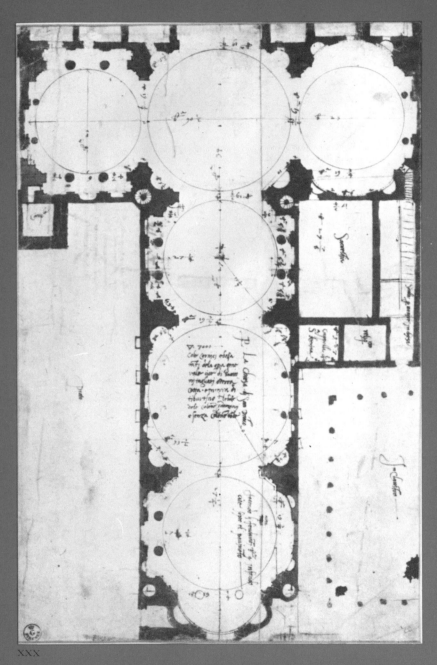

XXX

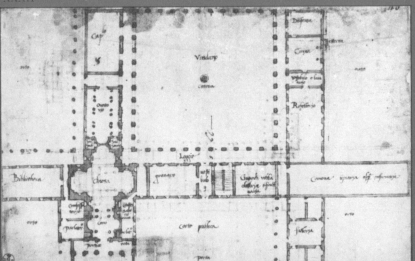

XXXI

XXXII

XXXIII

XXXIV. *Baldassarre Peruzzi: design for the Farnese palace of Caprarola.*
Uffizi, 200 A.
XXXV. *Baldassarre Peruzzi: design for the Farnese palace of Caprarola.*
Uffizi, 505 A.

XXXVI. *Baldassarre Peruzzi: design for a church. Uffizi, 495 A.*
XXXVII. *Baldassarre Peruzzi: architectural drawing. Uffizi, 529 A.*

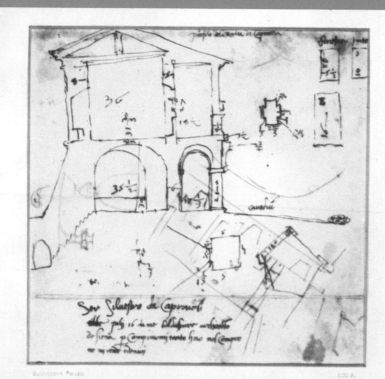

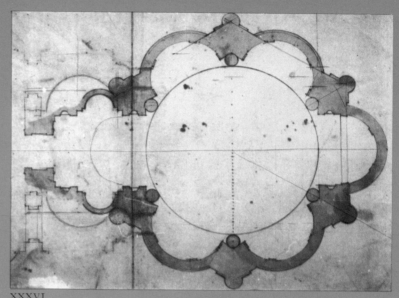

XXXVI

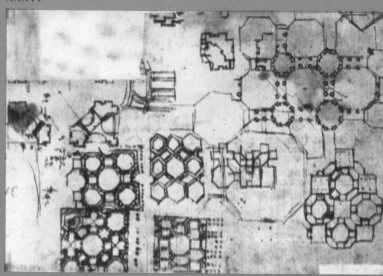

XXXVII

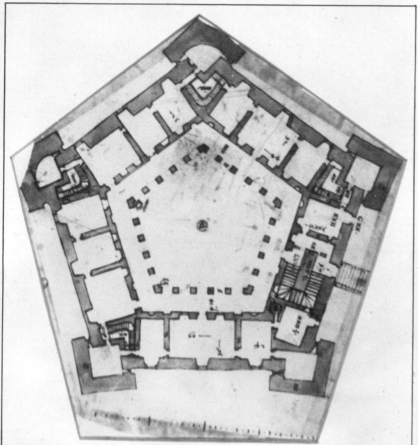

XXXIV–XXXV

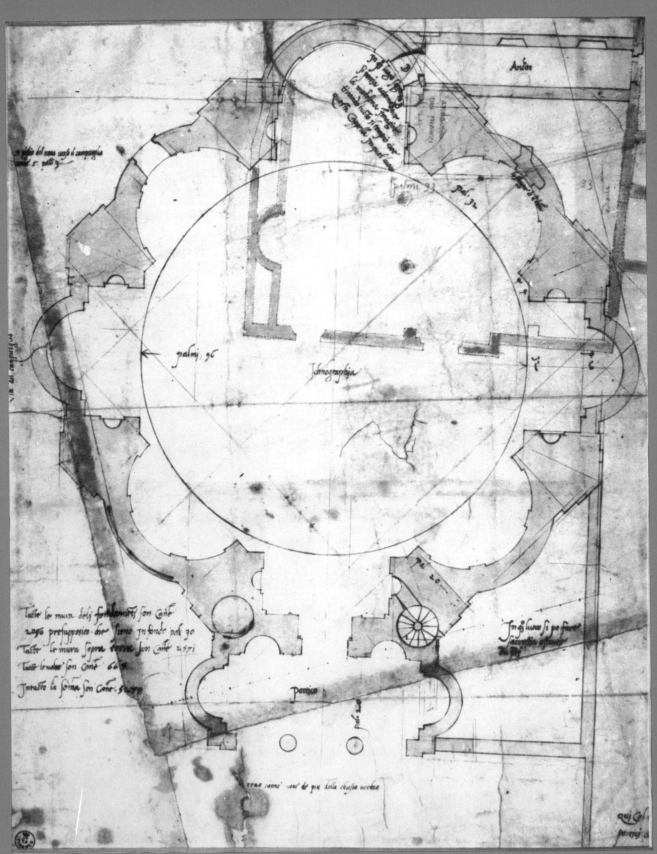

XXXIX

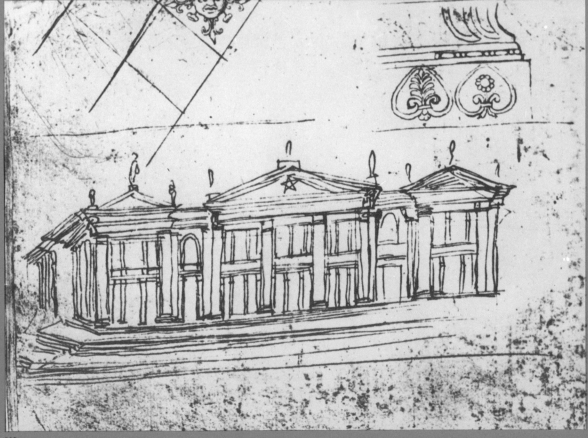

XL

XLI

XLII

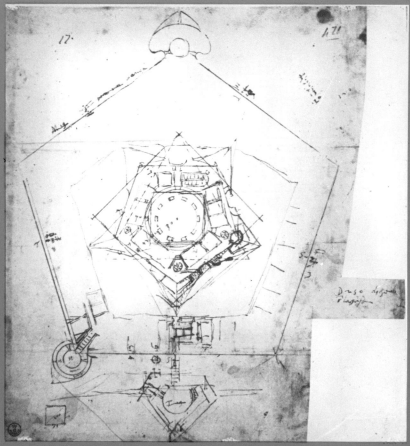

XLIII

XLIV. *Antonio da Sangallo the Younger: ground plan sketches and design for Santa Maria di Loreto, Rome. Uffizi, 786 A.*

XLV. *Antonio da Sangallo the Younger: ground plan sketches and design for Santa Maria di Loreto, Rome. Uffizi, 1368 A.*

XLVI. *Antonio da Sangallo the Younger: design for the Zecca, Rome. Uffizi, 867 A.*

XLVII. *Anonymous: relief of Antonio da Sangallo's model for St. Peter's.*

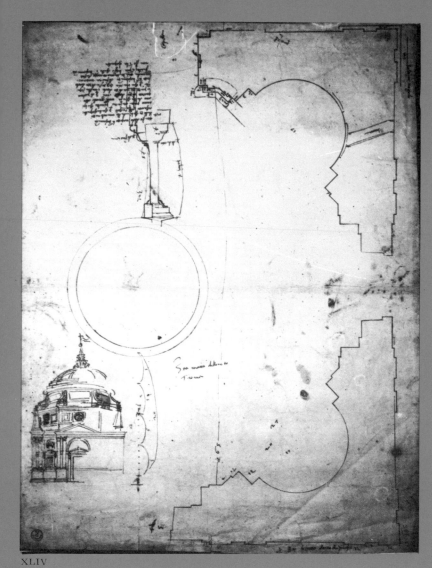

XLIV

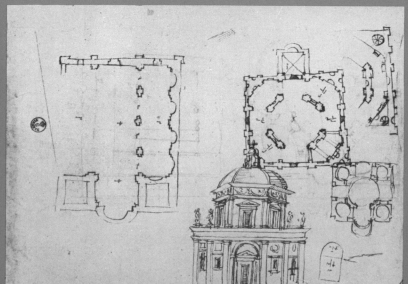

XLV

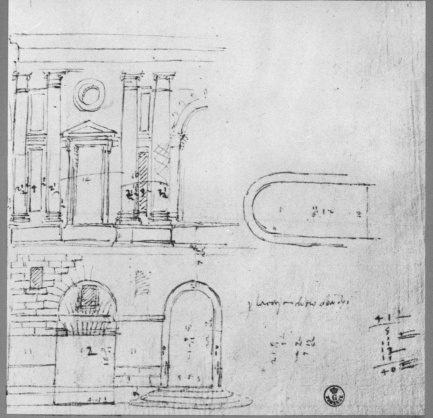

XLVI

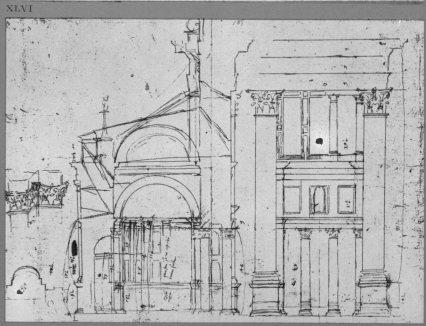

XLVII

XLVIII. *Antonio da Sangallo the Younger: studies for the palazzo of Cardinal Sanseverino. Uffizi, 1041 A.*
XLIX. *Antonio da Sangallo the Younger: façade sketch with architectural orders. Uffizi, 1859 A.*

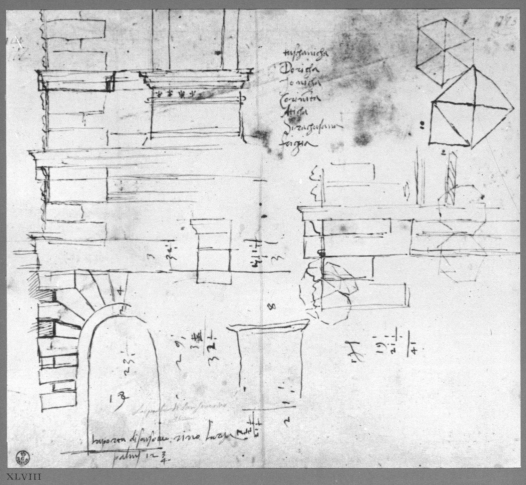

XLVIII

XLIX

L. *Antonio da Sangallo the Younger: exterior of the Del Pozzo house in Borgo. Uffizi, 210 A.*

LI. *Pirro Ligorio: architectural drawing. Turin, Archivio di Stato.*

LII. *Pirro Ligorio: archaeological reconstruction. Turin, Archivio di Stato.*
LIII. *Pirro Ligorio: archaeological reconstruction. Turin, Archivio di Stato.*

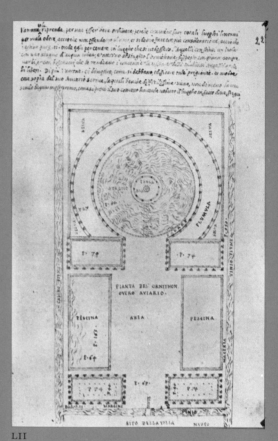

LII

LI

LIII

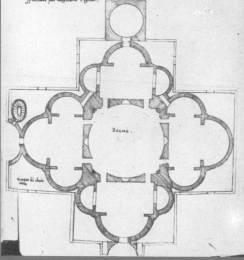

LV

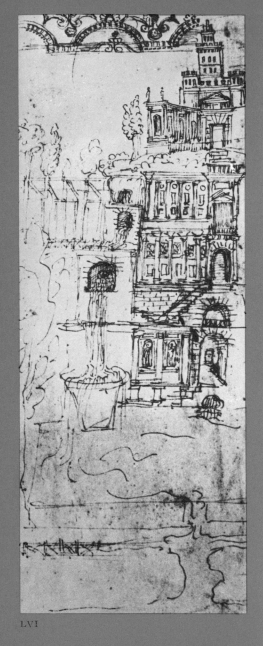

CLYTEMNESTRA
ET AGAMEMNONE

BIBLIOGRAPHY

1551 GIOVIO P., *Le vite di Leondecimo et d'Adriano VI. sommi Pontefici, et del cardinal Pompeo Colonna*, Florence.

1569 DOSIO G.A., *Urbis Romae aedificiorum illustrium quae supersunt reliquiae*.

1588 FRANCINO G., *Le cose meravigliose dell'alma città di Roma*, Venice.

1588 FULVIO A., *L'antichità di Roma di Andrea Fulvio con le aggiunte e annotazioni di Gerolamo Ferrucci*, Venice.

1642 BAGLIONE G., *Le vite de' Pittori, Scultori et Architetti dal Pontificato di Gregorio XIII dal 1572 in fino a' tempi di papa Urbano Ottavo nel 1642*, Rome.

1672 BELLORI G.P., *Le vite de' pittori, scultori ed architetti moderni*, Rome.

1694 FONTANA C., *Il tempio vaticano e la sua origine con gl'Edifitti più cospicui e moderni fatti dentro e fuori di Esso*, Rome.

1741 SEBASTIANI L., *Descrizione e relazione istorica del nobilissimo e real palazzo di Caprarola*, Rome.

1767–74 BALDINUCCI F., *Notizie de' professori del disegno da Cimabue in qua*, Florence, 20 vols.

1768 MILIZIA F., *Le vite de' più celebri architetti d'ogni nazione e d'ogni tempo precedute da un saggio sopra l'architettura*, Rome.

1784 STERN G., *Piante, elevazioni, profili e spaccati degli edifici della villa suburbana di Giulio III*, Rome.

1798 PERCIER C. - FONTAINE P.F.L., *Palais, maisons, et autres édifices modernes, dessinés à Rome*, Paris.

1822–5 BOTTARI M.G., *Raccolta di lettere sulla pittura, scultura ed architettura, scritte dai più celebri personaggi dei secoli XV, XVI, XVII*, Milan, 8 vols.

1828 WÖLFFLIN H., *Rinascimento e barocco. Ricerche intorno all'essenza e all'ordine dello stile barocco in Italia*, Florence.

1833 FONTANA G., *Raccolta delle migliori chiese di Roma e suburbane espresse in tavole disegnate ed incise da Giacomo Fontana e corredate di cenni storici e descrittivi*, Rome, 4 vols.

1838–41 NIBBY A., *Roma nell'anno MDCCCXXXVIII*, Rome, 4 vols.

1845 PONTANI C., *Opere architettoniche di Raffaello Sanzio*, Rome.

1868 GEYMÜLLER H., *Notizie sopra i progetti per la fabbrica di San Pietro in Roma desunte da fonti finora sconosciute*, in 'Il Buonarroti', vol. III, number VII (July), pp. 170-176, and number IX (September), pp. 215-233.

1868–74 LETAROUILLY P., *Edifices de Rome moderne*, Paris, 1 vol. (text), 3 vols. (plates).

1875–80 GEYMÜLLER H., *Die Ursprünglichen Entwürfe für St. Peter in Rom*, Vienna-Paris, vol. I (text), vol. II (plates).

1878 PODESTÀ B., *Carlo V a Roma nell'anno 1536*, in 'Archivio della Società romana di storia patria', 1 vol., pp. 303-344.

1878–85 VASARI G., *Le vite de' più eccellenti pittori, scultori ed architettori*, with notes and commentary by G. Milanesi, Florence, 9 vols.

1879 CLAYE D., *Etude sur la stabilité de la coupole projetée par Bramante*, Paris.

1879 DE ROSSI G.B., *Piante iconografiche e prospettiche di Roma, anteriori al secolo XVI*, Rome, 2 vols.

1880 FÖRSTER R., *Farnesina - Studien. Ein Beitrag zur Frage nach dem Verhältnis der Renaissance zur Antike*, Rostock.

1882 ARMELLINI M., *Un censimento della città di Roma sotto il pontificato di Leone X*, Rome.

1882 GEYMÜLLER H., *Cento disegni di Fra Giocondo*, Florence.

1884 GEYMÜLLER H., *Raffaello Sanzio studiato come architetto*, Milan.

1886 ALBERTINI F., *Opusculum de mirabilibus novae Urbis Romae*, Heilbronn.

1886 REDTENBACHER R., *Die Architektur der Italiänischen Renaissance*, Frankfurt.

1889 GNOLI D., *La Farnesina de' Baullari in Roma*, in 'Archivio Storico dell'Arte', year II, pp. 393-401.

1889 TESORONI D., *Il palazzo di Firenze e l'eredità di Balduino del Monte*, Rome.

1890 BERTOLOTTI A., *Nuovi documenti intorno all'architetto Antonio da Sangallo (il Giovane) ed alla sua famiglia*, in 'Il Buonarroti', series III, vol. IV, pp. 278-286.

1890 ERCULEI R., *La villa di Giulio III suoi usi e destinazioni*, Rome.

1891 GNOLI D., *La casa dell'orefice Giampietro Crivelli in Roma*, in 'Archivio Storico dell'Arte', year IV, number IV, pp. 236-242 and 287-290 (documents).

1892 GNOLI D., *La Cancelleria ed altri palazzi di Roma attribuiti a Bramante*, in 'Archivio Storico dell'Arte', year V, pp. 176-184 and 331-347.

1894 GNOLI D., *Descriptio Urbis o Censimento della popolazione di Roma avanti il sacco Borbonico*, in 'Archivio della R. Società Romana di Storia Patria', vol. XVII, pp. 375-521.

1895–1909 FREY K., *Studien zu Michelangiolo Buonarroti und zur Kunst seiner Zeit*, in 'Jahrbuch der Königlichen Preussischen Kunstsammlungen', vol. XV, pp. 91-103; vol. XVI, pp. 5-18 and 97-119; vol. XXIX, pp. 103-180.

1898 GNOLI D., *Bramante in Roma*, in 'Rivista d'Italia', year I, number IV, pp. 690-703.

1900 TOMASSETTI G., *Scoperte recenti nel palazzetto della Farnesina in via de' Baullari*, in 'Bollettino della Commissione Archeologica Comunale di Roma', year XXVIII, pp. 321-341.

1900–2 CLAUSSE G., *Les Sangallo architectes, peintres, sculpteurs, médailleurs du XVe et XVIe siècles*, Paris, 3 vols.

1901–40 VENTURI A., *Storia dell'Arte Italiana*, Milan, 11 vols.

1902 EGGER H., *Entwürfe Baldassarre Peruzzis für den Einzug Karls V in Rom*, in 'Jahrbuch der Kunsthistorischen Sammlungen des Allerhöchsten Kaiserhauses', vol. XXIII, pp. 1-44.

1902 MOLLAT G., *Thomas Le Roy (dit Régis) et le palazzetto de la Farnésine à Rome (via de' Baullari)*, extract from 'Annales de Saint-Louis-des-Français', year VI, number II, Rome.

1902 ROCCHI E., *Le piante iconografiche e prospettiche di Roma del secolo XVI*, Turin-Rome, 2 vols. (text and plates).

1902 SENI F.S., *La villa d'Este in Tivoli*, Rome.

1904 ASHBY T., *Sixteenth-century drawings of Roman buildings attributed to Andreas Coner*, in 'Papers of the British School of Rome', vol. II.

1905 Tomassetti G., *Il palazzo Vidoni in Roma appartenente al conte Filippo Vitali*, Rome.

1906 Willich H., *Giacomo Barozzi da Vignola*, Strasbourg.

1908 Ehrle F., *Roma prima di Sisto V. La pianta di Roma di Dupérac-Lafréry del 1577*.

1908 Giordani P., *Il Vignola a Roma*, in 'Memorie e studi intorno a Jacopo Barozzi Vignola', pp. 109-185.

1908 Wölfflin H., *Renaissance und Barock*, Munich.

1908-11 Hoffmann T., *Raffael in seiner Bedeutung als Architekt*, Zittau-Leipzig, 4 vols. (text), 4 vols. (plates).

1908-12 *Inventario dei monumenti di Roma*, Associazione artistica fra i cultori di architettura, Rome.

1910 Baldinucci G., *Palazzo Farnese in Caprarola illustrato nella storia e nell'arte*, Rome.

1911 Balestra G., *La fontana pubblica di Giulio III e il palazzo di Pio IV sulla via Flaminia*, Rome.

1911 Gnoli D., *Il palazzo Sacchetti in Roma*, in 'Bollettino d'Arte del Ministero della P. Istruzione', year V, number VI, pp. 201-206.

1911 Hewett A.E., *Ancora sul palazzo Sangallo*, in 'Bollettino d'Arte del Ministero della P. Istruzione', year V, number XI, Rome, pp. 439-440.

1911-16 Frey K., *Zur Baugeschichte des St. Peter. Mitteilungen aus der Reverendissima Fabbrica di S. Pietro*, in 'Jahrbuch der Königlichen Preussischen Kunstsammlungen', Berlin, appendix to vol. XXXI (1911), pp. 1-95; app. to vol. XXXIII (1913), pp. 1-153; app. to vol. XXXVII (1916), pp. 22-136.

1911-31 Egger H., *Römische Veduten Handzeichnungen aus dem XV-XVIII. Jahrhundert*, Vienna-Leipzig, 2 vols. (plates), 2 vols. (text).

1912 Gnoli D., *Pietro Roselli, architetto*, in 'Annuario dell'Associazione artistica fra i cultori di architettura', MCMX-MCMXI, pp. 70-73.

1912 Muñoz A., *La chiesa di S. Eligio degli Orefici e il suo recente restauro*, in 'Rassegna d'Arte', year VII, pp. 3 et seq.

1912 Rodocanachi E., *Rome au temps de Jules II et de Léon X*, Paris.

1912-13 Giovannoni G., *Chiese della seconda metà del Cinquecento in Roma*, in 'L'Arte', year XV, pp. 401-416; year XVII, pp. 20-31 and 81-106.

1913-16 Hülsen C. - Egger H., *Die Römischen Skizzenbücher von Marten van Heemskerck*, Berlin, 2 vols. (plates), 2 vols. (text).

1914 Giovannoni G., *Il palazzo dei Tribunali del Bramante in un disegno di Fra Giocondo*, in 'Bollettino d'Arte del Ministero della P. Istruzione', year VIII, number VI, pp. 185-195.

1914 Gnoli D., *Il palazzo di Giustizia di Bramante*, extract from 'Nuova Antologia', 16 April 1914.

1915 Frey D., *Bramantes St. Peter - Entwurf und seine Apokryphen*, in 'Bramante - Studien', vol. 1, Vienna.

1917 Hülsen C., *Römische Antikengärten des XVI. Jahrhunderts*, Heidelberg.

1920 Frey D., *Michelangelo-Studien*, Vienna.

1921 Pettorelli A., *Giulio Mazzoni da Piacenza, pittore e scultore*, Rome.

1923 Bargellini S., *Il palazzo di Pio IV sulla via Flaminia*, Milan-Rome.

1923 Biagi L., *Di Bartolomeo Ammannati ed alcune sue opere*, in 'L'Arte', year XXVI, pp. 49-66.

1925 Kent W.W., *The Life and Works of Baldassarre Peruzzi*, New York.

1925 Pastor L., *Die Stadt Rom zu Ende der Renaissance*, Freiburg im Breisgau.

1927 Ashby T., *The Capitol in Rome: its History and Development*, in 'Town Planning Review', XII, pp. 159-173.

1927 Boyer F., *La construction de la Villa Médicis*, in 'Revue de l'art', No. 51, pp. 3-14.

1927 Hermanin F., *La Farnesina*, presentation of A. Colasanti ..., presentation of Prince L. Chigi-Albani, Bergamo.

1928 Ehrle F., *Dalle carte e dai disegni di Virgilio Spada*, in 'Atti della Pontificia Accademia Romana di archeologia', series III, Memorie, volume II, pp. 45-98 bis.

1928 Greenwood W.E., *The Villa Madama: Rome*, London.

1929 Cecchelli C., *Palazzo Spada*, in 'Annuario dell'Associazione artistica fra i cultori di Architettura', pp. 39-54.

1929 Pernier A., *Il palazzo degli Alicornj a S. Pietro*, in 'Atti del I congresso nazionale di studi romani', pp. 725-731.

1930 Gnoli D., *Orti letterari nella Roma di Leone X*, in 'Nuova Accademia', number 1387 (1 January 1930), pp. 3-19; number 1388 (16 January 1930), pp. 137-148.

1932 Körte W., *Zur Peterskuppel des Michelangelo*, in 'Jahrbuch der Preussischen Kunstsammlungen', vol. LIII, pp. 90-112.

1932 Loukomski G.K., *Jules Romain*, Paris.

1934 Argan G.C., *Il problema di Bramante*, in 'Rassegna marchigiana', XII, pp. 212-234.

1934 Callari L., *Le ville di Roma*, Rome.

1934 Strinati R., *Palazzo 'Salviati' alla Lungara in Roma. Le pitture della 'cappella'*, in 'Bollettino d'Arte', year XXVIII, series III, No. I, pp. 37-44.

1934-5 Gombrich E., *Zum Werke Giulio Romanos*, in 'Jahrbuch der Kunsthistorischen Sammlungen in Wien', new series, vol. VIII, pp. 79-104; vol. IX, pp. 121-150.

1935 Ehrle F. - Egger H., *Der Vatikanische Palast in seiner Entwicklung bis zur Mitte des XV. Jahrhunderts*, Biblioteca Apostolica Vaticana, Vatican City.

1935 Giovannoni G., *Saggi sull'architettura italiana del Rinascimento*, Milan.

1935-6 Nava A., *Sui disegni architettonici per San Giovanni dei Fiorentini in Roma*, in 'Critica d'arte', vol. 1, pp. 102-108.

1936 Stefani E., *Villa Giulia, la primitiva sistemazione architettonica della facciata retrostante il ninfeo*, in 'Bollettino del Ministero dell'Educazione Nazionale', pp. 187 et seq.

1937 Apollonj B.M., *Fabbriche civili nel quartiere del Rinascimento in Roma*, Rome.

1937 Berra L., *Il testamento del medico di Leone X che costruì il palazzetto dei Borghi*, in 'Roma', November, pp. 420-426.

1937 Gnoli D., *Le palais Farnèse*, in 'Mélanges d'archéologie et d'histoire', pp. 200-210.

1937 Nava A., *La storia della chiesa di San Giovanni dei Fiorentini nei documenti del suo archivio*, in 'Arch. della R. Dep. romana di storia patria', LIX, pp. 337-362.

1937 Tomei P., *La palazzina di Giuliano della Rovere ai Santi Apostoli*, Rome.

1937 Tomei P., *Di due palazzi romani del Rinascimento*, in 'Rivista del R. Ist. di Arch. e storia dell'arte', year VI, numbers I-II, pp. 130-144.

1937 Tomei P., *La villa dei Papi alla Magliana*, extract from 'Roma', year XV, Rome.

1938 Apollonj B.M., *Il prospetto del palazzo romano del primo Cinquecento. Saggio sulla sua origine e su i suoi sviluppi*, in 'Atti del I congresso nazionale di storia dell'architettura', (October 1936), pp. 237-243.

1938 Gnoli D., *Facciate graffite e dipinte in Roma*, extract from 'Il Vasari', years VIII and IX, Arezzo.

1938 Lotz W., *Vignola - Zeichnungen*, in 'Jahrbuch der Preussischen Kunstsammlungen', vol. LIX, number II, pp. 97-115.

1938 Romano P., *Il quartiere del Rinascimento*, Rome.

1938 Tomei P., *Le case in serie nell'edilizia romana dal '400 al '700*, in 'Palladio', year II, number III, pp. 83-92.

1939 Giovannoni G., *Giovanni Mangone architetto*, in 'Palladio', year III, pp. 97-112.

1939 Lotz W., *Vignola-Studien*, Würzburg.

1939 Loukomski G.K., *The palazzo Sacchetti. The house and garden*, in 'The Burlington Magazine', vol. LXXIV, No. 182, pp. 131-132.

1939 Tomei P., *Contributi d'archivio. Un elenco dei palazzi di Roma del tempo di Clemente VIII*, in 'Palladio', year III, No. IV, pp. 163-174, and No. V, pp. 219-230.

1940 Bodoz E., *Studien zum architektonischen Werk des Bartolomeo Ammannati*, in 'Mitteilungen des Kunsthistorischen Institutes in Florenz', Florence.

1940 Bonfiglietti R., *Il palazzo di Firenze restaurato*, Rome.

1940 Ceccarelli G., *Strada Giulia*, Rome.

1940 Paschini P., *Roma del Rinascimento*, Bologna.

1940 Tomei P., *Guido Guidetti*, in 'Rivista del R. Istituto d'archeologia e storia dell'arte', year VIII, number I, pp. 62-83.

1940-1 De Camillis M., *Villa d'Este nelle descrizioni di U. Foglietta e M.A. Mureto*, in 'Atti e memorie della Società tiburtina di storia e d'arte', vol. XX-XXI, pp. 162-178.

1942 Clementi E., *I graffiti nella ornamentazione edilizia di Roma nel Rinascimento*, in 'Capitolium', year XVII, No. 2, pp. 47-53.

1942 Marchini G., *Giuliano da Sangallo*, Florence.

1942 Trinchier R., *Il palazzo Altemps, già Riario*, in 'Romana gens, Bollettino dell'associazione archeologica romana', No. 10.

1943 Bocchino G., *Annibale Lippi fu l'autore di Villa Medici?*, in 'L'Osservatore Romano', 18 February, p. 3.

1943 COOLIDGE J., *The Villa Giulia*, in 'The Art Bulletin', vol. XXV, No. 3, pp. 177-225.

1943 DE ANGELIS D'OSSAT G., *Gli archi trionfali ideati dal Peruzzi per la venuta a Roma di Carlo V*, in 'Capitolium', year XVIII, No. 9, pp. 287-294.

1947 GIOVANNONI G., *La facciata della chiesa di S. Spirito e S. Maria in Sassia*, in 'Bollettino del Centro di Studi di Storia dell'architettura', No. 5, pp. 4-5.

1947-1960 TOLNAY (DE) C., *Michelangelo*, Princeton, 5 vols.

1948 BAFILE M., *Villa Giulia, l'architettura, il giardino*, number XIV of 'Istituto di Arch. e Storia dell'Arte', Rome.

1948 FISCHEL O., *Raphael*, London, 2 vols.

1950 COLETTA G. - ROMITELLI A., *S. Eligio degli Orefici*, in 'L'Arte', year XIII, pp. 1-5.

1950 PECCHIAI P., *Il Campidoglio nel Cinquecento sulla scorta dei documenti*, Rome.

1951 LEFEVRE R., *Villa Madama a Roma*, Rome.

1952 BAFILE M., *I disegni di Villa Giulia nella Collezione Burlington Devonshire*, in 'Palladio', pp. 54-64.

1952 PECCHIAI P., *Il Gesù a Roma*, Rome.

1952 RICCI C., *Il tempietto di San Luigi de' Francesi*, in 'Rivista dell'Istituto nazionale d'archeologia e storia dell'arte', new series, year I, pp. 317-327.

1953 SCHIAVO A., *La vita e le opere architettoniche di Michelangelo*, Rome.

1954 ACKERMANN J.S., *The Cortile del Belvedere*, Vatican City.

1954 SIEBENHÜNER H., *Das Kapitol in Rom; Idee und Gestalt*, Munich.

1955 BRUSCHI A., *L'abitato di Bomarzo e la villa Orsini*, in 'Quaderni dell'istituto di storia dell'architettura', Nos. 7-8-9, pp. 3-18.

1955 FASOLO F., *Analisi stilistica del sacro bosco*, in 'Quaderni dell'istituto di storia dell'architettura', Nos. 7-8-9, pp. 33-60.

1955 LOTZ W., *Die ovalen Kirchenräume des Cinquecento*, in 'Römisches Jahrbuch für Kunstgeschichte', vol. VII, pp. 7-99.

1955 SIEBENHÜNER H., *S. Maria degli Angeli in Rom*, in 'Münchener Jahrbuch der bildenden Kunst', III series, vol. VI, pp. 179-206.

1956 ASTOLFI C., *I palazzi del Bufalo e Maurelli. L'Accademia colotiana*, in 'Studi romani', year IV, No. 6, pp. 644-651.

1956 CALVESI M., *Il sacro bosco di Bomarzo*, in 'Scritti di storia dell'arte in onore di Lionello Venturi', Rome, vol. I, pp. 369-402.

1956 FÖRSTER O.H., *Bramante*, Vienna-Munich.

1956 REDIG DE CAMPOS D., *Notizia sul palazzo Baldassini*, in 'Bollettino del centro studi per la storia dell'architettura', No. 10.

1956 SIEBENHÜNER H., *San Giovanni dei Fiorentini in Rom*, in 'Kunstgeschichtliche Studien für Hans Hauffmann', Berlin, pp. 172-191.

1957 D'ONOFRIO C., *Le fontane di Roma*, Rome.

1957 GNOLI D., *Bramante e il Palazzo della Cancelleria*, in 'Studi romani', (pubd. posthumously), pp. 318-338.

1957 MONTINI R.U., *Palazzo Baldassini restaurato*, in 'Studi romani', year V, No. I, pp. 39-56.

1957 MONTINI R.U. - AVERINI R., *Palazzo Baldassini e l'arte di Giovanni da Udine*, Rome.

1957 SAXL F., *The Villa Farnesina*, in 'F. Saxl Lectures', I, pp. 189-199, London.

1957 ZERI F., *Pittura e Controriforma. L'arte senza tempo di Scipione da Gaeta*, Turin.

1958 HARTT F., *Giulio Romano*, New Haven, 2 vols.

1958 MAGNUSON T., *Studies in Roman Quattrocento architecture*, Rome.

1959 CHASTEL A., *Art et humanisme à Florence au temps de Laurent le Magnifique*, Paris.

1959 DE ANGELIS D'OSSAT G., *Inedito palladiano e palazzetto romano*, in 'Strenna dei romanisti', pp. 57-59.

1959 GIOVANNONI G., *Antonio da Sangallo il Giovane*, Rome, 2 vols. (text and plates).

1960 BONELLI R., *Da Bramante a Michelangelo*, Venice.

1960 GIOSEFFI D., *La cupola vaticana. Un'ipotesi michelangiolesca*, Trieste.

1960 LAVAGNINO E., *Il palazzo Farnese a Roma*, in 'Le vie d'Italia', year LXVI, No. 12, pp. 1581-1592.

1960 PERICOLI RIDOLFINI C., *Le case romane con facciate graffite e dipinte*, catalogue of the exhibition, Rome.

1960 SCHIAVO A., *Palazzo Caffarelli*, in 'Capitolium', year XXXV, No. 11, pp. 3-6.

1960 SCHIAVO A., *L'architettura della Farnesina: I, La palazzina*, in 'Capitolium', year XXXV, No. 8, pp. 3-14.

1960 SCHIAVO A., *L'architettura della Farnesina: II, Le scuderie*, in 'Capitolium', year XXXV, No. 9, pp. 3-9.

1960 WALCHER CASOTTI M., *Il Vignola*, Trieste, 2 vols. (text and plates).

1961 ACKERMANN J.S., *The architecture of Michelangelo*, London, 2 vols.

1961 BATTISTI E., *Disegni cinquecenteschi su San Giovanni dei Fiorentini*, in 'Quaderni dell'istituto di storia dell'architettura dell'Università di Roma', essays in honour of Prof. V. Fasolo, VI-VII, numbers 31-48, pp. 185-194.

1961 FROMMEL C.L., *Die Farnesina und Peruzzis Architektonisches Frühwerk*, Berlin.

1961 HESS J., *Die Paepstliche Villa bei Aracœli*, 'Miscellanea Bibliothecae Hertzianae', Munich, pp. 239-254.

1961 LEFEVRE R., *La 'vigna' del cardinale Giulio de' Medici e il vescovo d'Aquino*, in 'Strenna dei romanisti', pp. 171-177.

1961 SHEARMAN J., *The Chigi Chapel in S. Maria del Popolo*, in 'Journal of the Warburg and Courtauld Institutes', vol. XXIV, Nos. 3-4, pp. 129-185.

1961 THELEN H., *Der Palazzo della Sapienza in Rom*, in 'Miscellanea Bibliothecae Hertzianae', Munich, pp. 285-307.

1961 VAN DAM VAN ISSELT H., *Wie is de Architect van Palazzo Spada te Rom*, in 'Mededelingen van het Nederlands Historisch Instituut te Rom', year XXXI, pp. 211-230.

1961 WASSERMANN J., *Palazzo Spada*, in 'The Art Bulletin', vol. XLIII, No. 1, pp. 58-63.

1962 BATTISTI E., *L'antirinascimento*, Milan.

1962 FRUTAZ A.P., *Le piante di Roma*, Rome, 3 vols.

1962 LAVAGNINO E., *La chiesa di Santo Spirito in Sassia e il mutare del gusto a Roma al tempo del Concilio di Trento*, Rome.

1962 MONACO M., *La Zecca vecchia in Banchi ora detta Palazzo del Banco di S. Spirito*, Rome.

1963 BRUSCHI A., *Nuovi dati documentari sulle opere orsiniane di Bomarzo*, in 'Quaderni dell'istituto di storia dell'architettura', series X, numbers 55-60, pp. 13-58.

1963 BRUSCHI A., *Il problema storico di Bomarzo*, in 'Palladio', new series, year XIII, numbers I-IV, pp. 85-114.

1963 GOLZIO V. - ZANDER G., *Le chiese di Roma dall' XI al XVI secolo*, Bologna.

1964 FROMMEL C.L., *S. Eligio und die Kuppel der Cappella Medici*, in 'Internationaler (XXI) Kongress für Kunstgeschichte', Stil und Überlieferung ..., vol. II, pp. 41-54, Bonn.

1964 LIGHTBOWN R.W., *Nicolas Audebert and the Villa d'Este*, in 'Journal of the Warburg and Courtauld Institutes', vol. XXVII, pp. 164-190.

1964 NEUERBURG N., *Raphael at Tivoli and the Villa Madama*, in 'Essays in memory of Karl Lehmann', New York, pp. 227-231.

1964 ROSENTHAL E., *The Antecedents of Bramante's Tempietto*, in 'Journal of the Society of Architectural Historians', vol. XXIII, No. 2, pp. 55-74.

1964 SCHIAVO A., *Il Palazzo della Cancelleria*, Rome.

1964 WITTKOWER R., *La cupola di S. Pietro di Michelangelo*, revised reprint taken from an article of 1933, Florence.

1964 WITTKOWER R., *Principi architettonici nell'età dell'Umanesimo*, Turin.

1965 AMADEI E., *Le porte di Roma*, in 'Capitolium', year XL, No. II, pp. 553-562.

1965 DE MAIO R., *Michelangelo e Paolo IV*, in 'Reformata reformanda', written in honour of Hubert Jedin, Münster, vol. I, pp. 635-656.

1965 HUEMER F., *Raphael and the Villa Madama*, in 'Essays in honor of Walter Friedlaender', New York, pp. 92-99.

1965 WURM H., *Der Palazzo Massimo alle Colonne*, Berlin.

1966 ALBERTI L.B., *L'Architettura* (De re aedificatoria), Latin text and translation edited by G. Orlandi, introduction and notes by P. Portoghesi; vol. I: Classici italiani di scienze tecniche e arti - Trattati di architettura, Milan.

1966 DE ANGELIS D'OSSAT G., *Il Campidoglio di Michelangelo*, in 'Atti del convegno di Studi michelangioleschi', (Florence-Rome 1964), pp. 366-378.

1966 DE ANGELIS D'OSSAT G., *Preludio romano del Bramante*, in 'Palladio', new series, year XVI, pp. 83-102.

1966 LAMB C., *Die Villa d'Este in Tivoli*, Munich.

1966 MARCONI P., *Contributo alla storia delle fortificazioni di Roma nel Cinquecento e nel Seicento*, in 'Quaderni dell'istituto di storia dell'architettura', XIII, numbers 73-78, pp. 109-130.

1966 TAFURI M., *L'architettura del Manierismo nel Cinquecento Europeo*, Rome.

1966 VAGNETTI M., *La perla degli insediamenti umani nel territorio: Caprarola*, in 'Quaderni dell'istituto di ricerca urbanologica e tecnica della pianificazione', No. 3, pp. 44-54.

1967 COFFIN D.R., *The plans of the Villa Madama*, in 'The Art Bulletin', No. 2, pp. 111-122.

1967 HESS J., *Kunstgeschichtliche Studien zu Renaissance und Barock*, Rome, 2 vols.

1967 MURRAY P., *Observations on Bramante's St. Peter's*, in 'Essays on the history of architecture presented to Rudolf Wittkower', London, pp. 53-59.

1967 WOLFF METTERNICH F.G., *Über die Massgrundlagen des Kuppelentwurfes Bramantes für die Peterskirche in Rom*, in 'Essays on the history of architecture presented to Rudolf Wittkower', London, pp. 40-52.

1967-8 FOSTER P., *Raphael on the Villa Madama. The text of a lost letter*, in 'Römisches Jahrbuch für Kunstgeschichte', XI, pp. 308-312.

1967-8 FROMMEL C.L., *Baldassarre Peruzzi als Maler und Zeichner*, in 'Römisches Jahrbuch für Kunstgeschichte', vol. II, Vienna-Munich.

1968 BENEDETTI S., *S. Maria di Loreto*, Le chiese di Roma illustrate, No. 100. Rome.

1968 FERNÁNDEZ ALONSO J., *S. Maria di Monserrato*, Le chiese di Roma illustrate, No. 103, Rome.

1968 SHEARMAN J., *Raphael as architect*, in 'The Journal of the Royal Society of Arts', No. 5141, pp. 388-409.

1969 FROMMEL C.L., *Bramantes 'Ninfeo' in Gennazzano*, in 'Römisches Jahrbuch für Kunstgeschichte', vol. 12, pp. 137-160.

1969 MARABOTTINI A., *Polidoro da Caravaggio*, Rome, 2 vols.

undated FERRERIO P., *Palazzi di Roma di più celebri architetti*, book I, Rome.

undated FOSSI M., *Bartolomeo Ammannati architetto*, publications of the Università degli Studi di Firenze, Facoltà di Magistero, vol. X, Florence.

INDEX

LIST OF ILLUSTRATIONS

LIST OF PLATES

449